■■■■

Settings of Silver ■■■■

■■■■

AN INTRODUCTION
TO JUDAISM

by
Stephen M. Wylen

Paulist Press / New York / New Jersey

Book design by Theresa M. Sparacio

Illustrations by Sheri Marcus.

Copyright © 1989 by Rabbi Stephen M. Wylen

Library of Congress Cataloging-in-Publication Data

Wylen, Stephen M., 1952–
    Settings of silver : an introduction to Judaism / by Stephen M.
Wylen.
      p. cm.
    Bibliography: p.
    Includes index.
    ISBN 0-8091-3071-8 : $14.95 (est.)
    1. Judaism—History. 2. Jews—History. I. Title.
BM155.2.W95   1989
296—dc20   89-9456
                                        CIP

Published by Paulist Press
997 Macarthur Boulevard
Mahwah, N.J. 07430

Printed and bound in the United States of America

Contents

Part Three:
JUDAISM THROUGH THE AGES

Shammai, Religious Concerns of the Pharisees, Institutions of the
Pharisees: Court, School and Synagogue

The New Sanhedrin, Judaism Without a Temple, Remembering the
Temple, Religious Authority, Holidays, Yavneh and Masada, Rabbinic
Judaism from Yohanan to Judah the Patriarch, Judaism and
Christianity, Rabbinic Judaism in Babylon, The Formation of the
Talmuds

The Structure of the Mishnah, A Text from the Mishnah, Analysis of
the Mishnah Text, The Babylonian Talmud, The Talmudic Mind,
Living by the Talmud, Modern Views of the Talmud

From Antiquity to the Middle Ages, From Babylon to Ashkenaz and
Sepharad, The Feudal System, The Jews in the Feudal System, Jewish-
Christian Relations in Feudal Society, The Jew as Money-lender, The
Jews of England, Jews in Christian Theology and Law, The Decline of
Ashkenazic Jewry, The Ghetto, Eastward Migrations, The Social Order
of Ashkenazic Jewry, Social Life in the Jewish Community, Rashi

Spain in the Middle Ages, The Culture of Moslem Spain, The
Reconquest, the Translators and the Expulsion, Statesmen, Jewish
Philosophy, The Conflict of Philosophy and Religion, Saadia Gaon
(892–942), Judah Halevi (c. 1080–1140), Moses Maimonides (1135–
1204), The Philosophy of Maimonides

Mysticism, Rabbinic Mysticism, Kabbalah and the Zohar, The
Doctrine of the Sefirot, Religious Tension in the Kabbalah, The
Lurianic Kabbalah, The Lurianic Concept of Creation, Redemption in
the Lurianic Kabbalah, Exile, Humankind in the Lurianic Kabbalah,
The Effect of the Lurianic Kabbalah, Shabbatei Zevi—The Mystical
Messiah

A Brief History of Polish Jewry, The Jews Under the Czars, The Three

Foci of Jewish Life: The Home, The Marketplace, The Bes Midrash, The Social Order of Polish Jewry, Hasidism: The Legend of the Baal Shem Tov, The Growth of Hasidism, The Doctrines of Hasidism, The Way of Hasidism, The Generations of Hasidism, Tzaddik and Hasid, Hasidim, Misnagdim and Modernists

Part Four:
JUDAISM IN THE MODERN AGE

To Cheryl:
Kol hasheli, shelach hu.

"We will make you ornaments of gold
in settings of silver."
                    —Song of Songs 1:11

Acknowledgements

The computer has greatly transformed the task of writing. I am most grateful to my computer support team: Ruth and David Wasser of Philadelphia, and Tom Pressman and Mike Owens of Strictly Business Computer Systems in Huntington, West Virginia. I am grateful to the members of the B'nai Sholom Congregation in Huntington, West Virginia for their support and encouragement. Many thanks are due to my students at Marshall University. Their questions, interests and concerns were my guide in deciding which subjects required attention in this book. I am grateful to my wife Cheryl, my children, and my extended family for their help and encouragement and for their willingness to donate so much of my time to the writing of this book. I hope that my efforts prove worthy of your confidence.

PART ONE:

What Is Judaism?

1

What Is A Jew?

Different Definitions

Judaism is more than a religion. Judaism is the way of life of the Jewish people. Culture, customs, ethics, sense of self—these are a part of Judaism as much as the faith and the rituals of the Jewish religion. Since Judaism is the expression of the life of a people, we begin with the question, "Who are these people?" What distinguishing features identify the Jewish people?

A Jew can be defined in more than one way. Within Jewish law, being Jewish is a kind of citizenship. One is a Jew if one is born of a Jewish mother[1] or has undergone a conversion. Conversion to Judaism is like a bestowal of citizenship—it makes one a member of the people. A person who fits the legal definition of a Jew is recognized as a fellow Jew by the Jewish community. Even if a Jew does not share the religious beliefs of Jews and does not participate in the customs and practices of Judaism, one is still considered a Jew if he or she fits the legal definition.

One could define a Jew religiously, according to the religious beliefs and practices of Judaism. A Jew is one who believes in the one God, creator and master of the universe, the God with whom the people Israel have a special relationship.[2]

---

[1]Some contemporary Jews would add: born of a Jewish father.

[2]The term Israel is a synonym for the Jewish people. In contemporary times, "Israel" is used to refer to the Jewish state. Properly speaking, the state is the State of Israel, the land is the Land of Israel, but the word Israel used alone refers to the people, wherever they live. In Jewish writings from before the founding of the modern State of Israel, the term Israel always refers to the people, not the nation.

Jews have been identified as a race. This is not true if by race we mean a people united by blood with specific genetic characteristics. One becomes a Jew through birth, but in every generation there have been those who departed from their Jewish identity and married into other groups, and those who have become Jewish and joined their genetic heritage to that of the Jewish people. If one were to go to Israel today one would see Jews of every different build and skin color. One would notice that by and large European Jews look European, Yemenite Jews look like Yemenites, Moroccan Jews look like other Moroccans, and so forth. The stereotype of the Jew with dark curly hair, a long nose and olive skin fails to recognize the heterogeneity of the Jewish people. To the extent that the stereotype is true, it would fit many other Mediterranean peoples as much as it would fit the Jews.

Many writings from the nineteenth century, Jewish and non-Jewish, identify the Jews as a race. While some of these mentions have in mind the discredited idea of a blood group, the term race was used in that time to describe what we today would call an ethnic group. An ethnic group is a community of people who share a common culture. Language, literature, foods, common concerns, certain personality characteristics—these and other aspects of human culture make up an ethnic identity. Jews do share the characteristics of an ethnic group. More properly, we may say that Jews make up a number of ethnic groups, since Jews from different parts of the world have cultural traits that are unique to their own Jewish communities. There are some cultural traits which all Jews have in common, such as reverence for a body of literature and devotion to a language and a land which are considered sacred.

Stereotypes

As a minority group with a distinct and different way of life, Jews have often been singled out for negative attention. Many people think of Jews in terms of negative stereotypes. Let us come to an understanding of some of these stereotypes now, so that we can set them aside.

In ancient times the Jews were the only people who worshiped a single, exclusive God, and the only people who worshiped without physical images of God. The Jews were resented by other peoples for not participating in the worship of all gods. This led to the accusation that Jews were anti-humanitarian, since sharing gods was considered to be an act of friendship and universalistic concern for other peoples.

When Christianity replaced the pagan religions of antiquity the old misunderstanding of Jews did not die out. Added to it was the resentment that the Jews, Jesus' own people, had not become Christian. Jews were protected under Christian law but were restricted in many ways. The laws in Christian lands called for Jews to be humiliated and despised in order to encourage Jewish conversions to Christianity. When Jews did not convert they were accused of stubbornness or spiritual blindness.

Before modern times there was little appreciation for the differences between people. Conformity to cultural standards was prized. The many unique Jewish customs and rituals aroused suspicion and fear among those who did not understand them.

In the Middle Ages Jews were assigned by kings and nobles to fill economic roles that were magnets for resentment from the common folk. Jews were used as bankers, tax collectors and estate managers. Interest rates were set by the kings, who taxed Jewish profits heavily for their own benefit, but public resentment was directed at the Jews. In some lands the ruling class purposely directed peasant hatred against the Jews in order to deflect criticism of their own rule. The Russian czars, for instance, encouraged anti-Semitism throughout their empire after the fall of other European monarchies, when they were trying to cling to power. The Nazis encouraged hatred and fear of Jews in order to gain public support for their bid to rule Germany and the world.

Sociologists have demonstrated how an oppressed people may adopt the negative view of itself which is perpetrated by the oppressors. Jews are certainly subject to this unfortunate phenomenon. We find among the Jews such negative self-stereotypes as the overbearing Jewish mother and the "Jewish American Princess," a materialistic and self-centered Jewish woman. Some have found in these stereotyped images an element of healthy self-criticism, but there is no doubt that such stereotypes damage the public image of the Jew, especially when they enter the public consciousness in literature and film. More serious damage can be done by self-hating Jews in positions of influence. For example, Karl Marx's severe criticism of Jews was motivated by a rejection of his own Jewish ancestry, but it has had a negative impact on the image of the Jew among Marxists everywhere.

Prejudiced stereotypes teach us very little about who Jews are and what they are like. Such stereotypes are a projection of the fantasies and fears of those who believe in them. Stereotypes tell us more about anti-Semites than about Jews.

Jewish Self-Stereotypes

There is another type of stereotype that is of value in understanding a people. These are the stereotypes that a people has about itself. These stereotypes may not be true of all or even most of the people, but they reveal the primary concerns of a people and the ideals to which they aspire.

We find in Jewish sayings that to be a Jew is to be charitable, compassionate, forgiving, and sexually modest. It is true that Jews excel in charitable giving. When Governor Peter Stuyvesant wished to keep a group of Jews from landing in New Amsterdam (the colony that became New York City) out of fear that this impoverished group would become a public burden, the Jews were able to point to an ancient history of never allowing a fellow Jew to depend on public charity. They were allowed into the city. In America, Jews generously support both Jewish charities and public causes of all kinds, beyond all proportion to the percentage of Jewish population.

Compassion for the unfortunate, even one's enemies, was always emphasized in Jewish culture and education. Jews were never to forget that at the beginning of their history they were slaves in Egypt. A Jew is expected to behave kindly toward foreigners, strangers, and the helpless in society. The Jews have often been oppressed in their history. They are expected to remember this as an example of how not to behave toward the powerless elements of society.

Family life and sexual morality broke down in the society of the Roman empire. Jews recognized the difference in their own society. They took pride in the strength of Jewish family life, based on the sacred bond between husband and wife and the Jewish laws which governed their relationship. In their eyes, the sexual restraint which Jews practiced was a mark of a superior way of life. In difficult times, Jews found strength in the bonds of family life.

The closely knit Jewish family and community encouraged education and personal achievement, while it discouraged crime and alcoholism. Jews have been admired for these traits. It is important to recognize, though, that these traits are not native to the Jew any more than to any other person. As traditional Jewish culture breaks down, Jews are as susceptible to the ills of society as are any other people.

A People Apart

Before modern times Jews lived in various lands as a distinct community, separate in many ways from the other people of the land. It was a simple matter to identify and define a Jew. Jews were distinguished, of course, by their religion. Jews were a distinct nationality as well. Jews were not considered to be citizens of the lands in which they lived. They were considered as exiles from the ancient nation of Judah, and Jews themselves concurred in this. Jews lived under a separate set of laws. The rulers of a nation established the taxes and other civil obligations of the Jewish community. The Jews controlled their own community affairs through their own elected officials and appointed rabbis. The Jewish community regulated its affairs according to Jewish law. The rulers of a nation often established laws requiring Jews to dress in a certain way and live in a certain area; they attempted to limit relationships between Jews and non-Jews. Jews were often restricted to certain professions which were reserved for Jews, generally in business and commerce. Jews lived and worked according to their own sacred calendar. Jewish dietary laws made it necessary for Jews to dine only among their fellow Jews. Often, Jews even spoke a different language than their neighbors. The Jews of Eastern Europe conversed in **Yiddish,** a Jewish dialect of medieval German, rather than in the language of the countries in which they lived. Many Jews in the Middle East whose ancestors originated in Spain continued to speak Ladino, the Jewish dialect of medieval Spanish. Jewish religious-intellectual culture was expressed in the ancient languages of Hebrew and Aramaic. This culture, with its languages, was taught in Jewish schools which were supported by the Jewish community.

In sum, the Jews constituted a separate, organic community which was almost completely self-contained. The Jewish community established for itself separate institutions to cover every requirement of culture and social organization.

Beginning in the eighteenth century, Jews were emancipated—that is, Jews were offered the opportunity to enter society on an equal basis without giving up being Jewish. The great majority of Jews welcomed emancipation, even though it meant the break-up of the traditional Jewish community. The Jew had to give up areas of distinctiveness in order to establish spheres of life in which he would relate to non-Jews as one individual to another. Jewishness was relegated to a restricted arena of life and culture. Being Jewish was no longer a total way of life, but a role which a person fulfilled as one aspect of his way of life.

The Role of Being Jewish: Different Options

Not all Jews chose to retain the same aspects of the former Jewish way of life. Some Jews kept Judaism as a religion, a set of beliefs and practices. Some Jews continued the attempt to abide by Jewish law within the limits of their new obligation to live under the laws of the nations in which they were granted citizenship. Some Jews chose to abandon traditional religion and law but retain the national aspects of being Jewish. Some Jews did not retain Jewish religion or nationality, but remained attached to the ethnic culture of the Jewish people. Outside of the area in which a Jew retained his distinctiveness, he related to the world as a human being among other human beings, in which his status as a Jew was not relevant.

The choice of which aspects of the Jewish way of life to retain was determined by national origin as much as by individual choice. In America Judaism is generally considered to be a religion, although most American Jews identify themselves by ethnicity rather than by religious faith. In Russia Jews are considered to be a nation rather than a religion. The Jews are one of the many nationalities which are officially recognized by the multi-national Soviet Union. In the Jewish state of Israel, Jews are naturally recognized as a nationality.

Many Jews combine a variety of Jewish roles in their Jewish identity. They may be ethnic culturalists, or religious nationalists. One Jew may keep the dietary laws because he considers them to be a divine commandment. Another may observe these laws because he thinks of them as an aspect of Jewish culture, but he may be willing to break these laws when it is inconvenient to observe them. Another Jew may consider the dietary laws an unnecessary remnant from the past. The conditions of modernism have made it difficult to determine the meaning of being Jewish.

As we continue in the study of Judaism, it would be useful to keep in mind this question: How have Jews in different times and places defined for themselves what is important about being Jewish?

Eras of Jewish History

The Jewish people have had a continuous history of nearly four thousand years. Judaism has continuously evolved over these many years. There have been periods of slow evolution in Jewish culture, practice and beliefs, and there have been periods of revolutionary change. For the sake of study, Jewish history may be divided into three periods, separated by events which caused great change in the Jewish way of life. These three periods are:

The Biblical Period, 1700 BCE–165 BCE
The Rabbinic Period, 165 BCE–1800 CE
The Modern Period, 1800 CE–present

The Biblical Period

The religion of ancient Israel was quite different from what we think of today as Judaism. Israel was unique in many ways, but her beliefs and practices were conditioned by the culture of the ancient Near East, a culture utterly foreign to modern people. Like their neighbors, the Israelites worshiped God through sacrifice in a Temple. Hereditary priests presided over the sacrifices and maintained the sacred traditions of the people.

The religion and history of biblical Israel is beyond the scope of this book. It is sufficient for us to note some of the major accomplishments of the people, accomplishments which had a lasting effect on the religious culture of the people.

Israel began as a loose confederation of tribes. These tribes were gradually united into a single nation. When some of the tribes of Israel disappeared through defeat or assimilation, the remaining people came to be known as Jews, after the largest tribe, Judah. The nation acquired a capital, the city of Jerusalem. A central Temple was built in Jerusalem for the worship of God. This Temple became the exclusive site for offering sacrifices to God. To this day, Jerusalem remains the national, religious and spiritual capital of the Jewish people.

The nation acquired a royal dynasty. The descendants of King David ruled over the Kingdom of Judah for many centuries. When the dynasty finally ended, Jews continued to look for a descendant of David to be their rightful earthly ruler. The time of King David, when the Jews were united and free from enemies and the nation and king served God willingly, became the vision of a golden age to which the Jews hoped to return in the future.

Merely to have survived the centuries was a great accomplishment for the Jews. The great empires of Assyria and Babylon swallowed and destroyed many small nations in the Middle East, including the northern tribes of Israel, the so-called Ten Lost Tribes. Many small nations lost their identity after Alexander the Great conquered the Persian empire and brought Greek culture to the Middle East, but the Jews survived. In 586 BCE the Babylonians burnt the Temple, destroyed Jerusalem and brought all the leaders of the Jews into exile in Babylon. The Jews managed to retain their identity, and seventy years later the Persians allowed those Jews who wished to return to rebuild their city and their Temple. By the end of the biblical period the Jews were acutely aware of the fact that they had outlasted empires much mightier and more numerous than themselves. They had seen the rise and fall of Assyria and Babylon, Persia and Greece. They remembered the experience of exile and return. This memory gave the Jewish people a concept of history and a feeling of their own eternal place in the scheme of history.

The Jewish people developed a Scripture during the biblical period. People in biblical times obviously did not live by the Bible; it had not yet been written. Historians generally agree that by 400 BCE, after the return from exile, the first elements of the Bible reached final form and were recognized as sacred Scripture. The date we have assigned as the end of the biblical period is the approximate time when the last books which entered the Bible were written. By the end of biblical times, Jews had a collection of books which they believed were given to them as the word of God. Judaism differs from the biblical religion of Israel in having this Scripture. At the conclusion of the biblical period, Jews ceased to seek out prophets to deliver a word from God. Instead they studied the scriptures, which were believed to contain a message from God which would cover every possible situation if it were properly interpreted.

The Rabbinic Period

A great transition took place in Jewish life and culture during the centuries 200 BCE to 100 CE. The culture of the ancient Near East gave way to Hellenistic culture, a blend of Greek and Near Eastern elements. The province of Judah was ruled from afar by Greek kings, descendants of the generals of Alexander the Great, and then by the Romans. The religious and cultural institutions of ancient Judaism wore away and eventually disappeared. Their place was taken by new institutions—the synagogue as a house of worship and study, rabbis whose religious authority was based on knowledge of Scripture, yeshivot (academies) where rabbis were taught how to interpret Scripture. The Sanhedrin, the High Court, had the final say in Jewish religious and legal matters. In the year 70 CE the Romans destroyed the Temple. The sacrifices and the functioning priesthood came to an end. Rabbis became the uncontested religious authority for Jews. They developed the religious way of life that we know as Judaism.

The laws, customs and practices established by the rabbis became the norm for all Jews from the first century until the dawn of the modern age. Jewish life went through many changes during these eighteen centuries, but the way of life established by the early rabbis persisted as the basis for Judaism. The Rabbinic Period may also be called the Normative period of Judaism. Normative Judaism is that way of life based on the laws and teachings of the rabbis.

The Modern Period

Jews were catapulted into the modern world by the political and social revolutions of eighteenth and nineteenth century Europe. Jews were struck by vast social changes so rapidly that Normative Judaism was unable to evolve to meet the new challenges. For most Jews, the forces of modernism brought eighteen centuries of Jewish continuity to an end. Modernism was a force as revolutionary as the destruction of the Temple had been. Many Jews were lost to Judaism in the period of adjustment. Many Jews attempted to hold on to as much tradition as they could, to resist the forces of modernism. Many Jews have attempted to restructure Judaism into a form which fits into the modern world. It is too early in modern history to tell what form or forms of Judaism will become normative for the future. The Jews of today, even the most adamant modernists, must still refer to the traditions of Normative Judaism as a standard for practice or as a measuring rod for change.

Biblical Judaism belongs to the distant past, and modern Judaism to the uncertain present and future. When we mention Judaism in this book without reference to a time period, we refer to the beliefs and practices of Normative Judaism. Modernist Jews may or may not be in agreement with these traditions. If we wish to discuss biblical precedents or modernist innovations, we will say so explicitly.

Jewish Beliefs:
The Six-Pointed Star

We are now ready to learn the beliefs and practices of Normative Judaism. It will be helpful to us to have a model for understanding the various aspects of Judaism and their relationship one to another. Our model will be the "Jewish star," the six-pointed star made up of two opposing triangles.

On the points of one triangle we place God, Torah and Israel. On the points of the other triangle we place the deeds of Creation, Revelation and Redemption. God creates the world, and God places the people Israel in this world to fulfill the purpose of his creation. God reveals the Torah, the word of God, to the people, so that they will know what to do in God's service. This is Revelation. By observing the Torah, the people Israel bring Redemption to the world. When Israel succeeds in this mission the star will be complete.

To understand Judaism, we must come to a deeper understanding of the meaning of God, Torah and Israel, and how they interact to bring the world from Creation through Revelation to Redemption.

2

Torah

The Jewish Scriptures

The Hebrew Scriptures, the Jewish Bible, contains twenty-four books. The Bible is divided into three sections—the Torah, the Prophets and the Writings. The proper Jewish name for the Bible, Tanak, is an acronym for the titles of the three sections—Torah, Nevi'im, Ketuvim. Christians call the Tanak the Old Testament, but this name is not favored by Jews.

The three sections of the Tanak have a descending order of sanctity. The Torah was believed to be the direct word of God, spoken to Moses on top of Mount Sinai. For this reason, the Torah is also called the Five Books of Moses. The books of the prophets were believed to have been revealed to them in the "spirit of prophecy." The message is from God, but the words are the prophet's own words. The Writings were believed to have been written in the "holy spirit." They were inspired by God but had a human authorship. It was permissible even in traditional Judaism to believe that the characters and events in the Writings might be fictional, although the message of the literature is a divine message.[1] The books of the Prophets and the Writings exist for inspirational purposes, but actual Jewish law and practice is derived solely from the five books of the Torah.

---

[1]See, for instance, the way in which Rashi comments on the Book of Ruth, and the statement in the Talmud that "there never was a Job."

The Meaning of Torah

The word Torah means "teaching" or "instruction" in Hebrew. The ancient Greek translation of the Tanak translated the word Torah as "nomos," "law," and so the Torah also came to be called "the Law."[2] The Torah is also called the Humash, after the Hebrew word for "five," and, in English, the Five Books of Moses. The five books are: Genesis, Exodus, Leviticus, Numbers and Deuteronomy. These names come from the ancient Greek translation, the Septuagint. The Hebrew names of the books, used by Jews, come from the first significant word in each book: Bereshit, Shemot, Vayikra, Bamidbar, Devarim. Jews also used descriptive names for some books. Leviticus was "Torat Cohanim"—"instruction for priests." Deuteronomy was "Mishneh Torah," "repetition of the Torah," since it repeats most of the laws found in the other books.

The word Torah has a broad meaning in Jewish usage. In the narrowest sense, Torah refers to the five written books of the Torah. In a broader sense, Torah refers to all of the interpretations, commentaries, extensions and applications of the Torah which have accrued over the centuries. In its broadest sense the word Torah refers to any teaching of divine wisdom, all of which can be thought of as ultimately deriving from the word of God. Thus, it was traditional for a Jew in Eastern Europe to greet another Jew with the Yiddish greeting, "Tell me a little Torah," which means, "Let us initiate a discussion on a Jewish topic." In this broad sense, any elevated or scholarly discussion on any topic of Jewish interest is a part of the Torah.

The Twofold Torah

Christians and Moslems accept the Tanak as part of their own sacred literature. Clearly, then, the mere acceptance of this Scripture does not make one a Jew. To be a Jew one must share the Jewish way of reading and interpreting Scripture. Rabbinic Judaism is based on the concept of the **twofold Torah.** The Torah has two parts, the Written Torah and the Oral Torah. The written Torah is the Five Books. The Oral Torah tells us how to live by the written Torah, based on the traditions which were handed down from generation to generation. The ancient rabbis taught Torah laws based on what they had learned from their teachers, rather than by deriva-

---

[2]The Christian Scriptures, the New Testament, uses the Greek name for the Torah. In the time of Jesus the third section of the Tanak had not yet been organized. The Scriptures for the Jews of that time were "the Law and the Prophets."

tion from scriptural texts. They believed that the traditions of their teachers derived from an unbroken chain of teachings that went all the way back to Moses. God taught Moses the Oral Torah at Mount Sinai, just as God gave him the Written Torah. The rabbis taught that whatever the rabbinic scholars said in their academies had already been taught to Moses on Mount Sinai. The traditions of the rabbis were eventually committed to writing in the Talmud, but they are still called the Oral Torah. Torah and Talmud together, the Written and Oral Torahs, make up the total Scriptures of the Jews.

The Bible

Jews do not put much stock in Bible-reading as a form of religious activity. In traditional Jewish society the Bible was the textbook of elementary education, which means that every Jewish male had a good knowledge of the biblical text. Once a student went beyond the elementary level, education centered on the Oral Torah. Since the Oral Torah contained the instructions for how to live by the Written Torah, there seemed little point in studying the Bible. One could study the laws of the rabbis and find out what the Bible really has to say to us.

As time went by, this feeling that Bible-reading is superfluous grew. By the late Middle Ages, the prejudice grew strong that Bible study was for "children and women," while learned men should concentrate their studies in Talmud and law codes. Once a Jew reached adulthood he would read the Bible only as liturgy. In the course of the religious cycle of the year a Jew would liturgically read all of the five books of the Torah, large portions of the Prophets, and most of the books of the Writings.

When an educated Jew reads the unadorned text of the Bible it seems "hollow" to him. The Jew does not share the belief of the Protestant that the voice of God speaks directly out of the scriptural text. God's voice is heard through tradition. Our learned Jew, when he reads the Bible, will wish to immediately run to the commentaries that summarize tradition in order to find out what the Bible is saying. Jews traditionally printed the Bible in a **Mikraot Gedolot,** an "expanded Scriptures." This book contains the text of the Bible in the middle of the page, surrounded by learned commentaries. With such a text a Jew can study the text of the Bible and the oral traditions together.

Most modernist movements of Judaism attempted to restore the Bible to the primacy that it had lost in rabbinic Judaism. We may mention Reform Judaism, Zionism, and the religious revival that struck pre-World War II Germany as three Bible-centered modern movements. The Bible

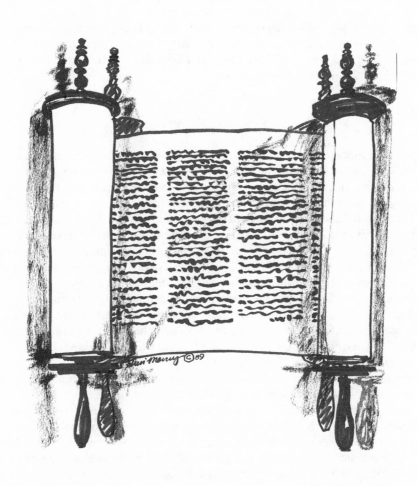

orientation of Reform Judaism has suffered from the general lack of Jewish education in America. Most American Jews know neither the rabbinic tradition nor the Bible. Many modernist Jews who are learned prefer to concentrate their learning in Jewish history, Jewish philosophy, and other such modern categories of learning, rather than in knowledge of sacred texts. In Israel Bible study has remained strong. Israelis perceive the Bible as the history book of their nation and, of course, the divine promises in the Bible justify the Jewish return to their ancient land. Both religious and secular Israelis find much of relevance and personal significance in the Bible. Since they speak Hebrew, Israelis find the Bible particularly accessible. They do not need translations.

Levels of Meaning

The rabbis believed that the Torah was word for word the actual word of God, including even the unusual spellings of some of the Hebrew words, and including even the form and style of the Hebrew letters. Even so, Jews were not biblical literalists in the same sense as modern-day Fundamentalists. They believed that every word in the Torah was true, but they did not believe that the message of Scripture was fully revealed in the literal sense of the words. It was generally agreed that "the Torah speaks in the language of humans" and "the Torah never departs from its simple meaning." In other words, the literal meaning is always a part of the message of Torah. But the literal meaning is not the only message, and it may not even be the most important message. In an important Jewish religious text of the thirteenth century[3] we find the daring statement, "If the Torah existed only for the sake of the stories it tells, we could write a better Torah ourselves." From this point of view, it is impossible that the eternal word of God should be concerned with events that occurred long ago, with no apparent relevance to the lives of later generations. If such texts exist in the Torah, it must be that they reveal their eternal truths on a symbolic level. Only by examining the text to discover its symbolic meaning do we uncover God's true intent in revealing the Scripture.

Symbolic interpretation was also used to reconcile human scientific knowledge with the divine teaching of the Torah. For example, if science tells us that the world was created over a long period of time, then the mention of seven days of creation in the Book of Genesis may be understood as a symbolic reference rather than as a literal truth. Although there are and have been Jews who insist on the scientific accuracy of the Torah,

---

[3]The *Zohar*.

there have also been those even in pre-modern times who had no difficulty upholding the divine origins of Torah while accepting scientific teachings that are in contradiction to the literal sense of the scriptural text. To modern Jews, Darwin's theory of evolution and the biblical account of Creation are not in conflict.

Rabbi Akiva, the great second century interpreter of Torah, taught that "there are seventy faces to the Torah." He meant that every verse of Torah could be interpreted seventy different ways, and each one of these ways would reveal a truth which is an aspect of God's message. Akiva compared the words of Torah to cut gemstones. A gem reveals a different light through every different facet, and yet it is a single stone with a single light from within. There is a unity to God's message, even while many different and even conflicting interpretations are possible, and each of these interpretations may reveal as aspect of God's truth.

Consider that when a mediocre novelist writes a novel, there is no meaning beyond that of the story itself. When a great writer creates a piece of literature, there are many levels of meaning. Consider how many messages have been discovered in Shakespeare's "Hamlet" or in Melville's *Moby Dick*. When God, the greatest of all authors beyond all comparison, writes a book, one would expect it to have a multitude of meanings and levels of meaning beyond our capacity ever to unfold them all.

"Pardes"

The Jewish mystics of the late Middle Ages identified four different levels of interpretation of Scripture. These four levels are together called "PaRDeS," the "garden," after the first letter of the name of each level— peshat, remez, derash, and sod. Peshat is the literal level of meaning. Remez is allegory, the means used by philosophers and scientists to derive scientific and rational truths from Scripture. Derash is the rabbinic method of interpretation by which we derive laws and the message of faith and hope. Sod is the meaning revealed only to the mystic. At the level of sod, the Torah reveals the nature of being itself, and the Torah becomes a pathway to the presence of God. The higher levels of understanding Torah are hidden, believed the mystics, because of the danger to those who dabble in knowledge of the divine without adequate maturity or learning.

Rabbinic interpretation of Torah was divided into two main categories, halakha and aggadah. Halakha is the legal interpretation of Scripture, the method by which required Jewish practices are derived from Scripture. Aggadah is everything else—ethical homilies, inspirational literature, doctrinal teachings, illustrative tales and the like. Halakhic interpretation of Torah must follow strict rules of interpretation, but in aggadah the literary imagination of the interpreter is given free reign.

Torah as Guidance

"Why did the Torah not begin with Chapter 12 of the Book of Exodus?" This was a favorite question in rabbinic commentary to the Torah. Regardless of the answer, the question reveals the rabbinic perspective on Torah. The most important thing about Torah is that it contains the laws which God has given for Israel to live by. So important is this function of Torah that the rabbis could wonder why there is so much Torah text before we get to the first laws given specifically to Israel, the laws of the Passover contained in Exodus, Chapter 12.

A divinely commanded law in the Torah is called a **mitzvah**, plural **mitzvot**. According to the aggadah there are 613 mitzvot in the Torah, 248 positive mitzvot (Thou shalt . . . !) and 365 negative mitzvot (Thou shalt not . . . !). There is a positive mitzvah for each bone in the human body,[4] to tell us that every limb of the body cries out, "Perform a mitzvah with me!" There is a negative mitzvah for every day in the year, to teach us that every day cries out, "Please do not sin on me!"

In English we speak of the Ten Commandments. These are called the Ten Words in the original Hebrew of the Torah. They are distinguished in that according to the Torah these were spoken in the hearing of all Israel, while the other commandments were given to Moses as an intermediary for the people. The Ten Commandments are not otherwise distinguished from any of the mitzvot in the Torah. The rabbis taught that one should be equally careful in the fulfillment of every commandment, for what seems minor to us may seem major to God.

The mitzvot are very general. They require a great deal of interpretation so that we will know how to actually observe them. We are told not to work on the Sabbath, but we do not know how to define work. We are told to honor our parents, but we are not told what deeds constitute honor for them. Rabbinic law fills in the details so that we will know how to perform the mitzvot properly.

The body of rabbinic law is called **halakha**. Every individual law is called *a* halakha. Reviewing their own work, the rabbis of old remarked that for some areas of law there are many mitzvot and only a small amount of halakha, while in other areas of law a few mitzvot generate mountains of halakha. Halakha literally means "the way." Halakha is the path one

---

[4]According to the counting of Aristotle. Modern anatomists identify more than this.

follows in order to live by God's intention. The rabbis attempted to be as specific as possible in halakha, to define the inner and outer limits of required and forbidden deeds. If one truly believes that one is living according to God's expressed will, one wants to be very careful not to transgress God's commandments even a little. At the same time, the rabbis took human and social realities into account. If it is a mitzvah to say a blessing before eating food, then one should say a blessing before eating any food in any amount. But it is ridiculous that one should say a blessing if one picks up a crumb and places it in his mouth. The rabbis debated whether the minimum quantity of food required for blessing should be equal to the bulk of an olive or the bulk of an egg, quantities well-known and easily estimated from human experience.

Although the rabbis attempted to be exact, they considered it a good thing to go beyond the letter of the law. They defined the minimum obligations of a person to God and to a fellow human being, but they considered it praiseworthy for a person to serve God and humanity beyond the minimum requirement. An ethical deed not required by halakha was considered to be **kiddush haShem,** a "sanctification of the Name of God." Rabbinic law attempted to establish standards beyond the minimum, to "build a fence around the Torah" that would keep a person far from transgression.

The development of halakha is the primary function of the Oral Torah. The Oral Torah was eventually written down in order to preserve the halakhic opinions of the rabbis. The first written volume of Oral Torah is the *Mishnah,* written about the year 200 CE by Rabbi Judah the Patriarch. The Mishnah is an encyclopedia of rabbinic legal opinions from the three previous centuries, organized by topic. Further rabbinic legal opinions, and old traditions not recorded in the Mishnah, are contained in the *Talmud.* There are two Talmuds. The Talmud of the Land of Israel was written down about 400 CE; the Talmud of Babylonia was written down about 500 CE. The Talmuds are organized as rabbinic discussions of each section of the Mishnah. The Talmuds contain a great deal of aggadah as well, but their primary purpose is the development and the recording of the halakha. After the publication of the Talmuds, all further halakha must be based on interpretation of the Talmud. The Babylonian Talmud in particular became the primary source for halakha. As new questions arose they were asked of great rabbis who were expert in the Talmud and other legal literature of Judaism. These rabbis would write **responsa,** legal essays, in which the new questions were answered. The customs of a community, **minhag,** also had the force of law and could not be overturned. The body of halakha established the Jewish way of life in the rabbinic period.

In summary: Torah provides mitzvot which are the basis of halakha. Halakha is based on the Talmud. The Talmud, combined with custom and the ongoing process of legal interpretation called responsa is the basis for the Jewish way of life.

Torah as Sacrament

Torah study is the most sacred activity. Torah study takes precedence over the pious service of God and the righteous service of humanity. In Jewish teaching we are told that a person cannot serve God properly or fulfill God's commandments unless he is learned in the Torah. In the Mishnah we are given a list of righteous deeds for which we reap rewards in this world and in the afterlife. The list includes acts of loving kindness, visiting the sick, giving hospitality to strangers, praying with sincerity, and more. At the conclusion we are told, "The study of Torah is equal to them all." The Jewish philosopher Judah Halevi explained the importance of Torah study with a parable of a pharmacy. In the hands of a trained pharmacist, the drugs in a pharmacy provide healing. If an ignorant person were to pose as a pharmacist and dispense drugs, he would provide death rather than healing. A person who has learned Torah serves God properly and brings healing into the world. A person who attempts to serve God without learning is likely to do more harm than good.

There is a rabbinic teaching in the Talmud: The world stands on three pillars—on Torah, on worship, and on deeds of loving kindness. The ordering of the three pillars is not accidental. Torah learning has priority.

The benefit of Torah study goes beyond its value as a tool for teaching the proper service of God. In Judaism, Torah study is a value in and of itself. The highest form of Torah study is "Torah l'shema"—"Torah for its own sake." This is Torah study unconnected to solving the practical problems of daily life and unconnected to the hope of acquisition of the power of knowledge. Rabbi Elijah of Vilna, a renowned scholar, was reported to have said, "If an angel were to offer me all the knowledge of the Torah at once, I would not accept it. For study, not knowledge, is the chief thing." The act of Torah study is believed to create character, to purify the soul, and to bring the student into relationship with God.

There is a Hasidic tale about Rabbi Zusya: Once Rabbi Zusya sat down with his disciples in a certain study house and he opened the Talmud to a certain page. All day long he never turned the page. The disciples, noticing this, waited in eager anticipation to hear of the problem that their rabbi had found in the page, and his resolution. When day after day went by and the rabbi was still on that same page, the disciples were puzzled.

Could anything be too hard for their rabbi to understand? Finally the disciples asked their rabbi what kept him so long. He replied to them, "I am so happy on this page; why should I turn to any other?" To Rabbi Zusya, advancement in knowledge and engagement in intellectual issues were not so important as the joy of study and the presence of the sacred that one discovers through study.

The Talmud is written in the form of a dialogue or debate between rabbinic authorities. The dialogue form is also used for the study of Torah. At Mount Sinai, God's word was revealed through divine speech to Moses, and afterward through the spirit of prophecy. Since the end of prophecy, taught the rabbis, God's word is revealed through the debates of the rabbinic sages. Even though the thoughts and words are those of the rabbis themselves, they are also the unfolding of the words which God gave at Mount Sinai.

This point is revealed in a daring legend found in the Talmud. Rabbi Eliezer[5] is in a dispute with the other Sages on a point of law. He is outvoted, but he refuses to yield. Rabbi Eliezer says, "If the law is according to me, let this tree prove it." He points to a tree, and the tree moves a hundred cubits. The others respond "The tree proves nothing." He says, "If I am right, let this stream prove it." The stream begins to flow backward. The others say, "The stream proves nothing." . . . Rabbi Eliezer says, "If I am right, let the heavens prove it." A voice came forth from heaven and said, "Why do you dispute with Rabbi Eliezer? The law is according to him." Rabbi Joshua rose to his feet and said, "It is not in heaven![6] The Torah has already been given on Mount Sinai, and we do not listen to voices from heaven. For it is already written in the Torah, 'After the majority must one incline.' "[7]

There is a postscript to the story. The next day Rabbi Nathan meets Elijah the Prophet.[8] Rabbi Nathan asks, "What was the Holy One, Blessed be He, doing at that moment?"[9] Elijah answered, "He was smiling and saying, 'My children have defeated me, my children have defeated me!' "

---

[5]Eliezer ben Hyrcanus, a member of the Sanhedrin at Yavneh in the late first and early second centuries.

[6]Rabbi Joshua quotes from the Torah, Deuteronomy 30:12. "It (God's commandment) is not in the heavens, that you should say, 'Who will go up to the heavens and get it for us and teach it to us?' . . . No, the matter is very close to you, in your mouth and your heart, that you may do it."

[7]Exodus 23:2. The full verse reads, "After the majority must one incline *not* to do evil." Rabbinic interpretation permits taking a text out of context to make an accepted point.

[8]In rabbinic legend, Elijah the Prophet is a messenger between Heaven and earth.

[9]That is, "Was God angry at the defiance of his word?".

When God took the Torah out of heaven and gave it to earth, God did so with the understanding that human scholars would unfold its meaning in earthly life. This intention is as much a part of revelation as is the original word of Scripture. Even God must follow these rules! In the end, God is depicted as a rabbinic master with his disciples—the master is pleased when his disciple becomes so skilled in Torah interpretation that he is able to overcome him in scriptural debate.

There is another Talmudic legend in which the scholars in the heavenly afterlife are debating a fine point of law, under the leadership of God. They are unable to decide the point, so they send for a certain rabbi. The Angel of Death goes to get the rabbi, and in his dying breath he calls out the answer to the question. Leaving aside the mythological elements of the legend, the point is that the Torah is given to the living, to flesh and blood human beings. Only before his death is the rabbi able to answer a question of law based on scriptural interpretation.

The question arises, "How can dialogue and debate reveal the word of God, when these are based on contradiction and God's word is unitary?" The rabbis were aware of this problem. In the earliest rabbinic times there were two major schools of thought among the rabbis, the School of Hillel and the School of Shammai. These two schools, following their masters, differed on many points of law. The final conclusion: "Both these and those are the word of the living God, but the law is according to Hillel." All the contradictory opinions of the rabbis, when they arise in good faith, are an aspect of divine revelation, but it is also part of God's plan that the opinion accepted by the majority becomes law for all time.

In Jewish printed editions of the Torah and the Talmud the text is printed together with commentaries. The commentaries were composed by the greatest Jewish scholars throughout the ages. The commentators often disagree with one another on the proper interpretation of the text. As one studies the text one is able to study the differing opinions of the commentators and draw one's own conclusions. In this way every Jew was able to participate in the ongoing dialogue of revelation, even when studying alone.

The preferred method of Torah study was for partners to join together and discuss the text, drawing out every possibility in the text to its furthest logical conclusions. This method of study through logical debate is called **pilpul,** literally, pepper. Pilpul engaged the full capacity of the human mind in the unfolding of God's word.

Torah as the Meaning of the Universe

In ancient Greek philosophy we find the concept of "logos," "the word," the ultimate idea, the ultimate meaning of the universe.[10] The rabbis of Greco-Roman times thought of the Torah as the logos of the universe, although they did not use the Greek term.

The Torah was believed to be pre-existent with God, as "black fire on white fire," before the Creation. The Book of Proverbs describes Wisdom as God's plaything, God's dear child since before the Creation. To the rabbis, this Wisdom could be none other than Torah. When God decided to create the universe, God looked into the Torah and created the universe according to the plan of what was written in it.

The Torah is the cause of the universe, in every sense of the word cause. Aristotle identified four types of cause: formal, material, active and final. We find in rabbinic writings that the Torah is attributed as the cause of all being in each of these four ways. God used the Torah as the blueprint for the Creation. Thus, Torah is the formal cause of the universe. When the people Israel came into being, when they entered their land and when they began to observe the laws of the Torah, they were fitting into the pattern established for the universe since its creation. To live according to the Torah is to live in harmony with the form of being itself.

The Torah is the active cause of the universe. Though the universe was commanded by God, Torah did the work, like the minister of a king. The Torah is the material cause of the universe. The twenty-two letters of the Hebrew alphabet which are the elements of the Torah were believed to be the twenty-two elements from which all matter is formed. The letters of the Torah were conceived of as a sort of Periodic Table.

The Torah is the final cause of the universe. The universe exists for the sake of Torah, so that the Torah may be fulfilled. One who observes Torah advances the purpose of the Creation. One who sins against the Torah hinders the purpose for which the world was created. The final end of Creation, of history, is a world filled with Torah, a world which is complete and all-good because Torah is the rule of all relationships. The Torah is thus conceived as being of cosmic significance.

---

[10]Those who know the New Testament may be familiar with the term from the Gospel of John. In the first verse of this book the Christ is described as the logos of the universe.

Torah as Salvation

It is often stated that "the difference between Christians and Jews is that Christians believe the Messiah has already come, while Jews are still waiting for him." Although well-meant, this statement is false. It presumes that Jews and Christians mean the same thing when we say "Messiah," but this is not the case. When a Christian says Messiah he means the Christ, the Savior. Jews do not believe that the purpose of the Messiah is to bring salvation from sin.[11] In Jewish belief it is Torah that brings salvation from sin. The Torah is already in the world; in Jewish eyes the means to salvation is ever at hand. Not faith in a Savior, but observance of the Torah, brings salvation to the individual. Jews and Christians both believe that their salvation is present and readily available. The difference between the Christian and Jewish concept of salvation is a difference in the concept of what it means to be human. One concept of humanity leads to the belief that faith in Christ brings salvation. A different concept leads to the belief that observance of mitzvot brings salvation. It is in their definition of humanity that the most significant difference between Christians and Jews is to be found.

The Torah Definition of Humanity

Jews believe that a human being is born neither good nor evil by nature. A newborn is **tabula rasa,** a blank slate, on which anything may be written. The human being is born with the capacity to do both good and evil, though certainly with a tendency to evil. The Jewish idea of the moral nature of humankind is not based on the Garden of Eden story, from which Christians derive the concept of Original Sin, but rather on the story of Cain and Abel. God says to Cain, "Sin crouches at the door; its urge is toward you, yet you may be its master" (Gen 4:7).

The Torah is the means to mastery over sin. Education determines whether a person will lean toward good or toward evil. Training in Torah tips the balance to the good. No human being is wholly good, but Torah allows a person to do enough good to outweigh the evil. In the end a person is weighed in the balance, and those who tip the balance to the good have saved their souls.

Torah learning improves the human heart, but this alone is not enough. A human being needs to be told what is good and what is evil. The mitzvot provide an absolute standard of good and evil. The Torah tells us

---

[11]We will discuss the Jewish understanding of the Messiah in a later chapter.

what is good, so that we may do it. A person need only obey the command-ments in the Torah, and even if his heart tries to draw him astray he will remain true to the path which God has laid out for him. If a person cannot overcome the will to do evil, even though he knows what God has com-manded, the Talmud says that he should immerse himself in the study of Torah, and this will purify his desires.

There is a well-defined psychology in the Talmud. A human being has two **yetzers,** impulses. There is a good yetzer and an evil yetzer. The Torah does more than suppress the evil yetzer; the Torah trains a person to use *both* yetzers in the service of God. The rabbis taught that if not for the evil yetzer a person would not engage in an occupation, build a house, or marry—all things which are an ultimate good. The mitzvot engage the evil desires and direct them to the fulfillment of God's commandments. We may compare the Talmudic psychology to Freud's idea of the id and the superego, desire and conscience. In the healthy person these two are merged into a strong and good ego.

The Torah Curriculum

Since Jews believe that the salvation of every individual requires knowledge of the Torah, it follows that every individual must be supplied with the means to salvation. Torah education is a necessity for every Jew. In ancient religions, religious knowledge was the province and property of the priests, the professional leaders of religion. This was also the case in biblical Judaism.[12] Early in the Rabbinic Period, a system of universal education was established for all male Jewish children. Tradition attri-butes the establishment of the schools to Simon bar Shetah, a Pharisee of the second century BCE. Jews had universal public education centuries before any other people, all because of the perceived need for every Jew to know the Torah.

The curriculum of the Jewish schools remained virtually constant for two millennia. Children began their education between the ages of three and five. The books of the Torah and the rest of the Tanak were the elementary school curriculum. The children began their education not with the Book of Genesis but with the Book of Leviticus. It may seem surprising that little children would be taught the dry priestly laws of Leviticus rather than the more interesting stories of Genesis. It may be that this was done to encourage the children to think of Torah primarily as

---

[12]See Ezekiel 44:23–24.

a book of laws and commandments rather than as a book of inspiration and history.

By the age of ten a child would know the written Scriptures virtually by heart. At this point the less promising students would conclude their formal education, while the brighter students would graduate from the **heder,** elementary school, to the **yeshiva,** a school of higher learning. In yeshiva the students would learn Mishnah, Talmud and halakha. The best students would go on to a higher yeshiva where they would learn Talmud in depth and the manner in which legal rulings are derived from the texts of the Oral Torah. The better students could look forward to rabbinic ordination and a position of authority in the community. The better students could also hope to be married to the daughters of the wealthy. Since the Jewish community admired learning above wealth, the wealthy gained status by giving their daughters to fine students and providing for them so that they were free to study. In this way Jewish society rewarded study of Torah above all other occupations. Even the poorest child could advance in society through the means of Torah scholarship.

We may admire the success of the traditional curriculum in serving the needs of the Jewish people for such a long period. At the same time, we must acknowledge the criticisms which were leveled against this curriculum in the past two centuries, with the advent of modernism.

The content of the curriculum created brilliant-minded people who had no practical, marketable skills. This fact contributed to the poverty and unemployment that were such a great problem for Jews as they entered modern society. Many Jews abandoned traditional studies in order to attend secular universities or trade schools. Now there are yeshivot in which secular and traditional religious studies are combined, but until fairly recently such a dual curriculum was unknown. There are still yeshivot where secular studies are forbidden, but most Jews have made their peace with the need for secular knowledge. A greater problem for Judaism today is the great number of Jews who receive very little religious education or none at all. Jews remain dedicated to education, as evidenced by the fact that ninety percent of American Jews attend college, but that dedication has largely been transferred to the secular realm.

Women and Torah Study

Perhaps the greatest criticism which modernists have leveled against traditional Jewish education is that it was reserved for males alone. Rabbinic law barred women from the higher levels of Torah study. Women were not taught the Hebrew and Aramaic languages, the languages of

Torah and Talmud. Women were permitted to read only inspirational literature and prayers composed especially for them, often by men.

The masculine orientation of traditional Jewish culture will be obvious as we discuss all aspects of Judaism. We will not repeat ourselves by raising the point again. It may be most important to raise the issue of women's religious rights here, since everything follows after education. Since Torah learning is the highest deed in Judaism, the source of salvation and the most admired occupation, it is natural that women would wish to participate. We know of some women who did become learned in Torah, but these were exceptional cases.

It seems obvious to the modernist Jew that women should have equal rights to learn and practice Judaism and to hold positions of authority within the community. Traditionalist Jews insist that law and custom are the will of God, not to be tampered with on account of contemporary values. In the modernist movements of Judaism in America today women have full educational rights, including the right to be ordained as rabbis. In the liberal Orthodox world women today have the opportunity to study Talmud, although they may not be ordained as rabbis. Even in the most traditional Jewish communities, where women are still barred from study and worship with men, women are granted many more opportunities for Jewish learning than were afforded them in the past.

In evaluating the role of women in the Jewish past, we might keep in mind that the attitude of the leaders of Jewish society reflected the perspective of the surrounding culture. Patriarchy was not peculiar to Judaism. Rather, it was a general characteristic of Western civilization. The rabbis of old were neither far-sighted nor regressive in their attitude to women, relative to the broader culture in which they lived. As for the present and future, the role of women in Jewish society will continue to be a subject of controversy. In the foreseeable future there will continue to be a broad spectrum of points of view, from the most traditional to the most egalitarian.

The Modern Torah Curriculum

The history of modern Judaism could be accurately traced in a history of curricular reform. The most moderate reformers at the beginning of the nineteenth century attempted to retain the traditional content of the curriculum—Torah and Talmud—while reforming the manner of presentation according to modern theories of education. They introduced instruction in Hebrew grammar to replace learning through word-for-word translation. They introduced an orderly presentation of materials. Some moderate reformers also attempted to broaden the curriculum with instruction in mathematics and science and with moral instruction based on study of traditional Jewish ethical texts. The intent of these moderate reformers was to improve the quality of Jewish education while creating a Jew who could make his way in the modern world and still be true to Jewish tradition. The watchword of this movement was "Torah v'daat" which means Torah and science or Torah combined with practical learning.

Even such moderate reforms were anathema to the adamant traditionalists. It was not unusual in the 1800s for a yeshiva student in Poland to be expelled if he were caught studying Hebrew grammar. It was known that if a student studied grammar he might then study modernist writings in Hebrew. He might then learn German, the better to advance in modern studies. He might then abandon Jewish tradition and run away to a German university. The adamant traditionalists thought it best to hold the line at the outset by refusing all curricular reform.

Those Jews who embraced modernism radically altered the curriculum. Talmud study was deemphasized or eliminated, while the Bible was given new emphasis. Jews were encouraged to engage in secular studies. The modern disciplines of philosophy and history were applied to the study of Judaism. Historical studies led to the view that Judaism was an evolving culture rather than an eternal divine law. The first large Jewish community to face the challenge of secular studies was in Germany. There, the **Wissenschaft des Judentums,** the Science of Judaism, was used to bolster the argument for changes in Jewish doctrine and practice which the modernists supported.

In America traditional Jewish education was difficult due to a lack of qualified instructors and because children attended public schools. In the early nineteenth century, American Jews followed the pattern of American Christians in establishing Sunday schools in which Jewish education could take place for a few hours each week. The curriculum was a Jewish catechism. Bible stories and the basic doctrines of Judaism were taught. The more traditional Jews who arrived in America in the late nineteenth century supplemented or replaced the Sunday school with a copy of the East European heder. Each day after school children would go to a Jewish school to study prayer book and Torah, using the familiar word-for-word translation method. Beyond teaching children to recite prayers by rote, this method had little success in America. In the twentieth century the Sunday school catechism was replaced with a curriculum based on Jewish history and customs. Constant curricular reform is typical of the Jewish religious school to this day, as America's Jews search for the curriculum that will express their modern concept of Judaism in a free society.

The influx of more traditional Jews in the twentieth century has led to the establishment of numerous Jewish day schools and yeshivot. Orthodox

Jews often attend a yeshiva rather than public high school. The Conservative Movement in America sponsors Jewish day schools as well. In recent years Reform Jews have also begun to establish Jewish day schools, despite their historic commitment to public education. There appears to be a growing movement among American Jews toward private schools that emphasize Jewish teachings, although the majority of American Jews still receive their Jewish education, limited though it may be, in synagogue-sponsored Sunday schools and afternoon schools.

The State of Israel maintains two separate school systems for traditional and secular Jews. In the "religious" schools Jewish texts are taught in the traditional manner, as a source of law for Jews to obey. In the "secular" schools Jewish texts are taught as a source of history and national culture. The different curricula reflect different perspectives on what it means to be Jewish in the world today.

3

God

Doctrines of Faith

We began our study with Torah rather than with God. Judaism is a religion of deeds more than doctrines. The beliefs of a Jew are inferred from what a Jew does. "There is no commandment unless there is one who commands." Thus, if we see a Jew fulfilling the mitzvot of the Torah, we presume that that Jew believes in God who gave the Torah. The learned rabbis of old paid great attention to drawing out the particulars of halakha, the law which they believed expressed the will of God. They did not pay such attention to the definition and description of Jewish beliefs about God. The rabbis tolerated much more diversity in matters of belief than is common in most religions, while insisting on conformity in religious practices. As long as a Jew lived by the Torah, he was not required to confirm his conformity to any standard of faith.

Rabbinic statements about the nature of God are scattered through numerous texts of midrash, rabbinic homilies on scriptural verses. The midrash is our greatest source for the doctrines of the rabbis. There is no attempt in the midrash to organize doctrines by subject matter, nor any attempt to resolve the numerous contradictions between one midrashic statement about God and another. The rabbinic language of faith was personal, informal, and generally stated in mythic or symbolic language that requires interpretation before much sense can be made of it.

When Jews have engaged in formal theology—that is, the attempt to develop an ordered philosophy which explains the nature of God—it has usually been under the influence of other cultures. In medieval Spain, Moslem and Christian intellectuals studied philosophy and engaged in formal theology. From their influence and in response to their challenges, learned Jews in Spain also began to practice theology, even to the point of developing lists of Jewish doctrines. It is worth noting, though, that each rabbinic philosopher had his own list, and the Jewish people as such never developed a consensus on formal doctrine. The most widely recognized list of Jewish doctrines is Maimonides' Thirteen Principles of Faith. These are:

1. The existence of God.
2. The unique unity of God. Not only is God one, but the oneness of God is unlike any other. God is not merely less than two, but one in a unique way.
3. God has no body or material being. All biblical references to parts of God's body (arms, eye, etc.) are to be taken as metaphors.
4. God is eternal. God exists before anything else did, and God will exist after all else is gone.
5. God alone may be worshiped. There is no intermediary between God and the worshiper.
6. We recognize the words of the prophets as a message from God.
7. Moses was the greatest of all the prophets. Moses alone received a word from God clearly, in a state of full wakefulness and awareness.
8. Moses received the entire Torah directly from God.
9. Nothing may ever be added to or subtracted from the Torah.
10. God is aware of all human deeds.
11. After death, God rewards the good and punishes the wicked.
12. God will send the Messiah. We must always hope for this, but we must not attempt to calculate the time of the coming of the Messiah.
13. In the Messianic Time all the dead will be resurrected to bodily life.

The final principle of Maimonides was the most controversial. His original list of Jewish principles did not include resurrection. After widespread protest, Maimonides included this in his list. After his death, Jews fought each other over whether Maimonides really believed in resurrection or had only said so under pressure. There were those who supported the doctrine and those who opposed it, although it had been a standard belief of Jews since the beginning of rabbinic times.

The Role of Theology in Judaism

The Thirteen Principles of Maimonides were written into a poem by an Italian Jewish poet. This poem was put to music and became a popular song which was sung at the conclusion of Jewish worship. This may be the final statement about the importance of creeds in Judaism, that they were sung more than studied.

Medieval Spain created other great Jewish theologians, although none was so influential as Maimonides. Judah Halevi, Hasdai Crescas, and Joseph Albo are worthy of mention. Gersonides was a great astronomer as well as a great Jewish theologian. Isaac Abravanel, the finance minister of Ferdinand and Isabella and a major force behind the voyage of Columbus, wrote a philosophical commentary to the Torah. The influence of the medieval Spanish religious philosophers was so great that Jews ever after expressed their beliefs about God in the terms which they established.

Philosophy and theology became important to Jews again in nineteenth and twentieth century Germany, as Jews began to integrate into modern Western culture. Jewish philosophers in Germany attempted to define the eternal beliefs of Judaism which could form a basis for modern Judaism. The philosopher Moses Mendelssohn was influential in the development of modern Judaism. Hermann Cohen, Sampson Raphael Hirsch, Leo Baeck, Abraham Joshua Heschel—these were some of the great German Jewish theologians. The philosopher Martin Buber had a tremendous influence on all modern philosophy. He may be the first Jewish philosopher since Maimonides to have such a widespread influence beyond the Jewish world.

The Unity of God

The most essential doctrine of Judaism is that God is one. All Jews are united in this belief, regardless of culture, time period or denomination. One could deny God and still be a Jew, but to deny the unity of God would be to remove oneself from the Jewish fold. The center of Jewish worship is the recitation of the verse from Deuteronomy 6:4 which affirms the oneness of God; "Hear, O Israel, the Lord is our God, the Lord is One."

Jewish philosophers realized long ago that an absolute Unity defies description. There is nothing that one can say to describe God. Maimonides teaches that all of our statements about God are metaphors which only tell us what God isn't, not what God is. When we say that God is one we say that God is not more than one, but God is not one in the same way that other things are one. When we say that God is powerful we say that God is not weak, but God is not powerful in the sense that created beings are powerful. The essence of God is always beyond our comprehension.

Essence and Effect

The things we can say about God are based on our own relationship to God. They are not a description of God's being but of God's effect upon us. In the Torah God's name is given as the four letters Yud, Heh, Vav, Heh. This unpronounceable name was said by the philosophers to represent the unknowable essence of God. God is also called by many appellations—Lord, Lord of Hosts, Elohim, El Elyon, El Shaddai, and the like. These names, said the philosophers, represent the various effects of God upon us, the ways in which God's actions impinge upon us. We are able to describe the deeds of God even though we do not know God's essence.

God is the Creator of the universe. Since God is good and God alone created everything, it follows that every created thing is good. Obviously there is evil in the world, but this evil is not created by God, nor does it derive from any force of creation equal to God. God alone is the source of all being.

God is the Revealer of the Torah. God gave the Torah and its proper interpretation to humankind. God's love for us is expressed in the gift of Torah. Our love for God is expressed through obedience to the Torah.

God is the Redeemer. God is made known in the world through his intervention in human history. God initiated the history of the people Israel through the choice of Abraham to father the people. The history of the nation begins when God redeems them from slavery in Egypt, gives them the Torah, and brings them into the Land of Israel. This act of redemption is representative of God's continuous acts of redemption. Ultimately, God will redeem the entire world. God's redeeming intervention in history ties together the beginning and end of time as we know it. The world begins with creation and ends with redemption. The events between creation and redemption are determined by God's revelation and the human response to it.

Relationship with God

Some modern Jewish thinkers have rejected the idea that God is unknowable. It is obvious to the reader of the Bible that ancient Jews believed that it was possible to have an intimate relationship with God. Abraham Joshua Heschel describes God as being above all a God of emotions, a God who truly cares. The sensitive person is able to feel the emotions of God. Heschel described the prophets of Israel as people whose own heart was filled with the feelings of God. They felt God's love for

Israel. They felt God's sorrow and anger when Israel did not respond to his commandments.

Martin Buber described God as a God of relationships. Not only can a person know God, but it is God who makes all relationships possible. The knowledge of God is not rational and intellectual. We do not know about God. Rather, God is known through direct and intimate relationship. God is always reaching out, always ready to relate to each person. When a person turns to God he finds that God is wholly present to him. God's presence makes it possible for us to enter into true relationship with other people and with all the things of this world.

Monotheism

The belief in one God is called monotheism. In ancient times Judaism was the only monotheistic religion. All other people were polytheists. That is, they believed in more than one God. Polytheists believe in an ultimate Divinity, or Godhead, which stands above all the individual gods. The difference between monotheism and polytheism is that the monotheist believes that the Divinity can be worshiped and related to directly, while the polytheist believes that Divinity becomes manifest in the world through numerous divine forces, each of which represents a partial aspect of Divinity. In polytheism a multitude of supernatural powers intervenes between the natural world and the Godhead.

This distinction is illustrated in a rabbinic tale about Abraham. Abraham is recognized as the first to recognize and worship the one God. The Torah introduces Abraham as a man of seventy who already has a relationship with God. The rabbis wondered how Abraham, living in a polytheistic culture, came to recognize God. According to the midrash, when Abraham was born the evil king Nimrod tried to have him killed. Abraham's father Terah hid him in a cave, where he passed his infancy. God caused food, drink and learning to pass directly into Abraham in the cave. When he was three years old Abraham crawled out of the cave and saw the world around him for the first time. It happened to be nighttime, and when Abraham saw the moon shining above the earth he said, "That must be God. I will worship it." All night Abraham bowed and prayed to the moon. Then the moon went down and the sun came up. "Now I see that I was wrong." said Abraham. "Not the moon but the sun is truly God." All day long Abraham worshiped the sun. Then the sun went down and the moon came up again. "This is foolish." said Abraham. "I will not worship the sun or the moon, but the One who created them both."

The polytheist perceives a world of contradictions. There is a god of war and a god of peace. There is a god of life and a god of death. There is a god of rain and a god of sunshine. The interaction of the contradictory forces in the world is explained by the interactions of the gods, each representing his own forces and either cooperating with or struggling against the other gods. The monotheist affirms that there is a unity above all seeming contradictions. There is an ultimate harmony to all creation. It must be admitted that this harmony is not readily apparent to one who observes life and the world. The recognition of this harmony requires a cognitive leap of the type taken by Abraham in the rabbinic legend. It is an affirmation of faith that the contradictions we face in life are only illusions or the result of a falling away from God's plan of creation. In the end, the perfect harmony which flows from a unitary God will prevail. The idea of "shalom," of harmony between all things in creation, flows from the idea of monotheism.

The unity of God means that there is a unity of ethics as well. In monotheism, contradictory laws of human behavior cannot be justified by the idea that each person follows a different god. One God establishes the same standards of behavior for all human beings. A person may be more or less obedient to the standards established by God, but the same standards apply to all people. One cannot choose to follow a god of war or a god of love, if one God created both war and love. Since all human beings are judged by a single standard the idea of humanity, of a single, united humankind, also flows from monotheism. It is worth noting that most ancient cultures, including that of the great philosophers of ancient Greece, did not think of people from other cultures as being truly human. Biblical Israel believed in their special relationship with God, but they also recognized God as the Creator of all humankind who extends his providential care to everyone. The requirement for justice in all human relationships follows from the ethical demands of monotheism.

Another distinction between monotheism and polytheism is the idea of human free will. In polytheistic religion fate stands above the gods, and even they must bow to its dictates. The manipulation of fate through magic allows the polytheist to gain control over the world of the gods. In monotheistic religion all events are seen as flowing from the will of God. Human beings are free to obey or disobey God's law, and by doing so they may change God's plan for them. Both God and humankind are free to determine the course of their own actions. What happens to a person is not determined by fate or by the whim of the gods, but by the judgment of a just God in response to a person's own actions.

Monotheism and Dualism

In early biblical times the prophets of Israel fought against the continuous influence of polytheistic religion. By the time of the Persian empire in the fourth century BCE we no longer hear of Jews being tempted by polytheism. New and greater religious challenges arose, however. The religion of the Persians was a Gnostic religion. The term Gnosticism is used to describe various religions in which there is a belief in two gods, a god of good and a god of evil. In Gnostic belief the world was created by the god of evil, while the god of good rules over the spiritual realm. There is a radical distinction between the material and the spiritual realm of human life, with all material concerns being relegated to the realm of evil. The concept of Satan came into Jewish religion from the Persian religion. Satan was made "safe" by assigning him the role of a faithful servant of God, the prosecuting attorney in God's heavenly court. The Gnostic influence caused many, however, to attribute to Satan independent power to do evil and frustrate the will of God.

In Gnostic religion the goal is to remove oneself from the material realm and live a spiritual life. One does this through "gnosis"—"secret knowledge" which is granted to the initiate to provide a pathway to the hidden realm of the spirit.

The rabbis in the first few centuries CE considered Gnosticism to be the greatest rival and threat to Jewish monotheism. The rabbis emphasized the goodness of all created things and the religious importance of material life, in opposition to Gnostic teachings. The rabbis fought against a distinction between the material and the spiritual; God can and must be served in both realms.

Mother and Daughters

Two new monotheistic religions arose and became the dominant religions of the Western world. Christianity arose in the first century and Islam in the seventh century. Although there are many differences between Judaism and Islam, Jews recognize that the Islamic idea of the one God is not essentially different from the Jewish God idea. The Christian idea of God is more troublesome for Jews to understand. Christians claim to be monotheists and are recognized as such in Jewish law, but the idea of a three-in-one God makes God divisible in a way not acceptable in Judaism. In Christian belief God the Father is Lord of Justice and God the Son is Lord of Mercy. Many Christians believe that Jews worship only the Father, and that the concept of mercy is unknown in Jewish religion. It is

important for Christians to recognize that Jews do not divide God in half and then worship only one half. Jews recognize the one God as the source of both justice and mercy.

There is a midrash which illustrates this point. According to the midrash God created many worlds and destroyed them before settling upon this world. God created a world of strict justice, but it could not stand. Then God created a world of strict mercy, but it could not stand. Finally God mixed mercy and justice together to create a world which could stand. This is compared to pouring water of different temperatures into a fine glass. If one pours boiling water into the glass, the glass will crack. If one pours icy water into the glass it will crack. If one mixes icy water with boiling water and then pours it into a glass, the glass will hold the water and remain whole. Thus, God mixed justice and mercy together to create a world that could remain whole. The midrash often speaks of God's "aspect of justice" and God's "aspect of mercy." The Creation was not possible without a continuing compromise between these two, both of which are aspects of the one God.

Idols

The second of the Ten Commandments forbids the making of physical images to represent God. Verbal imagery is not forbidden. The Bible and post-biblical Jewish literature abound in verbal images of God. God is called a father and a husband. God is called king and judge. God is depicted as sitting on a throne and as riding upon a cloud.

The rabbis stressed that the various biblical images of God should not be thought of as separate divine powers. We are taught in the midrash: God appeared to Israel at the crossing of the Red Sea as a mighty man of war, and at Mount Sinai as a kindly old man sitting upon a chair. Therefore God said to Israel, "I am the Lord your God, who brought you out of the land of Egypt" (the First Commandment), to teach us that God is always one and the same, no matter how many different ways God is perceived by us. The midrash teaches that the different images of God are human metaphors for understanding God. Our metaphors change as we relate to God in different ways and experience God in different ways. Shifting metaphors are useful to us, but they do not indicate any change in the nature and being of God.

In post-biblical times new metaphors were developed to express our understanding of God. The rabbis commonly spoke of God as The Holy One, Blessed be He, and as Master of the Universe. There is no feminine imagery for God in the Tanak, but the rabbis often spoke of the **Shekinah,** the "Indwelling," a feminine image for God which speaks of God's closeness to the world. Jewish mystics in the Middle Ages developed a rich vocabulary of verbal images for God. Thus we find in Jewish history a constant flow of metaphoric images for God. Old metaphors fall away and new ones come to replace them. Even as new names for God constantly arise, there is a continuous attempt to maintain the concept of the unity of God, to maintain that all names for God are human reflections upon a single and unchanging Divinity.

The philosopher Martin Buber defined an idol as a frozen metaphor. When one believes that one's image of God is not just a metaphor but a description of the true being of God, then that image becomes an idol. As long as one feels free to use a variety of metaphors for God, each one in proper response to the reality of the moment, there is no danger of turning images into idols.

The Problem of Evil and Injustice

Any observer of human life must notice that the good often suffer and the evil often prosper. In polytheistic religion this fact is easily explained as the decision of fate or as a sign of favor or disfavor from a particular god. In monotheistic religion, with its insistence that all the world is judged by a single just God, the injustice of life is not so easily dealt with. The justification of God is an overwhelming concern in monotheistic religion. Why are we unable to see in what way God justly rewards the good and punishes the evil?

An answer commonly given in the earlier books of the Tanak is that reward and punishment are inter-generational. If an evil person succeeds in life, he is reaping the reward of his good ancestors. If a good person suffers, it is on account of the evil deeds of his ancestors. This response loses acceptance in late biblical times, although it never entirely fades away. The rabbis believed in "the merit of the ancestors," God's forgiveness of Israel's sins in reward for the righteousness of Abraham, Isaac and Jacob. But this answer came to be regarded as not satisfactory in and of itself.

The prophet Ezekiel taught that each person receives reward or punishment from God only for his own deeds. (See Ezekiel 18.) Ezekiel denied that the deeds of a parent, whether good or bad, had any effect upon God's recompense to a child. God metes out reward and punishment to each person based upon his or her deeds alone.

Ezekiel's doctrine of individual reward and punishment opens the way for the doctrine of repentance, and Ezekiel himself draws this conclusion. If a person changes his deeds he becomes a new person, and is judged only on the basis of his new course of action. A person can turn from good to evil, in which case God will overlook the former good deeds and punish the evil. A person can turn from evil to do good, in which case God will forget the evil and grant reward for the good.

The idea of individual reward and punishment became basic to Judaism. But the abandonment of the notion of cross-generational reward and punishment left no way to explain the experienced reality of injustice. If good people do not suffer because of the sins of their ancestors, why do they suffer undeservedly?

The biblical Book of Job was written in the Persian period, about a century after the time of the prophet Ezekiel. The Book of Job can be seen as a response to the difficulty raised by Ezekiel's doctrine of individual reward and punishment. The book tells the story of the righteous Job who suffers for no apparent reason. The reader knows that he is merely being tested by God, but Job does not know this. Job cries out against the injustice done to him. He demands a court trial before God so that he can prove his innocence and the injustice of his sufferings. Job's friends, who came to comfort him in his affliction, attempt to assure Job that God does justly reward and punish. If Job is suffering, say his friends, then he must have committed some sin which justifies his punishment. Job denies this.

At the end of the story God speaks to Job and his comforters out of the whirlwind. God tells the comforters that they are wrong, that Job is indeed a just and good person. God tells Job of his greatness as Creator of the universe and assures Job that no human could possibly understand God's ways.

The Book of Job never answers the question it raises, except to tell us that the answer is beyond our comprehension. The only specific answer given in the Book of Job is a negative one—we may not say that there is no injustice in the world. We cannot explain the sufferings of the just by pointing to their imagined sinfulness. Injustice is not just an illusion. Despite the Book of Job, the human tendency to justify all of God's actions remained powerful. We find many rabbinic statements in which the rabbis attempted to justify their own sufferings and the sufferings of the Jewish people as God's just recompense for sins committed. The traditional liturgy includes the phrase "because of our sins we were exiled from our land."

The rabbis sought to explain the series of disasters that befell the Jewish people beginning with their unsuccessful rebellion against the Roman empire. How had God's people become so few? Why were they accorded second-class status in society? Why did the people lose sovereignty in their land and become exiles throughout the world, subject to the whim of foreign rulers?

One answer given was that the sufferings of Israel provided a vicarious atonement for all the peoples of the world. Israel, as God's people, was assigned the task of paying for the sins of the world through their own suffering. Another answer given was that the sufferings of Israel were "sufferings of love." Because God loves his people and trusts their faith in him, God tests them with great troubles. The midrash brings a parable of a potter and his pots. If the potter is unsure of the quality of his pots, he displays their quality by tapping them very lightly with the test-hammer. If the potter is certain that his pots are of the highest quality, he will strike them hard to display their value. God tests Israel with the greatest blows because God is certain that no matter how much they suffer they will not cease to worship him. Another given response to unjust suffering is that suffering is good for the sufferer. Suffering provides purification of the soul, and so ultimately it works to the benefit of the sufferer. The rabbis of old are recorded to have asked those of their colleagues who were suffering sickness or martyrdom if their sufferings were dear to them. Rabbi Akiva, who was tortured to death by the Romans in the arena, was recorded to have accepted his martyrdom as a precious opportunity for divine service.

Each of these various responses will provide consolation to some, but will seem inadequate and unsatisfactory to many others. It is recorded of Rabbi Ishmael that when the Romans tortured him he cried out for justice. He was silenced only when a heavenly voice told him that if he insisted on justice for himself, the whole created world would have to be brought to an end.

In the second century BCE we find a new response to the question of God's justice arising among the Jews. The belief arose that in a future time all people will be resurrected to new bodily life. The belief also arose that the eternal soul of each person is rewarded after death in a heavenly paradise or punished in a fiery hell. These beliefs replaced the biblical belief that all people, good and evil, sleep eternally in the underworld after death. The belief that reward and punishment are deferred until the afterlife and the time of resurrection gives a useful explanation for the injustice of this life. The rabbis taught the evildoers receive in this life the reward of their few good deeds, while the just receive the punishment for their few sins. The accounts are balanced in the afterlife.

The Jewish religious philosophers of the Middle Ages dealt with the problem of evil as a question of "providence," the nature of God's oversight of the world. They were faced with the challenge of contrasting the Jewish idea of a concerned God who intervenes in history with the Greek philosophical idea of a God who contemplates only his own being and whose only action in the universe is to guarantee the unchanging laws of cause and effect.

In his philosophy Maimonides classifies all the evils that can befall a person into four classes, based upon their cause. The most common type of evil, says Maimonides, is that which people do to themselves by improper living. A righteous person cannot complain of ill health if he eats and drinks too much. The second type of evil is that which people do to one another. Maimonides defends human free will. Just as God has granted us the ability to do his will without his assistance, so God has granted us the ability to do evil without his intervention. The suffering brought by wars, economic injustice and the like come to us from each other, and not from God. We cannot expect God to intervene to prevent the evil things we do to one another, even when they are very great. To do so would obviate the freedom of moral choice which God has granted to humankind.

The third type of evil is that which results from our nature. Since we have a mortal nature, we must die. Our death is not a judgment from God, but a natural event. Just as it is neither reward nor punishment for an ant to live according to the nature of ants, it is neither reward nor punishment when things happen to us according to our human nature, no matter how evil these events may seem to us from our own perspective.

The fourth class of evil is that which is visited upon us by God as punishment for our misdeeds. Such visitations, says Maimonides, are much fewer than is commonly supposed. Nearly all human misfortune derives from the first three causes.

The problem of injustice has been raised anew for Jews in the twentieth century by the Holocaust, the Nazi slaughter of six million European Jews during the Second World War. Some Jewish leaders have claimed that the religious responses of the past are not adequate to explain an evil of this magnitude. Attempts have been made to establish a Holocaust theology which will include this tragedy in our understanding of the relationship between God and the world, and between God and the people Israel. No one theology of the Holocaust has attained universal acceptance by the Jewish people, nor do all Jews agree that a new theology is required by the unimaginable evil we have seen in the twentieth century. The problem of injustice in a world created by a single just God will remain a central issue for Jewish theology. New answers will arise, and no one answer will solve the problem to the satisfaction of all.

4

Israel

B'rit

In Jewish teaching the relationship between God and humankind is understood to be a contractual relationship. The Hebrew word for such a relationship is **b'rit** (b'-reet). The usual English translation of b'rit is "covenant," an Old English word for "contract." B'rit expresses a mutual relationship between God and humankind. God fulfills his part of the contract, and humankind must fulfill its part. The partnership between God and humankind is intended to bring about the perfection of human life and society, and thus the redemption of the entire universe.

As expressed in the Torah, God's original b'rit with Adam was quite simple. Adam had to tend the Garden of Eden and observe the one mitzvah God had given him, not to eat of the trees in the middle of the garden. In return, God gave Adam eternal life and supplied all of his needs. Adam failed to fulfill the terms of the b'rit, and so God established a new b'rit. In the new b'rit with Adam people had to work hard to fulfill their material needs, and the eternity of humankind would be assured through birth rather than through immortality. Human beings were expected to live harmoniously among themselves and with all other creatures.

The descendants of Adam failed to live up to the terms of this b'rit. Finally God destroyed them all except for one righteous person, Noah, and his family. God established a new b'rit with Noah. For his part, God promised Noah never again to destroy the earth. The rainbow is the sign of God's covenant with Noah.

In rabbinic literature the terms of God's b'rit with Noah are called the Seven Laws given to Noah. These seven laws are not all explicitly found in

43

the written text of Torah, but the rabbis understood them all to be implied. The seven laws are:

1. The prohibition of idolatry.
2. The prohibition of blasphemy (cursing the name of God).
3. The prohibition of incest and adultery.
4. The prohibition of murder.
5. The prohibition of theft.
6. The prohibition of eating a limb from a living animal. An animal must be slaughtered before it is eaten.
7. The requirement to establish courts of justice. The taking of private revenge is thus prohibited.

The sixth prohibition follows the permission to eat meat that is given to Noah. The prohibition of murder is also connected to this permission—a person may slaughter an animal but not another person. The seventh prohibition follows the fourth. The given penalty for murder is death. In primitive societies this penalty is carried out through blood feud, in which the extended family of the murder victim seek out and kill the murderer or one of his relatives. The seventh law given to Noah requires that a murderer be brought to trial and that sentencing be carried out by the courts rather than by aggrieved relatives. Public law replaces private vengeance.

The Seven Laws of Noah are the terms of God's covenant with all humankind. They are what a modern anthropologist would call "natural law," the rules that are necessary for the establishment of any human society. All people, Jews and Gentiles, are responsible to fulfill the terms of this covenant. Gentiles in Jewish law are called Noahides—people living under Noah's covenant.

According to the Torah, the mass of humanity did not properly observe the covenant of Noah. In the succeeding generations people turned to idol-worship and to every sort of crime and sin. Having sworn not to uproot human society again, God established a new tactic. He would take one righteous individual and make a nation out of his descendants. God would give this nation his entire Torah. By their efforts and example this nation would establish the perfect society which would lead the world to redemption. God chose Abraham to be the father of the people Israel. God established a new b'rit with Abraham. God would make Abraham the father of a nation and give this nation the Land of Canaan, in exchange for which Abraham would worship only God and obey God's commandments. The sign of God's b'rit with Abraham is that all sons born to Abraham and his descendants would be circumcised on the eighth day after birth. This ritual is called **b'rit milah,** the covenant of circumcision.

When the nation was ready God established a covenant with them at Mount Sinai. The Torah provides the terms of this covenant, the Covenant of Sinai, under which the people Israel live. In exchange for observing all the laws of the Torah, Israel is God's chosen people. As long as Israel fufills the Torah God will fulfill his part of the covenant. When Israel fails to fulfill the Torah God punishes them. The success and progress of Israel in the world is dependent upon their fulfilling the terms of their covenant with God. The history of the people was thus to be understood not in terms of the interactions of nations and the forces of history but as a reflection of Israel's faithfulness to the terms of the b'rit. The Tanak is a history of the brit, a record of the consequences of Israel's obedience or disobedience to its terms.

As the bearers of the covenant, Israel are God's chosen people. The chosen people idea has been interpreted in different ways. At times the privilege of being God's chosen servants was emphasized. This was of particular importance when Jews were being persecuted and encouraged to abandon Judaism. At times the burden of divine service was emphasized, particularly in those eras when Jews have been able to interact freely with the non-Jewish community. The chosen people concept is not taken to mean that Jews are inherently superior to other people. It is taken to mean that the Jews have a unique opportunity to perfect themselves by observing the terms of the Torah.

There are Jewish texts which state that "all Jews have a place in the world to come"; membership in the covenant community provides automatic salvation. There are other texts which directly contradict this teaching, which state that it is more difficult for a Jew to achieve salvation. A Gentile is measured against the seven mitzvot given to Noah. According to Jewish teaching every Gentile who observes these laws is saved. It is not necessary to be Jewish to achieve salvation. A Jew is judged by all 613 mitzvot of the Torah. If one is a learned Jew the standard is applied even more strictly. Ironically, the more a person grows in covenantal relationship with God, the more that person places his soul in jeopardy. Salvation is easier for a Gentile than a Jew, easier for an ignoramus than for one learned in Torah.

Religion and Nationality

The covenant at Sinai was made not with individual Jews but with the Jewish people as a whole. The midrash states that when God established the b'rit at Sinai not only were all Israel gathered at the foot of the mountain, but God gathered every Jewish soul that would ever be born and brought them to Sinai to enter into the terms of the b'rit. Thus, every Jew is obligated from birth to observe the Torah.

Since the convenant was established with the people as a whole, it can only be fulfilled by the people as a whole. An individual Jew cannot fulfill the Torah on his own. Early in the rabbinic period the great teacher Hillel taught the maxim, "Do not separate yourself from the community!" This is one of the central maxims of Judaism. There are no monastic communities in Judaism. In Jewish teaching one cannot become spiritually perfect through self-isolation and self-denial. Every Jew was encouraged to engage in an occupation, to marry and have a family, to live in a Jewish community and participate actively in its affairs.

Many of the mitzvot in the Torah deal with the relationship between humankind and God. Many others deal with the relationship between one person and another. These mitzvot can only be fulfilled within a community of Jews, a community of people all living under the same covenantal terms. Not only in the ethical sphere but even in religious ritual there are many mitzvot that can only be fulfilled within a community. The rabbis defined ten persons as the minimum number of Jews required to establish a community. A group of ten or more Jews is called a **minyan**. Many of the prayers and rites of Judaism may only be performed in the presence of a minyan.

The traditional Jewish concept of the religious community is different from the concept found in America and some other modern countries that religion is a personal affair, the private faith of each individual. Many contemporary Jews apply this modern concept to their Jewish faith, at least to the extent that it enables them to participate fully as citizens of the nation while remaining Jewish. In Israel and in multi-national states such as the U.S.S.R., Jews are still thought of as a distinct nation. Traditional Judaism was the religion of a nation, and one could not be of the Jewish faith without also being a member of the Jewish people.

Since traditional Judaism is the religion of a nation, Judaism could only be observed and fulfilled in the context of national life. Jewish religion could not be separated from the Jewish land, language, law and culture. The Land of Israel, situated on the land-bridge between Asia and Africa, is the historic and natural home of the Jewish religion. The festivals, prayers, laws and practices of Judaism relate to the geography and climate of the Land of Israel. Jews continued to observe the harvest festival at the time of the harvest in Israel, even when they lived in lands that had a different harvest season. They continued to pray for rain at the time of year when the Land of Israel is in need of rain. Many of the mitzvot in the Torah, such as the commandment to let the land lie fallow every seventh year, are only operable within the land of Israel. In the Jewish religious consciousness, the Land of Israel is God's own possession. God gives and takes away this land in response to the moral quality of its inhabitants. No one but God truly owns the Land. God gave the Land of Israel, formerly Canaan, to the people Israel in fulfillment of his promise to Abraham and in fulfillment of his part in the covenant at Sinai.

The Hebrew language, as the language of the nation, is also essential to the practice of Judaism. Already in ancient times Jews ceased to use Hebrew in everyday speech. Aramaic, the language of ancient Babylon, became the common language of the Middle East. After Alexander the Great many Jews came to speak Greek, and a variety of other languages. From the Middle Ages on, most Jews spoke either a Jewish dialect of German, called Yiddish, or a Jewish dialect of Spanish, called Ladino. Through all this time, Hebrew continued to be the language of Jewish culture. Male Jewish children learned Hebrew so that they could read Scripture in the original. Many legends in the Talmud are written in Aramaic, but Hebrew remained the language of Jewish law. The prayers in the Jewish liturgy were all composed in Hebrew. It was considered permissible to pray in any language a person understood, but most desirable to pray in Hebrew. After Jews spread throughout the world, the Hebrew language provided a medium of communication and a force of unity between all Jews.

Jewish law was not just a religious law in the sense that we think of religion today. Jewish law was the law under which the Jewish nation lived. The Torah was the Constitution of the Jewish nation. The halakha was the body of the nation's laws. The **Sanhedrin,** the ancient high court of rabbis, served as Congress and Supreme Court of the Jewish nation. Although the Torah was considered divine in origin and its interpretation was given to religious leaders, it served all the purposes that secular law serves in modern America. Traditionally, rabbis were not so much pastors and spiritual leaders as they were lawyers, judges and legislators. Rabbis served these functions within the Jewish community.

The very term "Jew" is in origin national rather than religious. A Jew is a person from the Kingdom or Province of Judah. The first person in recorded history to be called a Jew is Mordecai in the Book of Esther, a book which tells of events during the Persian empire period. Judah was one of the 127 provinces of the Persian empire. In Persian times the term Jew replaced the earlier biblical term "children of Israel" to describe the members of this people. Jews lived in many lands, but always under their own national laws and with their own national culture.

In modern times, when Jews were first granted citizenship in the nation-states of America and Western Europe, some Jews actively rejected the idea that the Jews were any more a separate people. These Jews looked upon the national aspects of Judaism as a necessity to protect Judaism in its formative stages. Now that Judaism is fully developed, claimed these Jews, it could and should survive only as a religion, as a confession of faith. All of the religious movements of Western Judaism adopt this perspective to some extent, especially Reform Jews.

By now most Jews have become comfortable with their role as citizens. They no longer feel that their loyalty to the state has to be constantly proven. This makes contemporary Jews in Western countries more willing to reclaim some of the national aspects of Judaism as an integral part of their religion. Most American Jews give their heartfelt support to the State of Israel and express their solidarity with Jews throughout the world, even while functioning as loyal American citizens.

Kehila—The Community

Since the time of the Babylonian Exile in 586 BCE more Jews have lived outside the Land of Israel than within it. Even when Judah and Jerusalem were restored to Jewish rule under the Persians, not all Jews returned to live there. Over the centuries Jewish communities developed all over the civilized world. After the Romans destroyed the second Jewish state these communities carried on the Jewish way of life.

In ancient kingdoms and empires the modern national idea of one people living under one law was not known. There were many different laws. Different classes of citizens lived under separate laws, one law for nobility, another for peasants, another for each other social class. Empires imposed taxes and obedience on their subject nations but they did not require them to adopt the laws and customs of the rulers. Each subject people handled its internal affairs under its own laws and observed its own customs. In all the lands where Jews lived, they constituted a separate community. Jews would only live in those lands where they were free to live according to the Torah.

In all the centuries that Jews lived without a sovereign state of their own, the basic unit of Jewish self-government was the **kehila,** the community. All the Jews who lived in a given city constituted the kehila of that community. In some times and places the local kehilot (pl.) were organized into larger kehilot representing all the Jews of a given province or country. Each kehila was self-ruling and observed its own traditions and customs. The unity between all the kehilot was maintained by the fact that all of them accepted the authority of Torah and relied upon the rulings of the great teachers of Torah as the basis for their laws, rules and customs.

The citizens of each kehila established a ruling council. The council appointed rabbis to fill the positions of legal and religious authority in the community. The council had the power to tax the members of the kehila for both the taxes owed to the government and the taxes needed to pay for the community's own needs. The kehila established synagogues, schools, kosher meat-slaughtering houses, libraries for Jewish study, and whatever other institutions were required for the maintenance of Jewish life. When the government had business to conduct with the Jews it conducted that business through the leaders and representatives of the kehila.

In the Hebrew language a synagogue is called a **bet k'nesset,** a "house of assembly." The synagogue is also called a house of prayer and a house of study, but the primary name of the synagogue points to its original function as a community hall, a place for the members of the kehila to gather. Every kehila had its own synagogue supported from community funds. In larger communities there were also a variety of synagogues funded privately by voluntary groups such as trade associations, religious brotherhoods, or Jews who had immigrated from a common place of origin. Jewish men ideally spent their leisure time in informal study and discussion of the Torah. The **bet midrash** was established for this purpose. The bet midrash was a library full of tables and benches around which the men could gather before and after work to study. Those who could afford it could spend virtually all of their time in the bet midrash.

Elementary schools were established by individual teachers. The kehila would support a **Talmud Torah,** a community school for the children of those who could not afford to pay tuition. Every Jew was required to provide an education for his sons. A Jew who could afford tuition but would not send his sons to school could be enjoined by the court to pay tuition. The community school made sure that no one was deprived of an education on account of poverty.

If the community were large enough it would support a **yeshiva,** a school of higher Jewish learning. The members of the community would provide for the material needs of the students so that they would be free to study. The finest yeshivas would attract the best students from near and far. The next generation of rabbinical leaders would come out of these yeshivas.

Social services were provided by voluntary organizations within the kehila. Each kehila had a soup kitchen to feed the hungry and a community chest to provide money to the poor. There would be a hostel to provide hospitality to travelers and a poorhouse to shelter the homeless. There were societies to dower poor brides and other such needs. The leading citizens of the kehila were entitled to belong to the Holy Society, which maintained the community cemetery and provided for the burial of the dead.

The Modern Jewish Community

In the aftermath of the American and French revolutions the legally recognized kehila was abolished. In many countries Jews began to deal with their govenment as individual citizens rather than as members of a corporate community. In most modern countries Jews were still singled out by law for restrictive or injurious treatment, but even for this purpose Jews were now recognized by the government as individuals, not as members of a separate community. In the more enlightened countries there were fewer restrictions against Jews. Jewish law was no longer enforceable by the leaders of the community. Observance became a voluntary matter. Many Jews chose to live their lives within the bounds of halakha. Particularly in those countries which offered more social advancement to Jews, many were tempted to abandon Judaism, while others sought to restructure their Judaism along new lines that did not depend upon the community structure.

American law forbids the legal recognition of communities on the basis of faith. American Jews are no different from any other Americans before the law. In the United States more than in any other country Jews have organized their communities as voluntary religious associations. The primary mode of identification with the Jewish community in America is membership in a synagogue which serves primarily as a house of worship. About half of all American Jews do choose to belong to a synagogue. Unlike the synagogue of old which represented a local community, the American synagogue is organized around religious doctrines. Jews in one locale may travel to the synagogue in another locale if it better represents their religious perspectives.

In addition to serving as a house of worship, the other major function of the American synagogue is to provide for the religious education of children. The American synagogue is also a place for socializing and for adult study, but these functions have never taken on the significance that they had in the Jewish community of old.

American Jews have established community organizations outside the synagogue structure to meet community needs. Each Jewish community unites to raise charitable funds. Local federated charities pass on funds to the United Jewish Appeal, which distributes these funds in Israel, America and other countries according to needs. There are communal Jewish political organizations which serve to fight for social justice and against anti-Semitism, such as the American Jewish Committee. There are Jewish political organizations such as AIPAC which lobby for American support for the State of Israel. The B'nai Brith is a large Jewish men's organization which has lodges in many communities. Besides meeting social needs, the

B'nai Brith does much communal, educational and political work. Hadassah is a women's Zionist organization which supports health care in Israel.

Most American synagogues belong to national organizations which provide for a variety of communal needs. The major organizations are the Union of Orthodox Congregations (the largest of many Orthodox organizations), the United Synagogue (of the Conservative movement) and the Union of American Hebrew Congregations (of the Reform movement). The small but growing Reconstructionist movement claims recognition as a fourth major movement of American Judaism.

Many American Jewish communities have a Jewish Community Center, often supported by the local federated Jewish charitable organization. Some have predicted that in the future Federations and JCCs will replace synagogues as the dominant institutions in American Jewish life, bringing American Jews closer to the traditional communal framework. Although some see a trend to a greater degree of community organization, many Jews have opted for less formality and structure in their community. Since the late 1960s there has been growth in the **havurah** movement. A havurah is an association of Jews, limited in size, without any professional leadership and often without any building of their own. Havurot (pl.) meet for worship, study and Jewish celebration. In the havurah, the commitment of its members replaces the work of the rabbi and other professional communal leaders. Some havurot raise and distribute charitable funds from their own members, bypassing the formal communal organizations.

We have mentioned only a few of the Jewish organizations that exist in America. Jews in America have shown a knack for establishing numerous communal organizations, often with overlapping functions. It has been humorously stated that every Jew in America is president of something.

Outside the United States and Canada, the largest Jewish populations in the world since the Second World War are in the Soviet Union and the State of Israel. In the Soviet Union the government has effectively prevented the Jews from forming local or national community organizations— this despite the fact that as a recognized nationality the Jews have a legal right to their own press, theater and other expressions of national culture. In the State of Israel, the government and its institutions provide for the communal needs of Jewish citizens. National cultural institutions are Jewish in nature. Two public school systems are supported by the government, one for religious Jews and one for secular Jews. Synagogues and rabbis are provided from state funds.[1] The State of Israel perceives itself as the kehila not only of its citizens, but of Jews all over the world.

---

[1]Parallel religious and educational institutions are provided for the Christian and Moslem minorities.

Jews and Gentiles

Following the anthropology of the Book of Genesis, the Gentile nations of the world are known as the Seventy Nations. The biblical division of peoples is partly by geography and partly by language grouping. Modern Jews may still speak of the Seventy Nations, although the number is not taken literally today. The non-Jewish nations may also be referred to in Hebrew as "goyyim," "the nations." The Greek translation of goyyim, "Gentiles," is also used and is thought by some non-Hebrew-speaking Jews to be a more polite term.

As mentioned above, it is taught in Judaism that the righteous among all the Gentile nations have a place in the world to come. They may achieve their salvation by observing the Noahide laws. Since Jews believe that a Gentile makes his salvation more difficult rather than easier to obtain by becoming Jewish, Jews do not feel compelled to seek out converts to Judaism. According to the Talmud a person who comes on his own to convert to Judaism is to be repelled three times, in order to make sure that his motives are pure and his convictions are strong. If a person has withstood this test and is still interested in becoming Jewish after a period of study, then that person is accepted into the Jewish faith and the Jewish people. Despite the difficulties involved there have always been some men and women who have chosen Judaism.

The Pharisees, the predecessors of the rabbis, are reported to have actively sought out converts to Judaism. The missionary passion of early rabbinic Judaism was cooled by a number of factors. The defeat of the Jews in two rebellions against the Roman empire made Judaism less attractive to others. The rise of Christianity and Islam meant that most of the Gentiles with whom Jews came into contact were not idol-worshipers. They practiced a religion which according to Jewish teaching was acceptable to God.[2] When the Roman empire became Christian in the fourth century CE they made it illegal for any person to convert to Judaism. The penalty for the convert and for the Jew who supervised the conversion was death by burning. This law remained on the books in many Christian countries right into modern times. This penalty naturally cooled the missionary ardor of Jews. Over the centuries Jews in Christian and Moslem lands have frequently been pressured or forced to convert away from Judaism. The sympathy which Jews thus feel for the victims of conversionary pressures has also made Jews reluctant to proselytize others.

---

[2]Maimonides believed that Christianity and Islam were created by God specifically for the Gentile nations, just as God had created Judaism for the Jewish nation.

Early in its history the Christian movement made an historic decision that conversion to Christianity did not require one to join the Jewish people. One could become a Christian while retaining one's national identity. This decision is recorded in the Book of Acts. This decision facilitated the spread of Christianity to become the religion of many nations. The rabbis of the first century chose not to make a similar move. It seemed right to them that Judaism should be the religion of a single people, and whoever adopted the faith would become a member of that people and live by its laws. This decision determined that the Jews would remain few in number and small in influence on world events. On the other hand, the decision of the rabbis meant that the Jews would be free to live as a covenant community, united not only in spirit but also in all aspects of earthly human life. It meant that Judaism remained a religion tied to history, in which the passage from creation to redemption was indelibly tied to the communal life of the people and their rise and fall in the real world.

The decision to remain a single people did not mean that Jews had given up on the ideal of a united humankind. On the contrary, the idea of the one God contains within it the ideal of a united and peaceful world. The idea that all human beings are created in the image of God remained central in rabbinic Judaism. But the role of the Jews in human society was to be carried out from within Jewish society. The Torah defined the Jewish people as "a holy nation, a kingdom of priests." The rabbis took the priestly vocation of every Jew seriously, right up to demanding that every Jew observe the biblical rules of priestly living. The Jews were to serve humankind as a priest in biblical times served the nation of Israel. The Jews are to be teachers of God's law by exemplifying that law within their own communal life and by acts of goodness to others. An ethical deed performed to benefit a Gentile was considered an act of **kiddush haShem,** sanctification of the name of God. As a priest represented and taught faith in the one God, so every Jew was to represent and teach that faith. The sacrifices which the priests offered were believed to bring the nation of Israel close to God. By their divine service in observing the mitzvot, the Jews were to bring all of humankind into a close relationship with God. It was taught that the continuation of God's mercy and sustenance to all the world depended upon the faithfulness of Jews to the demands of the Torah. This belief gave cosmic significance to the practice of Judaism within the community. For a Jew, the best service of humankind was the practice of Judaism. In times of restriction and persecution, faithful Jews attempted to fulfill the Torah within the bounds of their own community, while living as peacefully as possible with their neighbors. In times of freedom, especially in modern times, Jews have attempted to extend the social principles of the Torah into the life of the broader community and that of the nations in which they live.

In pre-modern times Jews had no choice but to concentrate their ethical and social concerns on their own community. In contemporary Judaism there is much debate over the proper balance of particular and universal concern which Jews should express. Some Jewish leaders believe that too much emphasis on universal concerns weakens Jewish commitment, undermining the very source of Jewish concern for humanity. These leaders may also believe, on the basis of history, that the Gentile world is intractably hostile to Jewish concerns and so the Jews have a prior commitment to protect their own people. Other Jewish leaders believe that the world has changed. They see in modern freedom a new opportunity to bring the world closer to the perfected society which is envisioned in the Torah. To these Jewish leaders the service of humanity is the very justification for the existence of Judaism.

This same debate is carried on in the State of Israel in different terms. Some see the purpose of the State of Israel as providing her Jewish citizens with the same security and services which any state provides for her citizens. Others believe that the State of Israel should strive to be an exemplary society of perfect social justice. The hostility of Israel's neighbors to her continued existence has made it more difficult to see how Israel might fulfill this universalistic mission.

Judaism on Christianity

Christianity began as a sect of Judaism. The earliest Christians preached their message in the synagogues, seeking adherents from among their fellow Jews. The rabbinic leaders of Judaism were attempting to stamp out sectarianism and bring all of the many Jewish factions under their leadership. As recorded in the Christian Scriptures the rabbis (Pharisees and Scribes, lawyers) singled out Christianity for negative attention. While the early Christians probably felt this way from their own perspective, we have no reason to believe that the rabbis noted the small early Church except as one of many sectarian groups. In that period there were many claimants to the title of Messiah, some of whom gathered more followers than did the early Church.

The break between Judaism and Christianity occurred in stages, not all of which are clearly known to us. The apostle Paul brought his mission to the Gentiles, and it was among the Gentile nations that Christianity spread. Those Jews that did become Christian merged with the majority of Gentile Christians and soon lost their Jewish identity.

Paul defined Christianity not just in Christian terms, but in comparison to Judaism. Christianity was necessary, taught Paul, because Judaism does not work. Judaism was perceived as a failed precedent to Christianity. Judaism was portrayed as an incomplete religion, as Christianity without Christ. The historic Christian attempt to define Judaism in these terms has greatly complicated relations between the two religious groups. It is difficult to compare the two religions because of this, and because the two religions have a common Scripture and a common religious terminology but use them in different ways. Two thousand years of living in close proximity have also led to a great deal of mutual influence. Though they are two different religions, Judaism and Christianity are intertwined in many ways. For the Christian who is attempting to understand Judaism it is helpful to remember that Jews define their own religion differently than Christians define it, and Jews do not feel any gap in their religious life that could be filled with faith in Christ. A religious Jew finds answers to all of his religious questions within the teachings of Judaism.

The final break between Judaism and Christianity may have occurred during the Roman siege of Jerusalem in 69–70 CE. The Christians in Jerusalem removed to Damascus, separating their destiny from that of the Jews. Or the break may have occurred during the second Judean rebellion against Rome in 132–135 CE. The rabbinic leaders of the Jews proclaimed the leader of the rebellion, Simon Bar Kochba, as the Messiah. This may have proved unbearable to the Christian community, who then completed their separation from Judaism.

When the early Church leader John Chrysostom came to Damascus in the late fourth century he found that the strong Christian community there had close relations with the Jewish community. Christians relied on rabbis for amulets and for religious teachings and celebrated holidays with the Jews. Fearing that this situation would weaken Christian faith, Chrysostom preached a series of sermons against the Jews. He taught that the Jews were spiritually blind and rejected by God because they had not accepted Christ. He taught that Jews should be isolated socially and economically. Over the course of time this became the official attitude to Jews in Christian lands. When the Byzantine empire became officially Christian, Jews were isolated and restricted by law. The Church Father Augustine taught that the Jews were to be tolerated because of their position as God's people, but were to be despised and kept in low estate as a living example of the fate of those who reject Christ. This attitude remained official Christian doctrine until modern times, although often the restrictive laws were not enforced and Jews were granted more freedom and opportunity than Christian law dictated. Jews were treated harshly by modern democratic standards, but we should point out that in an age in which religious dissent was not tolerated, Jews fared better than Christian sectarians or followers of other religions, who were exterminated or persecuted out of existence.

In medieval Europe Jews were preserved for the valuable economic and social role they played in the feudal economy. Between the twelfth and the fourteenth century the Jews became less useful to the economy, while religious fanaticism was on the rise. Jews were subjected to increasing persecutions. Jews were eventually expelled from the countries of Western Europe. In Central Europe Jews were confined to walled-in ghettos and cut off from social relations with their neighbors.

The Middle Ages saw the rise of the **blood accusation,** the preposterous accusation that Jews use Christian blood to make Passover matzoh. The accusation was invented by two English monks who owed much money to Jewish moneylenders. Had they murdered these Jews, their debts would have reverted to the king. In order to escape their debts the monks planned a riot against the Jews in which the record of debts could be burned. The monks used the recent disappearance of a child in their locale to raise the accusation that the Jews had murdered him to use his blood in Jewish rituals. The blood accusation was repeatedly raised against Jews when it pleased governments to rouse the peasants against them. The last great occurrences of the blood accusation were in Damascus in 1848 and in Russia in 1903. International outrage in these two cases prevented anti-Jewish action and put the blood accusation finally to rest.

The modern age has been both the best and the worst for Jews in Christian lands. As nations were transformed by the ideals of the American and French revolutions, Jews were granted citizenship rights and equality, or at least relief from their worst disabilities. The Jewish community in the United States of America is the freest community ever to exist in the Diaspora.[3] On the other hand, the modern age saw the rise of anti-Semitism, the racial hatred of Jews, which culminated in the Holocaust. Six million Jews were exterminated, by far the largest slaughter of Jews ever. Since the Holocaust anti-Semitism has diminished but not disappeared. Much of the force of anti-Semitism has gone into anti-Zionism, the national hatred of Israel and, by extension, all Jews.

The Holocaust caused many Christian groups to reevaluate their teachings on the Jews. At the Second Vatican Council convened by Pope John XXIII the Church accepted the role of historic Christian teaching in leading to the Holocaust, and it took steps to initiate a new course. The Jews of today were not to be blamed for the death of Christ. The textbooks of Church schools were to be examined so that anti-Jewish teachings could be

---

[3]The lands outside the Land of Israel.

eliminated. A course of interfaith dialogue with Jews was initiated to increase interfaith understanding. Many Protestant churches have adopted similar proposals.

Dialogue between Jews and Christians is a reality today in America and throughout the world. Dialogue requires an attitude of mutual respect and recognition, a willingness to accept others as they are and listen to what they have to say. The Jewish agenda for interfaith dialogue generally includes: an end to missionary activities toward Jews, recognition of the validity of Judaism as a distinct religion, an examination of Christian attitudes and teachings which lead to anti-Semitism, a plea for support for the State of Israel. The Christian agenda generally includes the desire that Jews will listen and grant validity to the Christian belief in Jesus as the Christ.

Judaism on Jesus

Until modern times it was not possible for Jews to objectively study Christian beliefs. In the Middle Ages Jews were subjected to conversionary sermons and other tactics intended to pressure them into conversion. If a Jew came for instruction in Christianity he would be expected to convert. Jewish scholars were required by kings and nobles to engage in interfaith debates on terms highly disadvantageous to the Jewish point of view. These disputations were ordered for the amusement of the nobility or as a pretext to initiate a policy of persecution. All interfaith learning and discussion was carried on in a spirit of competition and conversionary fervor. Only in the past two centuries has the objective spirit of modern education made it possible to dispassionately and appreciatively study other religions.

In the late nineteenth and early twentieth centuries some Christian scholars in Germany and England began to study the Talmud and other basic works of rabbinic Judaism in an attempt to understand Judaism in its own terms. We might mention Strack, Danby, George Foot Moore and Travers Herford as the best known of these scholars. They ignored the anti-Jewish polemics of the New Testament in an attempt to understand early rabbinic Judaism as it appeared in the eyes of its adherents. They made it possible for students of Christian history to understand the Jewish origins of Christianity. Their work enabled Christians to study Judaism appreciatively.

In the early twentieth century Jewish scholars began to publish studies of the life and teachings of Jesus. Claude Montefiore, a wealthy English Jew, dedicated much of his time to the study of early Christianity. Though not a professional scholar, he was acquainted with many of the great Jewish and Christian scholars of his day, and he made use of their assistance in his work. Still popular is his *A Rabbinic Anthology*, a collection of selected rabbinic writings translated into English, organized around the major themes of the Gospels. A proper comparison of early Christinaity with rabbinic Judaism requires a knowledge of Greek, Hebrew and Aramaic. Montefiore wanted to enable the English reader to do his own comparative reading.

The Jewish historian Joseph Klausner wrote a biography of Jesus entitled *Jesus of Nazareth*, a book which is still read today. In the early decades of the twentieth century there was intense interest in reconstructing the biography of Jesus out of the materials presented in the Gospels. Most of these biographers presented a Jesus in their own image, and the Jewish biographers were no exception. They presented a Jesus who was a dedicated rabbinic Jew in his life and all of his teachings. Jesus' teachings were presented as reflecting the influence of the Hillelite school of Pharisaism, the same school of Pharisees who were the forerunners of rabbinic Judaism. As these biographers would have it, not Jesus but Paul was the first Christian. All of the Christian teachings which are contrary to Jewish teachings were seen to originate with the Apostle Paul, two decades after the crucifixion of Jesus. One might say that the Jewish scholars reclaimed Jesus as one of their own.

Contemporary scholarship has shown that the early biographers of Jesus, Christian and Jewish, did not sufficiently analyze their source materials. They also read many of their own wishes and opinions into their work. Today's historical scholars are much more cautious about what may be said about the historical Jesus. The New Testament and the Talmud are both recognized as religious documents which see history through the eyes of faith. All would agree today that Jesus' life and teachings reflected the Jewish environment in which he lived, but there is uncertainty about what may have been new in Jesus' teachings or contradictory to other Jewish teachings of the time. The New Testament and Talmud were composed in a time when Judaism and Christianity were already rivals, in a time when many of the Jewish sects active in Jesus' time had ceased to exist following the failed rebellion against Rome.

Contemporary reservations about the early Jewish historical judgment on Jesus have not gone beyond the scholarly world. Most Jews today would echo the earlier scholarly judgment that Jesus was a good Jew who never contradicted rabbinic teachings. They would say that Paul, not Jesus, was the first Christian. Asked what role Jesus plays in Jewish life, most today would respond with the statement made by earlier Jewish writers on Jesus that Jews can recognize him as a prophet. This statement, while nice and respectful of Christian sensibilities, has no basis in fact. It is a basic tenet of Judaism that prophecy ceased after the time of Ezra the Scribe, centuries before the time of Jesus. Only prophetic books written before the time of Ezra were included in the biblical books of the Prophets.

An interesting sidelight to the scholarly discussion on Jesus is provided by the work of the American Yiddish novelist Sholem Asch. Asch wrote two novels about the life of Jesus, *The Apostle* and *The Nazarene*. Asch was a well-known Jewish writer and these books were widely read in Yiddish and in English translation. Many of the tradition-minded Jews who read these works were scandalized by Asch's choice of subject, and he was accused of being a secret missionary. Asch was stung by the criticism. He later wrote a fictional biography of Moses in order to display his continuing loyalty to Judaism. Asch was in fact a loyal Jew who was simply fascinated by the Gospel story of Jesus. The earlier Jewish writers on Jesus had to overcome suspicion from Gentiles who feared that they were attempting to undermine Christian faith and from Jews who feared that they were assimilating to Christianity or secretly proselytizing Jews to Christian faith. Their restraint and objectivity in the face of criticism made it possible for a later generation of Jews to study the teachings of Christianity without fear. There are, of course, still many Jews and Christians who object to interfaith study and dialogue.

German New Testament scholarship after the First World War served the cause of the growing movement of anti-Semitism. Comparative studies were highly critical of Judaism. The German theologian Harnack wrote a book on Christianity in which he described Christianity as "Romantic Religion."[4] Leo Baeck, a leading German rabbi, faced the challenges raised by Harnack. In his essay "Romantic Religion"[5] Baeck criticized Romantic religion while praising Judaism as Classical religion. Baeck's essay can be seen by us as an attack not so much on Christianity as on that view of Christianity which made room for Nazism in Germany.

Another German-Jewish scholar, Martin Buber, compared Judaism and Christianity in his book *Two Types of Faith*. This book is of great importance because of Buber's popularity among Christian theologians. Buber's philosophy of dialogue made open-minded inter-faith dialogue and understanding an imperative. Though Buber makes his preference for Judaism clear, he shows a sympathetic appreciation of Christianity in his comparison of the Christian and Jewish ideals of faith. Buber calls Jesus

[4]The English translation of Harnack's book is entitled *What Is Christianity?*.

[5]This essay can be found in English translation in the book *Judaism and Christianity*, trans. Walter Kauffman, J.P.S., 1958.

his "great brother," a fellow Jew whose great and original teachings call for a response from his inner being.

Buber's response to Jesus has been widely praised in Christian circles, but Buber has also been criticized for his failure to deal with Jesus as the Christ. This far, though, a Jew cannot go and remain a Jew. A Jew can respond to the person Jesus of Nazareth, but the doctrine of the Christ was and will remain alien to Jewish religious thought. In response to calls for Jews to find a place for the doctrine of the Christ in their religion, Jews have asked for mutual respect for those differences which are basic to the two religions. Despite their similarities and their points of contact, Judaism and Christianity remain different religions with contradictory responses to the questions of religion.

Contemporary historical scholarship on Jesus has taken on a complexity which defies a simple summary. Students who wish to pursue the matter are encouraged to begin with the following two books:

Sandmel, Samuel, *We Jews and Jesus*, Oxford University Press, New York, 1973.
Vermes, Geza, *Jesus the Jew*, Fortress Press, Philadelphia, 1973.

PART TWO:

Jewish Faith and Practice

5

The Service of God

Varieties of Religious Duty

The Jewish way of life encompasses every aspect of human endeavor. There is a verse in the Book of Isaiah: God desired for his righteousness' sake to make the Torah great and glorious (Isaiah 42:21). This verse was interpreted in rabbinic Judaism to mean that God provided many opportunities for people to acquire righteousness by giving them a multitude of commandments covering every situation in life.[1] Whether a Jew is conducting business or preparing a meal or relaxing or doing any other thing a person might do, there are religious laws to give direction to that activity. The *Shulhan Aruk*, the great Jewish law code of the sixteenth century, even gives instruction for which shoe should be put on first in the morning. Through the observance of the commandments every act, even putting on shoes, is given divine and cosmic significance.[2]

The goal of the Jewish way of life is to extend the realm of the holy in human life. The holy may be defined as that part of life where there is awareness of the presence of God. The secular or unholy is that part of life where God's presence is ignored or kept at bay. Even if an act may not seem meaningful in itself, the consciousness of doing it in response to God's mitzvot raises the action to the service of God.

There are mitzvot of the hand, the heart and the mind—mitzvot

---

[1]Following the Hebrew, the verse was taken to mean "God desired for the sake of his righteous ones to make the Torah numerous (large, extensive) and glorious."

[2]Many modern-day Jews object to the extension of ritual rules to such acts as tying shoes. Many other Jews still find it meaningful to perform such acts according to religious law.

which cover deeds, beliefs and feelings, thought and speech. The mitzvot of the hand include deeds performed in the service of God such as worship and holiday observance, and also deeds performed in the service of humankind. Every good deed which serves humankind is considered to be a deed in the service of God as well. In the midrash there is a parable of a king whose subjects want to do something for him to show their devotion. The king says to his subjects, "What can you do for me? I have everything I need. But be good to my son the prince, and I will account it as devotion to me." In like manner God says to humankind, "What can you do for me? But be good to your fellow human beings, who are my children, and I will account it as service to me." It was considered a mitzvah to go beyond what is required in the law in the service of one's fellow. The rabbis called an act of gratuitous goodness **kiddush haShem,** the "sanctification of the Name of God." Every act of a Jew should ideally represent God's goodness to the world. The ultimate act of kiddush haShem is to give up one's life rather than deny God or be forced to commit a terrible sin.

The rabbis taught that one was not liable except for sins actually committed. Even so, they valued proper beliefs and feelings. There is a wealth of Jewish literature intended to train the heart in the love of God, the love of goodness, and the love of one's fellow human beings. The rabbis taught that one should not do good just because one feels like it, but out of the love and fear of God. The highest level of action is to do something because God has commanded it. "One should not say, I will do so-and-so because I want to; I will refrain from doing so-and-so because I do not want to do so anyway." Rather one should say, "I wish to do so-and-so, but my Father in heaven has commanded me not to."

In the Jewish culture words are thought to have great power. It has been pointed out that the Hebrew word for "word" is the same as the word for "thing." To say something is the same as doing it, so one must be careful what one thinks, what one intends and what one says. A pious Jew is careful not to take a vain oath and not to participate in malicious gossip. A pious Jew will attempt to deflect wrongful thoughts and intentions from the mind, to fill the consciousness with "Torah thoughts" and the consideration of how God might best be served.

A Jew is expected to study matters which help one to grow in Torah knowledge and the performance of mitzvot. In traditional society, this was the purpose of learning. Only in modern times have Jews widely adopted the habit of reading for pleasure or of studying only to broaden one's horizons. Time which could be devoted to the study of Torah was thought to be too valuable to expend on other matters. Subjects such as history, mathematics, natural science and philosophy were studied from the perspective of the light which they might cast upon the meaning of Torah.

THE SERVICE OF GOD

The Sacred Calendar

The Jewish way of life revolves around the sacred calendar. The calendar tells a Jew whether a day is a workday or a Sabbath, a holiday or a fast day. The cycle of the weeks, the months, the seasons and the years depends upon the calendar. The rabbis taught that the commandment to establish the calendar was the very first commandment given specifically to the Jewish people.[3]

The Jewish calendar is a luni-solar calendar. A solar calendar is based upon the solar year of 365 ¼ days. The Gregorian calendar used in the Western world is a solar calendar. A lunar calendar is based upon twelve lunar months of 29 ½ days. A lunar calendar year is 354 days long, about eleven days short of a solar year. A given date in the lunar calendar will march backward through the seasons at the rate of eleven days a year. The Islamic calendar is a lunar calendar.

The Jewish calendar is a lunar calendar adjusted to the seasons by the addition of a thirteenth month as needed. Every nineteen years there are seven leap years of thirteen months. The extra month is the last winter month, added to insure that in the Land of Israel the grain is ready for harvest by the spring festival of Passover. In ancient times the **intercalation** of years was done by observation, but in the fourth century or later a written, calibrated calendar made astronomical observation unnecessary.

The months in the Jewish calendar alternate between 29 and 30 days in length. There are two months which may have either 29 or 30 days. Thus an ordinary Jewish year may be 353, 354 or 355 days long. A leap year may be 383, 384 or 385 days long. The "intercalation" of months and years makes the Jewish calendar extremely complicated. It takes a trained expert to calculate the calendar properly.

In a solar calendar the new day begins at morning, with the appearance of the sun. Midnight, the start of the day in the Gregorian calendar, is the earliest moment of the morning. In a lunar calendar the new day begins in the evening. The Jewish day begins at sunset, defined as that time when at least three stars can be seen with one glance at the sky. A Jewish day goes from one sunset to the next. So, for instance, the Sabbath begins at sundown on Friday and ends at sundown on Saturday. In the Jewish calendar Saturday night is the beginning of the first day of the next week.

The seven day week is a uniquely Jewish development based on the religious observance of the Sabbath. The entire week of a Jew is thought of as the passage from one Sabbath to the next. The days of the week are named according to their distance from the Sabbath just past—First Day,

---

[3]Based upon Exodus 12:1: "This month you shall mark as the first of the months. . . ."

Second Day, and so forth. The week follows no astronomical or human pattern except for the Jewish Sabbath.[4] The week entered the calendar of the Western world through Julius Caesar. The Gregorian calendar is a minor adjustment of the calendar developed by Julius Caesar after he became emperor of Rome. Julius seems to have been fairly well acquainted with Jewish customs, and he borrowed the Jewish week as a way of organizing time in his new calendar.

Over the course of history Jews have used a variety of systems for numbering years. In biblical times Jews numbered from the year of the Exodus from Egypt. In Greek times Jews numbered from the beginning of the reign of the Seleucid dynasty which ruled the Middle East after Alexander the Great's conquests. From the Middle Ages on Jews began to number years since the Creation, according to the account of the generations given in the Torah. This number is not taken too literally even by those Jews who believe that the Creation story is literally true, since the count of the years between events in the Bible is often vague, but this system of numbering has been accepted by all Jews as a convenience. The Gregorian year "1980" is the year "5740 Since the Creation" in the Jewish calendar.

The Jewish calendar in use now is that favored by the rabbis in Judea during Roman times. It is uncertain how ancient this calendar is. There is much evidence that in biblical Israel a solar calendar was used. The lunar calendar may have come into use only after the Babylonian exile, in imitation of the Babylonian calendar. Various Jewish sectarian groups in Roman times had their own versions of the Jewish calendar which often differed widely from the rabbinic calendar. Like the rabbis, they believed that their calendar was the one commanded by God for the proper determination of the sacred times.

Calendars reflect astronomical realities such as the cycle of the year and the phases of the moon, but that is not their primary function. In human society our sense of the passage of time and its meaning comes to us from culture. The complex and relatively inaccurate Jewish calendar was developed not because simpler calendaric systems were unknown but because this system best suited Jewish needs. The ancient requirement for observation to determine the length of months and years helped to maintain the unity of a people that was scattered all over the civilized earth. Whoever had the power to declare the months and years had the authority to determine the calendar for all Jews. Any Jews who would not accept this central authority were identified as sectarians. This authority was probably centered in the Temple as long as it stood. After the Romans destroyed the

---

[4] The idea that the week is an approximate division of the month into fourths has no sound basis and has been generally rejected.

Temple in the year 70 CE the rabbinic Sanhedrin determined the calendar. The Talmud tells how in the century after the destruction of the Temple the President of the Sanhedrin, Rabban Gamaliel, asserted his authority by requiring the other rabbis to accept his calculation of the calendar. In the third century the center of Jewish learning was shifting from the Land of Israel to Babylon. The Babylonian rabbis wanted the authority to determine the calendar for themselves, but the leaders of the Sanhedrin would not allow them, maintaining the central position of Jewish leadership in the Land of Israel. The written calendar is attributed to the last President of the Sanhedrin. When the Sanhedrin was disbanding due to persecutions in the fourth century, the Nasi Hillel II created a written calendar rather than pass the authority to establish the calendar to the rabbis outside the Land of Israel.

Some modern reformers would like the Western world to switch to a simplifed calendar which would have a five-day week. They do not realize that the institution of the Sabbath is far more important to Western society than the mathematical convenience of having a year which is exactly divisible by weeks. A simplified calendar would require the establishment of occasional "non-days" which would not be numbered in the months or counted as days of any week. Non-days were known in some ancient societies. These days were believed to be ruled by evil spirits. No productive work was done on these days, and the usual morality and social order were not operative. Wild New Year's Eve parties are a remnant of this custom. By having no time which is "outside of time" in the Jewish calendar, the moral problems associated with non-days were eliminated.

Most modern-day Jews live by the Gregorian calendar as a matter of convenience. The Jewish calendar is used to mark religious occasions. This of course includes the holidays, which can only be determined by the Jewish calendar. It also includes the recognition of **Yahrzeit,** the death anniversary of loved ones, other significant life-cycle events, and important dates in post-biblical Jewish history. Most American Jews keep handy a calendar which gives both the Gregorian and Jewish dates and which marks both Jewish and secular American holidays. The American Jew lives in two cultures at once, and so he lives by two calendars at once.

The Life Cycle

The significant events in the life of a Jew from birth to death are recognized in sacred Jewish ritual. Eight days after birth a Jewish boy is entered into the covenant of Abraham in the ritual of circumcision. Appropriate blessings are recited by the father. The circumcision is performed by a **mohel,** an expert in this procedure.[5] This ceremony is called **b'rit milah,** the covenant of circumcision. The b'rit milah may be performed at home, in the synagogue, or in a special room at the hospital. At this time the child is given a name. Ashkenazic Jews usually name a child after a deceased relative. Sephardic Jews name after a living relative, often the grandfather of the child. Many American Jews have two different names. They have a secular name which they use in everyday situations and a Jewish name which is a Hebrew or Yiddish equivalent of the secular name. This Jewish name is used only on sacred occasions. The patronymic or last name is not used as part of the religious name. The Jewish custom is to call a person by his or her name followed by the name of the father, So-and-so **ben** (son of) so-and-so or so-and-so **bat** (daughter of) so-and-so. Girls are named when they are presented in the synagogue about a month after birth. In recent times some modern Jews have held a ceremony of naming and blessing for daughters on the eighth day after birth. It is common now for boys as well as girls to be presented in the synagogue, especially if the parents have not observed religious custom but have had their son medically circumcised in the hospital after birth. The ceremonies of b'rit milah and naming are followed by a joyous meal which is provided by the parents for friends and community members.

Education

The first day of a child's religious education begins around the age of five. In former times the child on his first day of school would be dressed in white and paraded on the shoulders of important members of the community. In a ceremonial lesson the child would be taught the first letter of the Hebrew alphabet. Then they would give him sweets to eat, so that the child would learn that Torah learning is sweet. In synagogue religious schools in America the ceremony of **consecration** is generally held on the fall festival of Simhat Torah. The new students in the religious school are called to the pulpit to recite the Shema Yisrael, after which the rabbi blesses them. The children are given a gift to mark the occasion, often a small paper copy of a Torah scroll.

At the age of thirteen for boys and twelve and a half for girls a child becomes **bar mitzvah**—"liable for the commandments." Before this age a child's behavior is the responsibility of the parents. Now the child is expected to have the maturity and knowledge to fulfill the mitzvot for

---

[5]In American Jewish communities where a mohel may not be available the rabbi will preside while a medical doctor will perform the circumcision.

himself. Now that the child is bar mitzvah he is privileged to fulfill commandments in the name of the public, which includes leading the community in worship. Some centuries ago it became the custom that on the Sabbath after the thirteenth birthday a boy would be called up to the **bimah** (pulpit) for the first time to recite the blessings over the public reading of the Torah. The boy recites the weekly reading from the Prophets, and often part of the week's Torah reading. The congregation would shower the child with sweets and a small repast would be served by the parents after worship in honor of the occasion. In modern times the ceremony of bar mitzvah has become exceedingly important and the celebration afterward has become second only to weddings in opulence. The bat mitzvah of girls is also now recognized in all but the most ultra-Orthodox communities, though in traditional congregations girls do not recite from Scripture.

Many modern Jews do not continue their child's religious education after Bar Mitzvah. In response to this unfortunate situation, Reform congregations in nineteenth century Germany replaced the ceremony of bar mitzvah with a ceremony of confirmation which is held at the age of fifteen or sixteen. The confirmation ceremony is held on the spring festival of Shavuot. In form it resembles a graduation ceremony. Members of the confirmation class lead the worship and give speeches. Confirmation is observed in all Reform congregations today, even though bar mitzvah observance has returned to these congregations. Some traditional congregations have also added a ceremony of confirmation, primarily as a mode of encouragement to continued Jewish study.

Conversion

One who is not born Jewish and wishes to become a Jew observes the ceremonies of **giur,** conversion. Rabbinic law establishes three requirements for giur—**milah** (circumcision, for men), **tevilah** (immersion in the **mikveh,** the ritual bath) and **kabbalat 'ol hamitzvot** (accepting the yoke of the commandments). A person must first engage in a period of study in order to learn about the commandments so he or she will be able to accept them. There is no set amount of study which is required; this is up to the discretion of the supervising rabbi. When the student is ready the ceremony of milah is performed. If a man is already circumcised a drop of blood is drawn in symbolic religious circumcision. A few days are given for recovery before the final ceremony of tevilah. A **bet din,** a court of three rabbis, is convened at the mikveh. The proselyte enters into the mikveh, a tub so constructed as to allow for complete immersion. The rabbis of the bet din symbolically ask a few questions on Jewish observance so that the proselyte can display knowledge of the mitzvot and readiness to observe them. If the proselyte is a woman the rabbis stand behind a wall or curtain. When the questions are properly answered the proselyte immerses in the water. Upon coming out, that person is recognized as a Jew. A Jew by choice is in no way distinguished from a Jew by birth. A Jew by choice is considered to be a descendant of Abraham, and if that Jew should cease to profess Judaism he or she would be considered not a Gentile but a Jew living outside the law. If he or she then wishes to return to Judaism, no new ceremony is required. The rule is "once a Jew, always a Jew," whether one became a Jew by birth or by conversion.

The modern Reform movement does not require milah or tevilah for conversion to Judaism. They require intensive study for at least a few months. When the proselyte is ready, the supervising rabbi convenes two additional witnesses. The proselyte answers a few questions regarding his or her free will and intention to join the Jewish people and accept the Jewish faith. He or she then recites the Shema Yisrael and is given a Hebrew name. He or she is then welcomed into the Jewish community.

The variant ceremonies for conversion have been a source of contention between the different movements of American Judaism. Efforts have been made to preserve the unity of the Jewish people by finding a way in which Jews by choice (a term preferred over "converts") from one movement can be accepted by all movements. As of this writing this remains one of the most serious issues confronting American Jews.

Marriage

The marriage rate has always been very high in Jewish society. Marriage is considered to be the natural state of a human being. An unmarried person is thought to be only half a person; in marriage two halves become one whole. The sexual relationship between husband and wife is considered to be no concession to human weakness but a gift of God and a pathway to holiness. The joy which husband and wife give to each other is a mitzvah. It has been said that the Torah served as portable home and government to the Jewish people during centuries of exile, preserving the Jewish people in times of trouble. The same could be said of the strong family life of traditional Jewish society, that it was a source of strength and salvation for the people.

The traditional age for marriage was about eighteen or twenty, though this has varied. Until modern times marriages were usually arranged by the parents of the bride and groom. A **shadkan,** a marriage broker, often helped to bring two families together. The shadkan has been a source of humor in modern parodies, but traditionally the shadkan was a leading citizen who performed this work without pay as a form of service to God. Most young Americans today would reject an arranged marriage, but the lower divorce rate in traditional society would indicate that parents often did a better job of choosing happily for their children than we do on our own today. Jewish law did provide that the bride and groom should meet before the arrangements were sealed, and each had the right of refusal.

Since the Middle Ages the legal engagement ceremony has been part of the marriage ceremony. Therefore the intent to marry is established by a contract, called **tenaim.** In traditional society a boy and girl were often promised to each other at the age of thirteen. There was a common custom in Eastern Europe for the future son-in-law to grow up in his in-laws' house. They would be responsible for his education. The bride's dowry often included a few years of full maintenance for the couple by her parents so that the groom could continue with his Torah studies.

The formal engagement contract was signed at the time of the marriage. This written contract is called a **ketubah.** The ketubah was established in early rabbinic times, primarily to protect the economic rights of wives. The ketubah establishes a bride-price. This amount is paid to the wife in case of divorce, or it comes to her as her inheritance out of the first and best part of her husband's estate upon his death. This prevented divorced and widowed women from becoming destitute.[6] The ketubah also established the dowry. It was traditional for the bride's family to provide the bedding and linens which the couple would need to establish their new household. The form of the ketubah, written in the Aramaic language, is established in Talmudic law. The details would vary depending upon the wealth and personal status of the bride and groom.

Today, all but the most traditional Jews choose their own spouse. They marry at the age usual in the general society. Dowry and bride-price are no longer observed. As in general society, wedding gifts and savings help the couple to establish their household. Traditional Jews still sign an Aramaic-language ketubah in the Talmudic form or a modern variation of it, but this has become a religious ritual without much legal application. In America the legal obligations of husbands to wives and wives to husbands are established by the statutes of the state.

In Talmudic law a wife is acquired by three means: by gift, by contract, and by cohabitation. The marriage ceremony includes all three. The gift is the wedding ring. The contract is the ketubah. Immediately after

---

[6] In comparison, it is worth noting that divorced women constitute the fastest growing proportion of the poor in America in the 1980s.

the ceremony the couple are secluded for a period of fifteen minutes, a symbolic cohabitation.

The marriage ceremony is called **kiddushin v'nisuin. Kiddushin,** "sanctification," is the legal engagement. **Nisuin,** marriage, is the permission to live together as husband and wife.

The ceremony may take place in the synagogue, in the home, or outdoors. The couple stands under a **huppah,** a wedding canopy. The huppah is an ancient tradition of unknown origin. It may symbolize the presence of God, or the new home which the couple will create. The groom is called **hattan;** the bride is called **kallah.** The hattan goes to the huppah in procession with the men. The kallah then goes to the huppah in procession with the women, who may all carry lighted candles. A rabbi officiates. The rabbi recites words of welcome and blessing, concluding with the blessing over wine. The kiddushin is sealed as the groom presents the ring to the bride and recites the words which establish their relationship. The ketubah is then read to separate kiddushin from nisuin. The nisuin consists of the **Sheva Berakot,** the seven blessings. These conclude with the blessing over wine, and again the bride and groom share from the cup. The rabbi pronounces them husband and wife. The groom then steps on a glass. When the glass shatters the guests shout "**mazal tov,**" "good luck." The new couple and guests then proceed to the wedding feast. Traditional Jews observe the wedding feast for seven nights. Each night the sheva berakot are repeated in honor of the new couple.

Reform Jews observe some variations of the traditional ceremony. The kiddushin and nisuin are completely intermixed. The bride generally presents a ring to the groom and recites a parallel formula. There is no reading of the ketubah, and instead of the traditional legal document a simple document of marriage is signed by the hattan and kallah and their witnesses. The bride and groom are generally accompanied to the huppah each by his or her own father and mother.

In addition to the customs we have mentioned here, Jews in different lands have developed their own unique marriage customs.

Divorce

The divorce rate among American Jews is lower than that of Americans in general. Divorce was uncommon in traditional Jewish society. That is remarkable when one considers how easy it is to acquire a divorce under Jewish law. Biblical law provides for a man to divorce his wife, and a man may do so for any cause. Rabbinic law allows a woman, for certain causes, to go before a court which will enjoin her husband to grant her a divorce. Since the Middle Ages the law provides that no woman may be divorced against her will; mutual consent is required. The **get,** the divorce decree, is presented by the husband to the wife. The **bet din,** the court of the three rabbis, serve only as witnesses and as experts to insure that all is done according to law.

A get may not be pre-made. It is written only for a specific man to give to a specific wife on a specific occasion. The husband is required to write the get himself; usually the husband appoints an expert to write the get on his behalf. The document is reviewed by the rabbis of the bet din to make sure that it is correct in all particulars. The husband drops the get into the hands of his wife, who takes legal possession of it by lifting it up and then carrying it under her arm to the door of the courtroom and back. When the wife takes possession, the divorce is complete. The court tears the document so that it may not be reused and keeps it on permanent file. This care is required to assure the legitimacy of children born to the woman from a later marriage.

American law licenses clergy to perform marriages but not divorces. Reform Jews accept civil divorce as religiously valid, obviating the need for a get. Orthodox and Conservative Jews require a get for divorce. They will not grant the husband or wife documentation of their get, which they need for remarriage, until their civil divorce is complete. A problem can arise for a traditionalist woman if after civil divorce her less traditional husband will not grant her a get. He may remarry under civil law, but she will not feel free to remarry until she receives a get. To solve this problem, the Conservative movement has included in its ketubah the obligation of the man to provide a get in case of divorce. This can be enforced as a contract in the civil courts.

Death

When a person dies that person's spouse, brothers and sisters, parents and children are considered to be mourners. Other relatives and friends are considered comforters, whose duty it is to provide for the needs of the mourners.

Death is defined in Jewish law as cessation of respiration. Law and tradition call for burial as soon as possible after death, within twenty-four hours if possible.

The body is prepared for burial by the **hevra kadisha,** the burial society. In modern times a funeral home often does the preparation as a professional service. The preparation is called **tahara,** "purification." The body is washed and then dressed in plain linen shrouds. The body is never left alone. An attendant stands by, reciting Psalms, until the time for the funeral.

Mourning is divided into **aninut,** the period before the burial, and **avelut,** the period after burial. Before the burial no consolation calls are made. Viewings are contrary to Jewish tradition. Tradition requires that the body be buried in the ground, following the words in the Torah that "from dust you came, and unto dust you shall return."

The funeral may be divided between a funeral parlor and graveside, or it may all take place at graveside. Persons of particular piety were traditionally honored by holding the funeral in the synagogue. At the funeral parlor Psalms are recited and the deceased is eulogized by family and friends or by the officiating rabbi. The **hesped,** the eulogy, is considered to be of great importance in the process of mourning. The memorial prayer for the soul of the deceased, **"El Male Rahamim,"** is recited as the congregation stands. The **Tsidduk Hadin,** "justification of the Divine judgment," is a liturgy which is recited at graveside. The body is lowered into the grave. The first shovels of earth are placed into the grave by the mourners, then by the comforters. After interment the **Kaddish** prayer is recited for the first time in memory of the departed. The Kaddish prayer is a prayer of sanctification of the name of God. It does not mention death, but since the Middle Ages it has been used as a mourner's prayer.

Jewish tradition does not allow the hard reality of death to be concealed. The body may not be embalmed and there is no public viewing of the body at the funeral. The coffin should be unadorned, of the plainest wood. Flowers are not permitted on the coffin or the grave. Comforters are encouraged to give money to charity in lieu of any other expense in honor of the dead. From ancient times to the present rabbis have discouraged the expenditure of large sums to memorialize the departed, except for charitable giving.

At the conclusion of the funeral the comforters line the way out of the cemetery. They may now speak words of consolation to the mourners. Immediately following the funeral the mourners and comforters gather for a meal, called the "meal of consolation." Having reached the depths of sorrow at the funeral, the mourners are now encouraged to begin the journey back to normal life.

With the burial the mourners pass from aninut to avelut. Avelut is divided into three periods—**shiva, sheloshim,** and **shana**—a week, thirty days, and a year. During the week of shiva the mourners remain in the house of mourning and refrain from all of their customary activities. During the sheloshim period the mourners return to their work but they refrain from participation in social events. During the period of a year a child recites the Kaddish prayer each day in memory of a departed parent.

The mourner must attend synagogue each day in order to recite Kaddish in a **minyan,** a community of worship. Tradition discourages the extension of mourning practices beyond the prescribed period. Life goes on, and the mourners are expected to return to normal life by passing through the stages of mourning. A widow is permitted to remarry after ninety days, a widower after the passage of three festivals (about seven months).[7]

Dietary Laws

A tremendous amount of human energy is expended in growing, purchasing, preparing and eating food. Maintaining the Jewish dietary laws requires constant awareness in the service of God throughout this process. The body of dietary laws is called **kashrut.** Food which is religiously acceptable is said to be **kosher,** meaning "correct, ritually acceptable." Food which is not kosher is called **treife,** which literally means carrion, an animal torn by beasts.

The biblical laws of kashrut are found in Chapter 11 of the Book of Leviticus and scattered throughout the Torah. The Torah allows the eating of only those beasts which both have a cloven hoof and chew the cud. This excludes many wild and domestic animals, including the pig, which has a cloven hoof but does not chew the cud. From the water, only those creatures which have both fins and scales may be eaten. This excludes shellfish and some kinds of fish which have skin rather than scales. Certain types of birds are forbidden. Since these species cannot be identified with certainty, only those birds which are known by tradition to be kosher may be eaten. All reptiles, amphibians and insects are forbidden, except for certain types of locusts which can no longer be identified.

There are rules concerning the permitted species. Animals which die of disease or which are torn by carnivores may not be eaten. The "sinew of the inner thigh," taken to mean the sciatic nerve, may not be eaten. A mother bird and its young, a mother beast and its young, may not be eaten on the same day.

In the vegetable kingdom no species is forbidden, but grafting and hybridizing are forbidden. Every species must remain distinct. It is forbidden to sow two different kinds of seed in the same field. When the sacrificial Temple stood it was required to set aside the tithes and offerings for

---

[7]The shorter period of time for women is probably because of the economic difficulties faced by widows in ancient times. The ninety day waiting period was the minimum required to establish the paternity of a child born soon after remarriage.

the priests, the Levites and the poor before consuming any vegetable foods.

In early rabbinic times the laws of kashrut were greatly extended. Three times the Torah forbids "boiling a kid in its mother's milk." Whatever that meant in its original context, the rabbis took it to mean that meat products and milk products may not be mixed. The threefold repetition was taken to mean that one may not cook them together, serve them together, or eat them together. A kosher home must have two different sets of pots and pans, plates and utensils. One set is for meat, one for dairy. Recipes and menus must take the separation into account. If a utensil is used improperly it must be purified or discarded. Foods which are neither meat nor milk, such as fish, eggs, vegetables and grains, are called **parve**. These may be eaten at any meal, although some Jews do not eat fish at a meat meal. Even though birds do not nurse their young, their flesh is considered meat. Poultry may not be consumed at a dairy meal.

Rabbinic law defines kosher slaughtering and health inspection. Slaughtering may be done only by a **shoket,** an individual who is highly trained and religiously pious. The shoket must use a sharp knife. The knife must cut through the neck, severing the artery, the windpipe and the nerve in one clean stroke. Various lesions on the lungs and other signs of disease make the animal treife. The shoket must inspect for these.

For a Jew who keeps a kosher home it is reason enough that God commanded these laws. Nevertheless there is great interest in explaining the reason for these laws, especially since unlike the laws of ethical behavior and social order the laws of kashrut do not serve an obvious purpose and their observance does not evoke admiration from others.

It is likely that in biblical times the dietary laws were only observed by the priesthood. They were observed by ordinary Jews only in connection to sacrifice and attendance at the Temple. They were laws of priestly purity. A distinguishing feature of the Pharisees, the forerunners of the rabbis, is that they lived as if they were Temple priests. They were therefore greatly concerned with the details of priestly food laws such as tithing. The Pharisees ate all of their meals as religious meals, in a state of priestly purity. The dietary laws were central to the spirituality of the Pharisees, their determination to take literally the notion that Israel is "a nation of priests, a holy nation." Strict observance of dietary laws was a pathway to holiness.

When the Temple was destroyed in the year 70 the Jews lost what had been their primary mode of relationship to God, the sacrifices. The rabbis replaced the sacrifices with other rituals and observances. Prayer in the synagogue, Torah study, mitzvah observance, deeds of loving-kindness, all replaced sacrifice as a mode of relating to God. The family dinner table was made into the primary replacement for the sacrificial altar. The rabbis called the family table the **Mikdash mu'at,** the "little Temple." The newly elaborate rituals of the dinner table replaced the elaborate and formal rituals of the Temple sacrifices. Seen in this way we can understand how the Jewish people probably needed and welcomed the rabbinic extensions of dietary law. Having lost what was dear to them, the ceremony of the sacrifices, the people were now granted a replacement ritual at which they themselves could preside. The people, in their kitchen and at their table, became the new priesthood; the laws of kashrut were their priestly rites.

The laws of kashrut helped to keep the scattered Jewish people distinct and united. The rabbis forbade the drinking of Gentile wine in order to prevent the social mixing that leads to intermarriage. Table fellowship is a source of friendship and unity between people. The dietary laws brought religious Jews into close relationships while they limited social contact with Gentiles and non-observant Jews. Religious table fellowship is practiced in many religions as a form of mystic union between the community and God. The Jewish dietary laws serve this purpose also.

The Reform movement of Judaism in the nineteenth century declared the dietary laws to be no longer in force. They did this largely because they considered the separatism enforced by kashrut to be undesirable and improper. They believed that Jews should mingle with general society, and they believed that the ethical message of Judaism would be transmitted to the world if Jews would mix with the Gentile public. The Conservative movement of Judaism compromised between the principles of observing kashrut and of mixing with the general public. They declared the laws of kashrut still in force but they reinterpreted these laws to permit social mixing. A Jew could eat in a non-kosher restaurant, for instance, as long as he did not eat meat. In modern times there are many Jews who do not keep kosher, some because they have adopted the principles of Reform Judaism and some because they are not observant.

Religious rationalists have sought to explain the dietary laws as health rules. This was particularly true in the nineteenth century when microbes were discovered and public health became a social concern. Many Jews today have adopted the idea that a clever priest in ancient Israel discovered the dangers of disease from uncooked pork and rotten meat and then promoted health rules by presenting them as religious commandments. This argument is highly unlikely. Some laws of kashrut do seem to promote hygiene, but others do not. There is no reason to believe that premodern Jews were any more aware than other peoples of the germs which cause disease. The idea that dietary laws are health laws was preferred by Jews who were looking for a rationale *not* to keep kosher, since refrigeration and proper cooking have made the old prohibitions no longer necessary. The laws of kashrut cannot be fully explained as rational rules. They are laws of holiness.

6

Jewish Worship

A Hundred Blessings

"A person should say a hundred blessings a day." This is an ancient Jewish teaching. A Jew is called to live with an attitude of constant gratitude for all of God's gifts. Gratitude to God is expressed by saying blessings. Of course a person does not go through the day counting the number of blessings he has recited. The point of the rabbis' teaching is that every day there are many things to be thankful for, and a person should seek every opportunity to express these thanks in words of blessing.

There are three kinds of occasion that call for a blessing. First, one recites a blessing when one performs a mitzvah. Second, the fulfillment of bodily needs and the enjoyment of material pleasures, such as eating and drinking, calls for words of blessing. Third, one recites a blessing when one experiences an event of great pleasure or great sorrow, in order to show that one accepts God's providence whether for good or for bad. No object receives blessing in Jewish practice; words of blessing are directed only to God. For instance one does not bless the Sabbath candles; one recites the blessing (of God) over the Sabbath candles. The formula for a **beraka,** a blessing, is: "Blessed be Thou, Lord our God, Ruler of the universe, who . . ." In the case of a beraka over the performance of a mitzvah, the formula is: "Blessed be Thou, Lord our God, Ruler of the universe, who has sanctified us by your commandments, and commanded us to . . ."

There are many specific blessings, especially in regard to eating. There is a blessing over fruits which grow from the ground, and another over fruits which grow from trees. There is a blessing over bread; whenever bread is served this blessing is sufficient to cover all foods at the table, with the exception of wine. The blessing over wine is recited whenever wine is served. There is a blessing over grain products other than bread. There is a blessing to cover all types of food not covered by the other blessings, such as meat, milk and eggs. This blessing is also recited before drinking water. The full blessing after meals is recited whenever bread is eaten at a meal. The blessing after meals contains four blessings, thanking God for food, for the Land of Israel, for the city of Jerusalem, and for God's merciful providence. There are special blessings to be recited upon seeing natural wonders such as thunder and lightning, a rainbow, or the ocean. The blessing over the ocean is not recited by one who lives by the ocean, but only by one who sees the ocean on rare occasions. There is a blessing to be recited upon seeing a great Torah scholar, and another to be recited upon seeing a person of great general wisdom.

We may come to understand a great deal about the rabbinic mind if we consider why the rabbis established so many different blessings. The rabbis could have established one single blessing for all types of food, but they chose to distinguish between many types of food. These various blessings are recorded in the Mishnah, in which the variety of blessings are taken for granted. We could present some theories as to why the rabbis established so many different blessings, but there may be more to be gained by making this fact an object of contemplation. Consider especially how when the rabbis determine the proper way to serve God they take into account human nature and the everyday realities of human life.

Daily Prayer

A Jew is obligated to pray three times a day—morning, afternoon and evening. Judaism is a liturgical religion, which means that there is an established order of prayers to be recited. The liturgy of Jewish worship is found in the **siddur,** the Jewish book of prayer. New prayers have been composed in every century, but the essential part of the Jewish worship service was established in early rabbinic times. There are two major portions to the worship service, the **Shema and Its Blessings** (also called the **"Keriat Shema"** [the recitation of the Shema] or, for short, just the **Shema**) and the **Amidah** ("standing" prayers). The Shema is said morning and evening; the Amidah is said morning, afternoon and evening. Originally the Shema and Amidah were recited separately, for a total of five periods of worship.

Jews gather in public worship to recite the liturgy, and also to read from the Torah. The Torah is divided into as many portions as there are

Sabbaths in a year. Each week, at the Sabbath morning worship service, that week's Torah portion is read. On Sabbath afternoon and on Monday and Thursday mornings a short reading from the coming week's Torah portion is recited. The reader reads from a **sefer Torah,** a parchment scroll containing the five books of the Torah handwritten by a scribe in the ancient manner. The sefer Torah is kept in the **aron hakodesh,** the "holy ark," which rests against the front wall so that the worshipers face it during prayer. The aron hakodesh is often large and beautifully decorated with carved wood, marble pillars, or other artifacts. Except during worship, the doors to the aron hakodesh are covered by a **paroket,** a curtain, which may be beautifully decorated with needlework.

There are special Torah readings for the holidays. On the Sabbath and on holidays a selection from the books of the Prophets is recited after the reading from the Torah. The reading from the Prophets is called the **Haftarah.** The Haftarah usually relates thematically to the subject of the Torah portion, or to the theme of the holiday or the season of the religious year. In the traditional synagogue there is an additional recitation of the Amidah on Sabbath and festival mornings, after the Torah service. This additional Amidah is called the **Musaf,** the "additional" service. It corresponds to the extra sacrifices which were offered in the ancient Temple on Sabbaths and holidays.

In many synagogues today worship is conducted in unison, but traditional Jewish worship is individual, a personal relationship between the worshiper and God. In traditional worship, the function of the worship leader is to keep all the worshipers in the same place in the liturgy, but each worshiper recites the prayers to himself. A Jew may recite the liturgy by himself wherever he may be at the time of prayer. Synagogue attendance is required only on Sabbaths and holidays, and when one is reciting the Kaddish prayer in memory of the departed, since this prayer requires a minyan. The liturgy was traditionally recited in a singsong chant, called **nusah.** There is a different nusah for weekdays, Sabbaths and holidays, so that the melody of worship is connected to the religious meaning of the day.

The traditional worshiper wears a **tallit** and **tefilin** in morning worship, and a **kipah,** also called **yarmulke,** in all worship. The kipah is a head-covering worn as a mark of respect, in accordance with Middle Eastern custom. Reform Jews prefer to follow the Western custom of removing the hat as a mark of respect. The tallit is a shawl worn over the shoulders. At each corner of the tallit a fringe is tied in fulfillment of the mitzvah (Numbers 15) that a Jew shall wear fringes on the corners of his garment. The fringes serve as a reminder of God's commandments. The tefilin are two leather boxes, tied with leather straps around the head and the left forearm. Words of Torah are contained in the boxes. The tefilin are worn in literal fulfillment of the commandment (Deuteronomy 6) that the words of Torah shall be a "sign upon your hand and a symbol on your forehead." Tefilin are not worn on Sabbaths and holidays.

Women

In rabbinic Judaism only men were obligated to pray. Women were not taught to understand the Hebrew of the liturgy. If women did come to the synagogue they would sit behind a curtain in the back or in a balcony. Jewish women did have their own traditions of prayer. A woman would pray for her family's welfare before lighting the Sabbath candles. Jewish women in Europe recited **tehinas,** "supplications," prayers composed in Yiddish especially for women. There were many printed books of tehinas. Women's prayer was more free-form than men's prayer, and given to the free expression of emotions.

There are many responses in the modern synagogue to the call for equality of women in religious matters. In non-Orthodox synagogues there is mixed seating and women and men share in the leadership of worship. Some Orthodox synagogues have placed the men's and women's sections side by side with a curtain down the center aisle in order to give women equality in seating. Only men lead the worship. Among very traditional Jews who believe in total separation of the sexes there are women's prayer groups who gather to pray the traditional liturgy. These women consider themselves to be praying voluntarily rather than by obligation, but as long as there are no men present they are free to perform all of the obligations of worship for themselves. The most strictly Orthodox believe that women may not take upon themselves the obligation of prayer; among these Jews women remain onlookers.

The Synagogue

The structure of the synagogue reflects its use. There is no architectural style which is required for a synagogue. The building may be in any shape and form and any size, from a grand hall to a small room. The synagogue is oriented so that the front wall faces Jerusalem.[1] The Holy Ark containing the Torah scrolls is kept on the front wall, the Eastern wall

---

[1]Reform Jews do not necessarily follow this procedure, but orient their building for the best land use.

for European and American Jews. In the modernist synagogue with a unison style of worship the **bimah** "pulpit," is before the ark, facing the congregation. The rabbi leads the service. In the traditional synagogue the bimah is in the center of the floor and the **hazzan,** the cantor who leads worship, faces in the same direction as the other worshipers. The benches or pews are oriented around the walls in the shape of the letter "U," with the opening toward the ark.

The Liturgy

The worship service begins with prayers and Psalms which help the worshiper to direct his attention toward God. Following these "warm-ups" the service proper begins with the call to worship. The leaders recites, in Hebrew, "Praise the Lord, who is to be praised!" The congregation responds, "Praised be the Lord forever and ever!" The worship service proceeds with the "Shema and Its Blessings."

At the center of this portion of worship is the Shema Yisrael and the three paragraphs from the Torah which accompany it: Deuteronomy 6:4–9, Deuteronomy 11:13–21 and Numbers 15:37–41. The Shema Yisrael is the verse of Deuteronomy 6:4, "Hear, O Israel, the Lord is our God, the Lord is One." We cannot say how these three paragraphs from the Torah became the central statement of Jewish worship. The early rabbis accepted this as ancient tradition. The first paragraph, including the Shema, commands the recognition of God and the love of God. It mentions the commandments to wear tefilin and to place a mezuzah on the doorposts of the house and gates.[2] The second paragraph mentions the gift of the Land of Israel and the reward and punishment which God will grant by blessing the land with rain or withholding rain. The third paragraph mentions the commandment to wear fringes and the Exodus from Egypt.[3]

The rabbis entitled the first paragraph "Accepting the yoke of Heaven." They called the second paragraph "Accepting the yoke of the mitzvot." They called the third paragraph "the paragraph of the fringes" or "the paragraph of the Exodus from Egypt." It is uncertain whether the third paragraph was included because it mentions the ritual commandment of the fringes, in parallel to the tefilin and mezuzah, or because it

---

[2] The **mezuzah** is a scroll containing this paragraph of the Torah, placed in a decorative box which is nailed to the doorpost in the entryway of the house.

[3] The "Exodus" is the name for the event which initiated the history of the people Israel, when God brought them out of slavery in Egypt. The story of this event is told in the Book of Exodus, the second book of the Torah, Chapters 1–15.

mentions the Exodus, in parallel to the love of God and the gift of the Land as aspects of the covenant.

Surrounding the three paragraphs of the Shema are three prayers. The two prayers before the Shema praise God as Creator of the universe and as Revealer of the Torah. The prayer after the Shema affirms the truth of the three paragraphs of the Shema and praises God as Redeemer, as exemplified by the Exodus from Egypt. In the evening worship there is a fourth prayer which asks God's protection in the night.

The Shema with its paragraphs and surrounding prayers summarizes the theology of Judaism. The Shema and Its Blessings is not prayer in the formal sense. The words are addressed not to God but to ourselves, telling us what to believe about God and defining the relationship between God and Israel. Israel's address to God is contained in the second part of the worship service, the Amidah.

The Amidah

The Amidah is called by three different names. It is called the **Amidah,** "standing," because the worshipers stand while reciting it. It is called the **Tefilah** "prayer," because the worshiper prays to God. It is called the **Shemone Esre,** the "eighteen" benedictions, because it contained that many prayers in its original form. The Amidah as we now have it contains nineteen benedictions. One prayer was added after the name Shemone Esre had already become common terminology in the first or second century CE.

The Amidah has three sections: the first three benedictions, the middle ones, and the final three. The first section contains prayers of praise, the middle section prayers of petition, the third section prayers of thanks. Praise, petition and thanks are the three forms of prayer, human address to God. The Amidah follows the pattern of a petitioner coming before a king. The petitioner first presents his credentials and praises the king for his great deeds. He then presents his requests to the king. He then thanks the king for granting his requests and for his goodness and kindness. The petitioner then takes his leave, asking for peace for himself, the king and the kingdom. In this pattern the first prayer of the Amidah mentions Abraham, Isaac and Jacob and announces the petitioner as one of their descendants. The next prayer praises God for his great deeds, especially that of resurrecting the dead. The third prayer praises God for his holiness. After the prayers of petition the petitioner thanks God for responding to prayer, thanks God for his goodness at all times, and prays for peace. After reciting the liturgy of the Amidah one may add his own prayers, whatever is in his heart to pray.

In the synagogue each Jew recites the Amidah silently by himself. The Amidah is then repeated out loud by the worship leader while the congregation responds "amen" at the conclusion of each benediction. The repetition of the Amidah was instituted for the sake of those who were not skilled at reciting prayers. The advent of printing made it possible for each worshiper to have a prayer book in his own hands, but the hallowed tradition of repeating the Amidah was retained. In the Reform synagogue the silent recitation of the Amidah was eliminated, and the congregation recites the Amidah once through in unison.

The middle benedictions of the Amidah, the prayers of petition, cover the following themes: wisdom, repentance, forgiveness, redemption, health, blessing of the land for good crops, in-gathering of the exiles, divine judgment, destruction of the wicked, mercy to the righteous, the rebuilding of Jerusalem, re-establishment of the dynasty of King David (coming of the Messiah), a wish that our prayers be heard.

We cannot say with certainty how these particular themes of prayer were chosen. In the latter part of the first century there was still discussion about where certain prayers belonged, indicating that the order of the Amidah had only recently been established by that time. We know that the prayer asking for the destruction of the wicked was established by the head of the Sanhedrin early in the second century for the purpose of driving sectarians out of the synagogue.[4] This prayer may have been the nineteenth benediction. Many modern scholars believe that the order of the prayers of petition follows the pattern of the redemption for which rabbinic Jews hoped. The first few prayers establish the order of the redemption of the individual. The latter prayers establish the order in which redemption will come to the nation as a whole.

The worship service concludes with the **Alenu** prayer. The Alenu originated as part of the liturgy for Rosh Hashanah, the Jewish new year, and later became part of every worship service. The first half of the Alenu recognizes the distinction of the Jewish people as the only worshipers of the true God. The latter half of the Alenu looks forward to a time when all people will worship God and all of humanity will be united as one. After the Alenu the mourners recite the Kaddish prayer and the congregation sings a concluding hymn.

On Sabbaths and holidays the middle portion of the Amidah, the prayers of petition, is not recited. It is considered improper to present

---

[4]Some think that the sectarians were the Christians, but there were many sectarian groups at that time and we cannot be certain who the rabbis had in mind.

petitions on such days. Instead of these middle blessings, a prayer is recited thanking God for the gift of the sacred day. The Amidah of Sabbaths and holidays contains a total of seven benedictions.[5]

Liturgical Innovation

From the time of their composition to the present, the Shema and the Amidah have constituted the essential liturgy of the Jewish people. New prayers did not replace the old but were added to them. Great poets wrote religious prayer-poems called **piyyutim** (sing. piyyut). Most Jews today continue to pray the traditional liturgy. The Reform movement eliminated most piyyutim and revised some of the traditional prayers. They reworded some prayers, often in the vernacular, while retaining the basic themes of the traditional liturgy. The liturgical changes made by the Reform movement will be discussed in more detail in a later chapter.

Development of the Liturgy

We do not know exactly how the Shema and the Amidah came into being. The Bible makes no mention of liturgical worship. Prayer was used in biblical times as an accompaniment to sacrifice or as a spontaneous outpouring of the heart on special occasions. The Mishnah (c. 200 CE), composed about four centuries after the last books of the Bible, presumes the existence of the Shema and the Amidah. The rabbinic debates in the Mishnah concern various details of how and when to recite the liturgy. They take for granted the existence of the liturgy, virtually in the form that it exists today. During those intervening centuries between the close of biblical literature and the beginnings of rabbinic literature a divine service of prayer somehow developed and became accepted by all Jews. After the destruction of the Temple in 70 CE, when sacrifices ceased, Judaism became the first of the world's religions in which prayer replaced sacrifice as the primary form of communion with God.

The "Shema and Its Blessings" is probably based upon the liturgy which was recited in the Temple in conjunction with the daily morning sacrifice. The rabbinic rule that the Shema should be recited twice a day, evening and morning, is based upon the verse in the first paragraph of the Shema, "You shall speak of them (words of Torah) . . . when you lie down

---

[5]The Amidah of Rosh Hashanah contains three benedictions in the middle portion, for a total of nine.

and when you rise up." In the Temple liturgy the Ten Commandments were recited before the Shema Yisrael. The rabbis changed that to a prayer thanking God for revealing all the mitzvot in the Torah, apparently to emphasize that every mitzvah is equally worthy of observance. This may have been directed at the Jewish-Christians who taught that only the Ten Commandments had to be observed, the other mitzvot having been made obsolete by the coming of the Christ.

The Amidah was recited in the morning and in the afternoon at the exact time of the daily morning and afternoon sacrifices.[6] The additional Amidah of the Sabbath and holidays is recited at the time when the additional Temple sacrifice was offered in honor of these days. It would seem from this that the Amidah was considered to take the place of the Temple sacrifices, but this is not clear. In the Talmud (c. 500 CE) there is extensive debate over whether the Amidah is "in place of sacrifice" or "an institution of the Patriarchs." The second argument is based on the rabbinic tradition that Abraham instituted the morning service, Isaac the afternoon service, and Jacob the evening service. The issue behind the debate is whether the recitation of the Amidah is a sacramental ritual, like the sacrifices, or a personal expression of devotion to God. If the former, then the Amidah if recited correctly is automatically effective in establishing communion with God. If the latter, then the Amidah is only effective if the one who recites it holds an attitude of prayerfulness and concentrated attention on its meaning. The rabbis did determine that one fulfills the obligation to recite the Sehma if one said the words and knew that one was obligated to say them, but one had only fulfilled the mitzvah to recite the Amidah if one concentrated on the meaning of the words. Sincerity and concentration are necessary to make prayer meaningful.

---

[6]The Amidah is recited in the evening service only because of the parallel with morning worship, when both Shema and Amidah are recited. Because of the secondary nature of the evening Amidah there is no leader's repetition in the traditional synagogue. The congregation recites the Amidah once through, in silent devotion.

7

The World To Come

Life after Death

In biblical times the people of Israel believed that the souls of the dead go to **Sheol,** the underworld, where they sleep forever in company with the ancestors. Good and bad alike go to the same end. A person lived on after death through the life of his or her descendants on earth.

After the close of biblical times the priestly Sadducees held to the biblical belief. The Pharisees developed the belief that at some time in the near or distant future God would bring all who had lived back to bodily life. This doctrine is called in English the "resurrection of the dead." The Christian Gospels depict Jesus debating with Sadducees over the doctrine of resurrection. Jesus defended this doctrine of the Pharisees.

The Greek philosophers believed in an eternal soul. The soul lives a heavenly existence after its release from the bonds of bodily life. The doctrine of the eternal soul presents a view of the afterlife which in some ways contradicts the doctrine of resurrection, but this doctrine was also accepted in rabbinic Judaism. It is not unlikely that Jews became interested in the nature of life after death due to their exposure to Greek thought during the centuries of Greek and Roman rule over Judah.

Doctrines and Beliefs

During the rabbinic period virtually all Jews shared an accepted set of doctrines concerning life after death. Jews believed that every person has an eternal soul which outlives the body. They believed that after death

God rewards the good and punishes the bad. They believed that in time to come God would bring all the dead back to life. The good would then be rewarded with eternal bodily life on earth, while the evil would go to eternal destruction.

The primary concern of Jews was to live this earthly life according to the Torah. The rabbis were more interested in defining halakha than in defining the details of the afterlife. Within the bounds of the general doctrines we have outlined many different beliefs about the afterlife are possible. A great variety of such beliefs existed. The rabbis made no attempt to unify Jewish beliefs in such matters. The Talmud quotes a variety of rabbinic masters concerning their beliefs about the nature of life after death. No attempt is made to judge between the different opinions.

One belief was that after death the souls of the righteous are kept in a box under the throne of God. Another belief is that the righteous sit upon thrones and enjoy the radiance of God's light. The former view sees the afterlife as a passive existence in which individual character and personality do not persist. The second opinion depicts an afterlife in which the individual has a more self-aware existence in eternity.

A more active view of the afterlife is the belief in the Yeshiva on High. On earth the Torah scholars sit in the yeshiva and discuss the meaning of the Torah; in heaven the righteous sit in the Yeshiva on High and continue to discuss the Torah. God sits as Dean of the Yeshiva on High, while the Patriarchs, Moses and the Prophets teach. A righteous Jew could look forward to listening and even participating as the greatest rabbis of all time clarified the fine points of Torah. Of course the laws of the Torah did not apply to life in heaven; the heavenly study of Torah was truly "Torah for its own sake."

The Jewish philosophers of the Middle Ages did not appreciate the projection of earthly pleasures into heavenly existence. The philosophers preferred to believe that the highest soul, the eternal soul, is not inborn but acquired through the study of wisdom. Upon death, the soul which a person has acquired becomes one with the eternal being of God, the source of all wisdom. The philosophers followed the teaching of Greek philosophy that a person has not one soul but a hierarchy of souls which govern the body. First there is the vegetative soul, which exists in all living things. Then there is the animal soul, which exists in all animals. Humans alone have a rational soul, which is activated to the extent that they acquire knowledge and become rational. Although most Jews were not philosophers, the beliefs of the philosophers became part of the Jewish store. In modified form, the doctrine of multiple souls was accepted into Judaism.

Reward and Punishment

The reward of the righteous is only vaguely defined in Jewish belief; the manner in which the wicked are punished is even more undefined. Do the souls of the wicked receive eternal punishment, or do they perish altogether upon death? This is never determined.

In midrash and Jewish folklore we find mention of **Gan Eden,** the "Garden of Eden," and **Gehinnom,** the "Valley of Hinnom." The Garden of Eden, Paradise, is the place where the righteous receive their reward. Gehinnom is a place of punishment. King Solomon established an altar to the Canaanite god Moloch in the Valley of Hinnom outside Jerusalem. There, according to the Bible, children were thrown into a fire as sacrifices to the god. This may be the origin of the concept of a fiery hell. Gehinnom is sometimes depicted as a hell, but more usually it is depicted as a purgatory in which ordinary persons pay for their sins for a year or less before going to their eternal reward. The idea of a hell ruled over by the Devil and his band of fallen angels is absent from Jewish religious teaching, although it does enter into Jewish folklore.

The World To Come

One of the most common themes in rabbinic literature is the contrast between "this world" and "the World to Come." In this world the righteous suffer, but in the World to Come there is reward for those who fulfill the mitzvot. In this world Israel is subjugated by the nations, but in the World to Come Israel will shine in all her glory as God's people. In this world God's power, God's mercy and justice are hidden from sight, but in the World to Come the light of God's presence will shine for all to see.

Even though the world to come is mentioned thousands of times in rabbinic literature, it is nowhere defined or described. The rabbinic literature gives us no clue to the relationship of the world to come to other Jewish eschatological[1] doctrines such as the Messiah, the resurrection, and the heavenly reward. The World to Come is reserved for a distant future; it is much better than this world, and "achieving life in the World to Come" is the ultimate reward of a good life.

Rabbinic law did not dictate many specifics about the afterlife, but we can see from the non-legal literature that during Roman times Jews were consumed with a desire to achieve a new life in a future world. We may

---

[1]**Eschatology** is the term for religious doctrines of the future life in heaven or on a transformed earth.

understand this as a response to the frustration of sacred Jewish hopes under the rule of the Romans. Roman oppression prevented the fulfill-ment of the promises made to Israel by the Torah and the Prophets. The Jewish people had lost their political sovereignty. They had become few in number, poor and downtrodden. God had not yet intervened to correct the situation, and there was no end to Roman domination in sight. The righ-teous could not receive their reward in this world. God's law could only be fulfilled in a future world which would be ruled by God's law of justice instead of by the Roman law of injustice.

Resurrection

There is only one mention of bodily resurrection in the Tanak, in the Book of Daniel. "Many of those that sleep in the dust of the earth will awake, some to eternal life, others to reproaches, to everlasting abhor-rence" (Daniel 12:2). The Book of Daniel was the last book of the Tanak to be written. Biblical historians date the book to about 170 BCE. At that time the Greek king of the Middle East, Antiochus IV, outlawed the Torah. Those Jews who abandoned the Torah lived at ease in Jerusalem, while those who defied the king's decree were hunted and slaughtered by the Greek garrisons. The doctrine of bodily resurrection arose at that time to justify the martyrdom of the innocent. A Jewish rebellion ending in 165 BCE brought an end to the persecution.

Some time later the Second Book of Maccabees was written to de-scribe the victory of the Jews. The First Book of Maccabees, written by the leaders of the rebellion, describes the military and political events of the rebellion. Second Maccabees is not so interested in battles and treaties as in tales of Jewish devotion and martyrdom during the persecution and the rebellion. One of the primary functions of this book was to spread and solidify belief in the new doctrine of bodily resurrection.[2] Within a century or so after the time of the Maccabees all Jews except the conservative Sadducees had come to accept this doctrine.

The doctrine of resurrection is controversial because it is contrary to logic and reason. It is not irrational; it is non-rational, not subject to logical proof. The rationalist may prefer the doctrine of the eternal afterlife of the soul, a doctrine which arose among philosophers. The great Jewish ratio-nalist of the Middle Ages, Maimonides, discussed resurrection in his writ-

---

[2]The rise of this doctrine must have been connected with the rise of the Pharisees, who begin to appear in Jewish history at about the same time. The Pharisees must have had their beginnings in the revolt of the Maccabees.

ings in such a way as to give the impression that he did not believe in it. He was pressured to write a defense of the doctrine of resurrection in response to criticism; in the Middle Ages one did not lightly deny traditional religious doctrine. It is very likely that Maimonides did not believe in resurrection, and he only made a slight bow to traditional Jewish piety in recognizing the doctrine of resurrection as a required Jewish doctrine. After Maimonides' death a great controversy broke out over his writings. This thirteenth century controversy was one of the most heated in Jewish history. It revolved primarily around the doctrine of resurrection. There were those who criticized Maimonides for not believing in resurrection, those who insisted that he did believe in the doctrine, and those who praised him for rejecting the belief in resurrection. The anti-Maimonists in France encouraged the king to burn the "heretical" books of Maimonides. The king did so, and then continued to burn Jewish books. The Jews were forced to close ranks against this new threat, and the controversy over the doctrine of resurrection came to an inconclusive end.

Modern Reform Jews reject the doctrine of resurrection for much the same reason as did the medieval philosophers, their preference for the rational doctrine of the afterlife of the soul. Reform Jews have eliminated all mention of bodily resurrection from their worship, and no longer look to return to earthly life in bodily form. Conservative Jews continue to recite the traditional prayers, which include the prayer for resurrection, but the English translation in Conservative prayerbooks usually obscures the reference to resurrection. It is doubtful that many modern Conservative Jews seriously believe in the doctrine of resurrection. In the modern Orthodox world the doctrine is not much discussed. Although Reform Jews are criticized in Orthodox circles for other changes in liturgy and doctrine, this change does not come up for mention. The doctrine of resurrection does not have the hold on contemporary Jews that it had on their ancestors, even among those modern Jews who have not formally rejected it.

The Messiah

In ancient Judah the ritual for the enthronement of a new king was to anoint his head with oil. One title for the king was **Mashiah,** "Messiah" in English, meaning "anointed one." To call the king of Judah the Messiah is equivalent to using the English phrase "the crowned heads" in reference to kings. The Messiah is not a supernatural creature nor an emanation from God but a flesh and blood human being, the rightful heir to the throne of Judah.

The kingdom of Judah had a stable dynasty from the tenth to the sixth centuries BCE. The dynasty was founded by David son of Jesse from the village of Bethlehem. The dynasty remained intact even through the exile in Babylon. Sometime after the return from exile the Persians dethroned King Zerubbabel and brought an end to the Davidic dynasty, in circumstances that are unknown to us.

Through the centuries of rule by the Persians, Greeks and Romans, the Jews retained the hope of a return to national sovereignty in their land. This hope was expressed as a hope for the Messiah, the heir of King David, to return to the throne. The prophets of Israel had criticized the kings for their failure to live by God's law. They had spoken hopefully of a future king who would fulfill all the terms of the covenant, bringing God's blessing and the fulfillment of God's promises to the nation. The Messiah now envisioned by the Jewish people would be a king who would fulfill the vision of the prophets. He would rule according to the Torah, creating a society of perfect justice. With God's help he would overthrow the "kingdom of wickedness," the secular empires, and initiate the "kingdom of God," the rule of God's law which would emanate from the lips of the righteous king.

Apocalyptic

There seemed little likelihood that the Jews would be able to overthrow the Roman empire and re-establish their king by themselves, in the course of natural events. It would take an act of God, a great miracle, to bring this about. Many Jews believed that the world as we know it would continue to exist for only a very short time. Then God would bring about a cataclysm in which the order of nature would be upended and human society would degenerate into chaos. The forces of evil would do battle with the forces of good. God would then send the Messiah to give a final defeat to the forces of evil and expunge them from the world. The immanent cataclysm which will end the world is called the **apocalypse.** Apocalyptic faith is the belief that the apocalypse is nearly upon us and so the only duty of humankind is to prepare for it.

In the first century CE there were numerous apocalyptic sects among the Jews of Judah, each with its own charistmatic leader. Much of the preaching of Jesus as recorded in the Gospels is apocalyptic in nature, and it is fairly clear that the followers of Jesus expected to see the end of the world in their lifetime. Apocalyptic beliefs of the type preached by Jesus were already well-known to the Jews from numerous other sects. Among these are the monastic group which lived by the Dead Sea, the Qumran community. Many of the writings of this community were preserved and have been rediscovered in modern times, throwing great light on the beliefs of the apocalyptic Jews. Other apocalyptic writings were preserved by the early Church in the Apocrypha and Pseudepigrapha, "biblical" books not accepted into the Hebrew Scriptures. There are also fragments of apocalyptic books which entered into collections of midrashic literature.

The apocalyptic sects disappeared or went underground after the failure of the Jewish rebellions against Rome in the first and second centuries CE. Even without the backing of organized sects, apocalyptic beliefs continued to influence both the Jewish and Christian religions. In both religions apocalyptic groups reappear from time to time, groups which believe that the end of the world is imminent.

The Vision of the End-Time

There is a rich folklore of apocalyptic. Every sect had its own version of how the end would come and what would occur before and after it. Despite the variations it is possible to give a general outline of the apocalypse with all the elements that became widely accepted among Jewish believers.

Following the prediction of the prophet Malachi,[3] the prophet Elijah will come to earth to pave the way for the coming of the Messiah. According to rabbinic folklore Elijah will answer all the difficult questions of the law which the rabbis were unable to decide upon, so that the law will be complete for the Messiah.

The end is preceded by times of terrible upheaval in the world. The forces of lawlessness and evil will become powerful, and the Jews will suffer terrible oppression. Many people will be killed or will fall away from the Torah during that time.

The forces of evil will gather together into a great army, the army of Gog and Magog.[4] The forces of good, few in number, will be led by Messiah ben Joseph, the Messiah descended from Joseph the son of Jacob. The two armies will fight six indecisive battles. The seventh and final battle is called Armageddon.[5] The forces of evil will have the upper hand in the final battle and the Messiah ben Joseph will be mortally wounded. Then God will send the Messiah ben David, the Messiah descended of

---

[3]Malachi 3:23–24.

[4]Using the terminology from the Book of Ezekiel.

[5]The name comes from Megiddo, a city in the Galilee which sits in a strategic valley. Many great battles were fought there in biblical times.

King David, who will miraculously turn the tide of battle and bring utter defeat to the forces of evil.

After the battle all who ever lived will be resurrected to bodily life in the Valley of Jehosaphat, east of the Temple Mount in Jerusalem. Those Jews who are buried in the Land of Israel will arise from the grave where they are buried, but other Jews will have to painfully burrow underground in order to rise up in the Land of Israel. After the resurrection comes the Last Judgment in which all who ever lived are judged on the scales of justice, with the Messiah presiding. Those judged to be evil go to eternal destruction, while those judged to be good are granted eternal life. They climb up from the Valley of Jehosaphat to the Temple Mount where they rebuild the Temple, the Third Temple which will last forever. God prepares a meal from the body of the primeval monster Leviathan for the Feast of the Righteous. Thus begins the Time of the Messiah, a time of peace, tranquility and material plenty on earth.

Anti-Apocalyptic

The apocalyptic vision we have presented here became standard in Jewish lore, although most Jews did not expect it anytime soon. Some Jews objected to the fantastic and mythological elements in this messianic lore. The foremost representative of this group is the great rationalist, Maimonides. In his book of Jewish law, the *Mishneh Torah*, Maimonides included a section on the Messiah. He advised that the Jews should not look for any supernatural events in connection with the Messiah. Rather, if a king comes who is accepted by the Jews, who restores Jewish sovereignty in their land and who rules according to the just laws of the Torah, then in retrospect the people may say that he is the Messiah.

The Messianic Impulse in Judaism

The doctrine of the Messiah was well established by the first century CE. Jews expected the Messiah to overthrow the rule of the Roman empire. Different sects of Jews had different doctrines of how this would take place. The apocalyptic sects believed in living a life of separatism and purity until God brings about his miracles. More militant sects believed that the coming of the Messiah must be initiated by human effort in armed rebellion against Rome. The Christian sect which arose in this century came to believe that their Messiah came not to end the oppression of the Jews but to provide salvation from sinfulness through faith in him. This doctrine did not respond to the messianic hopes of the Jews, a fact which became apparent as Christianity developed into a separate and distinct religion.

In the years 66–70 the militant messianists had their way, and the people of Judah rebelled against Rome. The expected miraculous deliverance did not come. The Jews were soundly defeated. In the wake of the destruction the Romans left a group of Pharisees, now called rabbis, in charge of internal Jewish affairs. The leader of this group was Johanan ben Zakkai, given the title Rabban. The rabbis taught that one should expect the Messiah and pray for his coming, but one should do nothing in the attempt to hasten his appearance. God would send the Messiah in his own good time. The responsibility of the Jewish people was to live faithfully according to the Torah until that time should come. The rabbis forbade all attempts to calculate the time of the coming of the Messiah. Johanan ben Zakkai taught, "If you are planting a tree and you hear that the Messiah has come, first finish planting the tree, then go to greet him." This is a teaching about priorities. The task of a Jew is to plant trees, to plan for the long-term future of humanity on earth. Awaiting the Messiah is a secondary and relatively unimportant concern.

Cycles of Messianism

The rabbis under Johanan ben Zakkai attempted to transform messianism from an activist doctrine to a quietist doctrine, a doctrine of patient waiting for a better world. They succeeded only for a short time. A generation later, in 132 CE, a new messianic rebellion broke out against the Romans, this time with the backing of the rabbis themselves. This rebellion ended in 135 with even greater death and devastation than the first rebellion. The surviving rabbis returned to a quietist and passive messianism which they made standard in Jewish teaching.

Through the centuries various Jewish groups returned to an activist messianism. They attempted to precipitate the coming of the Messiah through their own actions. Active messianism was especially attractive in times of great oppression and upheaval. Jewish history since the first century could be described as a cycle of messianic revolutions.[6] Periodically an individual would arise claiming to be the awaited Messiah. Some of these messianic claimants gathered a following in their city or country. A few managed to acquire international acclaim. In 1666 a Jew by the

---

[6]See Gershom Scholem, "The Messianic Idea in Judaism," in the book of essays by the same title, Schocken, N.Y., 1971.

name of Shabbetai Zevi was acclaimed as the Messiah by Jews throughout the world. All over Europe and the Mediterranean basin Jews prepared for a return to the Land of Israel. When it turned out that Zevi could not make good on his messianic promises there was widespread heartbreak among the Jews.

Secular Messianism

The modernist forms of Judaism that developed in the nineteenth century represent, in a sense, a new outbreak of messianic activism among the Jews. The modernists broke with rabbinic teaching in refusing to wait for God to send the Messiah. In fact, they denied that there would ever be a Messiah. They taught instead that the goals of Jewish messianism were achievable through human action alone. Messianism was transformed into a secular project for the improvement of Jewish and general society.

The Reform Movement which arose in Germany was the first modernist movement to disavow traditional messianic doctrine. The Reform Jews looked to a Messianic Age of perfect social justice rather than to a personal Messiah sent by God. The Reformers were full of the enthusiasm of the Enlightenment. They believed that the perfect world envisioned by the prophets could be achieved through advances in technology and social science. Technology would create a world of plenty. Social reform would insure that the plentiful goods of the world would be justly distributed. Education for all would bring an end to religious and national prejudices which are based on ignorance; Jews would be accepted in society on a basis of human equality. As for the particularistic aspects of Jewish messianism, the return to Jewish sovereignty in the Land of Israel, the Reformers had no interest in this. They saw a greater goal for themselves in being accepted as European citizens.

The Zionist movement, in contrast to the Reform movement, was created to fulfill the national goals of Jewish messianism. The Zionists believed that it was not necessary to wait for God to send the Messiah to initiate a return to the homeland. The Jews could emulate other modern nationalist movements in achieving national sovereignty for themselves. Resettlement and political work would accomplish what prayer and patience had failed to achieve, the restoration of the Jewish nation.

Many Eastern European Jews saw the Socialist movement as a secular way to fulfill the messianic Jewish goals of social justice. The Socialists rejected the religious program of the Reform Jews; they were divided on the nationalist program of Zionism. Some Jewish socialists believed that in the perfect Socialist future all national, religious and ethnic distinctions would fall away. Others saw in Zionism an opportunity to make the new Jewish state into a shining example of Socialism.

Socialism never had the attraction in America that it had in Europe, but the heavy Jewish involvement in the development of trade unions in America has its roots in Jewish socialism in Eastern Europe. American Jews in overwhelming proportions have supported liberal movements such as the New Deal of the 1930s and the Civil Rights Movement of the 1960s. To a great extent this support represents the continuing tendency of modern Jews to convert the messianic goals of traditional Jewish religion into secular social and political goals.

8

Shabbat

The seventh day of the week is **Shabbat,** the Sabbath, a day of complete rest. Shabbat is the most sacred of all the holy days in the Jewish calendar. Of all Jewish observances, only Shabbat is included in the Ten Commandments. The Jewish Shabbat has influenced all of Western culture. The Western calendar follows the seven-day week established by Shabbat. Christians observe Sunday as a day of rest, patterned on Shabbat. Moslems also observe a seven day week, with Friday as a day of special dedication to God, although the Moslem Friday is not a day of complete rest.

Shabbat Observance

The laws of Shabbat require that one refrain from all kinds of work. But Shabbat observance is not just a matter of what one does not do. Proper Shabbat observance requires entering into the spirit of the day through the traditional rituals and activities.

Shabbat begins on Friday evening with a short worship service. In America the worship service is often delayed until after the evening meal, in deference to the work schedule of American Jews. Sabbath dinner is the major activity of **Erev Shabbat,** the Eve of Shabbat.

The house is prepared on Friday afternoon. Everything is cleaned and the house is set in order. The table is set with the best of everything—the best dishes, the best flatware, flowers. Candlesticks and a silver wine goblet are placed on the table. The dinner will include either fish, chicken or meat, wine, and a braided loaf of white bread called **hallah.** Even the poorest family will have these things. In traditional Jewish society charitable funds were used to provide a festive Shabbat dinner for the poor. People would save all week in order to provide for Shabbat. Jews were so careful to fulfill this mitzvah that the rabbis in ancient Babylon worried that wealthy Gentiles would be upset with Jews for driving up the price of luxury food items on Fridays.

There is a legend which reflects the importance of the Shabbat dinner table. Two angels come from heaven every Friday evening, a good angel and a bad angel. They visit every Jewish home. In one home the children are scrubbed, dressed in clean clothes, and well-behaved. The husband and wife glow with holy affection. Everything in the house sparkles and shines. The good angel prays, "May the next Shabbat be just as this one." The bad angel, gritting his teeth, must say "Amen." In the next house everything is a mess and everyone is arguing and fighting. The bad angel prays, "May the next Shabbat be just as this one." The good angel, with tears in its eyes, must say "Amen."

The wife of the house recites the blessing over the Shabbat candles. In Orthodox homes this takes place one half hour before sundown, in order not to kindle light on Shabbat. In non-Orthodox homes the candles are generally lit as the family sits down to dinner. The husband of the house welcomes Shabbat with the blessing over wine. He recites the "Woman of Valor" (Proverbs 31) and blesses the children. He then holds up the hallah and recites the blessing over bread to start the meal. After the meal the Shabbat spirit is expressed through the singing of **zemirot,** Shabbat songs. Although zemirot are not prayers, the singing of them is considered a religious activity.

The Shabbat morning service is the major worship service of the week. The traditional service may be as long as four or five hours. Modernist Jews have shortened the service to one and a half or two hours. One of the functions of Shabbat rest is to give every Jew time for the sacred activities of worship and Torah study.

After morning services there is another kiddush in honor of the Shabbat, and lunch is eaten. The afternoon may be spent in rest, in study, or in visiting with friends. A third meal is eaten in the late afternoon. In twentieth century America nearly all people eat three meals a day, but through history most people have eaten two meals a day. The third meal of Shabbat is part of the enjoyment of the day of rest. In the late afternoon traditional Jews may return to the synagogue for the afternoon and evening service, at which the close of Shabbat is announced.

Jews bid farewell to Shabbat with the ceremony of **Havdalah.** Blessings are recited over three ritual objects: a twisted multi-wicked candle, a cup of wine, and a spice-box. With these objects we use the five senses which allow us to distinguish between the sacred and the profane. The hope of redemption is another theme of the havdalah ceremony. There is a saying that the Messiah will not come on Shabbat because he is already here. The Time of the Messiah is described as a time which will be "all Shabbat." As Shabbat departs there is hope that the Messiah will come and the Shabbat will not have to end. There is also a teaching that on Shabbat every Jew is granted an extra soul. The enjoyment of the flame, the wine and the spices gives consolation for the loss of this extra soul as it returns to heaven.

Shabbat Observance in America

Jewish immigrants found it much more difficult to properly observe Shabbat in America than in their former homes. American Jews work, attend school and live among the Gentile community which does not recognize Shabbat. Until the 1930s most Americans worked six days a week, with Saturday as a regular work day. Even after the five-day work week was established many American Jews were business people who could not make a living unless their shops were open on Saturday. In the past decades Sunday has more and more lost its character as a Christian day of rest, which makes it all the less likely that American Jews will recognize their own Sabbath.

During the period of great Jewish immigration (1881–1920) America was known to European Jews as a place where a Jew was unlikely to keep kosher or observe Shabbat. Many of the more pious Jews preferred the starvation and oppression of Europe, where they were at least able to preserve Jewish traditions. The pious ones remained in Eastern Europe until they were destroyed by the Nazi murderers or by the Communist regimes which did not allow the practice of Judaism. Those who came to America did not always overthrow all attachment to tradition, but most of them were willing to accommodate in order to raise themselves from poverty. It is estimated that only about twenty percent of American Jews attend Shabbat worship services, while perhaps half that number observe the full day of Shabbat rest.

Non-Orthodox religious leaders in America were willing to adjust Shabbat observances to the demands of American society. The major Shabbat worship service was shifted to Friday evening for the sake of those Jews who worked on Saturday. Often, a shortened Torah reading was also included in the Friday evening worship. The service was delayed until after the Shabbat meal to accommodate the longer time-span of the service and for the sake of those Jews who could not leave work early on Friday

afternoon. Some of the most radical congregations in the late nineteenth century even moved Shabbat to Sunday, but many Jews were outraged by this move, and the innovation was short-lived.

The Friday evening service moved the center of Shabbat evening observance from the home to the synagogue. The family now had to finish Shabbat dinner quickly in order to get to services. The social aspect of Shabbat eve was restored by having a social hour with refreshments after services. This custom is called **Oneg Shabbat,** the "joy of the Sabbath." The Oneg Shabbat is often an occasion for Jewish cultural activities, with a lecture or presentation on a Jewish theme.

The Oneg Shabbat had its origin in the practice of the great modern Israeli poet Haim Nahman Bialik. Bialik was not religious, but he did believe in living a Jewish way of life. On Friday evenings he would invite other writers and intellectuals to his home, where they would discuss their writings and important Jewish topics. The use of the Oneg Shabbat as a way of relating to the Jewish cultural heritage was encouraged in America by Mordecai Kaplan, the founder of the Reconstructionist movement in American Judaism.

In Reform Judaism Shabbat is retained as a day of rest and worship, but many of the traditional laws of Shabbat rest have been nullified. Driving, turning on lights, cooking and the like are permitted. In Conservative Judaism most of the traditions are considered still in force, though some adjustments have been made in response to modern society. For instance, driving is permitted if that is the only way a Jew can get to the synagogue for Shabbat worship, as is often the case in America's suburbs.

Shabbat in Israel

Israel was founded by Jewish nationalists who were often antireligious. Shabbat observance was not important to many of the pioneers of the State of Israel. Jewish law is not the law of the state, and Shabbat observance is not required by state law. Many of the Jews who have come to Israel since the founding of the state are more observant than the pioneers. They have pressured their government to make Shabbat more a part of the legal and social fabric of the country. For instance, it is their wish that El Al, the national air line of Israel, not fly on Shabbat. Many would like to see all shops and factories close down on Shabbat. This is a source of contention between the secularists and the religious in Israel. The laws of Shabbat were developed long before modern times, and in a time when Jews no longer had a sovereign state of their own. It is not clear how such modern national institutions as a police force, a hospital, the army, and the utility companies should observe Shabbat. As time goes by these questions are resolved in the laws of the state or by the individual institutions.

In very Orthodox neighborhoods the streets are barricaded to prevent driving and Shabbat observance is strictly enforced by the neighbors. In less Orthodox areas people may drive and do their chores. The Arab shopping districts are open on Shabbat, and many tourists and non-religious Israelis go to these areas. In Jerusalem, which has a large number of Orthodox inhabitants, the buses do not run on Shabbat. In other cities the buses stop on Friday night but continue again on Saturday morning. Many non-religious Israelis like to go to the beach on Shabbat, their only full day off from work.

Shabbat in Jerusalem is a special experience. At noon people get out of work. The food shops are jammed as people buy their necessities for Shabbat dinner. Every bus is packed with people hurrying home to prepare for Shabbat. An hour or two later the people of the city can be seen in their homes, scrubbing the floors, beating rugs, cooking, pulling laundry off the lines. The radio stations play Shabbat zemirot. When the chores are done a person might sit down to relax with the Friday paper, which like the Sunday paper in America is full of special features. In late afternoon the traffic ceases and the households settle into the peace of Shabbat. As the setting sun turns the sky red and makes the limestone buildings gleam like gold, Jewish men stream out of their homes to their synagogues or, in great numbers, to the Western Wall of the Temple Mount, the holiest site in Judaism. A city of half a million is as quiet and peaceful as a tiny village.

Development of the Laws of Shabbat

The written Torah contains only three specific rules regarding Shabbat observance. One is forbidden to work, to kindle fire, and to move from one's habitation. We have no record of how Shabbat was observed in early biblical times, but it is likely that the laws were taken literally. In the simple agricultural society of ancient Israel it would have been no great trouble to sit in the house all day on Shabbat, eating cold food and doing no work.

It would seem that from the time of settlement to the destruction of the first Temple (1200–586 BCE) Shabbat was not as significant as the observance of the Festivals and the New Moon, the first day of each month which was observed as a holy day. Shabbat observance first achieved special importance among the Jews of the Babylonian Exile.

In exile the Jews could no longer serve God through sacrifices, which could only be offered in Jerusalem. The synagogue and the service of prayer were still centuries away from development. How could the exile community continue to show their devotion to God in a foreign land? They could observe the dietary laws. They could circumcise their eight-day-old sons. They could observe Shabbat. These observances became the "sign of the covenant," the way for a Jew in exile to show continued solidarity with the Jewish people and with their God. Shabbat became the most important Jewish holy day. In the complex urban and commercial society of Babylon the laws of Shabbat observance underwent development. We can see the new perspective on Shabbat from the reaction of those Babylonian exiles who returned to the Land of Israel under Persian rule in the fifth century BCE.

The leader of the returning exiles was Ezra the Scribe. Ezra was authorized by the Persian government to rule the Jews of Judah. Ezra was shocked to discover that those Jews who had never gone into exile used Shabbat as a shopping day. The stores of Jerusalem were open and the farmers, who did no farm labor on Shabbat, came into town to shop. Commercial activity on Shabbat is not explicitly forbidden in the Torah, but it went against the practice of the Babylonian Jews. Ezra commanded that the gates of Jerusalem be closed on Shabbat and the shops shuttered. The exchange of money and goods was forbidden on Shabbat in Jewish law from then on; even the discussion of commerce and the making of verbal contracts was forbidden. We can see how the concept of work was interpreted in a new way by the Babylonian Jews in order to extend Shabbat observance from farmers to the urban business community.

During the Jewish rebellion against the Seleucid Greeks, which broke out in 168 BCE, the policy of the Greek soldiers was to seek out and destroy the rebel bands on Shabbat. The pious rebels would allow themselves to be slaughtered rather than desecrate the Shabbat by fighting. When the Maccabees took over leadership of the rebellion they decreed that Shabbat law permitted defensive warfare to protect one's life. This is the first example in recorded history of the process of Oral Torah that became the hallmark of rabbinic Judaism, and we might see in this legal ruling the work of the first Pharisees. In later rabbinic law it was a standard principle that one desecrates Shabbat to save a life. "Let them desecrate one Shabbat in order that they might observe many Shabbats!" said the rabbis.

Shabbat in Rabbinic Law

By the time of the writing of the Mishnah (200 CE) the rabbis had developed an extensive set of laws governing the observance of Shabbat.

They attempted to have a response for the many questions that could arise concerning proper Shabbat observance.

Since rest from work is the essential commandment of Shabbat the most obvious question is, "What is work?" The Oral Torah defines thirty-nine categories of work. These are: sowing, plowing, reaping, binding sheaves, threshing, winnowing, cleansing crops, grinding, sifting, kneading, baking, shearing wool, preparing wool, spinning, weaving, making two loops, weaving two threads, separating two threads, tying a knot, untying a knot, sewing two stitches, tearing, hunting a gazelle, slaughtering or preparing a skin, scraping or cutting a skin, writing two letters, erasing, building, pulling down, putting out a fire, lighting a fire, striking with a hammer, moving anything from one domain to another.[1]

The Mishnah does not explain the origins of this list nor the philosophy of law that went into its development. In the Talmud it is suggested that these are the thirty-nine labors required for the offering of sacrifice in the Temple. Modern scholars have suggested that forbidding these labors allows the world to exist in a state of nature without human artifice, or that these labors cover the three categories of making bread, making clothing, and writing a Torah scroll, the "indispensable bases of organized human life."[2]

Rabbinic law allows a fire which is kindled before Shabbat to remain burning through the Shabbat. One may feed a fire to keep it at a constant level. This interpretation allowed the kindling of Shabbat candles to give light to the home on Friday evening. It also allowed cooked food to be kept warm for eating on Shabbat, while the cookfire also provided warmth in the home. The rabbis considered Shabbat candles to be not only permitted but commanded, and so a blessing is recited when they are lit.

The rabbis interpreted the law against travel to forbid travel beyond the limits of one's own town. One could go a thousand paces beyond the limits of the town. Through a legal fiction one could establish a domicile at the Sabbath limit which would allow one to travel another thousand paces. As usual the rabbis do not record the reason for their legal ruling, but we note that in effect this allowed city dwellers to take a pleasant Shabbat stroll in the park-like public area outside the town limits. The rabbinic laws of Shabbat are naturally stated in terms of what is forbidden, but they had the effect of permitting as much as could be permitted within the

---

[1]A domain is a single piece of property, of any size. A public street is a domain. A private lot is a domain. To move an object from public to private, from private to public, or from private to private is to move from one domain to another.

[2]Robert Goldenberg, "Law and Spirit in Talmudic Religion," in *Jewish Spirituality from the Bible Through the Middle Ages*, ed. Arthur Green, Crossroad, N.Y., 1986.

bounds of divine law. Not only did rabbinic law make Shabbat observance pleasant for people, it also helped them to better maintain the joyous and worshipful spirit of Shabbat.

Rabbinic law established many "fences to the Torah," laws that would keep people from accidentally transgressing the essential Shabbat laws. The law forbade handling tools such as hammers or pens whose use is forbidden on Shabbat. The rabbis forbade playing musical instruments, since one would be tempted to tune them. They forbade bathing, since one would be tempted to wring out the towel after drying off. The refinements of rabbinic law attempted to mediate between the eternal commandments of God, the psychology of the human mind, and the ever-changing nature of human society. We may see an example of the interplay in the Mishnah's discussion of whether a man may wear a sword on Shabbat. The original question revolves around the question of whether a sword is an ornament which is worn (in which case it is permitted) or an instrument (in which case it is forbidden). The law is ultimately decided on an entirely different basis. A sword is forbidden because its function makes it inappropriate for the Shabbat, which is a celebration of peace.

Modern Applications of Rabbinic Law

Modern technology has brought us electric lights, automobiles, telephones, and many other things which did not exist in Talmudic times. The world has changed a great deal. The laws of Shabbat observance must be reinterpreted for the modern world.

Orthodox Jews apply the categories of traditional Jewish law to determine how new inventions may be used on Shabbat. Soon after electricity was tamed by Thomas Edison it was determined that electricity is fire. An electric light or appliance may not be turned on or off on Shabbat, since this is like kindling or extinguishing a fire. An automatic timer which is set before Shabbat may turn lights and appliances on and off. Machines are not required to observe Shabbat. Some kosher hotels are equipped with automatic elevators that stop on every floor during Shabbat.

A refrigerator door may be opened as long as the light bulb has been unscrewed before Shabbat, since the door is also a light switch. It is true that opening the refrigerator may cause the cooling motor to turn on, but this is only an indirect result of opening the door. One opened the refrigerator to take out food, not to make the refrigerator operate. Intention plays a role in determining what is and is not permitted.

Automobile travel is forbidden on Shabbat, since to run the car engine is to kindle fire. A doctor may drive on Shabbat to respond to a life-threatening emergency, but he may not drive back home.

The Reform movement takes the view that modern inventions have so changed society that the old rules of Shabbat observance no longer apply. While maintaining the concept of Shabbat as a day of rest, Reform Jews do not feel obligated to define work by the thirty-nine categories of the Mishnah, nor even by the three specific commandments in the Torah. They perceive these rules as being conditioned by the times in which they were developed and therefore not incumbent upon those who live in different times. Reform Jews will drive, use electrical appliances, kindle and use fire on Shabbat. The exact definition of forbidden work is left to each individual to resolve for oneself, though obviously such activities as working for money or doing onerous household chores would automatically be excluded. A religious Reform Jew feels that his or her primary obligation on Shabbat is to do things which maintain the Shabbat spirit.

The Spirit of Shabbat

The spirit of Shabbat can be summed up in three words: **Oneg, K'dusha,** and **M'nucha.** Oneg is "joy"; k'dusha is "holiness"; m'nucha is "rest."

The joy of Shabbat is a restrained and elevated joyfulness, not the kind of joy one experiences at a wild party but the kind of joy one feels in observing beautiful scenery. The joy of Shabbat is expressed through eating the fine foods of Shabbat dinner and eating the third meal on Shabbat afternoon. The joy of Shabbat is expressed in sociability and hospitality. Activities like strolling, napping and singing contribute to the joy of Shabbat. All the economic burdens and cares of the work week are set out of mind; there is nothing to interfere with the joyful feeling of Shabbat.

K'dusha, holiness, is expressed through worship. "Half the day you give to God, the other half God gives to you." On Shabbat one has the time to worship God properly, with full intention. There are no material concerns to force one to cut short the time for worship. Shabbat is a given to **imitatio dei,** the imitation of God. As God rested after the six days of Creation, so humankind now rests after six days of productive labor. As the mind of God is occupied with Torah and matters of holiness, on Shabbat the human mind is free to engage in Torah. Devout Jews attempt to avoid conversation on topics of passing concern on Shabbat; they direct all of their conversation to sacred matters. The public reading of the Torah and the study of Torah in social circles raises the human mind to the level of the divine.

Shabbat is a particularly suitable time for intimate relations between husband and wife. On Shabbat, heaven and earth are united, God and the world are united, in love. Husband and wife contribute to the sacred unity of the world through their own loving union. It was taught that husband and wife receive double credit in heaven for the mitzvah of sacred union when it is fulfilled on Shabbat.

God freed the people of Israel from slavery in Egypt so that they would be free to serve him. Nevertheless, most of the time they are not free to serve God. All week they must serve their employers or clients; they are enslaved to the material needs of human existence. On Shabbat the people are truly free of all other masters, free to engage in the service of God. They become like the angels, whose only task is to praise and serve God.

M'nucha, Shabbat rest, is more than just a time to restore the body through cessation from work. Shabbat rest does not exist so that one may work harder on the other days of the week. Rather, one works all week so that one will be able to rest on Shabbat. M'nucha is refreshment of the soul as much as it is rest for the body. During the week one tries to dominate nature, to master the elements and bend them to human will. On Shabbat, one lives in harmony with nature. In rabbinic law, if a house catches fire on Shabbat one may save the goods within the house, but one must let the house burn. We do not interfere with the natural course of events, whether they operate to the benefit or to the detriment of humankind.

There are many enjoyable leisure activities which are not permitted on Shabbat. It is fun to play baseball, but competitive sports do not contribute to the tranquility of mind which is a necessary aspect of Shabbat m'nucha.[3]

---

[3]An excellent exposition on the spirit of Shabbat is given in *The Sabbath* by Abraham Joshua Heschel, Farrar, Straus and Giroux, N.Y., 1951.

9

The Holy Days, Sin and Atonement

The Cycle of the Fall Holidays

The early fall is the penitential season in Judaism. A number of related holy days come one after another at this time of year. This period is called the **Yamim Nora'im,** the "Days of Awe." In English the Yamim Nora'im are often called the High Holy Days. This is the time to cleanse the soul and make a fresh start in life.

The Yamim Nora'im fall in the month of Tishre, the month of the fall equinox. The last summer month, the month of Elul, is a time of spiritual preparation for the coming Holy Days. This is the period of **selihot,** prayers requesting pardon for the sins of the past year. Sephardic Jews rise at midnight during the entire month of Elul to recite selihot prayers in the synagogue. Ashkenazic Jews generally hold one midnight selihot service on the Saturday night preceding Rosh Hashanah.

Rosh Hashanah is the Jewish New Year. It falls on the first day of the month of Tishre. Ten days later comes **Yom Kippur,** the Day of Atonement. The days in between are called the Ten Days of Repentance. Yom Kippur concludes the High Holy Days but then four days later, on the Fifteenth of Tishre, comes the fall harvest festival of **Sukkot** the Feast of Booths. Sukkot lasts for seven days. The eighth day after is **Shemini Atzeret,** the Eighth Day of Conclusion, which brings the festival season to a close. Shemini Atzeret is also celebrated as **Simhat Torah,** the Day of Rejoicing in the Torah.

In biblical times Rosh Hashanah and Yom Kippur were merely preludes to Sukkot, which was the major festival of the year. The atoning aspect of the Holy Days was related to the wish for a good harvest which was celebrated on Sukkot. After the destruction of the Temple, Sukkot lost some of its significance, while the Holy Days grew in importance. The rabbis gave a new character to these days, making them days of high spirituality. The mood of the Holy Days is solemn and uplifting.

Extra Day for Holidays

Because the calendar in ancient times could only be determined in the Land of Israel, there was uncertainty among Jews in the Diaspora as to which day was the correct day for observing the holidays. To be on the safe side, Jews in the Diaspora observed an extra day of every biblically commanded holy day. The only exception was Yom Kippur, a day of complete fasting, since it is beyond the ability of most people to fast for two days straight. One-day holidays were celebrated for two days, week-long holidays for eight days. When the calendar was written down in the fourth century the second day of holidays became technically unnecessary, but it was decided that since Jews in the Diaspora had been observing the extra day for centuries they should continue to follow their ancestral custom. Modern Reform Jews have eliminated the observance of the extra day, while Conservative and Orthodox Jews continue this practice.

Rosh Hashanah is observed for two days even in the Land of Israel. Rosh Hashanah is the only Jewish holiday that falls on the first day of the month. Even in the Land of Israel Jews could not be sure that they would hear when the Sanhedrin had declared the start of a new month in time to observe Rosh Hashanah properly. They observed two days so that they would have the right day whether the preceding month of Elul turned out to be a month of twenty-nine or thirty days.

Selihot

The custom of rising at midnight to recite penitential prayers seems to have arisen sometime in the Middle Ages. It was believed that midnight was a time of mercy, when God more readily heard the prayers of humankind. There was a Jewish legend that King David had a magic harp that would play at midnight to wake him up. He then spent the rest of the night until dawn engaged in Torah study and prayer. This practice is believed to purify the soul and bring one closer to God. The Jewish mystics of the late Middle Ages were especially fond of the custom of midnight prayer.

The custom of reciting selihot prayers fell into disuse in America. Since the 1960s there has been a resurgence of this practice, possibly following the new interest of American Jews in the beliefs and practices of the Jewish mystics of old. In the American synagogue the selihot service is often combined with a Jewish study or cultural program designed to raise Jewish consciousness as the Holy Days approach.

It is customary for Jews to visit the graves of their ancestors before or during the Holy Days. Remembering the piety of the ancestors helps bring one to repentance. At this time of year many Jewish charities make their annual appeal and, in America, many community charities make a special appeal to Jewish givers. The practice of charity provides atonement for sins. Jews give with special generosity during the penitential season. It is also customary at this time of year to patch up quarrels and to send greeting cards to all of one's friends and relatives. This custom follows the teaching that one cannot seek forgiveness for sins committed against God until he has first sought forgiveness for sins committed against one's fellow human beings. As the Holy Days approach everyone is anxious to be on good terms with all of his or her relatives, friends and associates.

The Season of Repentance

The drama of the penitential season is expressed in the legend of the Book of Life. According to the legend all the deeds of each person are written in the Book of Days, a ledger book which is kept in heaven. The mitzvot are written on the credit side, the sins on the debit side. Rosh Hashanah is the Day of Judgment. On this day God sits on his throne of justice and holds court. Satan, the Accuser, is the prosecuting attorney in God's court of justice. He mentions the sins of humankind and argues for conviction. The defending angels argue for acquittal. Those few human beings who are complete saints are written down in the Book of Life for good in the coming year. Those few who are utterly evil are written down for bad in the coming year. Most people are neither wholly good nor wholly bad, but somewhere in the middle. God judges them guilty for their sins, but God then waits to see if they will repent. During the Ten Days of Repentance, culminating in Yom Kippur, God looks for any sign of repentance. If a person repents God wipes away his sins and writes that person down for a good year in the Book of Life. At the end of the day of Yom Kippur the Book of Life is closed, but it is not yet sealed. God is so anxious to receive his people back in love that the book is left unsealed until after Sukkot, on the chance that even if a person did not repent on Yom Kippur he will repent afterward.

Rosh Hashanah

God has the right to establish laws and judge humankind because God is the Creator. Rosh Hashanah is celebrated as the day on which God created the world. God is recognized as King of the universe. The celebration of Rosh Hashanah has some things in common with ancient ceremonies in which the rulership of the king was annually renewed. It is customary on Rosh Hashanah to make the hallah, the festive loaf of bread, in the shape of a crown as a reminder of God's kingship.

Rosh Hashanah begins with a festive meal. Despite the serious purpose of the Holy Days they are also a joyous time, since we know that God's forgiveness is certain for those who repent. Blessings are recited over candles and over wine, as on Shabbat. It is customary to begin the meal with apples dipped in honey. This expresses the wish for a sweet new year.

The customary greeting on Rosh Hashanah is **L'shana Tova Tikatevu,** "May you be inscribed for a good new year."

The Mahzor

There are so many special prayers for the Holy Days that they cannot be included in the siddur which contains the weekday and Shabbat prayers. There is a special prayer book for the Holy Days called a **mahzor.** "Mahzor" means "cycle," so called because in earlier times the mahzor contained the prayers for all the holidays which arise in the cycle of the Jewish year. Nowadays the services for special days other than the High Holy Days are included in the siddur.

The Shofar

During the Amidah on Rosh Hashanah morning, and again during the Torah service, the **shofar** is blown. The shofar is the horn of a ram.[1] A total of a hundred blasts are blown on the shofar. The blowing of the shofar on Rosh Hashanah is commanded in the Torah. Many symbolic meanings have been ascribed to this custom.

Maimonides compared the shofar to an alarm clock. It calls upon

---

[1]Or of any other horned animal except for a cow. In some communities it is customary to use the long, beautiful horn of a gazelle. The ram's horn, though, is the most usual shofar.

people to wake up; it knocks them out of their self-content and calls them to look upon the sinfulness of their deeds so that they may repent.

Saadia Gaon, the great rabbi and philosopher of the tenth century, identified eight reasons for blowing the shofar. The shofar is a remembrance of the creation. It is blown like a herald's trumpet to announce the crowning of God as King. It is sounded as a warning, reminding us of the great danger we are in unless we repent. It is a remembrance of the revelation of the Torah at Mount Sinai, which was accompanied by the sound of the shofar. The shofar is a symbol of the words of the Prophets, who called Israel to repentance. The shofar was used as a war bugle in ancient times; now it reminds us of the war call of our enemies who will destroy us unless we prove worthy of God's protection.[2] The shofar reminds us of the binding of Isaac on the altar at Mount Moriah (Genesis 22); the merits of the patriarchs and of the ram which was sacrificed instead of Isaac have atoning power for us. Finally, the terrifying sound of the shofar inspires us to humility before our Creator.

The Scriptural Reading

The Torah reading for Rosh Hashanah is the **Akeda,** the "Binding" of Isaac (Genesis 22). The Akeda is believed to provide vicarious atonement for Israel. According to the midrash, Abraham refused to set down the sacrificial knife until God promised to account it to him as if he had sacrificed Isaac. God promised that whenever Israel recounted the story of the Akeda, God would account to their merit the atoning sacrifice of Isaac.

Special Prayers

The middle portion of the Amidah for Rosh Hashanah contains three sections. At the conclusion of each section the shofar is blown. The three sections are entitled Kingship, Remembrance and Shofar. The first section recognizes God as King and Judge of the world. The second section affirms that God knows and remembers all the deeds performed by every individual person. The third section recalls the important events of Israel's past and looks to the time of the final redemption, which will be accompanied by the blast of the shofar.

Jewish poets have composed numerous piyyutim for the Holy Days.

---

[2]A related interpretation is that the shofar calls us to war against our true enemy, which is the evil impulse within ourselves.

The most famous piyyut for Rosh Hashanah is the poem U'ntane Tokef. According to tradition it was written by Rabbi Amnon of Mayence. Rabbi Amnon was tortured for refusing to convert to Christianity after he made the mistake of telling his friend, the Bishop of Mayence, that he would consider conversion. Rabbi Amnon considered his tortures a just punishment for having implied that he might abandon Judaism. On Rosh Hashanah his tormenters brought him on a stretcher into the synagogue. In his dying minutes he spoke the words of U'ntane Tokef before the congregation. The next night he appeared to his student Eliezer in a dream and taught him the words to the poem. No words better summarize the mood and the religious themes of the Holy Days.[3]

> Let us proclaim the sacred power of this day;
> It is awesome and full of dread.
> For on this day Your dominion is exalted,
> Your throne is established in steadfast love;
> There in truth You reign. . . .
> You open the book of our days,
> and what is written there proclaims itself,
> for it bears the signature of every human being. . . .
> As the shepherd seeks out his flock,
> and makes the sheep pass under his staff,
> so do You muster and number and consider every soul,
> setting the bounds of every creature's life,
> and decreeing its destiny.
> On Rosh Hashanah it is written,
> on Yom Kippur it is sealed:
> How many shall pass on, how many shall come to be;
> who shall live and who shall die. . . .
> But **repentance, prayer and charity**
> temper judgement's severe decree.
> This is Your glory; You are
> slow to anger, ready to forgive.
> Lord, it is not the death of sinners You seek,
> but that they should turn from their ways and live. . . .
> Man's origin is dust, and dust is his end.
> Each of us is a shattered urn, grass that must wither,
> a flower that will fade, a shadow moving on,
> a cloud passing by,

---

[3]The selection which follows uses the translation found in *Gates of Repentance*, CCAR, N.Y., 1978. (Reprinted by permission.)

a particle of dust floating on the wind,
a dream soon forgotten.
But You are the King, the everlasting God!

The Observance of Yom Kippur

Yom Kippur is observed as a twenty-four hour fast. Nothing may pass the lips during that time, neither food nor water. The laws of Shabbat rest apply to Yom Kippur. There are many additional prayers on Yom Kippur which make the services very lengthy. The entire day is spent in the synagogue in prayer and penitence. There were some Jews in times of old who even stayed in the synagogue throughout the night of Yom Kippur, reciting Psalms. The usual evening, morning and afternoon services are extended with prayers of confession and many piyyutim. There are additional services as well. The **Avodah** service in the early afternoon recalls the penitential sacrifices offered by the High Priest in the ancient Temple. The **Yizkor**, "Memorial" service, is recited in memory of the martyrs of the Jewish people and in memory of deceased parents. The **Neilah** service concludes Yom Kippur. "Neilah" means "locking," referring to the closing of the gates of heaven which have been opened wide on Yom Kippur so that the prayers and penitence of Israel might rise before God.

On the eve of Yom Kippur, before sundown, a festive meal is eaten. It was taught that "One who feasts on the eve of Yom Kippur, God accounts it to him as if he fasted for two days." A light, joyous meal is taken at the conclusion of the fast. The joy of these meals recalls the words of Rabbi Akiva, the great second century rabbi: "Happy are you, O Israel! Who cleanses you of sin, and before whom are you cleansed? Before the Holy One, blessed be He."

Kol Nidre

The service for the eve of Yom Kippur begins with the chanting of the **Kol Nidre** prayer. Kol Nidre, "All Vows," is a prayer asking God to absolve us from vows which we are unable to fulfill. The leaders of the congregation hold the scrolls of the Torah and the congregation stands as the Kol Nidre is sung three times through by the cantor.

The Kol Nidre is first mentioned as a custom of Babylonian Jews in the early Middle Ages. Nearly as soon as the prayer arose it was opposed by leading rabbis, because it is contrary to Jewish law and ethical teaching.

A person is required to fulfill all vows. The absolution of vows can be provided by a rabbinic court under special circumstances, but a prayer of confession is insufficient to remove the obligation to fulfill a vow. A medieval French rabbi, failing in his own attempt to extinguish the custom of reciting Kol Nidre, lessened the ethical concern by changing the words so that one prayed for future absolution rather than for absolution of unfulfilled vows made in the past year. Later Jewish tradition further softened the ethical consideration by explaining Kol Nidre as a penitential prayer for Jews who had been forced to disavow Judaism and convert during the Spanish Inquisition. German Reform rabbis in the nineteenth century attempted once again to eliminate the custom of Kol Nidre. They failed, like their predecessors, due to the popularity of the prayer among the folk.

Since the late Middle Ages the popularity of Kol Nidre has resulted from the melody by which it is sung. Modern Jews pay little if any attention to the words of Kol Nidre, but the melody has the power to evoke the most powerful feelings of Jewish attachment, even in assimilated Jews. This power has been celebrated in American film in the classic movie "The Jazz Singer." In this movie a cantor's son falls away from Judaism to follow a secular singing career. He is drawn back to his Orthodox roots when he is called back to his synagogue to sing the Kol Nidre on Yom Kippur eve. There is a great element of truth in the story. The Kol Nidre service, as the Yom Kippur evening worship is called, draws to the synagogue many Jews who do not otherwise attend worship services. Synagogue attendance on Rosh Hashanah and Yom Kippur is many times greater than on other occasions, and the most crowded service is the Kol Nidre service.[4] The great German-Jewish educator and philosopher Franz Rosensweig was drawn back to Judaism by the melody of the Kol Nidre. In his time, in the early twentieth century, many German Jews underwent conversion in order to advance their careers. Rosensweig, who had just received his doctorate in philosophy, was considering this step so that he would be able to receive a faculty appointment in a German university. He attended synagogue for the first time in years on Kol Nidre night. As he listened to the melody of the Kol Nidre, he felt a rebirth of the Jewish feelings in his heart. He determined to pursue a different course for his future and he became a great Jewish educator, a leader of the Jewish revival that inspired the last generation of German Jewry.

---

[4] We may compare this American Jewish phenomenon to that of the "twice-a-year Christian" who attends church only on Christmas and Easter.

Confession

The prayers of confession are composed in the plural form. The entire community of Israel confess for the sins committed by any one of them. If a person were without sin his confession would be of special value to the community, since his righteousness would be a credit to them all.

The "short confession" is an alphabet of sins from Aleph to Tav (from "A" to "Z"). The long confession is a litany of sins. Each line begins with the words "For the sin which we have sinned against thee by . . ." The long confession concludes "For all these sins, O forgiving God, forgive us, pardon us, grant us atonement!" Besides participating in communal confession, it is considered proper for each person to privately review his life over the past year and repent the specific wrongs which he has committed.

A plea for divine forgiveness is offered in the prayer **Avinu Malkenu**, "Our Father, our King," which is recited on both Rosh Hashanah and Yom Kippur. According to legend this prayer originates with Rabbi Akiva. In ancient Israel public fasts were called by the Sanhedrin whenever the rains did not come in the fall, the rainy season. One year all the fasts and prayers were to no avail. The people called upon Rabbi Akiva to pray for them. He rose and said, "Our Father, our King, be gracious to us and answer us, for we have no merit. Deal charitably and kindly with us and save us!" Immediately, it started to rain. This prayer was kept from then on as a prayer of great efficacy in calling for God's mercy. Many petitions have been added to this one, each petition beginning "Our Father, our King . . ."

Teshuvah

The Hebrew word for repentance is **teshuvah.** Literally, teshuvah means "turning." To repent is to turn toward God, to turn toward a new path in life, to turn within one's own soul. The meaning of teshuvah has been explored in great depth in Jewish teachings. Teshuvah is believed to have unlimited power to effect the transformation of human life and of the world. There is a midrash that Adam met up with his son Cain. Adam said to Cain, "What are you doing here? I thought that God banished you forever after you killed your brother." Cain replied, "He did, but I performed teshuvah and God forgave me." Adam tore his hair and cried, "If only I had known the power of teshuvah, we would still be in the Garden of Eden!"

Every Jew is asked to imagine that his sins and his mitzvot are exactly balanced. A single act of teshuvah could be sufficient to turn his judgment to the good. Furthermore he should imagine that the sins and mitzvot of all Israel are exactly balanced. His own teshuvah may be significant to tip the balance of judgment for all Israel. Not only that, but he should imagine that the judgment of the entire universe is in balance. In that case a single act of teshuvah will be sufficient to save the entire world. Teshuvah is of cosmic significance.

Whole treatises have been written to explain the laws of teshuvah. The laws of teshuvah provide a good example of how the highest concepts of Jewish spirituality are expressed in law. Let us look at a sampling of these laws of teshuvah.

If one brings a sacrifice of atonement but does not perform teshuvah, the sacrifice is not accepted by God. Teshuvah is fully acceptable even without sacrifice. Although sacrifices of atonement were offered on Yom Kippur while the Temple stood, teshuvah alone and not sacrificial ritual is sufficient to atone for all sins.

There are three stages to teshuvah. First, a person must admit to having done wrong. It is possible to find all kinds of justification for our misdeeds, to excuse them or explain them away or to blame them on someone else. Teshuvah requires that one admit that his misdeeds were simply wrong; they should not have been done.

The second stage of teshuvah is to be truly sorry for the wrongs one has committed. This does not follow automatically from the first stage. One may be glad to have committed a wrong. One may confess, "I did it, and I would do it again." Teshuvah requires that one be filled with regret for having done wrong.

The third stage of teshuvah is to vow never to repeat the sin. This stage also is very difficult. Even if a person deeply regrets having committed a sin, the memory of the pleasure or gain which that sin brought might cause him to reserve to himself the option of repeating it at some future time. The rabbis taught that one who repents a sin without resolving to abandon it forever is like one who enters a ritual bath of purification with a lizard in his hand. At what point is he purified? Let him release the lizard and be pure!

If one has sinned against another person, one is required to make restitution if at all possible. One must seek the forgiveness of those who have been wronged. If you are asked to forgive, it is incumbent upon you to grant forgiveness. If one refuses to forgive, the sin is upon him.

If one says, "I will sin and Yom Kippur will atone for me," Yom Kippur will not atone for him.

Three things provide atonement: marriage, Yom Kippur and death. The law does not state what these things have in common, but the obvious connection is that after each of these events one is reborn into a new life;

one ceases to be the person that one was and becomes a new person. It was taught that in the case of the worst sins, for which restitution is impossible, Yom Kippur provides a third of atonement, regret and sufferings provide a third, and the eventual death of the sinner provides a third.

"The gates of repentance are always open." A person may repent at any time. Yom Kippur is set aside for repentance, but a person may repent on any day and be received. It is better to repent when one is young, but a person's deathbed repentance is fully acceptable. God will know if the repentance is sincere, even if a person waits until he is unable to do wrong anymore. The best repentance is when one ends up in the same situation in which he sinned before and does not repeat the sin.

No one is ever beyond repentance, but there are some sins for which it is difficult to repent. Those who stand aloof from the commuity, who mock the commandments and the teachings of the Sages, those who hate rebuke, those who commit murder and like crimes, are unlikely to repent.

If one has fulfilled the three stages of repentance in all sincerity and then goes out and sins, that sin is not to be considered a continuation of former sins. It is a new sin. One may not repent on Yom Kippur for sins committed before the previous Yom Kippur. One is required to believe that God has forgiven.

One who has repented his former ways and embarked on a new way of life is called a **baal teshuvah**, a "master of repentance." One may not mention his former sins to a baal teshuvah.

Modern Concepts of Teshuvah: Rosensweig

When the philosopher Franz Rosensweig decided to return to Judaism he had a long way to come. He was very assimilated to Gentile culture. He had very little knowledge of how to live as a Jew. Rosensweig embarked on a program of study. Every time he learned about a law or commandment he examined his heart to see if he was ready to observe it. If he could add this observance to his life he did so. If he found himself unwilling to observe this practice he did not reject it out of hand. He said to himself, "I am not yet ready to observe it." By taking the attitude of "not yet" Rosensweig held out to himself the hope that he would someday be able to observe all of Jewish tradition, even though from his assimilated background some aspects of traditional Judaism seemed undesirable to him at the time. To Rosensweig, the essential elements of teshuvah were education and the return to Jewish practice. Rosensweig was the father of the modern "baal teshuvah movement," the movement of non-practicing Jews into an Orthodox way of life. This movement has become a significant element in contemporary Jewish life. There are numerous yeshivas, especially in Jerusalem, whose curriculum is designed to train assimilated and uneducated Jews who desire a return to Jewish tradition. The Lubavitcher Hasidic sect, centered in Brooklyn, New York, is very strong in this movement. They have established outreach centers all over America and in many other countries to encourage young Jews to study and live an Orthodox way of life.

Martin Buber on Teshuvah

Rosensweig's contemporary and friend Martin Buber had a very different conception of teshuvah. Buber did not observe Jewish law and tradition. He believed that each person must act out of his own personal relationship with God. Teshuvah, the turning, is the turning of the total person toward God. Integrity, being a whole person, is the key to teshuvah. Buber defined sin as those deeds which cannot be done with integrity, those deeds which can only be performed by a divided self. If a person turns with his whole being to God he will find that God is always turning to him. Buber called the relationship of one person to another in complete integrity the "I-Thou" relationship. This is opposed to the "I-It" relationship in which we deal with one another in objective terms. We can have "I-It" relationships with other people—they are necessary—but we can only relate to God as a Thou. Teshuvah requires that a person turns to God with all of his being. The primary task of a person who desires "the turning" is to unite his own self. One must live with integrity.

Hermann Cohen on Teshuvah

Hermann Cohen was about half a generation older than Rosensweig or Buber. Like them, he was a German Jew. He had a successful career as a professor and philosopher; he was the renowned father of the Marburg school of neo-Kantian philosophy. Toward the end of his career Cohen turned his attention to Jewish topics. He described Judaism in the terms of modern philosophy. Cohen's teachings both inspired and reflected the beliefs of classical Reform Judaism.

Cohen contrasted the Jewish idea of sin to that of Christianity and of ancient paganism. To the pagan, sin is an inescapable fate. We may take the example of Oedipus, who was fated to kill his father and marry his mother. All of his efforts to the contrary could not help him to escape his fate. Paul defined sin for Christians as a state of being. People are born sinful and only a change in their state of being through the grace of God can remove sinfulness from them.

The greatness of the prophets of Israel, says Cohen, is that they defined sin as improper deeds. It is this definition which allows for the concept of teshuvah.

The prophet Ezekiel was the first to recognize that sinfulness is the result of misdeeds (Ezekiel 18). If a person changes his deeds, he has removed himself from his sin. The act of teshuvah is the act of correcting one's deeds.

Man is morally accountable to God. Ethical deeds are what God demands of humankind. The human effort to return to God must be expressed through the effort to perform good deeds.

But what of bad deeds already committed? Even if one now does good, what can undo wrongs which have been done? The greatness of God's love is shown in that God allows for reconciliation between himself and the doer of wrong deeds. This is possible because of another great realization of the prophets—all sin is error. If people had proper knowledge and if they had been able to use their divinely given ability to foresee the consequences of their actions, they would not sin. Sin can be forgiven because sin is error. God desires reconciliation with all sinners, but God cannot bestow forgiveness by grace alone. Reconciliation requires human effort. God's grace is available to the one who strives to liberate himself from doing wrong.

Cohen stressed that the liberation which comes from reconciliation with God is not a liberation from this world and its cares. Man is not released from earthly existence nor from pain and suffering, but only from errors and mistakes. People are released from the errors of the past so that they may do what is right and good—so that they may be ethical.

Studying and performing mitzvot, living with integrity, performing ethical deeds—the meaning of teshuvah for the modern Jew has been given greater depth by each of the three great philosophers we have studied. Each of these teachers has inspired great numbers of Jews to renew their efforts to live a Jewish life through the performance of teshuvah.

10

Passover

The Three Festivals

The Torah commands three festivals to be observed in the course of the year. These are **Pesah, Shavuot,** and **Sukkot.** Pesah is observed on the fifteenth day of the month of Nisan, the month of the spring equinox. The name Pesah is the term for the sacrificial lamb which was offered on the eve of the holiday. Pesah literally means to skip or "pass over"; hence the English name Passover for the holiday. The festival of Shavuot comes fifty days after Passover. The name Shavuot means "weeks." A week of weeks is counted out, forty-nine days, and the next day is Shavuot. The Greek name of the festival, Pentecost, means counting to fifty. Sukkot comes in the fall after the High Holy Days. The name Sukkot means "booths," a reference to the harvest booths which Jews build to eat and sleep in during the festival.

Passover is a week long. The first and last days are full holidays; the middle days are semi-holidays. Shavuot is one day long. Sukkot is a week long, with the eighth day of **Shemini Atzeret,** the "eighth day of conclusion," considered a separate holiday. Among traditional Jews in the Diaspora, Passover is observed for eight days, with the first two and last two days as full holidays. Shavuot is observed for two days. Sukkot-Shemini Atzeret is observed for nine days. The first two days and last two are full holidays. The second day of Shemini Atzeret is observed as **Simhat Torah,** the day of rejoicing in the Torah.

The three festivals form a unit. Each has a role in one of three cycles. Each of the festivals has an agricultural significance, an historical significance and a spiritual significance.

127

In agriculture, Pesah celebrates the birthing of lambs and the beginning of the grain harvest.[1] Shavuot celebrates the conclusion of the grain harvest and the ripening of the first summer fruits. Sukkot celebrates the fruit and vegetable harvest in the fall and the beginning of the rainy season, which lasts until Pesah.

Historically, the three festivals recall the important events at the beginning of Israel's history. Pesah recalls the Exodus from Egypt. Shavuot recalls the revelation of the Torah at Mount Sinai. Sukkot recalls the forty years of wandering in the desert prior to Israel's entry into the promised land.

Spiritually, Pesah celebrates God's role as Redeemer. On Shavuot God is recognized as Revealer. On Sukkot God is recognized as Creator.

Festival Laws and Customs

The three festivals are called the **Shalosh Regalim,** the "Three Pilgrimages." In ancient times these festivals were the occasion for farmers in Judah to make pilgrimage to Jerusalem in order to bring their agricultural offerings to the Temple. In addition to their religious significance, the festivals had a character something like a state fair. They provided an opportunity for farmers to sell their goods and purchase wares from the artisans and shopkeepers of Jerusalem.

The laws forbidding work on festivals are less restrictive than those forbidding work on Shabbat. Kindling fire is permitted on a festival. The food for that day may be cooked, although one may not cook on a festival food to be eaten later. On the intermediate days of a festival one is permitted to work at one's profession, although strenuous and unpleasant work should be avoided.

The joy of a festival has a different character than that of Shabbat. Festival joy is called **simha,** as opposed to the oneg of Shabbat. Simha is a more unrestrained joyousness. Simha is expressed through eating meat and drinking wine in a festive meal. It is expressed through gifts of clothing and jewelry to women, sweets and toys to children. Traditional Jews would await a festival to wear their new clothes, so that the pleasure could add to the joy of the holiday. The rabbis taught that the difference between gluttony and festive rejoicing is that the joy of a festival must be shared with those who cannot afford it. Charitable gifts to provide a festive meal for the poor are an essential part of festival celebration. With this under-

---

[1]The Land of Israel has a twelve-month agricultural cycle. Grain is planted in the fall and harvested in the spring.

stood, self-indulgence on a festival is not only permitted but encouraged. The simha of a festival is an aspect of the service of God as much as is the serious introspection of Yom Kippur. To rejoice on a festival is a mitzvah, commanded in the Torah. Because of this, mourning is forbidden on a festival. If one is observing shiva, the week of mourning, when a festival arrives, then shiva is interrupted and not resumed after the festival. On Shabbat, shiva is interrupted and then resumed.[2] The law presumes that sorrow is not displaced by Shabbat, while on a festival all sorrows are forgotten in the joy of God's happy day.

The synagogue services for the festivals are similar to those of Shabbat. The middle blessing of the Amidah is a prayer of thanks to God for giving the festivals. On Sukkot a special prayer for rain is included in the Amidah, and on Pesah there is a prayer for the dew which provides moisture for summer crops. On the last day of festivals Yizkor, the memorial service, is recited. The Torah readings for the festivals are selected from the portions of the Torah which describe their observance or which relate to the respective themes of creation, revelation and redemption.

The History of the Passover Celebration

The first Passover was observed on Israel's last night in Egypt before the Exodus. The Jews were instructed to sacrifice a lamb and place some of its blood on the doorpost. They were to roast the lamb and eat it in family groups. They were to be ready for travel, eating while standing up with their walking sticks in their hands. The Pesah sacrifice was to be eaten with **maror,** bitter herbs, and **matzoh,** unleavened bread. That night God's angel passed through Egypt killing the first-born males in order to force Pharaoh, king of Egypt, to release Israel from slavery and let them leave Egypt. This was the last of the ten plagues which God brought upon the Egyptians. When the angel saw the blood on the doorposts of Israelite houses it passed over those houses, sparing the inhabitants.[3]

The Passover was next celebrated on the eve of Israel's entrance into the promised land, and every year thereafter. The ritual of placing blood on the doorpost was not repeated, nor did people dress for travel. Those rules applied only to the first Passover. The people sacrificed a lamb, ate it with matzoh and maror, and recounted the story of the Exodus.

During the reign of King Josiah (sixth century BCE) the Passover

---

[2]Private aspects of mourning such as refraining from marital relations are still observed on Shabbat, but public mourning is not observed.

[3]See Exodus 12 and 13.

celebration was moved to the Temple in Jerusalem.[4] Until then it was a household celebration. Now, people brought their lambs to Jerusalem to be sacrificed in the Temple. They cooked them outdoors in the open places of the city and ate around their fires. This was the custom throughout the period of the Second Temple, until its destruction in 70 CE. After the destruction of Jerusalem the Passover was celebrated at home. No longer was a lamb sacrificed, since all sacrifice came to an end with the destruction of the Temple. Ordinary roasted meat or fowl replaced the Pesah lamb as the main dish. To this day the Passover is observed by family groups in the home.

The Seder

The discussion of the Exodus from Egypt is an important part of the Passover celebration. The Torah commands that a Jew shall tell his children about the wonders of the Exodus during the Passover feast. In the course of time a pattern developed for telling about the Exodus. This pattern is called the **seder,** Hebrew for "order," as in "order of service." The Passover feast came to be called the seder meal, or simply the seder. By the time the Second Temple was destroyed the pattern of the seder was well developed. The telling of the story became the essence of the Pesah celebration.

The pattern of the seder and the words to be spoken are contained in a book called the **haggadah,** the "telling." The haggadah stands with the Torah and the siddur (prayer book) as a text through which every Jew could absorb the message of Judaism. The haggadah outlines the essential elements of the seder. It contains scriptural passages, midrash, songs and hymns, blessings over the special foods that are eaten, and descriptions of the symbolic meaning of those foods. It is not necessary to stick to the text of the haggadah during the Passover seder. It is considered praiseworthy to depart from the text in order to delve more deeply into the meaning of the Exodus through group discussion.

The symbolic foods for the seder are placed on the set table. There is a large plate containing a roasted bone, a roasted egg, greens (such as parsley or celery), maror (bitter herbs) and **haroset,** a sweet sauce. There is a dish of salt water. Three pieces of matzoh are placed one on top of another. Each place is set with a wine cup from which four cups of wine will be drunk. A large wine cup is placed in the center of the table; this is called the cup of Elijah.

---

[4]See 2 Kings 23:21–23.

The order of the seder is as follows: blessing over the festival candles, first cup of wine, dip greens in salt water, eat matzoh, eat maror, eat maror on matzoh with haroset, tell the story of the Exodus, second cup of wine, dinner, blessing after the meal and third cup, Psalms and songs, conclusion and fourth cup.

The roasted bone is a remembrance of the Pesah sacrifice. The roasted egg recalls the musaf, the additional[5] sacrifice. The greens are a symbol of springtime. The salt water recalls the tears of slavery. The haroset recalls the mortar used to build the buildings which Pharaoh required of the Israelites.[6] The matzoh recalls the bread which the Israelites made for provision in the desert. They had to leave Egypt so quickly they did not have time to allow their bread to rise. The four cups of wine recall the four terms for redemption used in Exodus 6:6–8: "I will free you . . . and deliver you. . . . I will redeem you . . . and I will take you to be my people." The rabbis could not decide if God's further promise, "I will bring you into the land," was an aspect of the redemption from slavery in Egypt or a further benefit which God bestowed on the people. Since they could not decide if there should be a fifth cup of wine they left this cup of wine on the table for Elijah to decide when he comes to announce the final, messianic redemption.

The seder resembles in form the **symposium,** the dinner party common among the upper classes of Greece and, later, Rome. At a symposium the guests would be invited to discuss a particular subject. Each guest would be invited to offer a toast and discourse on the chosen subject. The seder is a symposium on the subject of the Exodus from Egypt.

Highlights from the Haggadah

Near the beginning of the seder the leader holds up the matzoh and recites the following formula: "This is the bread of affliction, the poor bread, which our ancestors ate in the land of Egypt. Let all who are hungry come and eat. Let all who are in want share in this Passover. Now we celebrate here, next year in the Land of Israel. Now we are still slaves. Next year may we all be free." This recitation reminds the participants that the theme of Pesah, God's redemption, is not just a theme of the ancient past. It is relevant to the present, to the needs of those who sit at

---

[5]The tamid was a daily sacrifice offered every morning in the Temple. The musaf was offered on Sabbaths and festivals in addition to the tamid.

[6]Despite the popular conception, the Israelite slaves did not build the pyramids.

the table. The participants are invited to join in the task of redemption by inviting the poor to join them at their feast.

The purpose of the seder is to tell the story of the Exodus to the next generation. One purpose of the unusual rituals of the seder is to arouse the curiosity of the children so that they will ask the meaning of the ceremony. This is a basic motivational technique so that the children will listen to the telling of the story. To make sure that the children participate, the questions for them to ask are included in the haggadah. The children are trained in advance to chant the words of the **arba kushiot,** the four puzzlements or, as they are called in English, the "four questions." The youngest child present asks, "Why is this night different from all other nights? On other nights we eat leavened or unleavened bread, this night only unleavened. On other nights we eat all kinds of vegetables; on this night, bitter herbs. On other nights we do not dip, on this night we dip twice.[7] On other nights we eat sitting up or reclining; tonight all recline."[8]

The Torah says four times to "tell your children on that day." The rabbis believed that there is no extraneous word in the Torah. If the commandment is repeated four different times, it must intend to tell us something new each time. The rabbis surmised that the Torah was talking about four different kinds of children. Thus arose the midrash of the Four Sons. The wise son asks about the laws and customs for the proper observance of Pesah. The wicked son asks why "you" are doing all this, excluding himself. The simple son asks, "What is this?" The fourth son is the son who does not know how to ask.

The father must reply to each son according to his type. He must teach the wise son. He must rebuke the wicked son. He must give a simple answer to the simple son. For the sake of the son who does not know how to ask he must tell the whole story of the Exodus, omitting nothing.

The midrash of the four sons teaches important lessons about Jewish values. The wise son already knows the story of Passover; his wisdom lies in realizing the importance of observing God's laws in exact detail. The wicked son is not a criminal but a scoffer. The wickedness of the wicked son lies in removing himself from identification with the Jewish people. The father tells him that had he been in Egypt, God would have left him

---

[7]The first dipping is the greens in salt water. The second dipping originally referred to the custom of dipping bitter lettuce in haroset. This is seldom done today, and the second dipping is taken to refer to the mixing of maror and haroset on matzoh.

[8]In Roman times Jews reclined on sofas at the seder table, as did noble Greeks and Romans at their banquets. This imitation of the nobility emphasized that on Pesah every Jew is a freedman. In modern times the leader of the seder reclines on a sofa or easy chair in remembrance of the former custom.

there. The father says, "We observe this seder because of what God did for *me* when I came forth out of Egypt."

Every Jew is required to look upon himself as if he himself had participated in the Exodus from Egypt. We have here another definition of a Jew, aside from the legal, religious, and national definitions which we discussed in Chapter One. A Jew is one who feels that he himself has experienced the Exodus from Egypt. A Jew is one who identifies with the historical experience of the Jewish people. Or we might describe this as a sort of internal conversion, an inner spiritual experience of God's redeeming power achieved through the sacred ritual of the seder. One who does not share this experience may still formally be a Jew but, like the wicked son, he is outside the community in any meaningful sense.

The haggadah tells a story: Rabbi Akiva and four other rabbis once held a seder that lasted until dawn, the maximum allowable time for a seder. Ostensibly this is a story about how five great rabbis fulfilled the mitzvah of discussing the Exodus at length. Those who are knowledgable in Jewish history are able to recognize that the five rabbis were actually planning a rebellion against Rome, the Bar Kochba rebellion which broke out in 132 CE. Rabbi Akiva was the religious leader of that rebellion. The story of the five rabbis actually tells how Jews applied the message of Passover to their own lives. They considered how they might be redeemed from slavery to the Pharaohs of their own time. The memory of the great redemption of the past, the Exodus from Egypt, gives inspiration to work for present redemption and gives hope for the messianic redemption of the future. The last words of the seder are, "Next year in Jerusalem," an expression of hope that before the next Passover the Jewish people will have been redeemed once and for all.

The hope for future redemption is expressed after the meal when the door is opened for Elijah the Prophet. This custom began in the Middle Ages to show the Christian neighbors of the Jews that there was nothing to hide in the activities of the seder. The neighbors were suspicious when the Jews, who lived as strangers in their midst, gathered in groups behind closed doors and observed strange rituals. The open door was intended to show that there was nothing to fear from the Jews. American Jews often invite Christian friends to their seder, not to dispel fear but to share the universal message of redemption, the hope for a time when all peoples will live in peace. The welcoming of Elijah, the forerunner of the Messiah, is another expression of that hope. Children are told that Elijah comes invisibly to each seder to take a sip from the cup that is set aside for him; when Elijah comes visibly, the time of the Messiah has arrived.

Half of the middle matzoh is hidden until the end of the seder. The children are invited to search for this piece of matzoh, called the **afikomen.**

The child who finds it receives a small prize. At the conclusion of the seder each participant eats a piece of the afikomen. The name comes from the Greek word for after-dinner entertainment, which usually involved drunkenness and bawdiness. The matzoh as afikomen was a reminder that the participants in the seder must stick to the subject and not allow their festive meal to degenerate into mere social entertainment. The seder must end in the same dignified manner in which it began.

Leavened and Unleavened Bread

During the entire week of Pesah leavened grain products may not be consumed. The five grains wheat, oats, rye, barley and spelt may not be consumed in any form unless it is certified that their flour has been kept dry before cooking to prevent natural leavening. Some Jewish communities begin to watch their grain from the time it ripens in the fields to insure against leavening. Leavening or leavened grain products are called **hametz.** Unleavened bread is called **matzoh.** It is a mitzvah to eat matzoh on the first day of Pesah. After that one may refrain from hametz and matzoh, if one so chooses. Jews from European countries also refrain from legumes, corn and rice, while Jews from Islamic countries eat these foods on Pesah.

Jewish women have developed ingenious recipes over the years to create delicious foods that are kosher for Pesah, including even cakes. Whipped egg whites are used to give lightness instead of leavening agents such as yeast or baking powder. Matzoh is ground into a powder and used for flour.

The house must be completely cleared of hametz before Pesah. Any hametz which remains in the house is locked out of sight. Traditional Jews observe a ceremony in which their hametz is symbolically sold to a Gentile, who returns it to the original owners when Pesah is over. In Israel, an Arab soldier in the Israeli army is chosen each year to become owner of all of the State of Israel's grain stores during the week of Pesah.

On the night before Pesah the children in each household are given a spoon, a feather and a candle. The children search for hametz with the candle. When they find some they sweep it into the spoon with the feather. The parents leave crumbs in strategic places to make sure that the children find some hametz. The hametz in the spoon is burned or scattered to the wind.

The Beta Yisrael, the Jews of Ethiopia, believe that no amount of house-cleaning can sufficiently remove all hametz. They live outdoors during the week of the holiday.

Song of Songs

On the Shabbat during Pesah the biblical book, the Song of Songs, is recited after the morning worship. The Song of Songs may also be recited on the first night of Pesah, at the conclusion of the seder. The Song of Songs is a book of love poetry. It was included in the Tanak because it was understood as an allegory for the love between God and Israel. God's love for Israel is displayed in the redemption from slavery in Egypt. The drama of redemption is perceived as a courtship and marriage, following the pattern expressed by the prophet Ezekiel (16:1–14). God found Israel as a young orphan girl. He gave her to Egypt to raise her for him. When Israel reached maturity God returned to consummate their relationship. God displayed his gallantry before Israel and won her love by bringing the plagues upon Egypt to free Israel from the grip of slavery. The passage through the split waters of the Red Sea was a ceremony of engagement. The marriage between God and Israel was carried out at Mount Sinai. The Torah is the ketubah, the marriage contract, between God and Israel. As in human marriage in ancient times, the wife promises to honor and obey her husband, while he promises to love, protect and provide for his wife. God gives Israel the Land of Israel as a wedding gift.

High Level of Passover Observance

Of all Jewish observances, Pesah is the most dear to modern Jews. In Israel and in America only about ten percent of Jews observe Shabbat as a day of rest. About half fast on Yom Kippur. Fully ninety percent of American Jews and ninety-five percent of Israelis attend a Passover seder.

We can only guess at why Pesah observance is so important to modern Jews. One obvious reason is that the seder is a home observance that brings families together. Many non-religious Jews observe the seder as a family gathering, without carrying out all of the required rituals. It may also be that the Jews observe the seder because the meaning of Pesah is so close to their own experience. Modern Jews have experienced redemption in their own lives. Most American Jews are only three or four generations removed from enslavement to the tyrannical and oppressive czars of Russia. By coming to America or Israel Jews escaped from the gas chambers of the Nazis. There are Jews who miraculously survived the concentration camps. Jews in Israel come from many countries in which they were oppressed and their lives were endangered. Now, in Israel and America, Jews live in freedom and dignity, in their own ancient homeland or in a democratic country of their own choosing. The Jews of today can truly relate to the miraculous escape from slavery into freedom.

Passover may also be so widely observed because the message of Passover is easily transferred to a secular context. The Jewish concept of redemption is a social and political concept. One is not redeemed from earthly concerns into a spiritual existence; one is redeemed from social inequality into a state of freedom. Contemporary American Jews, even if they are not religious, can identify the Passover celebration with their own acquisition of rights as American citizens and with their compulsion to struggle against anti-Semitism, racism, poverty and other forms of social inequality which persist in American society. Contemporary Israelis can relate the theme of Passover to the restoration of Jewish sovereignty in their own land.[9] Secular Jews may observe Pesah not as a time to give thanks to God for his deliverance but as a time to recall their own social and political ideals and their struggles to achieve them.

The Theology of Exile and Redemption

By the time rabbinic Judaism originated Jews could already look back on a history of over 1,500 years. They had seen successive empires rise to world prominence for a time, only to fall. Assyria, Babylon, Persia and Greece had each established an empire. Each had ruled for a time over the Land of Judah. Each had wrought destruction against the Jewish people, on occasion attempting to eliminate them altogether. The great empires had all vanished, and the Jews had outlasted them all. Now the Jews were ruled by Rome, the mightiest and most tyrannical empire of them all. On the basis of past experience the Jews had no doubt that eventually Rome's day too would pass and the Jewish people would survive. Jews saw all of history as a cycle of exile and redemption, of tyrannical rulers and divine deliverance. The following midrash illustrates this view:

> "(Jacob) had a dream; a stairway was set on the ground and its top reached to the sky, and angels of God were going up and down on it." (Gen 28:12) The rabbis taught: Jacob saw the guardian angels of the nations rising and descending. The angels of Assyria arose some steps, then fell off. The angel of Babylon rose and fell. The angels of Persia and of Greece rose and fell. Another angel rose much higher than all the rest and remained on

---

[9]Israelis living in farm communities have restored the celebration of springtime as a major theme of Passover.

his high perch. Jacob was afraid, but God told him, "Do not fear, for no matter how high this one climbs, and even if he climbs to the very vault of the heavens, I will throw him down from there."

God invited Jacob to climb the ladder, but after seeing what had happened to the angels of the nations he feared to climb. God said to Jacob, "Had you climbed, you would not have fallen. Since you did not climb, each of these nations shall dominate you for a time. But in the end, you shall rise above them all."

The biblical report of the Exodus from Egypt became the prototype by which Jews made sense out of their entire historical experience. God would allow one Pharaoh after another to arise in order to chastise Israel. The people would suffer exile in one Egypt after another. Whenever things became insufferable for Israel and they called out to God for deliverance, he would redeem them with a miraculous deliverance. Eventually the dominion of the tyrannical nations will end once and for all; God will bring all Israel back to their land and his appointed king, the Messiah, will rule over them. Jewish history begins and ends with God's redemption.

Roman oppression destroyed the institutions of Jewish leadership in the Land of Israel. The vast majority of Jews lived in "galut," in the exile, in one land or another. From Roman times until the dawn of the modern age Jews made few serious attempts to redeem themselves from exile. They patiently suffered the indignities of the exile. As the centuries passed they believed that although this exile was particularly long it did not otherwise depart from the pattern of the historical cycle of exile and redemption.

The cycle of exile and redemption is constant. In the big picture, Jews saw their history as consisting of three exiles and two redemptions. Jewish history begins with the exile in Egypt. Then came the first redemption. The Jews settled in their land and lived there for about five hundred years. Then came the Babylonian exile, the first exile from the Land of Israel. This exile lasted seventy years, ending in a new redemption in the time of Ezra and Nehemiah. Judah was restored and all Jews who wanted to returned to their land. The second exile began with the Romans and was to last until the coming of the Messiah. The next redemption would be the ultimate redemption, the end of history as we know it. Now that there is once again a sovereign Jewish state in the Land of Israel, most Jews see the third redemption as part of the process of history. Some Jews, though (and some Gentiles!), believe that the restoration of the Jewish state is the beginning of the end of history, the first stage in the coming of the Messiah.

There is a shorthand way to designate the periods of Jewish history in terms of the major cycles of exile and redemption. We speak of the First Temple, the First Exile, the Second Temple, the Second Exile, and the Third Temple or Messianic Age.

Jews believed that their lengthy exile was a punishment for their sins, for their failure to live up to the mitzvot. They said in their prayers, "On account of our sins we were exiled from our land." The nations had their own reasons for oppressing the Jews. The Jews themselves agreed that they deserved no more than to be treated as homeless exiles, though not for the reasons that the nations believed. The nations were only the instrument of God's will. When the time was ripe God would initiate another cycle of redemption, and the reward of those who waited would be more than equal to the sufferings of the exile. In the meantime, God caused his own presence on earth, the **Shekinah,** the indwelling spirit, to join Israel in exile. God shared the sufferings of his people. God regretted the cruelty of the nations in their excessive use of the power over the Jewish people which he had granted them. When the nations went too far, God intervened to save a remnant so that the Jewish people would survive to see their day of redemption.

Judah Halevi, the most popular of the medieval Jewish philosophers, had an interesting concept of exile and redemption. His book, the *Kuzari,* is written as a dialogue between the king of the Kazars, who is studying for conversion to Judaism, and the rabbi who teaches him. The king reproaches the Jews for not making every effort to return to their promised land immediately. The rabbi replies, "This is a severe reproach, O king of the Kazars. It is the sin which kept the divine promise with regard to the second Temple[10] from being fulfilled. God was ready to restore everything as before, if they had willingly consented to return. But only a part was ready to do so, while the majority and the aristocracy remained in Babylon, preferring dependence and slavery, and unwilling to leave their houses and their affairs. . . . Were we prepared to meet the God of our forefathers with a pure mind, we should find the same salvation as our fathers did in Egypt."[11]

Judah Halevi claims that, ironically, the sin which keeps Israel in exile is that they are willing to accept life in the exile. He points to the historic fact that most of the Jews from the first exile remained in Babylon. In truth he is addressing his own community, the Jews of twelfth century Spain. Spain was the greatest and richest land in the world at the time, the center of culture. The many Jews of Spain lived in comfort; the aristocrats of the community lived in true splendor. Judah Halevi claims that were the

---

[10]The promise that it would last forever, recorded in the biblical prophecies.
[11]*The Kuzari,* trans. Hartwig Hirschfeld, Schocken, N.Y., 1964, pp. 99–101.

Jews willing to give up all the advantages of Spain and undergo whatever hardships were necessary to return to the Land of Israel, God would redeem all the people from exile. As all the Jews in Egypt showed their willingness to be redeemed by their participation in the Passover, Judah Halevi urged all the Jews of his time to take action to express their willingness to bring the exile to an end.

Judah Halevi was ahead of his time in suggesting that the Jews could initiate the end of the exile by their own initiative. Most Jews believed that God was the sole master of history. God had determined the cycles of exile and redemption which were human history, and God would decide when to bring history to its triumphant conclusion in the final redemption.

Modernist Jews rejected the notion that Jews must passively await redemption. They determined to bring an end to exile, some by working to restore the Jewish state, others by working to find equality and acceptance in the lands where they lived. The success of these movements did not bring the old theology to an end, however. Religious Jews believe that human redemptive acts require God's help for their inspiration and their completion. Jews living in Jerusalem today no longer conclude their seder with the prayer, "Next year in Jerusalem." They pray, "Next year in Jerusalem restored!" "Jerusalem restored" is Jerusalem not as it is but as it should be, a place of peace and harmony, the center and symbol of world peace. This term distinguishes for the modern Jew between the "Third Temple," the restored State of Israel which is an historic act of redemption, and the "Messianic Age" of perfect peace and justice which Jews still hope for at the conclusion of human history.

11

Other Sacred Days

Shavuot

The festival of Shavuot is observed fifty days after Pesah, on the sixth day of the month of Sivan. The second day of Pesah is the first day for harvesting grain. In the time of the second Temple the harvest was begun with a formal ceremony in a barley field outside of Jerusalem. An **omer,** a "sheaf" of grain, was harvested and brought to the Temple as an offering to God. After that the farmers were free to begin their own harvest. By the time the barley was harvested the wheat would ripen. By Shavuot the harvest was completed. Each day during the harvest a sheaf was offered in the Temple. These days were called the days of the counting of the omer. After the destruction of the Temple, Jews continued to count off the fifty days of the omer. Decorative calendars were made for that purpose.

The date of Shavuot was an object of contention in early rabbinic times. The Sadducees claimed that the counting of the omer should begin the day after the Sabbath during Pesah. Shavuot would always then fall on a Sunday. The Pharisees contended that the counting should begin on the day after the first day of Pesah, which would make Shavuot always fall on the sixth of Sivan. The opinion of the Pharisees prevailed in the end.

When the Temple stood, Jews would prepare their first-ripened fruits and their grain offerings for the Shavuot pilgrimage. The offerings were placed in decorated baskets. The Jews of each district would go in parade to Jerusalem, accompanied by musicians and led by an ox with gilded horns and a wreath on its head. As the farmers entered the city the craftsmen and shopkeepers of Jerusalem would line the streets to greet the pilgrims and to advertise their wares. The farmers went directly up to the

141

Temple, where they placed their offerings on their shoulders and brought them to the priests. As they handed over their offerings they recited the litany of thanksgiving recorded in Deuteronomy 26:5–10. After they made their offering they would descend from the Temple mount and enjoy the festival in Jerusalem.

There was very little ritual left to observe for Shavuot after the Temple was destroyed, since the ritual of the festival was entirely Temple-centered. Shavuot decreased in importance. Jews came to celebrate Shavuout less as an agricultural festival and more as the festival of the giving of the Torah.

Jews decorate the synagogue with greens and flowers as a memorial of the first-fruits offerings. It is customary to eat no meat on Shavuot. The Torah is a Torah of peace; on the day of the giving of Torah God's peace extends also to the animal world. Dairy foods, fruits and vegetables are eaten at the Shavuot dinner. In traditional Jewish society Shavuot was the time for the consecration of new students. Another custom on Shavuot is to read the biblical Book of Ruth. The events in the Book of Ruth occur during the grain harvest. Also Ruth, as a convert to Judaism, accepted the Torah as did Israel at Mount Sinai.

Jewish mystics of the sixteenth century developed the custom of **Tikun Leil Shavuot.** This was an all-night study vigil. According to the midrash the Jews all fell asleep on the night before they received the Torah at Mount Sinai. They should have stayed up all night purifying themselves in preparation for their meeting with God, but instead they slept and even overslept the next morning. The mystics atoned for this action by staying up all night studying Torah on the eve of Shavuot. The curriculum of the Tikun included readings from each weekly Torah portion, from every book of the Tanak, and from each of the sixty tractates of the Talmud. This custom was believed to have the power to hasten the coming of the final redemption. Hence the term tikun, "repair," which the mystics used to describe the healing of the shattered relationship between God and the world.

In modern times many Jews ceased to observe Shavuot. The Reform movement in Germany attempted to revive the festival by making it the occasion for the new ritual of confirmation, the graduation of religious school students at age fifteen or sixteen. In Reform congregations today, and in some Conservative congregations, confirmation is the most significant ritual of Shavuot. In recent times neo-traditional Jews have revived the custom of Tikun Leil Shavuot. Usually these groups will develop their own curriculum for the evening rather than use the Tikun texts of the medieval mystics. They may ask each participant to prepare a presentation on a spiritual issue or an aspect of Jewish learning in which he or she has gained some insight.

Sukkot

While Pesah and Shavuot lost most of their agricultural significance since biblical times, Sukkot remained primarily a harvest festival. On Sukkot each Jewish family builds a **sukkah,** a shack of the sort which farmers in ancient Israel built in their fields as a resting place during harvest time. The sukkah must be a temporary type of structure. It must have at least three walls. The roof must be made entirely of natural materials, generally evergreen branches in America. The sukkah is decorated with fruits and vegetables. The building of the sukkah begins immediately after Yom Kippur, in order to start the new year with a mitzvah.

In the Middle Ages most Jews lived in cities. They did not have space in which to build a sukkah. Often Jews would have a removable section on the roof of their homes so that the area under it could serve as a sukkah. Sometimes Jews had to build a window box for a sukkah, just large enough to fit in the upper body. In modern America most Jews do not build a sukkah of their own. Each synagogue will build a sukkah in its courtyard, and some members of the congregation may build a sukkah and invite others to sit in it with them. One may live in the sukkah through the entire week of the festival, though this is seldom done today. More usually, those who have a sukkah will eat all of their meals in it. The mitzvah of sukkah is fulfilled by eating at least one meal in the sukkah during the festival.

Following Leviticus 23:40, it is a mitzvah on sukkot to wave the "four species" while reciting the appropriate blessings. The four species are a **lulav,** or palm branch, myrtle twigs, willow twigs, and an **etrog,** a costly and beautiful citrus fruit. The myrtle and willow are tied to the lulav and included with it, so that Jews say they are "waving the lulav and the etrog" when performing this ritual.

It is a mitzvah to glorify God by beautifying all of the rituals performed in worship. The rabbis applied this mitzvah in particular to the observance of sukkot. One should have a beautiful sukkah, a beautiful lulav and a beautiful etrog. In recent times the City of Jerusalem has established a "beautiful sukkah" contest which attracts many contestants. Jews will spend a great deal in order to acquire the largest and most attractive etrog with the loveliest color. Those who live in cities with large Jewish populations have the option of going to the markets and choosing their own. Others must order through the mail from dealers.

Until modern times enormous effort was required to bring fresh etrogs from the Mediterranean to the areas of Northern Europe where most Jews live. Nowadays most etrogs are shipped by air from Israel. The four species were probably originally used as the building materials for the sukkah, but since biblical times they have been used for the ceremony of waving, a symbol of the omnipresence of God and of his mercy in providing a bountiful harvest.

In ancient times the final day of Sukkot was the occasion for the water-drawing ceremony. A pitcher of water was drawn from Jerusalem's spring and poured upon the altar of the Temple. This was done in hope for a good rainy season. Israel depended upon good rains to prevent drought and starvation; the hilliness of the country made irrigation impossible until modern times. The water-drawing ceremony was the most joyous occasion in ancient Judaism. After the ceremony the people would dance, sing and rejoice in the Temple precinct until dawn. The usually dignified leaders of the Jewish people would perform acrobatic antics to amuse the people. This was truly the time of rejoicing before God.

Simhat Torah

The Torah does not command any rituals for Shemini Atzeret, the festival day which concludes the Holy Days—Sukkot season. Since late antiquity Jews have observed the second day of Shemini Atzeret as Simhat Torah, the "Rejoicing of the Torah." On Simhat Torah the annual cycle of the Torah readings is concluded and immediately restarted.

The public reading of the Torah began with Ezra the Scribe, the leader of the Babylonian exiles who returned to the Land of Israel. Over the course of time the text of the Torah was divided into set weekly portions. On the Sabbath seven people in turn are called to the pulpit to recite the blessings over the reading of the Torah. The reader must read at least three verses of Torah for each set of blessings. Each week's Torah portion must therefore be at least twenty-one verses long. Most of the Torah portions were that long or slightly longer. In ancient Judah no attempt was made to coordinate the Torah portions with the calendar year. It took about three and a half years to read through the entire Torah. The Jews would observe Simhat Torah each time a cycle was completed. The last few verses of Deuteronomy and the first few verses of Genesis were recited. This shows that the study of Torah is never completed. When one finishes one must immediately begin again.

In Babylon a different cycle of Torah readings developed. The weekly portions were much longer. The entire Torah was read each year. The custom developed of beginning the cycle at the conclusion of the Holy Days season. Simhat Torah was observed every year at the same time.

On Simhat Torah the Torah scrolls are paraded seven times around the synagogue. In some congregations this is done with solemnity and dignity. In other congregations the scrolls are paraded with raucous celebration and dancing. The children in the congregation join the parade, waving Simhat Torah flags. In former times it was the custom to place an apple atop the flag stick and a candle atop the apple. The children kept their candle lit through the parade, and ate the apple afterward.

Hanukah

Hanukah celebrates the successful revolt of the Maccabees against the Greek Middle Eastern empire. The Seleucid family, descended from one of Alexander the Great's generals, ruled over the Middle East from their capital in Antioch, Syria. The king Antiochus IV tried to unite the disparate subjects of his kingdom by encouraging them to adopt Greek customs and religion. This went against the former Hellenistic[1] custom of establishing Greek cities with Greek colonists while allowing the native populations to live under their own laws with their own traditional leaders. Jerusalem was made a Greek city, a "polis," with a gymnasium for the Greek education of the young. Some Jews enthusiastically greeted their city's new status, which offered many social and economic advantages to Jerusalem's citizens. The more traditional Jews resisted the changes. When Antiochus' policy met resistance, he outlawed the Torah and required Jews to adopt Greek laws and customs. The Temple in Jerusalem was placed under Greek priests and dedicated to the worship of Zeus.[2] Pigs were sacrificed on the altar. At that point, in 168 BCE, most of the Jewish population of Judah rebelled. Mattathias, a village priest from the village of Modin and head of the Hasmonean clan, became leader of the rebellion. When Mattathias died of old age the leadership passed to Judah, one of his five sons. Judah was nicknamed Maccabee, the "hammer." The rebels defeated the armies sent against them, and Antiochus could not spare more troops to put down the rebellion. In 165 BCE Antiochus made a treaty with the Jews granting them the right to live by their own laws and customs and giving possession of the Temple to the rebels.

---

[1]"Hellenistic" is the term used to describe the culture that developed when the Greeks became rulers of the Middle East. Hellenistic culture contained a mixture of Greek and Near Eastern elements.

[2]Ancient Greeks and Romans thought of Jews as exclusive worshipers of Zeus, the father of the gods.

Judah and his followers rededicated the Temple on the twenty-fifth day of the month of Kislev, the month of the winter solstice, three years to the day from when the Temple had been defiled. The rebels had been unable to observe Sukkot that year, so they made their rededication ceremony into a late eight-day observance of Sukkot. Judah declared that all Jews everywhere should celebrate these eight days every year in commemoration of his victory. The new holiday was called **Hanukah,** the Jewish term for a ceremony of dedication.

Hanukah is also called the Feast of Lights. The festival was celebrated by lighting bonfires in the streets. This custom probably derived from pagan rites welcoming the return of the sun, three days after the winter solstice.[3]

Judah's younger brother Simon eventually established himself as Prince[4] and High Priest of Judah. He founded a dynasty which lasted for eighty years, until the Romans swallowed Judah and put their favorite, Herod, on the throne. As the Greek empire fell apart the Hasmonean rulers established Judah as a virtually independent kingdom. They defeated their neighboring enemies, expanding the boundaries of Judah to equal those of the twelve tribes of ancient Israel. The Hasmoneans were successful rulers, but they were not all loved. They ruled in the absolute style of Greek monarchs and cruelly destroyed their enemies, including on occasion many Pharisees.

The Jewish rebellion against Rome in 66–70 CE was inspired in part by the victory of the Maccabees. After the war Rabban Yohanan ben Zakkai and his new Sanhedrin attempted to decrease the memory of the Hasmoneans in the minds of the people. All of the national holidays created by the Hasmoneans to commemorate events in their reign were cancelled by the rabbis, with the exception of Hanukah. The character of Hanukah was changed. In the rabbinic version of the holiday the victory of the Maccabees played no part. The Talmud asks, "What is Hanukah?" The response is a legend of a miracle relating to the rededication of the Temple. When the Maccabees went to rekindle the **menorah,** the sacred candlestick of seven branches, they found enough consecrated oil to last only one day. The oil miraculously lasted eight days until new oil could be prepared. Hanukah now celebrated not a military victory but God's miraculous intervention to preserve his people and his Torah.

---

[3]The Christian holiday of Christmas is also celebrated with the lighting of lights on the twenty-fifth day of the winter month. The similarities between Christmas and Hanukah are due to the fact that both holidays are revised versions of the same winter festival which was observed in many ancient religions.

[4]He had the powers of a king, but not being a descendant of King David, he dared not call himself King of Judah.

In the time of the rabbis the customs of Hanukah changed. Instead of lighting bonfires Jews lit candles or oil lamps indoors. The **hanukiah,** the Hanukah candelabrum, has space for nine lights. One light, the **shammas** or "servant," is used to light the others. On the first night one light is lit, on the second night two, and so on until on the last night all eight lights are lit. The Hanukah lights are a remembrance of the miracle of the oil. The lights are placed in the window to publicize the joy of the holiday and the miracle of Hanukah. As the candles are lit blessings are recited, one blessing over the commandment to light the candles and another in gratitude for the miracles by which God delivered the Jewish people in times past. While the candles burn, games of chance are permitted and children are allowed to play.[5] The **dreidle,** a four-sided top, is used to gamble for nuts or pennies. On the fifth night of Hanukah it was customary to give a gift of money to children. In Yiddish this gift is called **Hanukah gelt,** "Hanukah money." Fried foods are eaten in memory of the miracle of the oil. Ashkenazic Jews eat **latkes,** fried potato pancakes. Sephardic Jews eat fried donuts. Since Hanukah is not a biblically commanded holiday, work is permitted.

Hanukah was a minor holiday, but it has grown in importance in the past century. Among American Jews it is one of the most recognized holidays. In Israel Hanukah is a welcomed school holiday for children. The growing importance of Hanukah may be in part a reaction to the importance of Christmas, but Hanukah began to grow even before Christmas became the important holiday it now is to Christians. As Jews entered the modern world, Judah Maccabee and his revolt regained their place in the consciousness of the Jewish people. The Maccabees, who aggressively asserted their equality and their rights, became important symbols to modern Jews. Hanukah has come to symbolize the rights of Jews to have social equality while maintaining their own unique beliefs and customs. American Jews emphasize that the Maccabees fought for religious freedom, a freedom which is treasured by Americans as well. While Hanukah and Judah Maccabee have achieved great status, Hanukah gift-giving has increased greatly. In America, most Jewish children receive a gift on each of the eight nights of Hanukah.

Traditional Jews may still emphasize the miracle of the oil, while modernist Jews may emphasize the brave exploits of Judah Maccabee and his soldiers. What may be the greatest importance of Hanukah receives less notice; the events commemorated by Hanukah initiated the period of

[5]Before modern times boys studied and girls did household chores at all times. Opportunities to play were precious and scarce.

mediation between Greek culture and biblical Jewish culture that resulted in the development of rabbinic Judaism.

Purim

Hanukah and **Purim** are the two post-biblical festivals, the "minor festivals" on which work is permitted. Purim is celebrated on the fourteenth day of the last winter month of Adar. Purim celebrates the events told in the biblical Book of Esther. Mordecai, a Jewish courtier in the palace of the Persian king, thwarts a plot to destroy the Jews with the help of his cousin Esther, a favorite in the king's harem. The plan of the wicked prime minister Haman is exposed, and Mordecai is made prime minister in his stead. The main ritual of Purim is the public reading of the Book of Esther in the synagogue. The children in the congregation use noisemakers to drown out the name of Haman whenever it appears in the text. It is customary on Purim to exchange gifts of food with friends and to give gifts of food to the poor. The favorite food for Purim is a three-sided cookie called Haman's hat (or ear, or pocket). A satiric play, called in Yiddish a **Purim shpiel,** is put on by the wittiest members of the community. People dress in costumes, eat and drink. In modern America congregations often put on a Purim carnival for the children with games and prizes.

Purim is an upside-down holiday, on which excesses are permitted. Students are permitted to mock their teachers. Men masquerade as women and women as men. Drinking to excess is permitted and even encouraged. One is to get so drunk that one cannot tell the difference between "Blessed be Mordecai!" and "Cursed be Haman!" In general, Judaism discourages total abstinence from worldly pleasures, including alcohol, but encourages moderation. The ancient rabbis saw in self-denial a hint of the forbidden Gnostic belief that the material world was created by an evil anti-god. The rabbis taught that the moderate enjoyment of all material things shows a proper appreciation for the goodness of God's creation. The Jewish way of life requires tremendous self-control and repression of feelings in order to live up to the ethical demands of the Torah. It may be that the excesses of Purim are a necessity in order to release pent-up feelings and make it possible to maintain a life of self-control the rest of the year.

In Israel people take to the streets in great numbers on the night of Purim. Strangers bop each other on the head with plastic hammers that make a tooting sound when struck. On the day of Purim parents and grandparents parade their costumed children around town, indulging them in the toy stores and candy stores. Most little girls are dressed beautifully as Queen Esther, while the boys favor cowboy and spaceman costumes.

Tu B'Shevat and Lag B'Omer

The fifteenth day of Shevat (corresponding to February) and the thirty-third day of the counting of the Omer (in May) are minor observances in the Jewish calendar. **Tu B'Shevat** is the new year of the trees. When the Temple stood this day was the dividing day between one year and another for tithing the produce of trees. In modern times Tu B'Shevat is observed by donating money to the Jewish National Fund for planting trees in Israel.

The period of the omer between Pesah and Shavuot is observed by traditional Jews as a minor fast period. Weddings are not permitted during this period. An exception is made on the thirty-third day. According to legend, in the second century a plague killed many of the students of Rabbi Akiva. The plague lifted on **Lag B'Omer.** This explains both the fast and the lifting of it on this one day.[6] In former times Lag B'Omer was observed as a day of play for schoolboys. They would go into the fields and shoot arrows. This recalled the bravery of Rabbi Akiva and his students. When the Emperor Hadrian outlawed the Torah, Akiva and his students went out into the woods, pretending to go hunting. They would pull a Torah scroll out of a hollow tree and study in secret. If a Roman patrol came by they would put away the scroll and take up their bows and arrows. When they were finally caught, Rabbi Akiva stood his ground and allowed himself to be arrested so that his students could run away and escape.

Lag B'Omer is barely noticed among American Jews today. In Israel young adults observe the day with an all-night campfire. Youth groups gather to enjoy an evening of song and to reaffirm the ideals of their various youth movements.

Orthodox Jews who follow the mystical tradition gather on Mount Meron in the Galilee. They camp out by bonfires. On this day they give three-year-old children their first haircut and throw the hair into the fires. This is a memorial of the ancient sacrificial offerings from fruit trees (Leviticus 19:23–25).

---

[6]Modern historians discount the legend and explain the custom as a borrowing from Roman superstitions about lucky and unlucky days.

Tisha B'Av

The ninth day of the midsummer month of Av is a tragic day in Jewish history. In 586 BCE the first Temple was destroyed by the Babylonians on the ninth of Av. In 70 CE the Romans destroyed the second Temple on that same day. In 135 CE the Romans breached the walls of Simon Bar Kochba's last redoubt in Betar, also on the ninth of Av. In 1492 the Edict of Expulsion against the Jews of Spain was carried out on the ninth of Av.

The ninth of Av became a day of fasting after the destruction of the first Temple. Subsequent tragedies added to the sorrows which are mourned on that day. On the ninth of Av traditional Jews gather in the synagogue to recite the biblical Book of Lamentations, a series of dirges over the destruction of the first Temple. The prophet Jeremiah is said to be the author of this book.

In the nineteenth century Reform Jews nullified the observance of **Tisha B'Av.** They reasoned that it was no longer necessary to mourn the destruction of the Temple since they no longer prayed for its restoration. Subsequent events have shown that even in modern times great tragedies may still befall the Jewish people. The Holocaust has made the observance of Tisha B'Av more relevant to a new generation. Even if they no longer bemoan the specific events of the destruction of the Temples, they recognize the need for a day to mourn the tragedies that have befallen the Jewish people throughout their history.

Modern Observances

The face of Judaism has been permanently changed in the twentieth century by two events of surpassing significance, the Holocaust and the birth of the State of Israel. These two events have been recognized in two days which are rapidly reaching sacred status even though they are of recent origin.

Yom HaShoah, Holocaust Memorial Day, falls on the twenty-seventh day of the month of Nisan, shortly after the festival of Passover. The date is set to coincide with the outbreak of the Jewish rebellion in the Warsaw ghetto in 1943. Memorial candles are lit on this day in memory of the six million Jewish victims of the Nazis. Memorial services and study groups on the Holocaust are conducted in synagogues.

Yom HaAtzma'ut, Israel Independence Day, falls on the fifth day of the month of Iyyar, about a week after Holocaust Memorial Day. This is a day of rejoicing in commemoration of the rebirth of Jewish national independence on May 14, 1948. In Israel Yom HaAtzma'ut is a national holiday. Buildings are lit up with strings of colored light bulbs, and there are fireworks displays. Efforts are under way by religious leaders to develop appropriate rituals for the observance of the day. It has been suggested, for example, that on Yom HaAtzma'ut every Israeli should take a tour, to set foot on a part of Israeli soil where he or she has not yet been. This is based on God's commandment to Abraham to walk the length and breadth of the land in order to establish possession of it. It is also a way to increase the attachment between the land and its people.

In America's larger Jewish communities Yom Ha-atzma'ut is often celebrated with an Israel fair at a Jewish community center. The culture of Israel is celebrated in food, dance and song. Speakers encourage solidarity with the Jews of Israel. In synagogues there may be a service of thanksgiving which will include biblical passages that reflect the covenantal attachment between the people of Israel and their land.

PART THREE:

Judaism Through the Ages

12

Judaism in the First Century

Introduction

The religion practiced by Jews today has little in common with the religion of their ancestors in biblical times. If we wish to understand how Judaism as we know it came to be we must look not to the Bible, but to the Judaism of the first century. Judaism underwent much development in the centuries after the close of biblical history. The great events of the first century caused some of these developments to coalesce into a new definition of what it means to be a Jew.

In the early first century there was not one Judaism but many Judaisms. Biblical Judaism had branched into many different forms. Each of the main sects of Judaism had its own leaders, its own institutions, and its own idea of what God demanded of his people.

Some of the diversity in Judaism was created by competing sects. Some of the diversity was a result of the dispersion of the Jews. Jews lived in many different lands, participated in different cultures, and spoke different languages. Each Jewish community had its own history and its own religious response to the events it had experienced.

Nearly all Jews lived within one of the two empires which ruled the Western civilized world at that time. The Parthian Empire ruled from the Tigris-Euphrates river valley to the borders of India. The Roman empire ruled the entire Mediterranean Basin and Southern and Western Europe. In the Near East, Rome controlled Asia Minor (modern Turkey), Syria (including the Lebanon), Judea, and Egypt. Judea was one of the provinces of the Roman empire. The Roman empire was the largest, the mightiest, and the longest lasting empire in the history of human civilization.

Sources of Information

There are three primary sources of information about Judaism in the first century—the Talmud, the New Testament and the writings of Josephus. In addition to these sources we have the Dead Sea Scrolls and the non-canonical biblical books.[1] Unfortunately, none of our sources give us a completely accurate picture of the richly diverse Jewish world of that time. All of our sources are highly tendentious. Josephus wrote for Gentiles, to give them a sympathetic understanding of the Jewish people in terms that they would understand. The New Testament was written in retrospect at a time when the early Church was locked in an intense rivalry with the central Jewish leaders, the rabbis. The Talmud is also written in retrospect by rabbis who remembered one of the sects of first century Judaism, the Pharisees, as their honored forerunners. The Talmud and the New Testament are not histories, but religious documents, and they present history only as they find it useful in outlining their religious positions. We must piece together the actual story of first century Judaism from these sources, a difficult task. The result is that there are many different points of view about what really went on in that period, depending on which sources, if any, the historian believes to be most accurate, and to what degree the scholar is willing to accept as accurate the judgments that the writers of the sources made on the various Jewish sects.

Where Jews Lived

Outside the Land of Israel the largest Jewish community was probably that of Babylon in the Parthian empire. This Jewish community dated back to the Babylonian Exile; it was six hundred years old by the first century. A community that had existed for so long must surely have had well-established religious institutions. Due to an unfortunate lack of documents we have very little idea of how the Jews of Babylon lived before the third century CE. We do know that some of the greatest Torah scholars in

---

[1]These are books written near the end of the biblical period which were not accepted into the sacred Scriptures, either because they were written too late or because they presented unacceptable ideas or for other reasons. Many of these books were composed by sectarian groups.

the Land of Israel were born in Babylon. They came to Judea to study at the academies there. Although the Jews of Babylon lived under a different government, they spoke the same language as the Jews of Judea, Aramaic. This must must have helped to maintain close relations between the two communities. When the Jews rebelled against Rome they hoped that the Jews of Babylon would convince their government to join the battle, but they did not do so. The Babylonian Jews apparently saw the rebellion as a local political matter which had no relationship to their sense of religious connection with the Jews of Judea.

The largest Diaspora community in the Roman empire was in Egypt. Many Jews lived in Alexandria, the capital of Egypt and the cultural capital of the Eastern Mediterranean. We might compare Alexandria to New York City today. It was a cosmopolitan city with citizens from many lands, including a great many Jews. Alexandria had been founded by Ptolemy, the Greek general who became the monarch of Egypt after the death of Alexander the Great. Ptolemy ruled over Judea as well. Many Jews must have come into Egypt at that time, joining those who had gone to Egypt centuries earlier to escape from the Babylonians.

The Jews of Alexandria spoke Greek. They did not know Hebrew or Aramaic. They relied on a Greek translation of the Torah, the Septuagint, for their knowledge of Scripture. According to legend the Septuagint was commissioned by Ptolemy II, who wished to add the Jewish Scriptures to the great library of Alexandria. He brought seventy wise elders from Jerusalem to Egypt and locked each into a private room to write his translation of the Torah into Greek. When they were done, each manuscript agreed with the others word for word. This legend gave divine sanction to the use of a translation for sacred Scripture. This was a brave and novel innovation. It helped to preserve Judaism in a time when many religions became irrelevant because their sacred writings were in ancient languages that fell into disuse with the spread of Greek language and culture.

Because the Jews of Egypt spoke Greek, they received limited influence from the Jewish scholars in Judea. Their religion was heavily influenced by Greek thought. They saw the Torah as an allegory for many of the insights of Greek philosophy. We can see this in the writings of Alexandria's greatest Jewish leader and scholar, Philo.

There were Jewish settlements throughout the Roman empire, even as far away as Spain. Many Jews lived in the city of Rome. There was a large Jewish population on the island of Cyprus. There were many Jewish communities in Asia Minor. Jews may have constituted as much as ten percent of the population of the Roman and Parthian empires. The Jews did not become numerically few until their great losses in the rebellions against Rome. In the early first century Judaism spread by conversion as well as by emigration. The Pharisees attempted to bring many Gentiles to the Jewish religion. There was a class of people who worshiped the God of Israel but did not convert because they did not wish to observe all the customs of the Jews. These people were called "God-fearers." Roman women in particular were reported to be enamored of Judaism. Judaism appeared in their eyes as an exotic Eastern religion and a wise philosophy. Conversion to Judaism became less attractive after the Jewish rebellion, when in the eyes of many Gentiles Judaism became associated with sedition against Rome.

Jews in the Land of Israel

The Jewish population of Judea in the first century was about three million, about the same as in modern Israel. There was a large Gentile population in Judea as well. Judea was divided into many districts. Some were mainly Jewish, and some mainly Gentile.

The district of Judah consisted of Jerusalem and its surrounding hills. Jerusalem was the capital of Judea, the largest city and the center of religious life. The religious leaders and scholars of the Jewish people lived in Judah, in or near Jerusalem.

The hill district north of Judah was called Samaria. The Samaritans were descended from a mixed population which the Assyrians brought to Israel when they exiled the northern tribes of Israel in the seventh century BCE. Ezra and Nehemiah forbade intermarriage with the Samaritans, even though they lived by the Torah and worshiped God. The Samaritans in response had attempted to foil the building of the Second Temple. When that failed they built a rival temple on Mount Gerizim. The Hasmoneans had conquered and subjected the Samaritans and destroyed their temple. Religiously, Samaritans were considered to be not Gentiles but not exactly Jews either.

The seacoast west of Judah and Samaria was inhabited mainly by Gentiles. The Hasmonean kings had occasionally subjected the seacoast towns during their period of independence, but they had never brought them into the Jewish fold. The population were descendants of the Philistines, Greek colonists, and other Gentiles. The Romans administered Judea from the coastal city of Caesarea.

North of Samaria lay the Galilee, another Jewish area. The Galileans had been Jewish only a short time by the first century, having been subjected and converted to Judaism by the Hasmoneans. The Jews of Judah thought the Galileans to be strong on devotion to Judaism but sadly lacking in concern for the details of observance. Galilee was a stronghold of Jewish national feeling and anti-Roman sentiment. Many of the leaders of the rebellion and their followers came from the Galilee.

The area east of the Jordan River was also primarily Jewish. East of the Galilee lay the Decapolis, a cluster of towns with a large Jewish population. To the southeast of the Dead Sea lay Idumea. The Idumeans, or Edomites, had also been converted to Judaism by the Hasmoneans. Like the Galileans they had become devoted followers of the religion and offered many soldiers to the rebellion against Rome. The unpopular King Herod, appointed by Rome to rule over Judea, was an Idumean.

To the south and east of Judea lay the kingdom of the Nabateans, desert-dwellers who engaged in trade. To the north lay the much larger and more populous province of Syria, with its great cities of Damascus and Antioch. Antioch was a Greek city, the former capital of the Seleucid Greek empire of the Middle East. Since Rome had acquired her culture from Greece, the Greeks felt at home in the empire. Jews, on the other hand, chafed under Roman rule. The cultural conflict between Greeks and Jews in the Middle East created many problems for the Jews in the first century.

Hasmoneans and Romans

Let us review the historical background of the Roman province of Judea. We recall the rebellion of Judah Maccabee. The rebellion ended in 165 BCE when the Seleucid Greek king of Syria restored to the Jews the right to live by their own laws. In the decades which followed, the Seleucid empire fell apart under pressure from the expanding Roman empire. Different factions in Judah competed to control the country in the power vacuum left by the disintegrating empire. The surviving member of the Hasmonean family, Simon, defeated his rivals and made himself High Priest. He made Judah virtually independent of the Greek empire and made himself monarch as well, with the additional title of Nasi, Prince. The monarchy and the high priesthood had never in Jewish history been held by one person. There were critics, but Simon and his descendants silenced them, partly with a strong hand and partly with political and military success. The Hasmonean rulers consolidated their hold on Judah and managed to conquer all the surrounding petty kingdoms, extending the borders of their rule as far as the borders of King David's kingdom. The greater powers of Syria and Egypt were enmeshed in their own troubles, which gave the Hasmoneans great freedom of action. Although their family came to power defending Judaism against the Greeks, the Hasmoneans established their monarchy in the Greek style. They were absolute rulers. They hired mercenary soldiers. Court intrigues were resolved by murder and imprisonment of rivals. Internal dissent was harshly suppressed.

Simon was succeeded by John Hyrcanus and Alexander Yannai. After Yannai the reigns of power passed to the queen regent, Salome Alexandra. By the time of her death, the Roman empire had reached to the borders of Judea. The Roman general Pompey conquered Judah and included it in the Roman empire as the Province of Judea. Pompey entered the Temple, an act forbidden to Gentiles, and declared Judaism a godless religion when he found no idol in the sanctuary. Jews were scandalized by Pompey's behavior. This may be why they supported Julius Caesar in his civil war with Pompey for control of the Roman empire. Caesar returned the loyalty of the Jews with his friendship. When he became the ruler of Rome he passed edicts that allowed the Jews to freely practice their religion in a pagan empire. He allowed the Jews to substitute a daily sacrifice for the government in place of worship of the emperor, an act required of subject peoples as a sign of loyalty. He remitted taxes on the Sabbatical year when Jews planted no crops. The Roman legions in Judea kept their standards sheathed, since the Jews looked upon them as idols. When Caesar was assassinated, it was said that the mourning of the Jews could be heard throughout the city of Rome. The Jews might have gotten along well with the Romans, except that some of the succeeding Roman emperors were not so understanding of the special nature of the Jewish religion.

The Romans eliminated Judean independence in stages. First they removed the Hasmonean kings and appointed Herod, a king to their own liking. Then they divided Judea into different districts, giving each one its own ruler. They appointed a procurator, a Roman governor, to oversee the administration of the country. Finally they took away Judea's status as a province of the empire and made it a part of Syria, under the rule of the Syrian governor.

In 37 BCE Herod became king of Judea. Herod had no hereditary right to the throne. He became king only because of his connections in Rome. To legitimize his throne he married a Hasmonean, but later he had her and their sons killed. Having achieved his throne illegitimately, Herod was always insecure. He assassinated his political rivals. Herod attempted to purchase the love of his unwilling subjects with great public works. He rebuilt the Temple, making it more grand and beautiful than it had ever been. Herod was politically successful during his long reign, but he sowed the seeds of Judea's discontent.

After Herod's death (4 BCE) his kingdom was divided between his heirs. A decade later the Romans changed this arrangement and appointed a procurator, which put Judea under the direct control of Rome. The procurators appointed by Rome were mostly incompetent men. Some, such as Pontius Pilate (26–36 CE) and Felix (52–60 CE), became infamous for their greed and cruelty. Judea received some relief when Agrippa, a descendant of Herod, was appointed King of Judea (41 CE). Agrippa tried sincerely to rule well and to respect the sacred laws of the Torah. His untimely death (44 CE), probably by assassination, was a tragedy for Judea. After his death the Romans once again ruled Judea directly through procurators. The situation in Judea became more and more unbearable until, in 66 CE, the Judeans revolted against Rome. The failure of the revolt brought an end to Judea's status as a political entity. The Romans destroyed the capital of Jerusalem to the last stone. They renamed the country Palestine after the ancient Philistines, attempting to destroy the name and memory of Judea once and for all. After the war the center of Jewish life shifted to the coastal area. After the Bar Kochba rebellion (132–135 CE) Jewish life in Judah was utterly destroyed, and the center of Jewish life and learning shifted northward to the Galilee.

Government in Judea

There were three sources of government authority in Judea: the Temple priesthood, the monarchy, and the Sanhedrin.

Through the centuries after the return from exile in Babylon (c. 500 BCE) Judah was a theocracy, ruled by the high priest. The Jews were content to let the imperial power, the Persian and later Greek rulers, handle secular affairs of government. The high priest and the priestly bureaucracy in the Temple ran the internal affairs of the Jews.

When the Seleucid king Antiochus IV decided to Hellenize Judah he overthrew the high priest and put in his place a priest more willing to bend to his will. This began the politicization of the high priesthood, which never regained the honor and authority it enjoyed in Persian and early Greek times.

As we have mentioned, the Hasmonean high priest Simon granted himself royal authority as well. Thus began a return to the dual offices of king and high priest. During the Hasmonean period these two offices were sometimes combined in one person and sometimes held separately. Though the Hasmoneans were not in the line of succession of biblical kings and high priests, they gained legitimacy over time in the eyes of the people.

The Romans took control of both offices. They appointed kings or procurators of their own liking to run the secular government. The Roman rulers appointed and removed high priests as they wished, granting the office to compliant and unthreatening individuals or even selling it. The high priesthood became a fallen institution. Even so, the high priest retained great authority among the people. He was the one who offered the sacrifices that kept Israel in relationship with their God. The high priest presided in the Temple, and he was the living representative of the most ancient and honored office of the Jewish people.

The Sanhedrin was a court of seventy-one elders. It served as Congress and Supreme Court of the Jewish people, deciding issues of Jewish law. The Sanhedrin was the highest court of appeal. It gave the definitive interpretation of Torah law when interpretation was required. The rabbis traced the Sanhedrin back to the mythical Great Assembly which included Ezra and the last of the Prophets. The Sanhedrin may have arisen in that early period or it may have arisen only in Greek times—the Greek name for this assembly is evidence for the latter assumption. As time went by the Sanhedrin acquired greater authority. After the destruction of the Temple it became the sole institution of Jewish leadership. At that time, the members of the Sanhedrin were given the title "rabbi," the first formal use of that title in Judaism.

In the second and first centuries BCE the Sanhedrin was directed by a pair of sages. One was the **Nasi,** the Prince, the president of the Sanhedrin. The other was **Av Bet Din,** Father of the Court, the vice-president. The leaders of the majority and minority parties in the Sanhedrin held these positions.

We do not know exactly how the tasks of government were divided between the monarch or governor, the high priest, and the Sanhedrin. When the high priesthood came to an end with the destruction of the Temple in 70 CE, the threefold division of offices came to an end. The newly reconstituted Sanhedrin had complete authority over the internal affairs of the Jewish people. The members of the post-70 Sanhedrin were called by the title Rabbi. The Sanhedrin members were mostly from one political and religious sect, the Pharisees who belonged to the School of Hillel. The new Sanhedrin's president, now called by the title Rabban, was recognized by Rome and by the Jewish people as the highest Jewish authority.

When the rabbis looked back on Jewish history, they depicted a pre-70 Sanhedrin which was under the firm control of their ideological ancestors, the Pharisees, from the time of Queen Salome Alexandra. They claimed that their own school of Pharisaism, the School of Hillel, had always been in the majority among the Pharisees. They also claimed that the high priest had been stripped of all power. He had to perform all of his functions under the supervision of the Pharisees and according to their laws, because the Jewish masses all supported the Pharisees.

Some historians accept the rabbinic view of history at face value. Others, notably Jacob Neusner, believe that the historical tales in the Talmud represent a rabbinic fantasy of their own past. Neusner believes that until the year 70 the high priest and his Temple bureaucracy must have held considerable power in Judea, while the rival School of Shammai held precedence over the School of Hillel in the Sanhedrin.[2]

Religious Sects in First-Century Judea

Josephus says that there were three major "philosophies" or sects of Judaism in the first century—Sadducees, Pharisees and Essenes. He called the Zealots the "fourth philosophy." He gives a brief description of the beliefs of each group. These four sects are mentioned in other sources as well. Rabbinic, Greek and Christian sources give us the names of other sects or factions in Judea, including Boethusians, Scribes, Theraputae, Haverim and others. These seem to be either synonyms for the sects named by Josephus or the names of closely related groups or factions within the sects. Even though there is much we do not know, we are able to give a broad definition of each sect, its major institutions, and the doctrines it represented.

The Sadducees were an upper-class, priestly party. They were criticized by others for their aristocratic demeanor and their willingness to cooperate with the Romans in ruling the country. In religion and law the Sadducees stayed very close to the literal sense of the Torah. They rejected the doctrines of the Oral Torah and of the resurrection of the dead because they did not have firm support in the written Scriptures. It is likely that the legal tradition of the Sadducees represented Judaism as it had been practiced before the time of the Maccabees, when the high priest was the undisputed leader of the Jewish people. The Sadducees would then represent the group that rejected the many innovations brought about by the Jewish interaction with Greek culture.

Since the Sadducees were a priestly party, the Temple was their primary institution and the high priest was their leader. The Sadducees disappeared after the destruction of the Temple when they lost their institutional basis. There were conservative groups in the post-70 Sanhedrin, such as the B'nai Batyra, who might represent a continuation of the doctrines of the Sadducees.

---

[2]See Neusner's *From Politics to Piety: The Emergence of Pharisaic Judaism*, Ktav, N.Y., 1979. For another point of view see Solomon Zeitlin, *The Rise and Fall of the Judean State*, 3 vols., J.P.S.

The Essenes lived in monastic communities on the edge of civilization. Essenes rejected the official Temple leadership. They believed that
the Temple priests had gone astray, while they had retained the purity of
the priesthood in their communes. The Essenes believed that all human
society had become corrupt. They attempted to attain purity and goodness
by rejecting the world and re-creating society in their own tight-knit communities. It is likely that the Essenes were not a single organization, but
rather a variety of communities with similar ideas. Each community followed its own charismatic leader. John the Baptist may have been an
Essene. The community at Qumran, whose literature is well known to us
as the Dead Sea Scrolls, may have been an Essene community.

The Essenes were apocalyptics. They believed that the world had
become so filled with evil that God would soon bring it to an end. In their
small communities, the Essenes represented the chosen few who would be
the seed for the new human community that God would establish in a re-
created world. The Qumran community maintained a military pattern of
organization because they believed that they would be the soldiers of God
in the final battle between good and evil.

To maintain their purity the Essenes lived by a very strict interpretation of the Torah. The Qumran community forbade urination on the
Sabbath! Through celibacy, discipline, strict obedience to God's law, and
a simple life in the wilderness, the Essenes strove to be found worthy at the
last judgment.

The Essenes were inner-directed and other-worldly. They waited passively for God to bring about the end of evil. The Zealots were political
activists. They believed that God's kingdom would not come until the
Jews initiated the overthrow of Rome by military action. While the Zealots
agitated for rebellion they busied themselves assassinating those Jews that
they accused of complicity with Rome. They called themselves K'naim,
"Zealots," because of their "zeal" for God which inspired them to rebel
against Rome.

The Zealots had their day when the rebellion broke out in 66 CE. By
69 CE the Romans had captured the countryside and besieged Jerusalem.
Three Zealot armies within the city battled against each other and terror-
ized the populace. One of the groups burned the food stores of the city,
which would have been sufficient for a siege of many years, in order to
make the inhabitants of the city desperate enough to fight. The fighting
between the different Zealot armies made it easy for Rome to conquer
Jerusalem. One group of Zealots under the leadership of Eleazar ben Yair
escaped as Jerusalem fell. They fled to Masada, a fortress in the wilderness
of Judea that had been built by King Herod. The Zealots held out at
Masada for two more years. The Romans employed Jewish slaves to build

an earthen ramp up the side of the mountain of Masada so that they could attack the walls of the fortress. The Zealots could have stopped the construction by throwing rocks down upon the Jewish slaves, but they decided that they would no longer kill their fellow Jews. When the Romans finally breached the walls of Masada the defenders committed suicide rather than surrender their freedom.

In the retrospect of history it is generally agreed that the rebellion of 66–70 was unnecessary. The eagerness of the Zealots for war and their certainty that God would give them victory led to the death of over a million Jews and the destruction of Jerusalem and the Temple. The failure of the war meant the end of the party of the Zealots.

The Pharisees

The Pharisees are the most important to our investigation, since they are the forerunners of rabbinic Judaism. Pharisees first appear in history just after the revolt of the Maccabees, though their relation to the Maccabees is not clear. The early Pharisees had a tense relationship with the Hasmonean rulers of Judah. King Alexander Yannai (126–76 BCE) favored the Sadducees. He killed thousands of the Pharisees. According to rabbinic legend Yannai confessed on his deathbed that he had been wrong to persecute the Pharisees. Yannai ordered his successor, the queen regent Salome Alexandra, to support the Pharisees and to do as they say, since due to their popularity among the people Judah could not be governed successfully without their approval. It appears that at this time the Pharisees decided no longer to meddle in politics. They let the reigning powers be while they concentrated their attention on spreading their doctrines among the people. Because they refrained from criticizing their ruler, the Hasmoneans and later Herod and the Romans left them unmolested.

The rebellion of the Maccabees grew out of a conflict between Judaism and Hellenism. The Jews were challenged to follow either one path or the other. The Maccabean revolt was largely a civil war over whether Jews would adopt Hellenistic customs. The Pharisees developed a compromise solution. Pharisaism is a distinctively Jewish response to Hellenistic culture. The doctrines and the institutions of the Pharisees display close parallels to those of the Hellenistic world. The yeshiva resembles the Greek academy. The rabbi, or scholar of Torah, resembles the master philosopher. The method of the Oral Torah resembles Greek methods for the literary interpretation of sacred texts. And yet for all the resemblances, the Pharisees retained a close link to their roots in ancient Jewish tradition.

Through Pharisaism one could remain a Jew while being a part of what was, to a first-century Jew, the modern world.

Hillel and Shammai

In the middle of the first century BCE Hillel and Shammai were the leaders of the Sanhedrin. According to rabbinic tradition Hillel was Nasi, president, and Shammai was Av Bet Din, vice-president, of the Sanhedrin. Their names are not associated with any sect, but it seems certain that Hillel was a Pharisee. Shammai may have been the leader of the Sadducees, or he may have been the leader of the conservative wing of the Pharisaic movement.

Hillel and Shammai were the founders of two major schools of Torah interpretation, later called the House of Hillel and the House of Shammai. These two Houses were the major factions of the Sanhedrin in the first century. The Talmud records many legal disputes between the Houses of Hillel and Shammai. In nearly every case the Hillelites take the liberal position and the Shammaites take the conservative position. The Hillelites were more daring and innovative in their interpretation of Torah. Hillel is credited with establishing the "Seven Rules" of literary interpretation by which new laws could be derived from the text of the Torah. This was an essential step in the development of the Oral Torah. These rules were later expanded to thirteen, and then to thirty-two. The rules of interpretation permitted a more flexible reading of the Torah. The Shammaites insisted on a more literal interpretation of the Torah. We may compare the difference between the Houses of Hillel and Shammai to the difference between liberals and conservatives in America today. Political liberals favor a loose reading of the American Constitution which gives great leeway to the courts in deciding what the Constitution really means. Conservatives favor a narrow reading which stays as close as possible to the original intent of the words.[3]

The two Houses differed in their idea of the meaning of religious ritual. This difference is represented in a debate which is recorded in the Midrash. The Hillelites said, "The earth was created before the heavens." The Shammaites said, "The heavens were created before the earth." The issue of this debate is not the question of the order of creation, but the very

---

[3]The situation is repeated in the Sanhedrin of the second century. Rabbi Akiva, who headed the liberal wing of the rabbis, held that every extraneous word in the Torah was open to interpretation. Rabbi Ishmael, who led the conservative wing, insisted that "the Torah speaks in the language of men," and extraneous words are merely literary devices. As the liberalism of Hillel had predominated, so did the liberalism of Akiva.

relevant question of whether religious actions receive their meaning from "the heavens," from the fact that they are commanded by God, or from "the earth," the fact that they are ways for human beings to reach out to God. Are the religious practices of Judaism validated "from the heavens" or "from the earth"? Are religious practices sacraments or human responses to God?

The distinction is illustrated by the answers of Hillel and Shammai to the question, "When does Shabbat begin?" Shammai said, "When three stars appear in the sky on Friday evening." Hillel said, "When man recites kiddush." Pragmatically their answers are one, since man recites kiddush at the time when three stars appear in the sky. To Shammai, Shabbat is built into the order of the creation. Shabbat is Shabbat, a sacrament, even if no one recognizes it as such. To Hillel, Shabbat has no reality unless it is recognized as Shabbat by the human response to God's commandments. Shabbat is made on earth, not in heaven.

A sacrament is effective if it is performed with correct ritual, even if those who perform it pay no attention to the meaning of the ritual or do not understand it. The Hillelites believed that **kavannah**, the intention with which a ritual is performed, is what gives it its effectiveness.[4] Judaism generally follows the teaching of Hillel in this matter. We have seen that there are no sacred objects in Judaism; only God receives our blessing. We have seen that repentance, and not sacrifice, is the necessary condition for divine forgiveness. In contrast to priestly religion, Judaism after the time of Hillel is virtually devoid of sacraments. Hillel's development of the concept of kavannah was a major contribution to the development of the Jewish religion.

After the year 70 the House of Hillel dominated the Sanhedrin. The rabbis after that time taught that the contradictory teachings of Hillel and Shammai were both "the word of the living God," but the law follows the teachings of Hillel. The rabbis conceded that Hillel and Shammai were equal in scholarship and wisdom. They attributed the priority of Hillel's teachings to his character. Shammai was strict and rigid, while Hillel was gracious and loving. The difference between the two is illustrated in a Talmudic tale about a person who comes to Shammai with the intent of mocking Judaism. He says to Shammai, "I will convert to Judaism if you can teach me the whole Torah while standing on one foot." Shammai pushes the man away with a cubit-stick. The man then comes to Hillel and

---

[4]A Christian may understand the significance of this discussion by considering whether baptism is automatically effective, or only if one being baptized understands and accepts the meaning of baptism. This has been a matter of debate between Christians since the Protestant Reformation.

repeats his challenge. Hillel says to him, "What is hateful to you, do not do to others. The rest is commentary; go and learn it!" Hillel converts the man to Judaism on the spot. The man goes and studies Torah and becomes a learned and pious Jew. He announces that if not for Hillel his soul would have been lost.

The House of Hillel opposed direct confrontation with the Romans. They may have been motivated by the memory of the bitter experiences of the early Pharisees in their dealings with the government. They also may have been motivated by their approval of the Pax Romana. A contemporary of Hillel is attributed with the saying, "Pray for the peace of the government, for if not for the fear of it men would swallow each other alive." (Avot 3:2) The Pax Romana, the "Roman Peace," was the Roman law forbidding any kingdom within the empire from attacking any other. The Hillelites seem to have believed that the oppressive rule of Rome was preferable to the constant warfare between petty kingdoms that was the likely alternative. The determination of the Hillelites to stay out of Rome's way played a big role in their eventual rise to leadership of the Jewish people.

The Talmudic tractate *Pirke Avot*, the "Sayings of the Fathers," records the wise proverbs of the early Pharisees. A number of sayings attributed to Hillel are included in this collection. One of Hillel's sayings is generally regarded as the great summation of the ethical teachings of Judaism: "If I am not for myself, who will be for me? But if I am for myself alone, what am I? And if not now, when?" Hillel's most famous aphorism emphasizes the need to balance altruism against self-interest.

The later rabbis called Hillel and Shammai the "Fathers of the World." Hillel and Shammai were the founders of the system of religion which became Judaism in its classic post-biblical, rabbinic form. Hillel and Shammai did not invent Pharisaism, but in their time the doctrines of the Pharisees became normative for most Jews. Hillel was also credited with establishing a dynasty of hereditary leadership. After Hillel and Shammai there were no more pairs of leaders in the Sanhedrin. There was a single Nasi with great authority. With the exception of Yohanan ben Zakkai, every later Nasi was a direct descendant of Hillel. Hillel was said to have descended from King David on his mother's side, making the President of the Sanhedrin only a half-step removed from the throne of God's appointed king, the Messiah.

Religious Concerns of the Pharisees

The Pharisees believed that it was the vocation of every Jew to live as if he were a priest. They observed the laws of priestly purity. Originally these laws were observed only by the Temple priests within the confines of the Temple precinct, but the Pharisees observed the purity rules everywhere, at all times. The Pharisees ate only food that was fit for Temple offerings. They avoided contact with sources of ritual impurity such as reptiles, impure foods, and cemeteries. The Pharisees were very careful to make all the required agricultural offerings to the Temple. They measured and weighed their crops and food purchases to make sure that their tithes were exact. They suspected that those who tithed by estimation probably underestimated their Temple dues. The most distinctive feature of the Pharisees was that they ate every ordinary meal as if it were a sacrificial offering.

The Pharisees would not dine with people whose food might not have been properly tithed or prepared in purity. The Pharisees therefore would not break bread with an **Am Ha'aretz**, a Jewish peasant. The Pharisees considered themselves superior to the Am Ha'aretz, but they were not an exclusive group. The Pharisaic ideal was that all Jews would join them in their way of life. Unlike the priesthood, which was hereditary, anyone could become a Pharisee by adopting their concerns and by studying Torah with a Pharisaic sage.

Discipleship was important to the Pharisees. They kept their laws as oral traditions. The sage knew all these traditions. One became learned in the Torah teachings of the Pharisees by sitting at the feet of a master sage and memorizing his teachings. A disciple learned not only the knowledge but also the mannerisms of the master, who in his way of life represented a living Torah. The Pharisees believed that every Jew should dedicate sufficient time to become learned in the Torah even if this meant that he would not earn much of a living. They did believe, though, that Torah study should be combined with productive labor. According to legend, the great leaders of the Pharisees worked at humble professions. They were woodchoppers, water-drawers, donkey-drivers, and the like. They would work half a day to support the basic needs of their families, and the other half of the day they would study and teach. It is hard to believe that national leaders were truly so poor, but even if not literally true the legend represents an ideal. The young disciples were expected to live a very simple life in order to dedicate their time to the pursuit of Torah.

The teachings of the Pharisees are the original core of the Oral Torah. Until the time of the Pharisees, Torah learning was in the hands of the priests (see Ezekiel 44:23–24). The Oral Torah of the Pharisees differed from the priestly laws of the Sadducees in content and also in form. We presume that in the schools of the priests the laws were learned in the ancient manner, connected to the verses of Scripture from which they were derived. The Pharisees taught each law not as it was derived from biblical proof-texts but in the name of the teacher from whom they learned it. This gave the Oral Torah an authority equal to and independent from the written Torah. Instead of proceeding in the order of the laws of Scripture, the laws of the Oral Torah were organized by subject matter or by mnemonic devices. This assisted in the memorization of the many laws. This was important because it was forbidden to commit the oral traditions to writing. The Oral Torah also differed from priestly tradition in relying upon logical rules of literary interpretation for the derivation of law in new situations. These rules are the Seven Rules of Hillel which we have mentioned, and the others which were added later. These rules include the argument from a minor situation to a more serious situation (if the law is so in such a case, it is even more surely so in such another case), the comparison of similar expressions (if the law is so in this situation, then in this other situation where the Torah uses a similar expression it must also be so), the argument from a general situation to a particular situation and from the particular to the general, and so forth. When an urgent situation called for a new law that could not be derived from the Torah by these rules, a new regulation could be decreed on the authority of a great sage. Hillel is credited with two such regulations. One of these eliminated the cancellation of debts on the sabbatical year. This was done because the wealthy would not make loans as the sabbatical year approached, with the result that the Torah law of debt cancellation was leaving the poor worse off instead of better off. We may also attribute this regulation to the growing importance of commercial activity in the Judean economy. The cancellation of debts was good for farmers but it was ruinous for businessmen who depended on credit to acquire capital. It has been argued on the basis of this and other evidence that the Pharisees represented the interests of the growing urban class against the landed gentry who supported the Sadducees.

The Pharisees also differed from the Sadducees in their belief in future resurrection and the world-to-come. The religious life of the Pharisees was directed toward attaining merit in the world to come, even if that meant foregoing honor, wealth and safety in this world.

Institutions of the Pharisees: Court, School and Synagogue

The Pharisees expressed their political authority through their presence on the Sanhedrin and in the lower courts. As scholars of the law, the Pharisees and their close associates[5] adjudicated disputes in civil, criminal

---

[5]The Scribes, always mentioned in association with the Pharisees in the Gospels, may have been the class of educated civil servants in the Judean government.

and religious law according to their traditions of Torah interpretation. Until the year 70 the authority of the courts was dependent upon the authority of the Temple, but after 70 the Sanhedrin became the central institution of Jewish self-government.

Schools were important in the religion of the Pharisees. If every Jew was to live as a priest, he would need a priestly education. The educational system of Judea was reputed to have been established by the early Pharisees. In the time of Queen Salome Alexandra the Pharisees established a network of elementary schools to fulfill their ideal that every Jew should be learned in the Torah. The better students advanced to the yeshiva, or academy, where they became disciples of the sages and learned the Oral Torah. The greatest Pharisaic scholars opened their own academies. Hillel was said to have studied in the academy of Shemaiah and Avtalion, who led the Sanhedrin in the previous generation. Hillel's greatness is attributed to his having been an industrious student who learned well the teachings of his masters. In the yeshivas established by the more patrician Pharisees tuition was charged. Other yeshivas were open to all, regardless of ability to pay. Rabbi Akiva, the great second century rabbi, remembered the difficulty he had raising the tuition at his first yeshiva, until he transferred to a free school. When he established his own yeshiva, Akiva sat under a fig tree and taught in the open, so that anyone who wanted to could come and learn. Yohanan ben Zakkai met with his students on the steps leading up to the Temple, one of the busiest pathways in the city of Jerusalem.

The synagogue was established by the Pharisees as a place for the public study of the Torah.[6] This was an aspect of the Pharisaic program to democratize the priestly vocation. Because there were too many priests in Judea to serve all at once in the Temple, the country was divided into twenty-four districts. The priests from each district served for two weeks at a time in Jerusalem. While the priests of a district were serving, the Pharisees held an assembly in the chief town of that district. At the hours that the priests offered the sacrifices, the public gathered to hear the scholars recite from the Torah the passages which command those sacrifices. This recitation was a symbolic equivalent of participation in the priestly rituals. The scholars also preached, explaining the teachings of Judaism by interpreting passages from the Torah. Eventually the synagogue building was established for this public study. By the time of the destruction of the Temple there were synagogues in every town, and nu-

---

[6]Many older history books theorize that the synagogue began in the Babylonian Exile four hundred years earlier, but neither literature nor archaeology displays any evidence of synagogues arising before the rise of the Pharisees in Judah.

merous synagogues in the cities. The synagogue replaced the Temple as the place for communion with God. Communion was now achieved through study and prayer rather than through sacrifice.

The Pharisaic institutions of the court, the academy and the synagogue became the institutions of rabbinic Judaism. These institutions underwent many developments, but they remained the primary institutions of the Jewish community up to modern times.

13

70 CE—
The Turning Point

The New Sanhedrin

In the summer of the year 70 the Roman siege of Jerusalem was nearly over. There was no food in the city, and the Romans were about to breach the walls. Under their general Vespasian, the Roman legions had already subdued the rest of the country. The remaining armies of the rebel Zealots were holed up in Jerusalem. The Zealots would let no one leave the city, forcing the people to fight to the end.

The Talmud tells a legend of how Yohanan ben Zakkai devised a plan to get out of Jerusalem so that he could negotiate with the Romans. He pretended to be ill, and then his disciples put out the word that he had died. They put him in a coffin and carried him outside the city gates. At the gates of the city the rebel guards, suspecting deception, wished to pierce the coffin with their spears. The disciples said to them, "Shall the Romans say that this is how they treated the body of their master?" The guards allowed them out of the city.

When Yohanan reached the Roman camp he came to the tent of Vespasian and said to him, "Hail to you, O Emperor!" Vespasian replied, "Why do you call me a king if I am not a king? And if I am a king, why did you not come to me before?" Yohanan replied, "You are a king, and I did not come before because the rebels would not let me." Just then a messenger came into the tent, announcing that the emperor was dead, and the citizens of Rome had elected Vespasian to succeed him.

Vespasian told Yohanan, "I am off to Rome, and my son Titus will take my place. Since you were the first to address me as Emperor, you may make a wish and I will grant it." Yohanan replied, "Give me the town of Yavneh and spare the lives of the sages and the descendants of Hillel (the hereditary heads of the Sanhedrin)." Vespasian granted this wish.

In reality, Yohanan did not need prophetic insight to know that Vespasian would be emperor. The general's agents had been busy in Rome for some time arranging for him to receive the throne. Nor did Vespasian grant Yohanan the right to rule the Jews on a royal impulse. Yohanan and his circle, the Pharisees of the School of Hillel, were known to be opposed to rebellion against Rome, and they had enough authority among the people to restore order to Judea.

Soon after the war ended Yohanan ben Zakkai re-established the Sanhedrin in the village of Yavneh, on the coastal plain west of Jerusalem. Yohanan now had the title of Rabban, "master," and the members of the Sanhedrin were called rabbis. The "Patriarch," the president of the Sanhedrin, was granted nearly royal power over the Jewish people in Judea. The new Sanhedrin set about the task of restoring the Jewish people and the Jewish religion after the terrible destruction of the rebellion.

Yohanan ben Zakkai was said to have been the youngest of Hillel's disciples. This is doubtful since they lived in different centuries, but Yohanan was the leading scholar of the House of Hillel. The new Sanhedrin which Yohanan convened was dominated by Hillelites. The other sects and factions of Judaism had disappeared or lost their power base in the rebellion. The Judaism of the future, rabbinic Judaism, was the creation of the Hillelite Pharisees in the post-70 Sanhedrin.

The Sanhedrin faced a difficult task. They had to re-create Judaism without a Temple. Every religion in the world had temples for sacrifice and a priesthood to officiate in the temples. There was no religion without sacrifice. The Jews had lost their Temple once before, centuries earlier, but at that time the Jews were content to wait until they could rebuild. This time, considering the power of the Roman empire and its determination not to allow the Temple to be rebuilt, the Jews would have to either disappear or develop a religion that did not depend upon sacrifice. The Jews in the year 70 could easily have decided that Judaism had come to an end with the destruction of the Temple. That they did not do so is largely attributable to the genius of Yohanan ben Zakkai and the rabbis of Yavneh.

Judaism Without a Temple

The rabbis were surely as overcome with sorrow as anyone over the great tragedy that had befallen the Jews. But for them, the destruction of the Temple was in many ways a benefit. It allowed them to promote the practices and doctrines of the Pharisees as a way of life for all Jews. The Pharisees had already developed a way of life that made the Temple unnecessary. They had been living "as if" they were priests. They had observed the laws of priestly purity everywhere, extending the sanctity of the Temple precinct into the entire world. Now that the Temple was gone, the Jews could continue to live as if they were all priests, and they could recognize God's holy presence anywhere in the world.

The sacrifices had been offered as a way to achieve forgiveness of sins and as a way to enter communion with God. The rabbis taught that these same goals could be achieved by other means. Obedience to the mitzvot established a connection between God and humankind and brought God's grace upon his people. Teshuvah, repentance, brought divine forgiveness. The rituals of the table and the service of prayer were an offering to God as pleasing as the burnt offerings of the sacrifices had been.

The Talmud tells us that once Yohanan ben Zakkai and his disciple Rabbi Joshua were walking through the ruins of Jerusalem. When Joshua saw the ruins of the Temple he cried out, "Woe to us that it has been destroyed, the place where Israel found atonement for their sins!" Yohanan ben Zakkai replied to him, "My son, do not let it grieve you! We have atonement equal to that other. And what is it? It is deeds of loving-kindness, as it is written in Scripture, 'For I desire mercy, and not sacrifice' " (Hos 6:6).

The Torah says that before God redeemed Israel from Egypt he required them to sacrifice the Passover lamb. God commanded Israel to set aside the lamb four days before it was to be sacrificed. Why was this necessary? The rabbis taught that God commanded the taking of the lamb so that Israel would have a mitzvah to perform. The merit of fulfilling the mitzvah made Israel worthy of the redemption from Egypt.[1] The point is that the fulfillment of God's commandments, not sacrifice, earns redemption for Israel. This was the message of the rabbis; observing the Torah is the true offering to God, making sacrifice unnecessary.

Remembering the Temple

After the destruction of the Temple, sects arose that practiced severe self-denial in mourning over the catastrophe. They refrained from all joyous activities, from meat and wine, from marriage. The rabbis decreed that such severe expressions of sorrow were not proper. They ordained that Jews should continue to seek the joy in life and in the service of God, making only a small symbolic act of regret at each joyous occasion in

---

[1] *Mekhilta*, Piskha, Ch. 5.

remembrance of the Temple. The rabbis wanted the Jews to adopt a positive attitude to life and the future. This was necessary for the continuation of the Jewish people.

The rabbis established as doctrine that the Temple would one day be rebuilt, but this would not occur until God had determined the time. Prayers for the restoration of the Temple were included in the liturgy, but the rabbis did nothing to encourage rebuilding projects. There was an attempt to rebuild the Temple in the fourth century, but it came to nothing. Until the Messiah comes to restore the Temple all the Torah laws dealing with the Temple and the sacrifices were suspended. The rabbis decreed that the Jews no longer needed to offer the priestly dues and tithes. This meant that the priests, the hereditary leaders of the Jews since antiquity, now had to earn a living in the ordinary manner, like any nonpriest. The priesthood was reduced to a merely symbolic honor.

The Temple remained important in the Jewish consciousness as a symbol of the messianic restoration. But after the passage of a few generations the sacrificial service no longer had any reality in the Jewish religious consciousness. If Jews today had the opportunity to actually rebuild the Temple, only a small percentage would desire to do so. Some of the medieval Jewish philosophers taught that God had never desired a Temple; it was only a temporary expedient to slowly wean Israel away from the pagan practice of sacrifice. Most modern Jews take the attitude that the Temple disappeared at just that time when the growth of the Jewish religion made it extraneous. The rabbis of old would not have openly said so, but their actions reveal that they may have shared this attitude.

Religious Authority

Yohanan ben Zakkai established that the authority of the Sanhedrin in Yavneh was in no way inferior to the former authority of the Temple and its leaders. A few years after the Sanhedrin was established, Rosh Hashanah fell on a Shabbat. The shofar is not blown when Rosh Hashanah falls on Shabbat, but it was blown in the Temple precinct. (Activities otherwise forbidden on Shabbat were permitted in conjunction with the Temple service.) Yohanan granted himself the right to blow the shofar in Yavneh, where the Sanhedrin met. By doing so he established that the Sanhedrin held the same authority that had formerly been held by the Temple priesthood.[2] By giving themselves this authority the rabbis gave

---

[2]It is interesting to contrast Yohanan's attitude with that of Jews in the fourth century, when the Sanhedrin was abolished. The Jews of that time declared that without a

themselves the right to restructure Judaism. This was necessary to develop the practices which would replace sacrifice in Jewish observance. Had the rabbis been more conservative in their attitude to authority, Judaism would have remained a Temple religion without a temple. Instead, the rabbis never doubted that in their innovative practices they were unfolding the meaning of the Torah as it had been intended since the revelation at Mount Sinai. In their own eyes they were not innovating or making a revolution, but making explicit the message that God had built into the Torah for them to reveal. The rabbis believed that their authority came to them from God.

Holidays

Until the year 70 holiday observance centered around the Temple. The holiness of the holy days was recognized in the special additional sacrifices which were offered in those days. All who were able went to Jerusalem to bring their offerings and observe the priests perform their rituals. The rabbis transformed the practices and the meaning of the holidays. The agricultural aspects of the holidays was de-emphasized, since the festival offerings of the farmers had ceased. The holidays became more important for their association with Jewish history than for their relationship to the cycle of nature. The rabbis of Yavneh also emphasized the way in which the holidays symbolize the ongoing relationship between God and humankind. To use a modern term, one might say that the rabbis spiritualized the holidays.

The Hasmoneans had established various national holidays to celebrate important events in the history of independent Judah. The rabbis eliminated all of these holidays from the sacred calendar except for Hanukah. They revised the meaning of Hanukah to stress the miracles of God rather than the bravery of Jewish fighters. The rabbis' attitudes to national holidays was probably related to their attitude to the rule of Rome. The rabbis taught patient waiting for divine deliverance. They taught that the Jews must accept the domination of the Gentile nations until God chose to send the Messiah. The example of the Maccabees ran counter to this doctrine.

New practices were developed to replace the sacrifices on the holidays. Observance was transferred to the home and the synagogue. On

---

Sanhedrin, the shofar may no longer be blown anywhere on Shabbat. They took the attitude that the institutions which replaced the Sanhedrin were spiritually inferior to it. Until modern times, no Jews dared grant themselves the authority to contradict an enactment of the Sanhedrin.

Passover Jews would now hold a seder in their homes. On Sukkot they would build a harvest booth in their own yard. Instead of offering special sacrifices the Jews would offer special prayers on the holidays in their local synagogues.

Yavneh and Masada

To the modern Jew Yavneh and Masada arise as two powerful and contrasting symbols of the Jewish response to living in an unredeemed world. The promise of the covenant has not yet been fulfilled. The Jews still live in subjection to more powerful nations which sometimes persecute and even kill them. Masada symbolizes the determination of Jews to be masters of their own fate. Masada represents the idea that in an unredeemed world Jews must sometimes protect themselves by doing unredeeming acts such as taking up arms in self-defense. The Israeli army conducts the induction ceremony for new soldiers on top of the hill of Masada. This represents their determination that "Masada shall not fall again." They will protect Jewish independence and self-determination with their lives, if necessary.

Yavneh represents a way of accommodation and adjustment. Yavneh represents a self-conscious removal of the Jews from the stage of world events in order to concentrate Jewish attention on a supra-historical event, the redemption of the Jewish people and the world. In the perspective of Yavneh the redemption cannot be brought about by historic acts. The Jews must busy themselves with obedience to the divine commandments in order to earn the divine grace that will cause God to fulfill his promise to Israel. Until that time the Jews must meekly submit to the dominion of the Gentile nations, for this is the will of God. In the perspective of Yavneh, the Jews need only that independence which will allow them to live according to the Torah without interference.

It is obvious that after the year 70 the rabbis in Yavneh succeeded to preserve Judaism while the Zealots on Masada failed. To some modern Jews this reveals the eternal wisdom of the Yavnean perspective. Other modern Jews are no longer willing to live with the compromises that Yavneh demands. The Holocaust revealed that accommodation may no longer be an adequate response to oppression. To these Jews there was nothing wrong with the perspective of Masada except for its failure to unite all Jews in the enterprise for Jewish independence.

Masada, or Yavneh, or is there a third choice, a symbol for another kind of action that Jews have not yet explored? This question confronts the modern Jew as he considers the proper relationship between the Jewish people and the world at large.

Rabbinic Judaism from Yohanan to Judah the Patriarch

The work begun by Yohanan ben Zakkai was continued under his successor, Rabban Gamaliel II. Under Rabban Gamaliel the new patterns of Jewish law, worship and practice became firmly established. The greatest scholar in the Sanhedrin of Gamaliel was Rabbi Akiva. As a young man Akiva was an ignorant shepherd in Babylon. He married Rachel, the daughter of the wealthy landowner for whom he worked. Rachel saw the potential in Akiva and she encouraged him to study Torah. Legend says that Akiva sat in the first grade next to his son to learn the alphabet. He advanced quickly and was soon recognized as the greatest rabbinic scholar. He acquired many disciples. Rabbi Akiva followed a very liberal pattern of Torah interpretation that permitted the derivation of new law by interpreting conjunctions such as "and" or "but." Even the decorations which by tradition are placed over certain letters in the written text of the Torah were subject to interpretation. Because of his humble origins Akiva was aware of the impact of rabbinic law on the life of the common people, and he took this into consideration in his interpretations of the Torah.

The Roman empire reached the height of its glory under the emperors Trajan and Hadrian who ruled in the second century. The Roman government paid scant heed to the religious requirements of its Jewish subjects. At one point Rabbi Akiva led a delegation of rabbis to Rome seeking relief for Jewish grievances, but none was offered. Hadrian responded to the "rebelliousness" of the Jews by outlawing the teaching and practice of the Torah. At that point the Jews of Judea joined in open rebellion. Rabbi Akiva gave his validation to the messianic claims of Simon Bar Kochba, the military leader of the rebellion. The rebellion lasted from 132 to 135. Bar Kochba's army retreated to its final redoubt in Betar, a fortress west of Jerusalem. The Romans stormed the fort and slaughtered a frightful number of Jews, as many as half a million. During the rebellion Rabbi Akiva and many of his fellow rabbis were arrested. They were tortured to death in the Roman arena. The line of rabbinic ordination very nearly came to an end, but some rabbis survived the rebellion. Five years after the rebellion the Romans restored the Patriarchate and the Sanhedrin. Since Judah was utterly wasted, the Sanhedrin and the rabbinical academies now met in the Galilee. The Sanhedrin eventually settled in the city of Tiberias on the Sea of Galilee, where it remained until its dissolution in the fourth century.

Rabbi Judah ha-Nasi (c. 135–220) was the most powerful of the patriarchs. He maintained excellent relations with the Roman government. Legend says that he was a close personal friend of the emperor Antoninus Pius. Rabbi Judah had great personal wealth. He was popular with the masses. He had absolute authority over the Jews of Judea. He was a king in all but title, and the rabbis of the time had to do his bidding. His legal rulings were absolute in his time and they became law for all time in the literature of the Oral Torah. In rabbinic legal literature Judah the Patriarch is called "Rabbi"; no other identification is needed.

Judah organized a written encyclopedia of much of the Oral Torah. Rabbinic tradition insisted that the Oral Torah remain distinct from the Written Torah. The Oral Torah could not be written down, but had to be committed to memory. As the Oral Torah grew through the years, some rabbis developed the practice of maintaining written notes which would help them remember all of the laws. They still taught orally, but they referred to these notes in preparing their lectures to the disciples. These written notes were called "mishnah," from the Hebrew verb "to teach." Judah used a set of notes handed down from Rabbi Akiva and other written materials plus his own extensive rabbinic knowledge to prepare a written mishnah collection. The encyclopedia of Rabbi Judah, called the **Mishnah,** grew in recognition. Within a few generations it was recognized as the essential text of the Oral Torah. Later rabbis depended on it and felt obligated to decide legal questions in accordance with what they found in the Mishnah; contrary traditions were discarded. The continued development of the Oral Torah revolved around interpretation of the Mishnah.

Judaism and Christianity

Christianity and rabbinic Judaism grew and developed at the same time. Although Christianity had become a separate religion, it shared with rabbinic Judaism a Scripture, the Tanak. Both the Christians and the rabbis believed that they possessed the tradition for the proper interpretation of this Scripture. The rabbis called their interpretation the Oral Torah. The Christians called theirs the New Testament. The Mishnah and the New Testament were written down and canonized at about the same time. The rabbis claimed that one could not comprehend the Tanak or know how to live by it without the Oral Torah. The Christians made a similar claim for the New Testament.

Christian theological tradition regards Judaism as the religion of the Old Testament and Christianity as the religion of the New Testament. This tradition has caused many Christians to compare Christianity with Judaism by comparing the Tanak with the New Testament. Such a comparison is historically invalid because it ignores the vast tradition of interpretation of the Tanak that occurred within Judaism over the centuries between the closing of the Tanak and the writing of the New Testament. A proper comparison of Christianity with Judaism requires a comparison of the New Testament with the Mishnah and other early rabbinic literature.

For example, one hears of a contrast between the New Testament message of mercy and the Old Testament law of "an eye for an eye." To make this comparison meaningful, we must ask how the rabbis interpreted this Old Testament law, and we must also ask what the rabbis taught about mercy and forgiveness. We find that in rabbinic law the point is made that "an eye for an eye" cannot be taken literally. Since no two people are alike, no two eyes are alike. What if a one-eyed man poked out the eye of a two-eyed man? The scriptural law is interpreted to mean that the courts must fine the aggressor to provide just monetary compensation for the suffering, medical expenses and loss of time and income of the injured party. We also find that the rabbis taught the value of forgiveness; in fact they taught that to be quick to forgive was an ethical obligation. "An eye for an eye" means that the courts must dispense justice. The injured individual is encouraged to forgive and to love his enemy.

Both Judaism and Christianity are rooted in the Tanak, which Christians call the Old Testament. They also share a stock of scriptural interpretations which developed during the first few centuries after the canonization[3] of the Torah. The early Christians developed some aspects of the scriptural tradition and mixed them with other religious ideas to form Christianity. Other aspects of scriptural tradition were taken up into rabbinic Judaism. Many teachings from scriptural tradition were shared by both religious communities. We see, for instance, that even though Jews and Christians had completely different concepts of the Messiah, they agreed on which verses from Scripture ought to be interpreted messianically. That was an aspect of their common heritage.

Rabbinic Judaism in Babylon

Rabbi Judah the Patriarch sent two of his students, Rav and Samuel, to establish rabbinic academies in Babylon. Judah may have foreseen that the Roman empire would not continue to be as tolerant of Judaism as it was in his time. Academies of Babylon, outside the reach of the Romans, would assure the continuation of rabbinic teaching if the great academies in the Galilee should close. Academies were established in Babylon in the towns of Sura and Nehardea. The Nehardean academy was later moved to Pumbeditha. The head of each academy was called by the title **Gaon**.

The Jews of Babylon lived in relative freedom under their Parthian

---

[3]Canonization is the process by which a book becomes recognized as sacred Scripture.

rulers. When the Sassanians took over from the Parthians in the third century they briefly attempted to spread their own religion to their subjects, but they soon returned to the tolerant policy of their predecessors. The Jews of Babylon had control over their own affairs. The **Exilarch** was the king of the Jews in Babylon. He answered to the rulers, and all Jews were under his rule. They paid the taxes, obeyed the laws and went to the courts of the Jewish administration. The rabbis who came out of the academies were appointed as administrators and judges in the Jewish community. The Gaonim (pl.) grew in power and authority, so that the two academies and the court of the exilarch became three nearly equal sources of leadership for the Jews of Babylon.

When in the fourth century the Roman empire became officially Christian, the Jews were severely persecuted. The Sanhedrin was dissolved and the academies in Galilee were closed. Babylon gradually became the world center of Judaism. The authority of the Gaonate extended beyond Babylon to Jewish communities throughout the world. For many centuries thereafter the Gaon of the ascendant academy was recognized as the leading religious authority for Jews everywhere. The Gaonate maintained contact with Jews in the medieval communities that formed in Europe and North Africa after the fall of Rome. The Gaonim encouraged Jews everywhere to follow rabbinic teaching as they had developed it in their academies in Babylon. As the Middle Ages began, the teachings of the Babylonian rabbis became the standard of law and practice for Jews throughout the world.

The Formation of the Talmuds

The process of developing the Oral Torah continued through the centuries. Each generation of rabbis faced new situations which called for new interpretations of the Torah. The process of rabbinic interpretation had become firmly established. It was accepted that the rabbis developed Torah law by right of a chain of tradition that went back to Moses.

In the fourth century the Torah academies in Galilee were closed by the government. The rabbinic scholars of the time attempted to preserve the most important rabbinic teachings from the two centuries since the writing down of the Mishnah. Probably using the records of the academies as well as their own memorized knowledge, the rabbis hurriedly composed a written text. After each portion of the Mishnah they recorded discussions and legal opinions loosely based upon the topic in that mishnah. This newly written material was called **gemarra,** from an Aramaic word for "study" or "learning." The Mishnah together with its gemarra is called

Talmud. This Talmud is variously known as the Jerusalem Talmud,[4] the Palestinian Talmud, or the Talmud of the Land of Israel.

The process of rabbinic interpretation continued in the academies in Babylon. In the fifth century, during a period of persecution, the Babylonian rabbis attempted to record and preserve their laws and interpretations of the Mishnah. A gemarra was composed in Babylon from the records of the academies in Sura and Pumbeditha. When the persecutions ended a group of rabbis edited the text of the Gemarra and completed it. The Mishnah with the Gemarra of Babylon is called the Babylonian Talmud.

The Talmud of Babylon became the standard Talmud; an unattributed reference to the Talmud always refers to the Talmud of Babylon. There were a number of reasons that the Babylonian Talmud was preferred. It is much more extensive than the Talmud of the Land of Israel, nearly ten times larger. It is a much smoother and more comprehensible document, having been written more gradually and having been subjected to more editing. The power of the Gaonim helped to spread the Babylonian Talmud to other lands. The Babylonian Talmud presumes the situation of Jews living in relative autonomy under foreign domination in the Diaspora. Since this was the situation of Jews everywhere in the world outside the Land of Israel, the Babylonian Talmud was more applicable to their lives than the Talmud of the Land of Israel. For all these reasons the Babylonian Talmud was preferred.

The Babylonian Talmud was written down in about the year 500 CE. It soon became the chief object of rabbinic study. The Talmud was accepted as the final and complete compilation of the Oral Torah, the completion of the sacred Scriptures. After the Talmud was written down, learning the Talmud and how to interpret it became the essence of rabbinic education. Until the dawn of the modern age, all Jewish life was based upon the Talmud.

---

[4]Inaccurately, since it was composed in the Galilee.

14

Rabbinic Literature

The Structure of the Mishnah

The Mishnah is divided into six books, or "orders." These are entitled: Seeds, Feasts, Women, Damages, Sacred Things, Purity. Each order of the Mishnah is further divided into topical sections, called **tractates.** There are sixty tractates in the Mishnah. Each tractate is divided into chapters, and each chapter is divided into sections of a few sentences each which discuss a particular legal ruling. Each section is called a "mishnah" or a "halakha." An individual mishnah is identified by the title of the tractate in which it is found, the chapter number, and the number of the individual mishnah within the chapter. For example, "Berakot 3:1" refers to the tractate Berakot in the order Seeds, the third chapter, the first mishnah in the chapter.

The order Seeds deals primarily with agricultural laws. It also deals with prayer, following the logic that blessings are recited over food.

The order Feasts gives the laws for Shabbat and the holidays of the Jewish year.

The order Women covers domestic law, including marriage and divorce. There are also tractates dealing with vows and with the Nazirite vow of abstinence. They are included in this order since marriage is a type of vow.

The fourth order, Damages, deals with civil and criminal law and the establishment of courts. Also included in this order is the tractate **Pirke Avot,** "Sayings of the Fathers." Pirke Avot is a collection of the wise sayings of the early masters. It serves as an ethical guide and incidentally as a history of the rabbinic movement.

The fifth order, Holy Things, gives the laws concerning animals and other objects made holy by being dedicated as Temple offerings.

The sixth order, Purity, gives the laws for what makes objects and persons ritually impure and what returns them to a state of purity.

All of the Oral Torah is organized under the six major headings of the Orders of the Mishnah.

A Text from the Mishnah

(Berakot 1:1) (A) From what time in the evening may the "Shema" be recited? (B) From the time when the priests enter (the Temple) to eat heave-offering until the first watch (of the night). (C) So says Rabbi Eliezer. (D) But the Sages say, "Until midnight." (E) Raban Gamaliel says, "Until the crack of dawn." (F) His sons once returned from a wedding feast. They said to him, "We have not recited the Shema." He said to them, "If the dawn has not yet risen you are required to recite it." (G) (It is a general rule) that whenever the Sages say, "Until midnight." The obligation of fulfillment lasts until the crack of dawn. (H) The obligation of burning the fat pieces and appendages (of the sacrificial animals) lasts until the crack of dawn, and for all (the sacrifices) that must be consumed on that very day, the obligation lasts until the crack of dawn. (I) If so, then why have the Sages said, "Until midnight"? (J) To keep a person far from transgression.

Analysis of the Mishnah Text

The above is the opening mishnah of the Mishnah. We notice immediately how strange and difficult this text is. There are a number of reasons why the Mishnah text appears to be so difficult and intimidating:

1. The Mishnah represents the world view of rabbinic Judaism, a world view very different from that of contemporary America, or even of contemporary Judaism.
2. The Mishnah, although written, displays its character as an oral tradition. Nothing is written out in complete prose. We have before us only the notes which serve as reminders to those who have this material committed to memory. The concise, disjointed style of the Mishnah is called an "elliptical" style. This means that much information is left out and must be filled in by the reader.

3. The Mishnah has no beginning, middle and end. Every part of it presumes a knowledge of every other part. The whole presumes a knowledge of how Judaism is lived and practiced in the first centuries of the Common Era, including a detailed knowledge of the Temple sacrificial system.
4. The early rabbis shared a set of concerns which are not always relevant to us.
5. The rabbis had a large technical vocabulary for their legal doctrines and religious practices. Translation is not sufficient to explain the meaning of these technical terms. Some of the technical terms in the above mishnah are:

Shema—the recitation of the Shema Yisrael with its accompanying Torah paragraphs and surrounding blessings. A Jew is obligated to recite this evening and morning.

Heave-offering—a portion of the sacrifices which was set aside as priestly dues. The priests would sit down to dinner in the Temple precinct each evening to partake of the holy offerings.

Obligation—a commandment of the Torah, a requirement which God has placed upon the Jewish people.

Fat Pieces and Appendages—the inedible portions of the edible sacrifices. These were saved throughout the day and burned each night on the altar fire when the sacrifices were completed.

The hand of the editor in creating this text is easily visible. We can identify nine related pieces of material which the editor has stitched together into this text. These pieces are noted in the text with capital letters in parentheses. (The pieces are not marked off in the original text.)[1] The pieces are:

(A) A question is raised. What is the time for the recitation of the evening Shema?
(B) An answer is given, anonymously. We may say the evening Shema anytime after sunset. Sunset is defined not astronomically but according to what the Temple priests were doing at that time of day, beginning their evening meal of holy offerings. The Shema must be recited before the night is one-third over. This time is also defined in terms of Temple activity. The Temple guard was divided into three watches of the night.

---

[1]We are indebted to Jacob Neusner for his method of identifying the component parts of a rabbinic text.

(C) The answer is identified as being the legal opinion of Rabbi Eliezer.

(D) An alternative answer is given as the opinion of the majority. The Mishnah identifies a generally accepted opinion as being the opinion of "the Sages." It is presumed that this, and not the opinion of Rabbi Eliezer, is the law to be followed. There is no dispute about when one may begin to recite the Shema, but the majority allow the Shema to be recited until the night is half over.

(E) A third opinion is given and identified as that of Rabban Gamaliel. Rabban Gamaliel says that the evening Shema may be recited throughout the entire evening, which goes until the "crack of dawn" when the first light appears in the Eastern sky.

(F) A story is told. The story lends credence to the opinion of Rabban Gamaliel by giving a precedent when his ruling was actually applied.

(G) A general principle of law is established based on the specific example of the evening Shema. Any mitzvah which must be performed in the evening may be fulfilled at any time before the crack of dawn.

(H) There is a logical contradiction in the law. The Sages say that the mitzvah *must* be fulfilled by midnight. Rabban Gamaliel says that the mitzvah *may* be performed until dawn. A question is raised concerning this contradiction. The questioner presumes that the opinion of the Sages must be respected, but the opinion of Rabban Gamaliel is the law. This question must derive from a time when the prior material in the mishnah is already known to the rabbis in its present form.

(I) An answer is given to the question. The answer resolves the contradiction that was noted, and grants authority to both the opinions of the Sages and of Rabban Gamaliel. The resolution of the contradiction lies in an understanding of human nature.

A mitzvah is of greater value when it is performed in a timely manner. It is praiseworthy to fulfill a mitzvah at the first possible moment, to "rush to the performance of a mitzvah." It is perfectly acceptable, though, if one does not rush to the performance but one does fulfill a mitzvah within the span of its proper time. It is possible that one who has ignored the first possible opportunity to fulfill a mitzvah will procrastinate and delay until the last possible opportunity. Since it takes about fifteen minutes to recite the Shema, one who is in the habit of staying up all night may say to himself, "I will wait until the last fifteen minutes before dawn, and then I will recite the Shema." This is within the law, but there is danger that a person will delay too long and the proper time will pass before the mitzvah is completely fulfilled. It is wise to establish an inner boundary law well within the proper time-frame in order to insure that a mitzvah is performed in a timely manner. For an evening mitzvah, this inner boundary is

established as midnight. If the inner boundary is accidentally transgressed (such as in the case illustrated by the story) one can still fulfill the divine commandment up until the last possible moment without loss of divine credit.

Besides establishing a wise principle of observance, parts (H) and (I) fulfill a function commonly found in sacred literature, that of resolving a seeming contradiction between two sacred texts. In this case, the sacred texts are the contrary opinions of the Sages and of Rabban Gamaliel. The resolution of the contradiction is that it is not really a contradiction—one text is giving the law "a priori" and the other "ex post facto."

The Babylonian Talmud

The editors of the Talmud organized it in the form of a debate or discussion on the points raised in the Mishnah. There is a gemarra to most of the tractates in the first four orders of the Mishnah. There is no gemarra to the orders Holy Things and Purities. The laws in these two orders apply only when the Temple is standing; no new issues concerning these laws were raised in later times. In the gemarra the rabbis ask questions about the Mishnah text, attempt to resolve contradictions, and extend the law to new issues. They quote old traditions which were not included in the Mishnah. They tell aggadot, stories, which illustrate points and which give the world view, the folklore and the historical sense of the rabbis.

The basic unit of Talmud text is the **sugya**. A sugya is a discussion on a particular point in which rabbis argue the different sides of an issue. The Talmud does not record actual debates, although the actual discussions in the academies must have followed a similar pattern. The Talmudic debate is an editorial convention, the form in which the writers of the Talmud collected and wrote down their traditions. In a Talmudic sugya a third century rabbi might raise a question which is answered by a second century rabbi. A rabbi from the fourth century might then raise an objection, which is answered by a rabbi from yet another time.

The Talmudic discussion moves from topic to topic in the manner of human conversation. Because of this, any subject might arise at any place in the Talmud. The pattern which the Mishnah gives to the Oral Torah is undone by the gemarra. Because the gemarra raises issues in an almost random pattern, one cannot become expert in Talmudic law without being well versed in the entire Talmud. This is a prodigious intellectual task.

The gemarra is much greater in length than the Mishnah. The Mishnah is about the same length as the Tanak. The gemarra is more than ten times this long. According to the standard pagination, the Talmud fills over three thousand two-sided pages. A complete set of the Talmud is printed in numerous volumes and fills a bookshelf about three feet long. The gemarra on the one mishnah that we have studied fills nine two-sided folio pages.

The Talmudic Mind

Talmud study requires a sharp, analytical mind. The student of Talmud must be able to decode the elliptical language and pick apart the arguments of the rabbis in order to recognize the fine logical distinctions behind the rabbinic arguments. Talmud study is excellent training for the intellectual capacities of the human mind. The Talmud represents the belief that the human mind is capable of penetrating the mind of God. By raising the intellect to a high level and concentrating it on sacred concerns, Talmud study enables the student to perceive God's intentions for human society.

The Talmud represents religion on a practical level. It always deals with real human issues and concerns. Talmudic debate is concerned with real situations in which choices must be made about how to act. The Talmud does not give a complete, abstract overview of the meaning of existence as in a philosophical treatise. The Talmud deals with life as it is lived, one issue at a time. Every possible issue is dealt with only as it is raised by circumstance.

The Talmud does not distinguish between important and unimportant areas of human concern. Minute ritual matters are as much a part of God's law as are the great ethical commandments. The Talmud lavishes attention upon all areas of divine law.

The Talmud encourages skepticism. There is no question which may not be asked. To the contrary, the mind rises toward God only by asking questions. The Talmud is engaged in a search for truth. Truth is revealed in dialectic, in honest debate between sincere and scholarly seekers after truth. An objection may be raised to any point, and every objection must be answered. There is no doctrine that is not subject to refinement through questioning.

During the centuries since the return from the Babylonian exile the Torah had served as the constitution of the Jewish state and the Jewish people. The Oral Torah developed as the laws which interpreted that constitution. After the Talmud was completed, it became the constitution of the Jewish communities throughout the world. The Talmud was considered to be the ultimate revelation of the meaning of Torah. New legal decisions were derived from the Talmud. There was no need to refer back to the Written Torah for legal precedent, since the entire message of the Written Torah was made explicit in the Oral Torah, the Talmud.

Living by the Talmud

The Talmud was completed about the year 500. For the next five centuries Jewish communities throughout the world depended upon the Babylonian academies for the answers to their religious questions. When a question arose for which the local rabbis had no answer, they would write to the Gaon in Babylon. Based on his knowledge of the Talmud and the ongoing studies in the academies, the Gaon would come up with a definitive answer which he would publish. This question and answer is called a **responsa.** When academies for Talmud study opened up in Spain and Northern Europe in the high Middle Ages the great rabbis in those regions also engaged in responsa and published their legal decisions. The responsa, based on study of the Talmud, kept the halakha up to date. Responsa continues up to this very day. Those rabbinic scholars who engage in responsa must be very knowledgeable in the Talmud and they must also be learned in the precedents established by earlier responsa. They must be recognized by a broad spectrum of the community as authorities in Jewish law.

It is no easy matter to derive legal rulings from the Talmud. As we have seen, the Talmud is not a book of laws but a book of legal discussions. The derivation of law from the Talmud requires great knowledge and a highly developed ability to analyze the text of the Talmud. Periodically, great rabbinic scholars have attempted to make the laws and customs of Judaism more accessible to the masses. This is accomplished by writing commentaries or codes of law.

A commentary is written to be studied alongside the text of the Talmud. A Talmudic commentary may explain the logic of the rabbinic discussion and present a conclusion as later Jewish law has determined it. A commentary may make the Talmud more comprehensible by filling out the elliptical language with a more complete statement of the issues and the situation in which they arise. A commentary may also participate in the process of Talmudic dialectic, entering into the debate of the rabbis with new thoughts and opinions. Commentaries constitute a sort of Talmud to the Talmud.

The greatest commentary to the Talmud is that of **Rashi,** Rabbi

Solomon ben Isaac (1040–1105). Rashi was the founder of a great yeshiva in Troyes, in the Champagne district of France. His students and descendants composed another commentary which complemented his own. Rashi's followers are called the **Tosafists**; their commentary is called **Tosafot**, "Additions." The first printed edition of the Talmud and every edition since has been printed with Rashi's commentary on the inside of the page and the Tosafot on the outside of the page.

Codes of law attempt to give a summary of the legal decisions of the Talmud, circumventing the complexities of Talmudic dialectic. The greatest codes of law were written by Sephardic rabbis, rabbis of medieval Spain. Maimonides wrote a code entitled the **Mishneh Torah**, the "Repetition of the Torah." He divided all the subjects of Jewish law into fourteen different topic areas, with a book for each topic. Jacob ben Asher (d. 1340) wrote a code in which he combined all the laws into four major categories. He called his code the **Arba Turim**, the "Four Columns," after the four columns of jewels which adorned the breastplate of the high priest in the ancient Temple. Rabbi Joseph Caro (1488–1575), an exile from Spain who lived in Zefat in the Galilee, wrote a commentary on the Arba Turim. At the conclusion of this work he compiled a summary of all of the legal decisions found in his commentary. This work was entitled the **Shulhan Aruk**, the "Set Table." The Shulhan Aruk became recognized as a code of law in its own right, the last of the great codes of Jewish law. The Shulhan Aruk attracted its own commentators. In later times and to this very day, adherence to the Shulhan Aruk became the litmus test of Jewish orthodoxy.

The great codes came out of the Sephardic world, while the great commentaries came out of the Ashkenazic world. This is probably due to the different social order in the two Jewish societies. In the Sephardic world there was a small upper class of wealthy and educated Jews and a large mass of poorly educated ordinary Jews. The upper classes became extremely learned, but the simple people were not likely to ever approach the study of Talmud. A code of law gave an unambiguous pattern for Jewish living to Jews who had no more learning than a simple reading knowledge of Hebrew and Scripture. In the Ashkenazic world the restrictive laws under which Jews lived placed all Jews in a few professions. Virtually all Ashkenazic Jews were what we today would call "middle-class," and most had the leisure to acquire a fair amount of education. A commentary allowed a reasonably well-educated Jew to study the Talmud, even if not on the level of the great scholars who were capable of understanding the text in their own way. Commentaries are also interpretive and directive, but they give the reader a greater sense of participation in the sacred process of dialogue than does a code of law.

Modern Views of the Talmud

For an Orthodox Jew today the Talmud remains the ultimate resource for the Jewish way of life. Talmud study is the highest religious activity. The Orthodox Jew lives under the law, the halakha, that is based upon the Talmud. The medieval commentaries and codes are accepted as the proper explanation of how to understand the Talmud and live by it.

Jewish modernists in the nineteenth century rebelled against the primacy of the Talmud, since the Talmud was the source of the way of life they wished to change. Reform Jews in the West and Zionists in Eastern Europe, with very different programs for modernizing Judaism, both attempted to restore the Bible as the direct source of Jewish inspiration.[2]

Non-Orthodox Jews today do not agree that the Talmud is the only and complete unfolding of the message of the Torah. However, very few would share the negative feelings toward the Talmud expressed by the early rebels against traditional Judaism. Rather, the Jewish modernist sees the Talmud as a valuable contribution to the Jewish spirit and the Jewish way of life, offered by the rabbis of the early centuries of the common era. They perceive the great commentaries and codes as revealing not the message of the Talmud, but the spiritual greatness of the medieval Talmudic scholars. In other words, they see the Talmud and Talmudism as part of the continuous historical development of Judaism, rather than as the unfolding of the message which was entirely contained in the original revelation at Mount Sinai. The modernist Jew recognizes that contemporary Judaism owes a great debt to the Talmud, but he also believes that to some extent he is living in the post-Talmudic age. The Jewish modernist makes religious decisions which are not necessarily based upon the Talmud.

Orthodox Jews in the contemporary world continue to make Talmud study the highest level of the Jewish curriculum. Among the Orthodox there are programs to make Talmud study in the traditional manner available to high school and college students and to adults in all walks of life. Among non-Orthodox Jews in the world today few other than professional scholars and rabbis study the Talmud. Most American Jews have only a vague idea of what the Talmud is. Even if most modern Jews have no learning in the Talmud and do not respect its authority, the Jewish customs and traditions which they practice, from holiday celebrations to marriage and funeral customs to the ethical ideals they hold dear, have their source in the Talmud.

---

[2]It is interesting to compare this with the Protestant Reformation, in which Luther and other reformers held up the Bible against Church tradition, using the Bible as a tool for change. One might say that the Bible is a very revolutionary book!

15

Jews in the Middle Ages

From Antiquity to the Middle Ages

The Roman empire reached the height of its political and economic greatness in the reigns of the emperors Trajan and Hadrian early in the second century. From that point on the empire underwent a slow decline. In these centuries of decline the Western world underwent such great social changes that we recognize in this period one of the great shifts in human history, from the era of antiquity to the era of the Middle Ages. The culture of Greece and Rome and the even more ancient cultures of the Near East disappeared. The learning, the world-view and the accomplishments of antiquity were forgotten. Tribes from Northern Europe overran the Roman empire in Western and Southern Europe. The ancient world was replaced, over a period of centuries, by the world-view of two new religions, Christianity and Islam.

The Roman emperor Constantine (c. 288–337) was the first Christian emperor. The Christian religion, which had been growing for three centuries, was legalized by Constantine. Christianity became the new uniting force for the peoples of the empire. Constantine united the beliefs of the various Christian sects at the Council of Nicea in 325. He suppressed those Christian sects which did not agree with the now official version of Christianity. He also attempted to suppress Judaism.

Constantine moved the capital of the empire to Constantinople (modern-day Istanbul). Western Europe was gradually abandoned to invading Germanic tribes who founded loose-knit nations in the areas of Spain, France, Germany, England and Italy. These peoples gradually adopted Christianity. The Christians in these lands were under the supreme religious leadership of the Bishop of Rome, the Pope, while Christians in the Eastern Roman empire accepted the leadership of patriarchs seated in various cities. These two branches of Christianity are called today Roman Catholic and Eastern Orthodox.[1]

In the centuries after Constantine most of the people in the old Roman empire, and many in Babylon and Persia, became Christian. The situation changed with the rise of a new world religion, Islam. The founding prophet of Islam, Muhammad (c. 570–632), was born a simple cameldriver in Arabia. He united the tribes of Arabia under his new monotheistic religion. Moslems date the founding of their religion from 622 CE, when Muhammad fled for his life from the city of Mecca. He returned in triumph to conquer Mecca and make it the holy city of Islam. The new converts united Arabia and then swept out of Arabia on a path of conquest and conversion. The Moslems allowed Jews and Christians, as monotheists, to live. They gave to pagans the choice of death or conversion to Islam. In a short time the religion of Islam was predominant in North Africa and Spain, the Middle East, Northern India, and in East Asia as far as Indonesia and the Philippines.

The Muslims accepted the Hebrew Scriptures and the Christian New Testament as holy books. They added their own sacred scriptures, the Koran, said to be dictated to the prophet Muhammad by the Archangel Gabriel. Moslems accept Jesus as one of the prophets, but not as God incarnate nor as a Savior. Muhammad is said by Muslims to be the "seal of the prophets," and Islam the final statement of monotheistic faith.

The Jew in the Middle Ages found himself in a very different world than the world of antiquity. Before, Judaism was the only monotheistic religion. Now Jews found themselves living between two great and numerous monotheistic peoples, the Christians and the Moslems. Each of these religions recognizes Judaism as its foundation, but claims to have superseded it. The change in world religions affected the very foundation on which the Jew was accepted in Gentile society, and it also shifted the foundations of Jewish belief concerning relations with Gentiles.

The world economy had also changed greatly. The Roman empire had developed a sophisticated commercial economy. In the early Middle Ages the world was thrown back into a system of local economies based primarily on subsistence agriculture. The Jews were to find a special niche in this new economic structure.

The Jews had become very few in number by the early Middle Ages. Roman persecutions had led to the death of many Jews. Many Jews suc-

---

[1]The various Protestant denominations did not arise until the sixteenth century. These denominations arose in various Roman Catholic lands in protest against the doctrines and the central authority of the Church.

cumbed to the restrictive laws and intense conversionary pressures of the Christians and Moslems. Judaism is the only ancient religion of the Western world which survived the shift from antiquity to medievalism; it only barely did so. Fortunately for them the Jews were tolerated and given a role in medieval society. They recovered in numbers, though they remained a small people. They established new Jewish cultures suited to the society of the Middle Ages. Creative responses led to new and sometimes radically different expressions of the ancient spirit of Judaism.

From Babylon to Ashkenaz and Sepharad

From the fourth century and for many centuries afterward, the center of Jewish life was in Babylon, the land in which the Talmud was developed. The Babylonian Jewish community easily survived the shift of rulership from the Gnostic Persians to the Moslem Arabs. Like most peoples under Arab rule, they adopted Arabic as their common tongue. The Aramaic of the Talmud became a language of learning, as had happened to Hebrew centuries before. In parallel to the centralized religious rulership of the Moslems, the Gaonim acquired great centralized powers over all the Jews of Babylon. After the tenth century, though, the Gaonate experienced a decline. The centers of Jewish life and learning shifted westward. In the Islamic world, Spain became the center of Jewish population and Jewish learning. Spain was called **Sepharad** by the Jews. In the Christian world a center of Jewish life and learning was formed in the Rhineland, in Northern France and in Germany. This area was called by the Jews **Ashkenaz**. The Jews of Ashkenaz and Sepharad each developed their own Jewish way of life and became independent of the declining centers in Babylon. To this day most Jews consider themselves to be Ashkenazic or Sephardic, depending on their ancestry, and there are numerous religious and cultural differences between them.[2]

The Feudal System

Feudalism was the economic and social system of Christian Europe in the Middle Ages. The feudal system was based on land and agriculture.

---

[2]Many Jewish communities, such as those of Italy, Iraq (Babylon) and Yemen, have their own continuous histories independent of Sepharad and Ashkenaz. Still, in general usage Jews from Christendom are called Ashkenazic and those from Moslem lands are called Sephardic.

The nobility owned the land. They were under the nominal rulership of a king. The serfs worked the land. They also owned the land, in the sense that it was theirs to work, but the land also owned them. A serf could not move from the manor of his lord. Villagers such as millers, potters and smiths served the simple needs of the serfs for manufactured goods. Below the level of the villagers were slaves. Landless members of the nobility served in the higher levels of the clergy and as knights, the military class.

In the Middle Ages the concept of citizenship was unknown. There was no such thing as a nation of citizens with rights guaranteed to them by the state. Each person had a lord. A person's loyalty was not to a state but to the service of his lord. The rights and obligations of a person were determined in a charter granted by the lord. Special rights and obligations could be granted to individuals, but by and large rights and obligations were determined by the social class of the individuals in a given fiefdom. The famous Magna Charta (1215), for example, determined the rights and obligations of the English nobility in their relationship to their lord, the king of England.

The Jews in the Feudal System

The Jews of medieval Europe were a chartered community, a social class in their own right. Thus, the Jew related to the state and society as a whole not as an individual but as a member of his class, the Jewish community. The Jews served as the middle class of medieval Europe. They were the traders, the craftsmen and the bankers. This system was amenable to both the Christians and the Jews. Their professions allowed Jews a degree of independence and a decent livelihood. The feudal system, based on land, would have been disrupted by traders freely moving about; since the Jews were already outside the social system by virtue of their different faith, the nobility found it convenient to use Jews for commerce and banking. The term "merchant" was often used in the Middle Ages as a synonym for Jew, so concentrated were the Jews in this area of the economy.[3] Since commerce and ready capital could bring prosperity to a region, the nobility sometimes courted Jews by offering them more generous rights and lower taxes than in neighboring feifdoms, hoping thus to attract Jews to their lands.

The status of Jews was something of an anomaly in the feudal system. The Jews stood outside the land system and the parallel hierarchical system of the Catholic Church. The Jews claimed the status of knights, since

---

[3]For example Shakespeare's play, *The Merchant of Venice*.

they had freedom of movement and gave their fealty directly to a nobleman or king. Others claimed that the status of Jews was lower than that of serfs, since Jews were forbidden to own or live on the land.[4]

The Jews were granted the right to earn a living by their occupations, usually limited to commerce and banking. They were granted the right, which they insisted on, to be judged in their own courts according to their own laws. The Jews lived according to rabbinic law and their own customs. The Torah was the constitution of the Jewish community.

The primary civil obligation of the Jews was to pay taxes, which were often quite heavy. The lord established the rates of interest for Jewish money-lenders, and then taxed away most of the profits. The Jews were circumscribed by many laws and rules of the church and state which were intended to keep Jews in a low and humble state and to limit social relationships between Jews and Christians. The Church was always anxious that the life of the Jews should not seem pleasant or desirable to Christians. Where relations were good and the Jewish population was valued, these nuisance laws were often not enforced.[5] Thus, we find it written in complaint that although the Church forbade a Christian to be attended by a Jewish doctor, many high churchmen themselves preferred to go to a Jew for medical care.[6]

Jewish-Christian Relations in Feudal Society

Modern people often think of the Middle Ages as a time of great oppression and suffering for Jews. This view needs to be modified. It is true that the Jews often owed heavy dues to their rulers and were treated as a class rather than as individuals, but this is true of all people in feudal society. When Jews were oppressed in one place, they were able to remove to another place. Wherever Jews settled, they went by invitation, and at least initially they were welcomed. It was only as the feudal system began to fall apart and a class of Christians arose who wished to compete economically against the Jews that the Jews began to suffer as a group.

As cities arose in Europe the class of freedmen, or burghers, took control of the skilled trades. Jews were then excluded from these occupations by the guilds, or trade unions. Jews were excluded from the guilds,

---

[4]This rule was not always strictly enforced.

[5]Hitler culled his Nuremberg Laws, limiting the rights of German Jews in the 1930s, from the medieval codes of law which limited Jewish rights and relations with Gentiles.

[6]See Jacob R. Marcus, *The Jew in the Medieval World*, Harper and Row, N.Y., 1938, for examples of laws governing relations between Jews and Christians, and their enforcement or lack of it.

which were also religious organizations. The Italian cities of Venice and Genoa took over the international trade which had been controlled for centuries by Jews. These cities later moved into banking. Jews were reduced to petty money-lending and trade in second-hand goods. When the Jews became impoverished they became less desirable to the nobility. The peasantry came to resent the Jews, who were used by the nobility for the unpopular tasks of collecting taxes and managing estates. The Jews became expendable. The decline of Ashkenazic Jewry accelerated in the fourteenth century. Before this time the Jews lived very happily on the whole in Western Europe, and often enjoyed cordial relations with their Christian neighbors. Jews dressed like their neighbors, enjoyed the same entertainments, and shared the same world-view in all but religious matters.[7]

The Jew as Money-lender

In an advanced commercial economy such as that of the United States, banking is perceived as an honorable and useful profession. People recognize credit as a way of increasing their personal wealth and the wealth of society by enabling them to acquire durable goods and means for production which would otherwise be beyond their reach. In a primitive agricultural society banking is not honored, and bankers are considered to be socially unproductive. The medieval Church forbade lending money for interest, reflecting both the perceptions of an agricultural society and the biblical commandment which forbids such loans. Since society could not exist without money-lending, the Church gave this economic role to Jews. Jews were able to fulfill this role because Jewish law allowed lending at interest to non-Jews, and because Jewish law, which had developed in the sophisticated commercial society of the Roman empire, distinguished between commercial loans and charitable, private loans. For the latter one could not charge interest but for the former, a loan made to a person so that he can invest for profit, interest was permitted.

Jews in the Middle Ages had a variety of attitudes toward their role as money-lenders. Some shared the attitude that banking was unethical and unproductive; they bemoaned the fact that Jews were required by Christian law to carry on this trade. Others took an attitude similar to that held in society today, that lending money at interest bestowed a benefit upon society and was therefore an honorable and productive profession.[8]

---

[7]For a perspective on this matter, see Israel Abrahams, *Jewish Life in the Middle Ages*, Atheneum, N.Y.

[8]For a review of Jewish attitudes to money-lending see Abravanel's commentary to Deuteronomy.

The Jews of England

The Jews of England were placed into the stereotyped role of the medieval Jew more than in any other country. In other areas of Europe Jewish communities developed along with the feudal societies around them. There were many local variations in the rights and occupations granted to the Jews, and many exceptions to the usual rules. There were places where Jews engaged in agriculture, for instance, despite the fact that Christian law forbade this to Jews.

There were no Jews in England until 1066, when William the Conqueror, the Duke of Normandy, conquered England. William brought to England a whole new nobility from his home fiefdom. He structured a new society in England along the classic lines of the feudal concept of a perfect society. William brought Jews from Normandy to England and granted them the sole occupation of money-lending. All Jews in England were the king's men; the nobility did not have their own Jews. This sytem was highly restrictive for the Jews, but it gave the king an effective means of control over the nobility through his absolute control of the banking system. Whenever a Jew died, all the debts owed him reverted directly to the king. It is estimated that ten percent of the royal revenues of England came directly from the Jews.[9]

It is no wonder that the Jews became a pawn in the contest for power between the nobility and the king of England. When the kings of England had squeezed all the money they could out of the Jews,[10] leaving them impoverished and politically useless, they offered up the Jews as a sacrifice to public resentments. In the year 1290 King Edward I expelled the Jews from England.

Jews were never legally readmitted to England, a fact which curiously worked to their benefit. When, in the early modern age, other nations of Western and Central Europe passed laws admitting Jews into society, these laws retained some of the medieval restrictions against Jews. In England, where the return of Jews was tolerated but not enacted into law, there were no restrictions limiting where Jews could live and the occupations they could enter, making the Jews of England the freest Jews in all of European society.

---

[9]Abrahams.

[10]A major step in the impoverishment of the Jews came when King Richard the Lion-Hearted was imprisoned in Austria and held for ransom during his return from the Crusades. The Jews of England were required to come up with the enormous sum of money needed for the ransom of the king.

Jews in Christian Theology and Law

The ideal of tolerance for minorities, so precious to Americans, was unknown in the Middle Ages. Conformity to traditional social practices and accepted beliefs was highly prized; unusual behavior and doctrines which varied from accepted religious beliefs were not tolerated. Within Christian society, movements deemed heretical were strongly suppressed. It was thought proper for the good of society to execute heretics, teachers of new or variant doctrines. It is remarkable, then, that the Jews were tolerated in medieval society. The Jews had a different religion altogether, contrary to Christianity, and due to their religion the Jews practiced social customs which seemed strange and mysterious to their neighbors. The toleration granted to the Jews can only partially be ascribed to their economic usefulness. This unusual toleration is also attributable to Christian doctrine.

The Jewish Scriptures were retained by the Christians as part of their own Scriptures, the Old Testament. Although the Christians believed that the Jewish covenant with God had been superseded by the new covenant in Christ, they believed that the Jews were still God's chosen people. As the chosen people, Jews were under God's protection.

Christians believed that at the second coming of Christ the Jews would convert to Christianity. This would be the final triumph of Christianity; God's own people, the people from whom Jesus came, would recognize the error of their ways. The Jews were to be preserved until the coming of that day. It was against Christian law to kill or to forcibly convert a Jew.

Since Judaism was perceived as only an incomplete form of Christianity, it was hard for Christians to imagine why Jews persisted in their own religion. The solution for Christians was to believe that Jews are "spiritually blind," unable to see the truth. The Jews were to be subjected to constant conversionary pressure to encourage them to see the light. The Jews were to be kept in a position of subjection and degradation as an abject example to Christians of what happens to those who do not accept Christ.

The Church considered itself to be the protector of the Jews. The Pope, the nominal head of all Western Christians, protected the lives of Jews and the rights of Jews to practice their religion and live according to their laws. When there were local outbreaks against the Jews, these were carried out in defiance of the position of the leaders of the Church. On the other hand, when Jews were forcibly baptized, the Church generally required the reluctant new Christians to abandon Judaism and practice as Christians.

After the thirteenth century the attitude of tolerance for Jews decreased. The Jews ceased to hold an honored position in Christian theology. As some Church leaders became more sophisticated in their knowledge of Judaism they became aware that Judaism as practiced in the Middle Ages was significantly different from biblical religion, giving rise to doubts that the Jews in their midst were truly the chosen people of the Old Testament. Church and secular leaders became fearful that Jewish influence would weaken Christian faith.

Pope Innocent III decreed in 1215 that all Jews were to wear a pointed dunce cap in public, and a yellow badge on their coats. The purpose of these infamous enactments was to make Jews appear ridiculous, thus decreasing the attraction of Judaism for Christians. Where relations between Jews and Christians were good this legislation, like earlier Church legislation against the Jews, was not strictly enforced.

Suspicion against Jews increased with the Protestant Reformation. Jews were thought by many Church leaders to be a sect of Protestants rather than a distinct and protected religion. The Jews became victims in the rivalry between Catholics and Protestants.

As various suspicions arose against the Jews, Jews were called upon to defend their faith in public debate. These debates between Christian and Jewish scholars were called **disputations**. The first great disputation, the Disputation of Paris in 1240, was initiated by a convert from Judaism named Nicholas Donin. Donin denounced the Talmud to the King and Queen of France. Rabbi Yehiel of Paris was called upon to defend the Talmud. Despite the efforts of Yehiel and his fellow rabbinic scholars the Talmud was condemned. Forty cartloads of Talmudic books, confiscated from the Jews of France, were burned in a public spectacle.

Another great disputation was that between the rabbi Nahmanides (Moses ben Nahman) and the converted Jew Pablo Christiani in Barcelona, Spain in 1253. Nahmanides succeeded in answering the charges brought against the Jews, but the disputation left him exhausted and broken. He left Spain, and died shortly thereafter in Jerusalem.

The Decline of Ashkenazic Jewry

We have mentioned above how Ashkenazic Jews were displaced from their economic position in medieval society, while the Church came to find the continuing presence of Jews in the midst of Christian society less religiously relevant and more of an annoyance. From the eleventh century on, Ashkenazic Jewry underwent a gradual decline until this community virtually disappeared.

The Crusades were one of the first significant events in the decline of Ashkenazic Jewry, although they affected only some communities. In 1099, when the Crusaders conquered Jerusalem, they slaughtered all the Jews of the city. At the start of the Second Crusade (1147–1149) some Rhineland communities were entirely wiped out. The leader of this Crusade, Bernard of Clairvaux, attempted to defend the Jews from attack but the mobs, inflamed with indignity at the "infidels," could not be held back. Given the choice of baptism or death, whole communities of Jews chose to meet a martyr's death. Despite the carnage, the communities destroyed in the Crusades were restored by Jews immigrating from other cities.

Far worse for the Jews was the Black Death, a virulent outbreak of the plague which killed about a third of the population of Europe in 1348. Angry mobs, looking for a cause and a cure for this terrible epidemic, accused the Jews of poisoning wells. Many Jewish communities were destroyed.

Eventually the Jews were expelled from the lands of Western Europe. The Jews were expelled from England in 1215. In France during the fourteenth century Jews were expelled at various times from royal lands and from the lands of various nobles, with their properties confiscated at each turn, until there were virtually no Jews left in France. In the German states, also, local expulsions were combined with periodic massacres and expropriations until few Jews were left. When the Christians completed their reconquest of Spain from the Moslems in 1492 they expelled all the Jews. The Spanish Expulsion was a particularly great tragedy for the Jews; the Jewish population of Spain was large, they had nowhere else to go, and they retained the memory of the former greatness of their community. The Spanish Expulsion will be discussed in more detail in Chapter Sixteen.

The Ghetto

The final indignity placed upon the remaining Jewish communities in central Europe was the establishment of the **ghetto**. This was a walled-in area of the city in which all Jews were required to reside. Jews could exit the ghetto only for permitted economic activity. This provided a way for a city to gain economically from the Jews while limiting social relations. The first ghetto was built in Venice in 1516. The Jewish quarter of that city was located next to the "Giotto," an iron foundry; this is how the ghetto acquired its name. At first the Jews did not object to the ghetto, which afforded them some protection from mobs and from the forces of assimilation. As time went by the ghettos became more crowded. Living conditions became intolerable, but the ghettos were not allowed to expand. Jews were reduced to living in squalor, while they lost touch with the changes and developments brought about by the Renaissance, the Reformation and the beginnings of the modern age. The Jews of Europe were forced by a wall to maintain a medieval way of life long after the rest of European society had abandoned the medieval world view.

Eastward Migrations

The Jews of Ashkenaz fall out of the record of history after the dispersion of the various communities in the fourteenth century. From the sixteenth century on, historical records show a well-formed Jewish community in Poland. These Jews spoke the Jewish dialect of medieval German which came to be known as **Yiddish.** It is apparent that after their expulsion from Western Europe groups of Jews made their way eastward and reformed their communities in the East. In the fifteenth and sixteenth centuries Poland (actually the kingdom of Poland and grand duchy of Lithuania) was the largest kingdom in Europe. The Polish kingdom constituted much of what is now the Soviet Union and its satellite states. The Polish society and economy were less advanced than in Western Europe; the Poles were still in the early stages of feudalism that England, France and Germany had passed through five centuries earlier. The Polish kings welcomed Jewish settlement, since Jews could establish trade and bring prosperity to the kingdom. The Jews took much the same social and economic position in Poland that they had held in feudal Ashkenaz.

The Social Order of Ashkenazic Jewry

Each Jewish community in Christian Europe was self-ruling. The community was chartered by the king or the local nobleman. The community dealt with their ruler through elected leaders. The community handled all of its own internal affairs. They were not answerable to any other authority of the civil government or of the Jewish people. A great rabbinic scholar might have the authority to impose his religious and legal opinions on other communities, if they accept his teachings, but no one had the power to impose a ruling from outside a given community. The community was called the **kahal.** The term kahal refers to all the Jews of a given locale, and also to the internal government of that community.

The elected leaders of the kahal appointed a communal rabbi, rabbinic judges, a slaughterer for kosher meat, a synagogue caretaker, and all the other religious and communal officers. These served at the pleasure of the kahal. The Middle Ages saw the rise of a professional rabbinate. Until that time rabbis made their living in another occupation or by serving as civic officials. The medieval Jewish communities felt the need to have individuals serve full-time as rabbis. Since Talmudic law forbids one to take payment for being a scholar of Torah, the kahal paid the rabbi the income he could have made if he were not taking all of his time with his rabbinic occupation—a legal loophole which allowed for the changing needs of the times. The professional rabbinate has existed ever since among the Jewish people. The rabbi was not a pastor and worship leader, but a reservoir of knowledge of the laws and traditions of Judaism. Many Ashkenazic Jews were learned in Talmud and held the honorary title of "rabbi," but only one rabbi served as the official rabbi of the community.

The leaders of the kahal established a **bet din,** or court of three judges. These three judges were selected from the leading citizens of the town, and may or may not have included the rabbi. The bet din handled all civil suits between Jews. In some places they were also entitled to handle criminal cases and to adjudicate civil suits between Christians and Jews. In some places the civil authorities reserved the right to mete out punishments. In other places the bet din could enforce its own verdicts, even up to the death penalty.[11]

The kahal imposed taxes on its members both to pay its dues to the civil authorities and to support its own institutions. The most usual form of taxation was a luxury tax, which fell most heavily upon the rich. The kahal could impose fines upon its members as punishment or when necessary to pay the heavy dues owed to the government.

The leaders of the kahal governed through **takanot,** ordinances. Any Jew living in a kahal had, in theory, freely granted the kahal the right to establish the laws by which he or she would live. Every Jew was obligated therefore to obey the ordinances of the community leaders. A Jewish traveler could live by the rules of his own community, but if he chose to settle in a new community, he had to pledge allegiance to its ordinances.[12] Considering the level of local control, it is remarkable that Jewish communities throughout the world remained relatively unified. There were differences between the practices of communities, and these sometimes upset

---

[11]Although the Talmudic sages had great reservations about the use of the death penalty, medieval Jewish communities generally shared the view of their neighbors that this was an appropriate response to crimes against the social order.

[12]For a review of medieval Jewish theories of law and community see Irving R. Agus, *Rabbi Meir of Rothenberg,* Ktav, N.Y., 1970, Chapter IVa, "Appendix."

rabbinic authorities, but these differences would seem small to us in historical perspective.

Social Life in the Jewish Community

Social services were provided by voluntary societies. Such a society
was called a **hevra**. There would be a hevra for caring for the sick, one for
providing hospitality to travelers, one for dowering poor brides, and so on
to meet every conceivable need of the community. The most honored
society, to which the community leaders belonged, was the **hevra kaddisha,** "holy society," which took care of all funeral arrangements and
maintained the cemetery. Only in very recent times has this sacred obligation been handed over to professional funeral directors.

The kahal was responsible to see that every Jewish boy received an
education. Those who could afford it were required to pay tuition to send
their children to a private school. Those who could not afford it sent their
sons to the free school maintained by the kahal. A larger community might
be graced with a yeshiva, an academy of Talmudic learning. A great
teacher might attract students from all over Ashkenaz to study at his
yeshiva. Such great yeshivot arose under Rashi (Rabbi Solomon Yitzhaki)
(1040–1105) in Troyes in Northern France and in Rothenberg in Germany
under Rabbi Meir ben Baruch (1220–1293).

Before the imposition of the ghetto, Jews lived and dressed much like
their neighbors. They enjoyed the same entertainments, including jousting
and dancing. There were great public entertainments at weddings and on
festivals, particularly on the festival of Purim. Cards became very popular
after their introduction in Europe, and many community ordinances attempted to limit card-playing. The game of chess was very popular and
was considered more respectable than cards. Some rabbis were renowned
as great chess players. Jews were subject to the same whims of fashion as
their neighbors, and there are many community ordinances which attempt
to limit the ostentation of fashionable clothes.

Jewish domestic life was characterized by tranquility and good relations between husband and wife, parents and children. Although divorce
was permitted, it was rare. Jewish men abhorred the practice of wife-
beating. Modesty and chastity were expected of both sexes. The legal
rights of women were extended by Rabbi Gershom (960–1028). In a famous takanah (ordinance) he forbade bigamy, which seems not to have
been practiced anyway, and he ruled that a woman could not be divorced
without her consent.

Rashi

Rabbi Solomon ben Isaac (1040–1105), better known by the acronym of Rashi, was the greatest rabbi and teacher of Ashkenazi Jewry. As a young man he studied in the most renowned Talmudic academies of his time, in Mainz and Worms. He founded his own yeshiva when he returned to his home town of Troyes in the Champagne district of France. Rashi's academy superseded those of his teachers. Rashi established a method for the study of Torah which became standard for medieval Jewry and which strongly influences Jewish study of sacred texts to this very day. After his death, Rashi's students and descendants remained the leading rabbis of Ashkenaz for the next few generations. Rashi's disciples are known as the Tosafists—literally, those who add on—since they added to the teachings established by Rashi.

Rashi spread his influence far and wide through the commentaries which he wrote to the Tanak and the Talmud. In his Torah commentary Rashi distinguished the plain meaning of the text from the midrashic explanations of the rabbinic era. His goal was always to identify and explain the plain sense of the text. Rashi also gave many quotations from rabbinic-period midrash in his commentary, but he was careful to distinguish the midrash from the "peshat," the literal meaning. Rashi's commentary assumes the presumptions of Jewish devotion and piety, that the whole Torah was given to Moses on Mount Sinai and that the main purpose of the Torah is to give the mitzvot to Israel so that they may observe them. Rashi's commentary to the Torah and other biblical books became enormously popular. In a short time it became the basis for all further Jewish commentary on Scripture, and more than two hundred super-commentaries on Rashi's commentary have been published. In later times Jewish schoolchildren learned Scripture in conjunction with Rashi's commentary, so that Rashi's explanations became for Jews the essential meaning of Scripture itself.

Rashi's commentary on the Talmud attempts to elucidate the many difficulties and contradictions to be found in the text of the Talmud. Rashi's commentary makes the Talmud a more unified and vivid document than it is in itself. Rashi's primary purpose was to ease the task of studying and understanding the Talmud, not to decide Jewish law. Still, in many places Rashi elucidates the legal issues in the Talmud text, and Rashi was recognized by other rabbis as an important legist. In his commentary to the Talmud Rashi reflects the world view and the legal issues of his own day. In this way Rashi's commentary took a sacred text which had been composed in late antiquity in the Middle East and made it a relevant document for medieval Jews in Europe. Since the invention of the printing press, virtually every edition of the Talmud has been composed of three major columns. The text of the Talmud is in the center column, Rashi's commentary is on the inside of the page, and the commentary of the Tosafists is on the outside of the page. Virtually every Jewish printing of the Bible in Hebrew has also included Rashi's commentary. The Jewish teachings of Ashkenazic Jewry have been incorporated into the sacred texts through the commentaries of their greatest representative, Rashi.

16

The Golden Age of Spain and Medieval Jewish Philosophy

Spain in the Middle Ages

Early in the Middle Ages the tribe of the Visigoths invaded Spain and became the rulers of the nation. The Visigoths adopted the Roman Catholic faith. In the eighth century the Moslems invaded Spain and took over the whole of the country except for the mountainous regions of the North, which remained in Christian hands. For a period of about two centuries the Moslem caliph of Cordova was the ruler of all of the Iberian peninsula. In the eleventh century the caliphate broke up into a number of petty kingdoms. The Christians began the gradual process of reconquering Spain, pushing down from the North. The Christian part of Spain was also made up of petty kingdoms. This condition continued until 1492. King Ferdinand and Queen Isabella united all of Iberia except for Portugal under their rulership. In 1492 they conquered Granada, the last Moslem kingdom in Spain.

The division of Spain into different kingdoms with different religions established ideal conditions for Jews to flourish. Since all parts of Spain contained numerous Moslems and Christians, religious tolerance was necessary for successful rulership, whether the rulers were Moslem or Christian. The Jews were valued as a numerically significant minority who could bring prosperity and strength to a kingdom. If Christian or Moslem religious fanaticism took hold in one kingdom it was easy for the Jews of that region to move to another region of Spain where the rulers practiced toleration. When Christians and Moslems were at odds, it was to the benefit of either side to win the loyalty of the Jews. In many kingdoms of Spain the Jews enjoyed at various times a level of toleration not to be matched until the advent of the modern democratic state. It was not so unusual in Spain that a Christian, a Moslem and a Jew could enjoy each other's company while discussing the differences and similarities in their religions; this was an unusual climate of religious toleration and understanding even by modern standards.

The Culture of Moslem Spain

Spain reached the highest level of material prosperity and intellectual culture anywhere in the medieval world. The rulers and the intellectual class in Moslem Spain preserved and studied the scholarly teachings of antiquity which had been lost and forgotten in the Christian world. The works of Plato and Aristotle, the sciences, philosophy, grammar and rhetoric—these were all studied in Moslem Spain. In ancient times the rabbis had resisted the study of Greek writings. They considered Greek philosophy to be part of the forbidden pagan culture which threatened to engulf Judaism. Now, in Spain, surrounded by fellow monotheists who were studying the wisdom of ancient Greece, the Jews engaged in the study of philosophy. They reinterpreted Judaism according to the categories of Greek thought. This led to one of the great intellectual revolutions in Judaism.

The Jews of Spain enjoyed economic prosperity. They were numerically great, nearly a million strong. They had a degree of respect and power in the kingdoms where they lived. The Jews were free to engage in all walks of economic and social life. They were part of the most advanced, scientifically oriented culture in the world. This era is called by Jewish historians the Golden Age in Spain.

Not all Sephardic Jews participated equally in the benefits of the Golden Age. The Jews of Spain were not compressed into one social class like the Ashkenazi Jews. Spanish society was hierarchical, with a small, powerful and highly educated upper class and a large mass of common people. Philosophical studies and interfaith toleration were most common in the upper classes of society. The masses lived within the cultural confines of their religious traditions.

The Reconquest, the Translators, and the Expulsion

The Christians reconquered Spain in gradual stages over a period of centuries. The great city of Toledo was conquered by the Christians in 1085. After the capture of Toledo new rulers arose in Moslem Spain who were less tolerant of Jews. Fortunately for the Jews, the Christian rulers at that time welcomed Jewish settlement in their lands. The Christian rulers were anxious to acquire the philosophy and science which had been developed in Moslem Spain. The best way for them to do this was to fill their courts with Jews who knew the traditions of Greek learning, and who had the knowledge of languages to translate these works from Arabic or Hebrew into Latin. This era is known in Spain as the "Era of the Translators." Sephardic Jews were directly responsible for the beginnings of the Renaissance in Christian Europe due to their work in bringing the wisdom of antiquity to the attention of the Christian rulers of Spain. Alphonse the Wise, king of Castile (1221–1284), was a great patron of learning who sponsored many Jewish scholars.

As the Moslems lost strength in Spain the Christians lost their attitude of toleration. In 1391 there was an outbreak of anti-Jewish rioting throughout Spain. Many Spanish Jews accepted baptism to avoid bodily harm. These "conversos" or New Christians[1] continued to practice Judaism fairly openly, although nominally they were now Christians. They married only among themselves or among Jewish relatives who underwent an insincere conversion of their own for the sake of the marriage. For the next century these New Christians made up a large element in the Jewish population of Spain. In a culture where secular knowledge and material prosperity were more important than religious tradition, it seemed no great problem to be somewhat Christian and somewhat Jewish.

In 1492 King Ferdinand and Queen Isabella conquered Granada, the last Moslem kingdom in Spain. The religious fervor of Spanish Christians, which had been growing for some time, was renewed with the victory. The Spanish determined that the New Christians would henceforth be required to take their religion seriously. In order to remove the major detriment to their religious convictions, the king and queen issued an edict of expulsion against the Jews. The Jews of Spain were greatly devoted to their country and the life they lived in it; they were not so willing to go as the Ashkenazi Jews had been. Besides, the Jews were still a numerous and important group in Spain. They were proud of their heritage. Many more Jews

---

[1] Their fellow Jews called them **Marranos,** an uncomplimentary term, on account of their reluctance to stand fast for their faith.

underwent conversion rather than leave Spain. Many Jews went over to Portugal. These received a fate worse than in Spain. In 1496 an edict of expulsion was decreed against the Jews of Portugal. Before they could depart the country, the entire Jewish population was forcibly dragged to the baptismal font in 1497. They were henceforth required by their king and the Church to live as Christians, although these Jews of Portugal were precisely those who were most determined to remain true to Judaism.

Those Jews who attempted to leave Spain found it difficult to get out. Very few ships were willing to take them, and very few countries were willing to receive them. Those who had been baptized were watched closely. They were arrested for attempting to return to Judaism if they were caught trying to leave the country. Eventually some Spanish Jews escaped to the growing Turkish empire, some to the cities of Italy which were willing to accept them, and some to Holland. Amsterdam became the largest center of Spanish and Portuguese Jews. Having fought their own battle for Protestantism and for freedom from Spanish rule, the Dutch welcomed the Jews. Some Spanish Jews moved to France or England, where they quietly and gradually reverted to Jewish practices. Many of Columbus' crew were Jews looking for a new place to settle. There is strong evidence that Columbus himself was a secret Spanish Jew who had removed to Italy in order to revert to Judaism.

Most Spanish and Portuguese Jews had no choice but to remain in Iberia. They consoled themselves that they could continue to practice Judaism in their homes. This hope was shattered when the Holy Inquisition came to Spain. The Inquisition had been established to root out heresy in Catholic countries, largely in response to the Protestant revolution. In Spain, the Inquisition managed to take control of the country. They arrested anyone suspected of the secret practice of Judaism. Those arrested were tortured into confession, after which their possessions became the property of the Office of the Inquisition. Those who returned to Judaism after confession were burned at the stake. Over the course of centuries the Inquisition rooted out the secret Jews from Spain and Portugal. In the process they destroyed the prosperity and world power which Spain had formerly enjoyed.

The Spanish Expulsion was viewed by those who experienced it, and by later Jewish historians, as one of the greatest tragedies in Jewish history. It ranks with the Roman wars of antiquity and with the Chmielnicki massacres and the Nazi Holocaust of later times. Even so, the ferment caused by the expulsion had some positive results. It led to the return of Jews to Western Europe and the entry of Jews into the New World. The Spanish Jews brought with them such tremendous talents and such great traditions of scientific knowledge that they were allowed into countries which formerly did not welcome Jews. This talented group of people brought forth many advances which helped to usher in the modern age. Among the exiles from Spain was Barukh (Benedict) Spinoza, the father of modern philosophy. There were many doctors and scientists, political and economic leaders, who created important advances in their fields. The Spanish Expulsion also led to new currents in Jewish thought and practice, particularly in the area of religious mysticism, as we shall see.

Statesmen

The Jewish people had been relatively powerless for centuries, but some Spanish Jews attained positions of great political influence. Hasdai ibn Shaprut (915–970) was personal physician to the caliph. He was a member of the inner circle of advisors in the court. Samuel ibn Nagdela (993–1055) was vizier, or prime minister, of the kingdom of Granada. He ran the country and led its armies in battle. He was highly successful as a general and as an administrator, bringing wealth, power and glory to his nation. The Jews of Spain called him Samuel the Prince and acknowledged him as their leader.

Hasdai and Samuel and other powerful Jews who came after them followed the pattern of other Spanish nobles in being patrons of learning. They supported Jewish scholars who applied the categories of Greek and Arabic learning to Jewish topics. They supported the development of secular and religious poetry in the Hebrew language and the study of Hebrew grammar, as well as traditional Talmud studies. These leaders gave a great boost to Jewish scholarship in Spain, and to the development of Hebrew letters. Medieval Spain produced the only great body of Jewish secular literature until the modern age.

Isaac Abravanel (1437–1508) was the greatest among the Spanish Jews at the time of the exile. In his lifetime he served as a high minister to five kings in Portugal, Spain and Naples, Italy. He convinced Ferdinand and Isabella to send Columbus on his voyage. The king and queen pleaded with Abravanel to remain in Spain as their valued minister of finance. When he was unable to convince them to rescind the Edict of Expulsion, Abravanel threw in his lot with his fellow Jews and joined the exile.

Abravanel had a tremendously broad education. He was a scholar in the Bible and the Talmud. He knew the works of the great Jewish philosophers of the Golden Age, as well as the important Moslem philosophers and Christian theologians. He was well acquainted with the sciences. In his commentaries to the Torah and other scriptural books he displayed his broad knowledge and the wisdom he had acquired through his lifetime of involvement in affairs of state.

In later life Abravanel became disgusted with political affairs, which had caused such damage to his people. He wrote a commentary on Genesis to complete his writings on the Torah. He came to believe that God would soon send the messiah to redeem his people from the misery of the exile. Abravanel's last works were essays attempting to prove that the time of the Messiah was near.

Dona Gracia Nasi was a new Christian who remained devoted to Judaism. As a young widow she turned an inheritance into a huge fortune. She managed to escape from Spain without losing her fortune. She resettled in Constantinople, which had recently been conquered by the rising Turkish empire. She used her wealth and power to support Jewish learning and to assist other Spanish exiles. Her son Joseph, duke of Naxos, was in the inner circle of advisors to the Turkish pasha. Joseph used his immense power to punish the Spanish for their treatment of the Jews and to assist his co-religionists in Italy and in the Turkish empire.

Jewish Philosophy

The curriculum of the philosopher included all the categories of knowledge which were known at the time. In the Middle Ages it was believed that there was only so much knowledge in the world and a person could acquire all of it, as broadly if not as perfectly as God's own knowledge of everything. The student began with the study of grammar and mathematics. From grammar the student progressed to literary analysis. From mathematics the student progressed to the natural sciences, including astronomy, zoology, and physics. The student also learned political science and ethics, the science of proper human relations. The advanced student went on to metaphysics, the study of being itself and the causes of being and becoming all the way to the ultimate cause in God.

The religious philosopher learned all of these subjects as they had been taught by the ancient philosophers and their medieval interpreters. There were two main schools of thought, Aristotelianism and neo-Platonism. The Aristotelians followed the teachings of Aristotle. The neo-Platonists followed the teachings of Plato as they had been interpreted by Plotinus. The Aristotelians were more scientific and purely rational, while the neo-Platonists were more spiritually oriented. There were many differences between the two schools of thought, but they had in common the philosopher's method of learning, advancing logically from premises to conclusions.

The religious philosopher went on to apply the learning of the ancient Greeks to the interpretation of his own religion and the proof of its doctrines. The Jewish philosophers applied the study of grammar to a linguistic analysis of the Bible. They sought a rational basis for the belief system of Judaism. They interpreted Jewish law as a way of promoting ethical action, correct beliefs, and a well-ordered society.

The religious philosopher had a twofold task. The first task was to understand reality as it is, using the tools of human reason. The second task was to show that the divinely revealed doctrines of religion are in harmony with rationally discovered truths. The religious philosopher had to defend the doctrines of his religion against those beliefs of the Greeks which were not in accord with his religion, and also against the truth claims of the philosophers of other religions.

The Conflict of Philosophy and Religion

It was no easy matter to harmonize philosophy with the traditional teachings of Judaism. The conclusions about reality which came from philosophy often contradicted or cast doubt on the teachings of the Bible and rabbinic doctrines. The popularity of philosophy weakened and endangered traditional faith based on belief that the Torah is a divinely revealed truth which is above human questioning.

The Greek philosophers taught that God is one. A Jew would certainly agree with this, but the God of the philosophers was quite different from the God of the Bible. Aristotle defined God as the "unmoved mover," the cause without effect, who constantly and endlessly contemplates his own perfect nature. Such a God does not cause supernatural miracles nor display concern for human affairs, as God is depicted in the Hebrew Scriptures and the Talmud. Aristotle claimed that the physical universe was eternal and uncreated, a challenge to the belief of Jews that God's power and rule over the universe derives from God's action as Creator. The religious philosopher had to demonstrate rationally that God could create the universe in time and show providential care for humankind.

The ancient philosophers believed that a human being achieved eternity through knowledge. The eternal soul of a person consists of the eternal truths which that person has learned in his lifetime. One who has not studied philosophy has no eternity; there is nothing left after his body dies and the breath of life dissipates. Judaism taught that eternal afterlife is granted to those who are good and denied to those who do evil. Does God reward knowledge, or obedience to the commandments? Is faith in eternal reward for goodness only a "useful myth," like the myth in Plato's *Republic*, to teach proper behavior to the uneducated?

In addition to an afterlife in a spiritual heaven, Jews also looked forward to a return to bodily life at the time of the Messiah. The doctrine of the Messiah and the doctrine of bodily resurrection are non-rational beliefs, not subject to analysis. The pure rationalist may have difficulty accepting these doctrines at face value.

Jewish, Christian and Moslem philosophers were all acutely aware of these conflicts between philosophy and religion. They attempted to keep their teachings out of the hands of the masses for fear that the masses would either abandon religion or revolt at the heresy and impiety of the philosophers. The philosophers desired for their own sake and the sake of the students of philosophy to demonstrate as much as possible that philosophy was not contrary to religion. When they perceived contradictions they attempted to bend or reinterpret traditional doctrines to bring them more in line with the teachings of philosophy.

Saadia Gaon (892–942)

Saadia was one of the last of the great gaonim, the heads of the academies in Babylon. In the time of Saadia there was a great schism among the Jews. The sect of Karaites arose in Babylon and spread to other centers of Jewish population. The Karaites rejected the Talmud and the entire rabbinic tradition. They attempted to live literally by the five books of the written Torah. The Karaites used philosophy to support their contention that rabbinic doctrines were without basis.

Saadia arose to defend the Talmud. Besides being a great Talmudic scholar, Saadia was expertly trained in the teachings of Arab philosophy in his time. The major school of Arabic philosophy was the Kalam. The Kalamists remained closer to pious religious notions than did the later schools of Aristotelians and neo-Platonists. The Kalamists taught that nature remained constant not because of laws of cause and effect in nature, but because God willed it to be so. Still, despite their face of piety, the Kalamists subjected religious doctrines to the test of reason.

Saadia wrote a book, *The Book of Doctrines and Beliefs*. Saadia showed that the basic doctrines of Judaism were consistent with human reason. Saadia discussed the subjects of Creation, God's unity, divine law, the human mind and human free will, reward and punishment, afterlife and the Messiah.

Karaism continued to exist right up until modern times, but Saadia broke the back of the movement with his defense of rabbinic Judaism. The Karaites eventually faded into obscurity. In the process of defending the Talmud, Saadia introduced Greek-Arabic philosophy into the realm of Jewish studies.

Judah Halevi (c. 1080–1140)

Judah Halevi is known as "the sweet singer of Zion." He is one of the greatest poets ever in the Hebrew language. His famous poems include odes of longing for a return to Zion. In later life Judah Halevi left Spain for the arduous journey to Palestine. According to legend he was struck dead by an Arab horseman as he stood at the gates of Jerusalem, reciting his poetry. The legend is probably not true, but it is a fitting tale for the life of a great poet.

Judah Halevi was born in Toledo, the cultural capital of Spain. The great event in his lifetime was the capture of Toledo by the Christians in 1085. In the ensuing era of adjustments throughout Spain there was a revival of religious piety, and philosophy fell into temporary disfavor. Judah Halevi's own philosophy reflects this attitude.

Like many great Jewish scholars of Spain, Judah Halevi made his living as a physician. Besides studying medicine and philosophy, he studied Talmud in the greatest academies of his time, in southern Spain. He was acknowledged as the greatest scholar of his age; he lived an aristocratic life. Judah Halevi regretted the misfortunes of the majority of his Jewish brethren who did not have the advantages that he had and who suffered in the conflict between Moslems and Christians. He also regretted the wealth and splendor of Spain which he believed were preventing the Jews from fulfilling the divine command to return to Zion. A return to the Land of Israel was politically impossible in those times, but with his poet's heart Judah Halevi imagined that if only the Jews would all return to their ancient homeland immediately, their troubles would cease and God's promises to Israel would be fulfilled.

In Judah Halevi's time the Jews of Spain were heartened to hear that, in a world divided between Christians and Moslems, there was a kingdom that had chosen to become Jewish. This was the kingdom of the Kazars, on the Caspian Sea. News of this distant land, where Jews lived a sovereign existence, filled the Jews of Spain with hope and pride. Judah Halevi wrote his book of Jewish philosophy, the *Kuzari*, as an imaginary dialogue between the king of the Kazars and the rabbi who trained him in Jewish teachings. The dialogue form is an effective tool for teaching a point of view; the author has the questioner raise whatever doubts he wishes to raise and has the respondent give an answer which arouses the sympathy and the agreement of the questioner.

In the opening to the *Kuzari*, the king of the Kazars decides to worship the one God. In a dream-vision he is told that his intentions are good but his practices are not in accordance with God's will. The Kuzari, the king of the Kazars, invites to his court a philosopher, a Christian, a Moslem and a Jew. The *Kuzari* rejects the philosopher because all philosophers disagree with one another, a sure sign that human reason is inadequate to determine the true nature of God. After hearing from the representatives of the three monotheistic religions, the *Kuzari* chooses to convert to Judaism. In the rest of the book, the *Kuzari* learns Judaism from the rabbi who has trained him for conversion. The Judaism espoused by the rabbi demonstrates the Jewish philosophy of Judah Halevi.

Judah Halevi argues that the Jews have something more accurate than human reason to teach metaphysical truths; the Jews have an unquestioned historical tradition which goes back to the revelation of the Torah at Mount Sinai. Since no one can question the truth of this revelation, which was seen by a multitude and recorded in history, everything said in the Torah must be true. Judah Halevi then endeavors to show that what the Torah teaches is an internally consistent philosophy. The philosophy of Judah Halevi is loosely identified with neo-Platonism, but is in many ways his own unique system of thought.

The philosophers taught that a human being has three types of soul—a vegetative soul which gives life, an animate soul which gives powers of locomotion, and a rational soul which gives the power of decision. The rational soul is unique to humans, and is the part of the person that survives death. The rational soul exists only in potential; for it to be actualized, a person must acquire reason through the study of philosophy. The rational soul acquires eternity through its connection to the Active Intellect, the highest intelligence or "angel" under God. The Active Intellect runs the world, which is beneath God's notice, much as a vizier handles the daily concerns of a kingdom while the king concerns himself with royal matters.

Judah Halevi taught that there is a higher spiritual entity below God, the Divine Influence. As the Active Intellect relates and responds to the rational soul, the Divine Influence relates and responds to the performance of mitzvot, divine commandments. Every Jew is born with an additional level of soul which corresponds to the Divine Influence. As a Jew performs mitzvot he actualizes this potential soul and rises to a higher level of being. A Jew actualizes this soul more fully by using the Hebrew language, and even more by living in the Land of Israel. When the majority of the Jews live in the Land of Israel, the Divine Influence is received with sufficient strength to create prophecy. Prophecy will thus be renewed, and the Jews will rise to their full glory in this world, when they return to their own land, their own language, and their own divinely commanded way of life.

In the latter half of his book, Judah Halevi describes the religious life in terms which are at once philosophical and poetic. His description of Jewish religious life as the pinnacle of human living is the greatest strength of his book. The *Kuzari* was translated from Arabic into Hebrew soon after its composition. For obvious reasons, it became the most popular of all works of Jewish philosophy. It is widely read even today.

Judah Halevi's doctrine of Jewish superiority, inherent in his idea of a special Jewish soul, is contradictory to the biblical and rabbinic teaching of the unity of humankind. It is not acceptable from the perspective of pure ethics. It is understandable, though, as a source of pride for people who were being crushed between two numerous and powerful world religions. Judah Halevi's philosophy made Jews proud of their people and their religious way of life.

Moses Maimonides (1135–1204)
(Rabbi Moses ben Maimon, also called the Rambam)

Moses Maimonides was the greatest of all the Jewish philosophers of the Middle Ages, and the only one to receive world recognition as one of the great philosophers in history. His great philosophical work was the *Moreh Nevuchim,* the *Guide for the Perplexed.* In this work Maimonides harmonized the teachings of Aristotelian philosophy, the purest rationalism, with the teachings of Judaism. In the process, Maimonides transformed the teachings and ideas of Judaism for all time. The greatness of his influence is recognized in the saying which arose soon after his death, "From Moses until Moses there was no one like Moses." Maimonides was like Moses in more than name; he brought as it were a whole new Torah into the world with his philosophical interpretation of Judaism.

In addition to his work in philosophy Maimonides was one of the greatest Torah scholars of all time. He wrote a commentary on the Mishnah and an enumeration of the 613 mitzvot. He wrote a code of Jewish law, the first of the great Sephardic law codes. He called his law code the *Mishneh Torah,* the "Second Torah." Although it is a listing of laws, the Mishneh Torah also contains many of Maimonides' philosophical ideas, presented in the form of required and forbidden beliefs. The Mishneh Torah divides all of Jewish law into fourteen chapters, putting into Jewish law an organizational pattern which does not exist in the Talmud. Maimonides wrote the Moreh Nevuchim in Arabic, but he wrote the Mishneh Torah in a clear and simple Hebrew. This law code is one of the greatest examples in history of Hebrew literary style and pure, clear language. Maimonides intended that a Jew would no longer have to struggle with the Talmud or rely on the unreliable opinion of his local rabbi; he could look into the Mishneh Torah and find the answer to every question of religion.

Maimonides was born in Cordova. He received an education in Torah, philosophy and the medical profession. In addition to his other accomplishments he was a leading medical doctor and researcher. The doctor's oath he composed is used today by some medical schools instead of the Hippocratic oath.

When Maimonides was a young man, Cordova was taken over by a fanatical Moslem sect from Morocco. Maimonides and his family converted to Islam to save their lives and then escaped to North Africa, where they reverted to Judaism. Maimonides settled in Egypt, where he was court physician to the great Mameluke ruler Saladin. He lived the rest of his life in Egypt. He achieved great fame in his lifetime, and was acknowledged as the leader of all the Jews in Islamic lands. Although he attracted criticism for his radical ideas, he remained so popular in life and death that many Sephardic Jewish communities still hold an annual festival in his honor.

The Philosophy of Maimonides

Maimonides taught that human reason, properly applied, leads to knowledge of the truth as surely as does divine revelation. Since truth is one, the teachings of the Torah and the teachings of philosophy cannot be in contradiction to one another. When the Torah appears to contradict the findings of science and reason, we must interpret the Torah allegorically rather than literally in order to remove the contradiction.

Let us take, for example, the story of the seven days of Creation. Aristotle had recognized that time is a measure of motion. The time period we call a "day" is a measure of the (apparent) motion of the sun around the earth. Since the sun was not created until the fourth day, it follows that the term "day" cannot be understood literally, at least in reference to the first three "days" of Creation. Now that we have established that the story of Creation uses allegorical language, we are free to interpret the story symbolically. Thanks to the attitude of Maimonides, most Jews in the modern age had no difficulty accepting Darwin's theory of evolution. They have been able to interpret the story of Creation so that it does not necessarily contradict the findings of modern science. Maimonides had a more difficult task in his time, since Aristotle had taught that the universe was eternal and uncreated. Maimonides was unable to disprove Aristotle's arguments for an uncreated universe through logic. In this case he concluded that since there are strong rational arguments both for and against a created universe, we must have faith in the Torah.[2]

---

[2]The weakness of his arguments suggests that perhaps Maimonides agreed with Aristotle, but was reluctant to say so in writing.

Maimonides taught that when the Torah states that God created man in his image, the meaning is not in a physical image but in a moral image—with a free will, capable of choosing between right and wrong, good and evil. God has no physical being. The descriptive terms in the Torah which describe God in terms of human physique must be understood as metaphors. When we say that God sees we do not mean that God has eyes, but that God knows all. When the Torah speaks of God's arm, the meaning is that God is infinitely powerful. After Maimonides, most Jews ceased to imagine God as in Michelangelo's famous painting in the Sistine Chapel. Jews came to take for granted that God has no shape or form.

Maimonides said that God is so infinite and transcendent, so above human comprehension, that there is nothing we can say about God that is accurate. We can only say what God is not. For example, we can say accurately that God is not many. If we say in the positive that God is one we are only partially right; God's uniqueness is unlike the uniqueness of anything else of which we have knowledge, that we may describe as being "one." All terms which describe God are metaphors, describing not so much God as he is but rather God as we experience him.

Aristotle taught that God is unaware of the particulars of worldly events; God is above such knowledge. God eternally contemplates his own being, which contains all eternal truths. Maimonides did not go this far, but in his philosophy he did describe a God who is far removed from the intimate God of personal relationships depicted in the Torah. Maimonides taught that God is not much involved in the daily events of human life.

In his discussion of "providence," God's oversight of the universe, Maimonides classifies the disasters that might befall a person into four categories. Some bad things happen because of the harm which people do to themselves; they do not eat properly, they live riotously, and then they complain of God's injustice if their health fails them. Some bad things happen because of the evil things which people do to each other. God has granted humankind complete free will. We can be as good as we wish or as evil as we wish, and God does not intervene if we have chosen to be evil and do harm to the innocent. Some bad things happen because of our nature. For example: we are mortal, therefore we die. Nobody would think it evil for an ant to suffer the fate of ants or for a tiger to suffer the fate of tigers, and we should not think it evil if the accidents which humans are prone to by nature should befall us. The last class of events are those which occur because of a divine judgment, to punish evildoers for their wickedness. Such divine intervention is much more rare than the other three classes of events, says Maimonides, and we may suspect that by "rare" Maimonides implies that it never actually happens that God acts in this way.

To Maimonides, God's providence is revealed in the unchanging laws of nature. In fact, says Maimonides, the verse in the Psalms which says that one must "know the Lord in all his ways" is a commandment to study science, since the ordering of nature is the work of God. God is known through natural, and not supernatural, events. In a similar vein, Maimonides says that one who is sick must pray for health, but if he does not also go to a doctor, then he is a heretic. God has provided us with healing by giving humans the ability to acquire medical knowledge, and we show our faith in God by letting the doctor apply his abilities.

One may well wonder what benefit there is in observing the commandments of the Torah, if God acts as Maimonides says. The reward for observance is only indirect in Maimonides' teaching. The commandments cause one to live a temperate life which then allows one the opportunity for study and contemplation. The ultimate reward is reserved for those who acquire knowledge of true things. The human soul which they actualize for themselves by acquiring knowledge joins with God's knowledge after death, existing into eternity. This is not a pleasing or emotionally satisfying concept of the afterlife, but Maimonides has little patience for those who want pleasure or emotional satisfaction rather than knowledge.

Maimonides looked down on the common folk with their simple piety and their material view of reward and punishment. In his life he was so great that none would dare criticize him, but after his death his work was criticized on account of his contempt for the unlearned and on account of his suspected heresies. When the Ibn Tibbon family of translators, living in Spain, translated the *Guide for the Perplexed* into Hebrew, Ashkenazic Jews were able to read this work. Living in the pious society of medieval Christendom, the Ashkenazic rabbis were greatly offended by the doubts which Maimonides cast on traditional doctrines, especially the doctrine of bodily resurrection. A great controversy broke out in France, the Maimonidean–anti-Maimonidean controversy. By request, the king of France burned Maimonides' books. The controversy only ended when the king went on to burn all Jewish books, and the Jews had to close ranks to defend themselves.

In the "Introduction" to the *Guide*, Maimonides wrote that he was writing this book for the benefit of those students who had been drawn away from Judaism by their love of philosophy. His intent was to show them that Judaism and rational philosophy were not contradictory, but harmonious with one another. Maimonides wrote that none should read this book until they were well-versed in all the lower disciplines of learning, and in traditional Jewish lore, lest they misunderstand and be led into heresy or falsehood.

Maimonides intentionally wrote in vague language so that none but a fellow philosopher would understand what he was saying. One not trained in philosophy would read the *Guide* in such a way that he would find in it only a verification of his accepted religious doctrines. To this day there are those who think that Maimonides wrote his book to turn philosophers back to Jewish piety, and others who believe that Maimonides was attempting to turn pious Jews into philosophers. Whatever his intent, there is no doubt that after Maimonides, Jewish views of God, humanity and the world were forever transformed by concepts drawn from rational philosophy.

The scientific ideas of Aristotle upon which Maimonides depended have long since been disproved and replaced by modern science. And yet, even today the work of Maimonides provides inspiration for those seeking a bridge between secular knowledge and religious doctrines. Maimonides was a major source for the work of Thomas Aquinas, who brought Aristotelian philosophy to the medieval Christian world. In the eighteenth and nineteenth centuries, when modern science and philosophy ushered in the age of secularism in Europe, the study of Maimonides' *Guide* induced many a young Talmud student to go out into the world in search of this modern knowledge.

17

Mysticism

Mysticism

At the same time that rational philosophy was flourishing among the Jews of Spain, another school of religious thought was quietly developing. Schools of mystics were combining neo-Platonic philosophy with elements of Jewish tradition and their own original thoughts. The result was the **Kabbalah,** a mystical doctrine that was to become one of the dominant modes in Jewish religious thought from the time of the Spanish exile until the dawn of the modern era.

Mysticism can be defined as the science of the metaphysical world. The natural scientist attempts to define with mathematical precision the things of the natural world, their forms and their relationships. The mystic attempts to understand with great precision the things of the supernatural world and their relationships. The mystic attempts to define the various orders of the heavens—the spiritual world—and the angels, the creatures which inhabit the spiritual realm. The mystic attempts to describe the anatomy of the being of God.

We may further define mysticism as the attempt of the individual person to come into intimate contact with God. The mystic studies the supernatural realms so that he may learn how to rise through those realms in order to directly encounter God. The mystic then descends back into the material world, bringing with him the understanding that he has gained in his meeting with God.

The religious experience of the mystic is necessarily solitary and individualistic. The mystic must travel alone into and again out of the spiritual realm. Nevertheless, mysticism tends to arise among circles of practitioners who are deeply entrenched in organized religion. The spiritual journey of the mystic is given meaning as it is explained by, and helps to explain, the major topics and concerns of a given religion.

Rabbinic Mysticism

We generally think of the sages of the Talmudic period as legalists who expressed their religious convictions in the study and development of religious law, but many of the greatest lawyers were also practicing mystics. We do not know all the details of rabbinic mysticism, but we know that there were two general areas of mystical speculation. The "ma'asey bereshit," or "work of creation," was the mystical study of the spiritual state of the created universe in relationship to its Creator. The "ma'asey merkavah," or "work of the chariot," was the mystical study of the nature of the various heavens and the throne of God which sits in the highest heaven. Numerous fragmentary texts of merkavah mysticism have come down to us. They include elaborate descriptions of the various types of angels who reside in each heaven, and the tasks which they perform in the divine service. Merkavah mysticism was based on the text of the biblical book of Ezekiel, Chapter 1, in which the prophet describes his vision of the divine throne. Some merkavah texts describe the "ascent of Moses" into the heavens to receive the Torah. This is in marked contrast to the concept in the written Torah, which emphasizes that Moses did not ascend into the heavens but stayed on the mountain top, while God bent the heavens earthward to meet with Moses. The merkavah mystics clearly were allowing certain concepts which were considered by the biblical writers to be dangerous to monotheistic religion. In rabbinic times Judaism was no longer in danger of being engulfed by other religions. There was no fear that Jews would deify Moses or worship angels. Therefore, this form of speculation was now permitted to the learned. A rich and specific angelology developed. Metatron is prince of the angels, the vizier in the heavenly court. The archangel Gabriel is the protecting angel of the Jewish people. Each of the other nations had their own protecting angels, which they mistook for gods and worshiped. Numerous other angels were named and assigned to various roles in the heavenly bureaucracy.

Mystical speculation was thought to be dangerous to those who were not masters of the traditional, non-mystical aspects of Jewish lore. A teacher was not permitted to teach mysticism in public, as halakha and midrash were taught. He could teach only a single disciple at a time, in secret, and only if he were convinced that the disciple was able to withstand the power of mysticism. This secrecy, and the reluctance to write down dangerous and nearly heretical speculations, is one reason that our knowledge of rabbinic mysticism is limited.

A story is told in the Talmud: "There were four who walked in the garden. (One) entered and died. (One) entered and went insane. (One) cut off the young shoots.[1] Only Rabbi Akiva entered in peace and returned in peace." The most common interpretation of this story is that it refers to the practice of rabbinic mysticism, and its attendant dangers. One who was not sufficiently grounded in the practice of Judaism and who was not sufficiently mature and stable could die, go insane, or lose his faith as a result of engaging in mysticism. The rule eventually developed that before one could begin the study of mysticism he had to be at least forty years old, married, and learned and well-practiced in the halakha.

Kabbalah and the Zohar

A new form of mysticism arose among the Jews of medieval Spain. This school of mysticism was called the Kabbalah, which means "received tradition." This name represents either extreme modesty or deliberate misdirection, for the Kabbalah was not at all traditional. It represented a radically new interpretation of Judaism. The practitioners of Kabbalah continued in all outward forms as traditional Jews, but their sense of what they were doing and why they were doing it was drastically different from that of previous practitioners of rabbinical Judaism.

The Kabbalah originated in the twelfth century in Provence and Catalonia, in Southern France and Northern Spain. The Catalonian city of Gerona was an important center for the early Kabbalists. As with earlier schools of Jewish mysticism, and mystical movements in general, Kabbalism was an elitist enterprise. It was limited to small circles of initiates who learned from one another. The earliest Kabbalists produced books, but these did not have a wide circulation and would not have meant much to those not initiated into Kabbalistic doctrines.

Around the year 1280 a new book of Kabbalah was written by Moses deLeone, a Jew of Castile in central Spain. This book was entitled the **Zohar**, the "Book of Splendors." The Zohar is pseudepigraphic—it claims to be authored by Rabbi Simeon bar Yohai, an important rabbi of the second century. The Zohar was written in Aramaic, in a conscious imitation of the language of Talmudic Judaism. The Zohar is a mystical commentary to the Torah, explaining how the Torah is to be understood in its secret and "truest" Kabbalistic meaning.

---

[1]That is, he became a heretic and misled the young students with his teachings.

Remarkably, the Zohar became a popular book. The Zohar was studied by ever-wider circles of Jews, far beyond the circles of the initiates. The book was circulated all over the Jewish world, among Ashkenazic as well as Sephardic Jews. In each generation the Zohar received a wider following, especially after the Spanish Expulsion. Eventually it came to be considered a third and necessary text of the revealed Torah, along with the written Scriptures and the Talmud. When the Jews of Yemen came out of the mountains to be transported to Israel in the early 1950s, they had to leave their homes in a hurry. Many of them brought nothing with them but their family copy of the Zohar.

The Zohar retained its importance until the modern age. Modernist Jews abhorred mysticism as a form of medievalism which they believed was preventing Jews from entering modern society and enjoying its benefits. The early modern historians of Judaism in the nineteenth century downplayed the importance of Kabbalism and the Zohar. They portrayed Kabbalism as an aberration from "authentic" Judaism, and oddity of concern to only a few obscure groups of practitioners. The scholar Gershom Scholem, in his ground-breaking studies, revealed to the modern world that Kabbalism was in truth the central doctrine of Judaism for centuries. Thanks to Scholem and those who have followed in his footsteps, the modern world has a new appreciation not only of the importance of Kabbalah to Judaism, but also of the depth of its message. Kabbalism is recognized in many circles as a significant movement in the history of human spirituality.

The Doctrine of the Sefirot

The Kabbalists taught that God created the world through a process of emanation. At first God existed in his wholly transcendent and infinite unity—the Ein Sof, the "Infinite Nothing," the Godhead. Then God caused a series of emanations, ten in number, to flow out of the Ein Sof. The first of these is called Keter, or Crown. Out of Keter flowed the next emanation, and so forth. The final emanation is Malchut, Kingship. Malchut is identified with the rabbinical concept of the Shekinah, God's indwelling presence in the created universe. As the Ein Sof represents God as utterly transcendent and unknowable, Malchut symbolizes God as the personal and knowable God of religion.

These ten emanations are called **sefirot** (sing. sefirah). The sefirot are not creations; the process of emanation occurs wholly within the being of God. Only after the process of emanation does the created universe come into being, as a reflection on a lower level of being of the process that has occurred within God's being.

The ten sefirot are sometimes depicted as concentric circles, and sometimes as a tree, the "Tree of Life," with a central trunk and branches to the right and left. The right side represents love of God and divine mercy. The left side represents strict judgment and fear of God. The left side represents evil in that evil is defined as judgment untempered by mercy. The central column of sefirot represents the harmonizing of opposites. All of the higher sefirot are brought together in the ninth sefirah, Yesod or Foundation, which is the source of the created world.

In the process of Creation the divine light flowed from a point in the Ein Sof into the sefirot. The light became words and the words then became things, the matter and form of the created universe. These words are the Torah. The Torah is thus the form and pattern of Creation, which is a reflection of the form and pattern of the inner life of God in the sefirot. In the created world the Torah dresses herself in earthly garments and appears as laws and stories. The Kabbalist who knows how to interpret the Torah in the mystical way is able to see through the earthly garments and perceive the heavenly Torah. The Kabbalists taught that "the entire Torah is the name of God." To know the name of a thing is to know its essence. Thus, one who understood the mystical meaning of the Torah understood the essence of God, to the highest extent that this is knowable to humankind. Every word in the Torah became for the Kabbalists another symbolic term for one or another of the sefirot. To one who understood these symbols, the Torah stories revealed the interactions of the sefirot in the divine realm. In the hands of the Kabbalists the Torah became not just a revelation from God, but the revelation of God.

Religious Tension in the Kabbalah

The doctrines of the Kabbalah come dangerously close to heresy on numerous counts. The doctrine of the sefirot seems to allow for multiplicity within divinity, in contrast to the monotheism of Judaism. The Kabbalists were aware of this danger and insisted that, paradoxically, all the sefirot were manifestations of the ultimate unity of God which remains somehow uncompromised.

The Kabbalistic doctrine of good and evil is remarkably similar to the ancient dualistic religion of Gnosticism. The ancient rabbis had fought a lengthy battle against the influence of Gnosticism. In the Kabbalah many of the doctrines of Gnosticism were reinvented, achieving now a degree of acceptance within Judaism. While the rabbis had insisted that God was

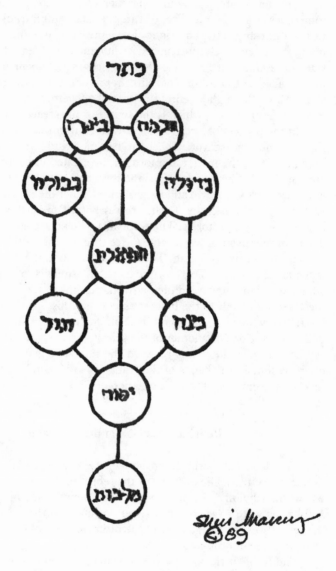

wholly good, the Kabbalists believed that evil was rooted in God's own being, in the sefirah of Judgment. The Kabbalists adopted the Gnostic notion that matter is inherently evil, while goodness and ultimately redemption are to be found in the spiritual realm.

Kabbalism also came close to the heresy of pantheism, the belief that everything is God. Some Kabbalists insisted on maintaining an absolute distinction between the realm of divinity and the realm of creation. For others, the created world is another emanation of God, and is therefore a part of God. If so, then every human being contains the divine within himself.

The Kabbalistic concept of the Torah contained the seeds for a potential rebellion against the strictures of the divine commandments. The Kabbalists taught that in the heavenly Torah there are no "do's and don't's"; in that Torah the letters realign themselves to form a message of love and freedom, unrestricted by judgment and the fear of God. There were counter-balancing tendencies which made many Kabbalists the strictest of all observers of Jewish law. Nevertheless the anti-nomian (anti-legal) tendencies of Kabbalah broke forth in a mystical messianic movement of the seventeenth century, as we shall see.

If the practitioners of Kabbalah had given in to their tendencies to Gnosticism, pantheism and antinomianism, then their religious faith might have lost its connection to historical Judaism. But, many Kabbalists were conscious of the tensions between their doctrines on the one hand and the monotheism of rabbinic Judaism and the even more pure monotheism of Jewish philosophy on the other hand. The Kabbalists struggled to remain within the fold, always insisting that at the last step the complete unity of God was confirmed. The contradictions and paradoxes within Kabbalism make it even more difficult to comprehend, but they also undoubtedly lend to the depth, the attractiveness, and the spiritual power of the Kabbalah.

The Lurianic Kabbalah

The Kabbalah underwent a great transformation in the century after the Spanish Expulsion. Until this time the Kabbalists concentrated on understanding the processes of Creation and Revelation. They pursued a private and personal revelation through their mystical ascent and return to the source of all being. After the Expulsion from Spain the sufferings of the exiles became so acute that they sought and yearned for a speedy redemption. The Kabbalists now attempted to formulate a mystical process by which they could hasten the final redemption of Israel.

This new form of Kabbalah jelled around the figure of Rabbi Isaac Luria (1534–1572). Isaac Luria was known as Ashkenazic Rabbi Isaac and is often called by the acronym "Ari," which means "lion" in Hebrew.

Isaac Luria was the central figure and teacher of a group of Kabbalists who gathered in the city of Zefat (Safed) in the Galilee in the north of the Land of Israel. In the decades after the Spanish Expulsion this circle became a magnet for exiled Spanish Jews who were interested in the study of Kabbalah and the pursuit of an ascetic life of holiness. The city of Zefat was chosen because it provides a beautiful view of Mount Meron, the legendary burial place of Rabbi Simeon bar Yochai, the reputed author of the Zohar. It is an irony of history that these Kabbalists gathered in their ancient homeland, there to bemoan the exile of Israel which they experienced sharply on account of their expulsion from their beloved Spain. At this time the Land of Israel was part of the Turkish empire, which welcomed many Spanish exiles.

Isaac Luria's short life became a matter of legend. It was said that Elijah the Prophet appeared in person to hold him at his circumcision. He was said to know the languages of all things, animate and inanimate; he often engaged in discussion with birds and invisible spirits and with the souls of those saintly rabbis of antiquity whose names had become attached to Kabbalistic literature. The Ari never wrote a book of his own, but his teachings were preserved and publicized by his followers, particularly Haim Vital.

The Kabbalists of Zefat dedicated their lives to study, contemplation and practice. They considered prayer to be of special importance in spiritual life. They developed a system of **kavannah** in prayer. In their system this term no longer held its rabbinic meaning of concentration and intention. It now meant the ability to direct one's prayer so that it would fulfill the mystical purpose of hastening the final redemption. On the eve of the Sabbath the Kabbalists of Zefat would dress in white and go out to the edge of the town to greet and accompany the Sabbath. They conceived of the Sabbath as a bride and associated her with the tenth sefirah, the Shekinah. The peace of the Sabbath brought harmony in the world of the sefirot, symbolized by the marriage of the Shekinah to her husband, Yesod, the ninth sefirah. This mystical marriage is symbolically celebrated in the hymn "Lekha Dodi" which was composed for the ceremony of welcoming the Sabbath Queen. The ceremony of "Kabbalat Shabbat," welcoming the Sabbath, was added to the Jewish liturgy in every community. This was the last great addition to the traditional order of prayer. The Kabbalists brought to Judaism the feminine imagery of divinity which had been expunged in biblical times because of the need to eliminate the concept of male and female gods.

The Lurianic Concept of Creation

Before the Creation God was all of existence. How could there be room for a world when everything was filled with God's being? The first step of Creation was **tzimtzum,** "contraction." God contracted his being so as to leave a space devoid of the presence of God. Creation begins with a void, the absence of God.

The next step of Creation was the emanation of the sefirot, as in standard Kabbalistic doctrine. Each sefirah was successively farther from the Eternal, more coarse, less spiritual. Below the sefirot the heavenly realms were created. The process concluded with the creation of the material universe, which stands at the furthest reach from the Godhead.

It was God's intention to fill his creation with the light of his presence. God shone his light into the highest sefirah, from which it flowed into the next and so on down the line. Then, a catastrophe! The lower sefirot, coarse as they were, were unable to contain the pure light of divinity. Like a cold glass into which hot water is poured, they shattered. This is called **shevirat ha-kelim,** the "shattering of the vessels." The pathways were broken, so that the divine light was no longer able to flow freely between God and his creation. Sparks of holiness were trapped in evil **kelipot,** "shells" of material existence.

Through the shattering of the vessels, God was separated from the world of his creation. More, the lowest sefirah was trapped in the created universe, unable to restore her connection to the sefirot above. The midrash states that "God caused his Shekinah (Presence) to go into exile with his people." What the rabbis stated as a symbol of God's empathy becomes a literal reality in the Lurianic Kabbalah. The exile of Israel in the world below is a necessary reflection of what is happening in the worlds above. God is in exile from his own being. The exile of Israel can only end when the exile of God has come to an end.

Redemption in the Lurianic Kabbalah

Since the time of Creation, God has been busy restoring the pathways between the sefirot and setting free the captured sparks of holiness from their shells. This process is called **tikun olam,** the "repair of the universe." God cannot fulfill this task on his own. Tikun requires help from below. The task of humankind is to restore the vessels to their wholeness. This task falls primarily upon the people Israel. Among the people Israel, it falls primarily upon those who are adept in the Kabbalah.

Proper observance of the mitzvot in the Torah is the way of tikun.

Each time a Jew observes a mitzvah in the proper way, sparks are released from their shells and the pathways of divine light are restored. Each time a Jew transgresses a mitzvah, the pathways are obstructed and shattered further. Every mitzvah has its own function in the restoration of wholeness to the universe, so every mitzvah is equally important. The doctrine of tikun gives a powerful new rationale for both ethical living and ritual observance. In living according to the Torah a person not only acquires merit for his own soul; he also benefits humankind, the cosmos, and even God, who is dependent upon him for tikun. The most effective worker for tikun is the Kabbalist, who knows the mystery of every mitzvah and holds the keys to unlock its redeeming power.

The doctrine of tikun gave a great sense of empowerment to the suffering Jews. In this world they were powerless to oppose the nations which persecuted them and shoved them from one exile to another. The Jews had in their possession, though, the only power that really counts—the power to redeem the world. Even the nations which persecuted the Jews were dependent upon the Jews for their own redemption, though they did not realize it.

Exile

Exile was now seen to be more than just the political status of the Jews. Exile does not result from the accidents of history. It doe not result from the sins of Israel, as rabbinic theology had taught. Rather, exile is the current state of being of the universe. God is in exile from himself, which explains the painful absence of God from so much of human life. The cosmos is in a state of exile, which explains why there is disharmony in nature and the life of all creatures is a struggle against others for survival. The nations are in exile from each other, which is why they are always at war with one another. People are in exile from one another, which is why there is social injustice in society. The exile of Israel is one manifestation of an exile which shows itself on every level of existence because of God's own exile. Tikun olam will solve all of these problems at once by striking to the root of the problem. The redemption of Israel is the redemption of the universe, the restoration of the flow of divine light into the world. God will be whole again, as he was before the Creation.

The restored universe will in one way be more perfect than the universe before Creation, which was filled with God's being. God created the universe to expunge from his being a grain of evil, as it were, a bit of unrestrained judgment. In the universe of tikun, judgment will be locked in the grip of mercy, and so evil will be eliminated.

Humankind in the Lurianic Kabbalah

Adam contained the soul of all humanity. If Adam had been obedient to God's command in the Garden of Eden, the process of tikun olam would have been immediately completed. Adam's sin initiated a new shattering of the vessels, greater than the one at the time of Creation. Adam's soul, which derived from the divine light, was correspondingly shattered. The soul of each human being is a spark from the soul of Adam. In the process of tikun, each human being is returning his own soul to the unity of the soul of Adam. In the Messianic time all of humanity will be literally united.

The sefirot exist in the soul of each person in a replica of the sefirot within the being of God. This is the meaning of "God created man in his image." As the exile of the Shekinah is reflected in the exile of Israel, so is it reflected in the exile of a person from his own true being. That state of mind which the modern social psychologist would call "alienation," the Kabbalist would call "exile" within the human soul. The modern social critic bemoans the alienation of the individual from his work, from society, from true relationship with other human beings. The process of tikun creates wholeness in the human soul even as it creates wholeness in the cosmos and in the being of God.

The Effect of the Lurianic Kabbalah

The Lurianic Kabbalah uses the same symbols to address humankind on the cosmic and spiritual level, the social-political level, and the individual psychological level, all at once. The Kabbalah responded to all of the pressing issues on each of these levels that Jews were facing in the sixteenth century. The set of doctrines that had been established for an elite group of ascetic mystics soon spread beyond the borders of Zefat and the Land of Israel to other Jewish communities. Though the Kabbalah had developed within the Sephardic culture, the large Ashkenazi community in Poland found it equally enticing. Undoubtedly, most Jews did not comprehend the details of this esoteric doctrine, nor did they receive mystical visions, but in a popular form the Lurianic Kabbalah captured the imagination of virtually all of world Jewry.

The Kabbalah gave a new and significant rationale for remaining Jewish in an age when Jews were persecuted and many Jews were tempted to succumb to baptism. The Kabbalah gave Jews a new reason to observe Jewish law down to its finest details; the spiritual power of this observance was the force of tikun olam, the force that would bring the redemption of the universe.

It is not surprising, then, that the Lurianic Kabbalah inspired the last and greatest code of Jewish law. Among the disciples in Zefat was the visionary mystic **Joseph Caro** (1488–1575). Caro claimed to have received the inspiration and message for his work from the Archangel Gabriel.

Caro wrote a learned commentary on the law code **Arbah Turim** of Rabbi Asher ben Yehiel. In a separate volume Caro published all of his legal conclusions. This volume was entitled the **Shulhan Aruk**, the "Set Table." The title was an invitation for Jews to dine, to study this book, and in a simple way, without rabbinic dialectics, to learn what a Jew must do in the observance of God's law.

There were many objections to Caro's work, but over the course of time its authority was accepted. Rabbi Moses Isserles wrote an Ashkenazic commentary to the Shulhan Aruk called the **Mapa**, the "Tablecloth." This commentary pointed out the many differences in Ashkenazic observance, making the Shulhan Aruk useful for Ashkenazic Jews. When the modern age began and many Jews rebelled against the rabbinic-legal definition of Judaism, the traditionalists responded by raising up the Shulhan Aruk as the ultimate definition of who a Jew is and what a Jew does. This code of law is much used by modern Orthodox Jews. New rabbinic responsa are coded according to the section of the Shulhan Aruk in which related laws are found.

Shabbetai Zevi—the Mystical Messiah

The Jews in the mid-seventeenth century were ripe for a new messianic movement. Jews were engaging in intense messianic speculation due to the spread of the Lurianic Kabbalah. The major Jewish populations were suffering from awful persecutions, raising hopes among Jews that they were living through the evil times of the "last days" before God would send the Messiah to redeem them from their troubles. The Sephardic Jews, with the retrospect of history, were realizing the full extent of the tragedy of their expulsion from Spain. The Ashkenazic Jews, concentrated in Poland, were being massacred in the Cossack wars of rebellion against the Poles. Messianic speculation centered around the coming of the year 1666, which many Jews as well as many Christians believed would be the year of the Apocalypse.

Shabbetai Zevi (1626–1676) arose in 1665 and claimed to be the long-awaited Messiah. He justified his claims through an elaboration of the doctrines of the Kabbalah. Shabbetai had a brilliant prophet and publicist,

Nathan of Gaza, who made his name great throughout the Jewish world. In every generation claimants to the throne of the Messiah had arisen. Some had gained a following for a time in one locale or another. Shabbetai Zevi gained a broader and more devoted following than any messianic claimant since the Bar Kochba rebellion against Rome. Jews from throughout the Jewish world, including many learned rabbis, announced that Shabbetai Zevi was authentic. Jews from all over Europe and the Turkish empire abandoned their work and their worldly goods and prepared to follow Shabbetai Zevi to the Holy Land.

Shabbetai Zevi was born in Smyrna, Turkey, in a family of merchants. As a young man he showed genius as a student of the Talmud. He turned to the study of the Kabbalah, and began to engage in often bizarre mystical practices. His messianic claims and his strange practices, which often were contrary to Jewish law, led to his banishment from Smyrna. He embarked on a period of wandering which led to his meeting with Nathan of Gaza, who encouraged his messianic claims. Despite the opposition of many rabbis, Jews from all over came to believe in Shabbetai. Soon, those rabbis who opposed him did not dare to speak out, for fear of the passions of the people.

In the summer of 1666 Shabbetai Zevi announced that he was marching on Constantinople to knock the turban off the head of the Turkish sultan and re-establish Jewish sovereignty in the Land of Israel.

The Sultan had Shabbetai Zevi arrested. In September of 1666 the sultan had the messianic claimant brought before him. The sultan gave him the choice of having his head cut off, or converting to Islam and receiving a government stipend for life. Shabbetai Zevi chose conversion.

His followers were devastated by this turn of events. The Jews were thrown back into the grip of a despair made worse by the disappointment of their hopes. Some Jews continued to believe in Shabbetai Zevi. These Jews formed cultish groups. Jacob Frank in Poland gathered a group who engaged in outrageous practices, taking to a perverted extreme the Kabbalistic concept that the Torah would be inverted in the Time of the Messiah. Many Frankists converted to Christianity around 1760, but continued to believe in Shabbetai Zevi and to secretly practice their strange religion.

The majority of Shabbetai Zevi's followers grimly accepted the fact that they had been deceived. In Southern Poland, the Kabbalistic messianic hopes of the Jews were gathered and redirected by the Hasidic movement. Hasidism rose from the ashes of Sabbatianism to become one of the great spiritual forces in Jewish history. We will learn more about Hasidism in the next chapter.

18

Jewish Life
in Eastern Europe

A Brief History of Polish Jewry

The Jews of Eastern Europe constituted the largest concentration of Jews in the world for about four hundred years, from the mid-1500s until the Second World War. The Jews began to appear in significant numbers in the kingdom of Poland in the sixteenth century. We have no sure evidence of where these Jews came from or how they got to Poland. It would appear that most of them emigrated from central Europe as persecutions and expulsions increased there. The Jews came to constitute a significant proportion of the population in Poland.

In the sixteenth century Poland was the largest kingdom in Europe. It stretched from Germany in the West to the Crimea and Russia in the East. Most of the territory that is now in the western republics of the U.S.S.R., and the Russian satellite states, at that time was part of Poland.

Poland was centuries behind Western Europe in economic development. The economy was primarily agricultural. The society was feudal. Jews moved into the commercial roles which they had formerly held in the West. The Polish kings and nobility welcomed Jews as part of their strategy to develop the country. Jews were granted moderate taxation and generous self-rule in order to entice them to come to Poland.

As long as Poland was on the rise all was well for the Jews, and Jews enjoyed excellent relations with the Polish lords and the people. Sadly, though, Poland underwent a long period of decline from which she has never recovered to this day. Poland lost her empire, then her power, then her independence. In Poland's political and economic decline the Jews suffered most of all. Poles no longer willingly granted Jews a place in the economy. Anti-Jewish feeling became a major force in Polish society. Many Jews were thrust into unemployment and poverty.

The first step in Poland's decline was the revolt of the Ukraine in 1648 under the leadership of the Cossack, Bogdan Chmielnicki. The Ukrainians were Orthodox Christians, like most Slavic peoples, while the Poles were Roman Catholic. Thus, the Cossack rebellion became something of a holy war in which Jews were caught in the middle. Waves of Cossack horsemen, called Heidemaks, rode into southern Poland, capturing cities and slaughtering their people. Although Jews fought in the defense of Poland, they were often not protected by the Poles. All told, a third of a million Jews died in the Chmielnicki rebellion. Many of these were cruelly tortured to death after being captured. It was the worst slaughter of Jews from the Roman wars of antiquity until the Nazi Holocaust of modern times.

The Chmielnicki rebellion devasted Jewish society in southern Poland. Jewish life in Lithuania, in the North, was largely unaffected. From this different historical experience arose the cultural differences between the "Litvak" and the "Galitzianer." The Litvaks maintained a society based on Jewish learning, while the Galicians became known for their religious fervor and messianic yearnings. Shabbetai Zevi found many followers among Galician Jews who were suffering the after-effects of the Chmielnicki rebellion, and this region became the homeland for the later Hasidic movement.

In the 1700s, at about the same time that America was fighting for independence, Poland was being attacked and dismembered by her neighbors. In three stages, Poland was gulped up by Prussia, Austria-Hungary and Russia. Independent Poland was no more, and Polish Jews were separated among three different kingdoms.

The partition of Poland opened up new lands for Jewish settlement. There followed a great explosion in the world Jewish population, from perhaps three million in the 1700s to as many as eighteen million on the eve of World War II. The Jewish communities took on a different character, depending upon which nation ruled over them. The Jews in Germany and Austria-Hungary became more Western, while those in the Russian territories remained Eastern. In the heart of Poland the frontier shifted among the three conquering states, depending upon their relative power and fortunes in war. There was never again an independent Poland except briefly during the time of Napoleon and again between the two World Wars.[1]

---

[1]Poland today, though nominally independent, is a closely controlled satellite of the U.S.S.R.

The Jews Under the Czars

Most Polish Jews ended up under Russian rule. This was a great disaster for them. Wherever Jews lived, they had always gone by invitation. At least initially, they were welcomed. The Russians never wanted Jews. It was illegal for a Jew to live in Russia. The Czarina Catherine the Great (1729–1796) had always expelled Jews from newly conquered territories, but there was no way she could expel the vast number of Jews she acquired in the conquest of Poland. Instead, she established an area in the western and southwestern areas of the empire in which Jews could live. This area was called the **Pale of Settlement.** She established restrictive and punitive laws to keep the Jews poor, isolated, and at the bottom of society.

Czar Nicholas I (1796–1855), developed a three-part plan to deal with the Jews. One third would be forced to emigrate, one third would be forced to convert to Russian Orthodoxy, and one third would be killed. Nicholas established the **cantonist** system, by which young Jewish boys were taken into the Russian army for a period of twenty years or more. The army did not permit Jewish observance. If a Jew were still alive after that much time it was unlikely that he would even remember that he was Jewish.

The Russian government encouraged anti-Jewish feeling among the peasants. The czars hoped in this way to deflect their rebellious frustration and prevent a revolution. From time to time and place to place the government would initiate a **pogrom,** an anti-Jewish riot. A pogrom might begin in a certain village after a priest, who was in the employ of the government, gave an anti-Jewish sermon in church. Paid agents would agitate against the Jews. Free liquor might be distributed in the village to encourage foolish bravery. In the pogrom some Jews would be beaten and some might be killed; houses would be burned and property destroyed.

Relations were not always bad between Jews and their Gentile neighbors. We might consider the example of the **Shabbes goy,** a common institution in Eastern Europe. The Shabbes goy was a Gentile who came to a Jewish home on Friday night to perform the evening chores which the Jews could not do on the Sabbath. The Shabbes goy received no payment for his troubles, though he might be offered a slice of hallah and a glass of brandy as a sign of friendship and gratitude. The Shabbes goy performed his chores solely as an act of friendship to his Jewish neighbor.

The czar Alexander II (118818–81) was a liberal. He emancipated the peasants, who until 1861 were still owned by their noble masters. Alexander II removed most of the oppressive laws against the Jews. Jews were allowed to live anywhere in Russia and were granted many rights which had been denied to them. When Alexander II was assassinated by radicals, his successor, Alexander III, restored the Pale of Settlement and all of the former laws against the Jews. The so-called May Laws of 1881 which brought back the old status quo were accompanied by many unusually ferocious pogroms. In that year most Jews gave up hope that Russia would ever improve as a home for Jews, and large numbers of Jews began to emigrate. Most of those who left Russia came to America, though Jews also went to South America, to Western Europe, and to Palestine, which was then under Turkish rule. Jewish emigration continued at a rapid rate for the next thirty or forty years, until the avenues of escape were cut off by World War I, the Russian revolution, and restrictive immigration laws in America.

Most Russian Jews welcomed the Bolshevik Revolution in 1917. Not that they were Communists, though some were, but anything had to be better than the czars! Lenin wanted Jews to assimilate into Russian society and disappear. He hoped to accomplish this by eliminating all restrictions against Jews, giving them full rights as Soviet citizens.

Lenin's successor, Joseph Stalin, attempted to return Jews to a lower status in Russian society, not by law but by not granting to Jews the rights which the Soviet constitution guaranteed to them. Stalin was about to initiate a new anti-Jewish campaign when he died in 1953. Even though Stalin was no friend of the Jews, Russian Jews in his time could be thankful that they had been saved from Hitler. They appreciated their country for her great sacrifices in the war against Germany. Over a million Soviet Jews were killed when the Nazis invaded Russia, but most Russian Jews were saved.

Between the two World Wars Russia was pushed back from her empire. Many Jews found themselves living in newly independent Poland or Lithuania. This was a time of great changes, as the forces of modernism impinged upon the Jewish way of life. In communist Russia the government discouraged any expression of religion, making Jewish tradition all but impossible to observe. It is hard to say what might have become of Jewish society in Eastern Europe. During the Second World War the Nazis killed six million Jews, including nearly the entire Jewish populations of Poland, Lithuania, Hungary, and other East European countries. Those who remained alive were trapped behind the Iron Curtain, where they were denied access to Jewish learning of any kind. Jewish life in Eastern Europe came to a shockingly sudden and tragic end.

The Three Foci of Jewish Life:
The Home

Jewish life in Eastern Europe centered around three institutions—the home, the marketplace, and the **bes midrash**, the "study-house." The home rather than the synagogue was the center of religious life and practice. The activities of the household and the relations between its members were defined according to tradition and religious law. Life at home gave the Jew his sense of dignity and importance as a human being. In the world outside a Jew might be one of a downtrodden minority, but at home he could feel like one of God's chosen people.

The father was like an honored nobleman in the house when he was home, but he was often out. All day he worked to make a living, unless he was a scholar or the rare man of leisure. Morning and evening he would go to the synagogue for daily prayers. If his life afforded him spare time, much of it would be spent in study at the bes midrash.

The mother was ruler of the home and, one might say, the priestess of its religious rites. She was responsible to see that the kitchen was kosher, that Shabbat and all holidays were properly observed, and that the children were being raised as proper Jews. Although she had little formal schooling, the mother learned her lessons in apprenticeship to her own mother. The task of a daughter was to help with all matters of household management in preparation for the day when she would have her own home.

The task of a son was to learn Torah. The child would begin his attendance at heder at an early age. At about the age of twelve, if he were bright or fortunate, he would go on to a yeshiva. Otherwise he would begin to learn the trade by which he would make his living.

Boys and girls were often engaged to each other in their early teens. The boy would go to live in the house of his future father-in-law, who would be responsible for the final years of his education. When they got married at the age of eighteen, husband and wife had already lived like brother and sister for a few years. While we have no statistics, it seems from literary evidence and from the rarity of divorce that these arrangements led to great affection and stability in married life.

The Marketplace

The economy in Eastern Europe was based primarily on primitive agriculture, right up to the twentieth century. There was very little commerce and industry. The class of urban freedmen who displaced the Jews

in the economy of Western Europe never developed to the same extent in the East. The Jews served as the middle class in Polish society. They worked in commerce, shopkeeping and various trades.

The land was owned by the nobleman, the squire or "pan." The peasants lived on the land and worked it. The Jews lived in the **shtetl,** the village, and served the commercial needs of the peasants. Jews were not permitted to own land or to live on the land and work it.

Jews rented concessions from the nobleman, the mill and the inn and the other small commercial ventures of the estate. The **arrendar,** or estate manager, handled all the business affairs of the nobleman so that he was free to engage in government or to enjoy his social affairs in the city. The arrendar would generally be the most prosperous Jew in the shtetl, and the one who would intercede for the Jews with the government when that was necessary. Some Jews became prosperous engaging in international trade in the agricultural and forest products of Poland. Most of the Jews, though, were petty shopkeepers or tradesmen.

If a Jew were fortunate, he might own a general store on the market square of the shtetl. If less fortunate, he might peddle his goods from a cart in the open air of the marketplace. The least fortunate might have to make their living from a single barrel of apples or other produce which they would hope to sell for a small profit on market day.

If a woman had a husband who was a Torah scholar, she would handle the business in the marketplace by herself. In this way she would free her husband from work so that he could study Torah all the time. This was considered a great honor for both husband and wife.

On market days the peasants came into the shtetl. There they would sell their farm products to Jewish dealers and purchase their needs from Jewish shopkeepers. The peasants might then retire to the inn for some drinks and relaxation before returning home.[2] Life was difficult for peasant and Jew alike. The peasants had at least this advantage, that since they lived on the land they were not in danger of starvation. The Jews had always to fear that if business were bad they might have to go hungry. Despite this disadvantage, the Jews preferred their life to that of the peasants. The peasant lived a brutal life of back-breaking labor, with no opportunity for education. The Jews were literate, gentle and refined.

---

[2]Alcoholism was the bane of society among East European workers and peasants, as it is to this day. For unknown reasons, Jews in Eastern Europe were nearly free of this vice. It may be that Jewish culture discouraged drinking to excess. It may be that since the Jews always had to be on guard against a pogrom, they could not afford to get drunk. No physiological reason has been discovered for the low rate of alcoholism in traditional Jewish society.

They worked more with their heads than with their hands. In comparison to the society around them, the Jews considered their shtetl culture to be uniquely virtuous. Indeed, the shtetl culture created a person who stands out in the history of humankind for his love of God, love of peace, and love of learning, and for his compassion toward his fellow human being.

As Poland declined politically she declined economically. The decline of Poland led to anti-Semitism, much as racism and isolationism increase in America in times of economic recession. Poverty and unemployment increased greatly among the Jews. Russian restrictions against the Jews made poverty even worse. It is estimated that at the turn of the twentieth century as many as one third of all Eastern European Jews were permanently unemployed. Many of the rest barely scratched out a living. Jews left Eastern Europe in droves not just to escape oppression and the Russian military draft, but also to escape from starvation and hopeless poverty.

The Bes Midrash

Constant poverty and oppression have caused many societies to break down, but Jewish society in the shtetl was not based upon wealth or rank. The purpose of life was to serve God, and the highest service of God was to become learned in the Torah. Jewish society in Eastern Europe was centered around its schools and libraries. Many Jews, if given the choice, would gladly have passed up the opportunity for riches in exchange for the leisure and ability to study.

Talmud study was the principal activity in shtetl culture and the end to which all other activities were the means. The ideal was that every Jewish male would be learned in the Talmud. As much time as a man could take away from earning his living, he would go to the bes midrash. The bes midrash was a library, but it was not quiet like a modern library. The men would bend over a book together in pairs or in study groups and debate the meaning of a passage in the holy books, in the attempt to draw out every possible meaning of the text. The most learned would study the Talmud and its commentaries. The less learned would study the Mishnah or one of the great anthologies of rabbinic teaching such as the *Ein Yaakov* or the *Menorat Hamaor*. The least learned would study Rashi's commentary to the Torah. Everyone would study.

. . . all professions, the bakers, the butchers, the shoemakers, etc., have their own **shtibl** (study room) in the Jewish district; and every free moment which can be taken off from their work is given to the study of the Torah. And when they get together in intimate groups, one urges the other: *"Sog mir a shtickl Torah—* Tell me a little Torah."

An old book saved from the countless libraries recently burned in Europe . . . bears the stamp, "The Society of Wood-Choppers for the Study of Mishnah in Berditshev."[3]

In the shtetl we would find characters such as the **matmid,** or eternal student. The matmid would sit in the bes midrash day and night. He had no home or worldly possessions. When he got tired he would doze a short time on a bench. Townspeople would send him food to eat at his study table. Many a young man or old man dedicated a few years of his life to eternal study.

Also in the shtetl we would find the **ilui,** or child prodigy. The ilui memorized the Bible and the Talmud by the age of ten or twelve. Since there was no one in town who could teach him anymore, and he was too young to teach or to go off to a great yeshiva, the ilui was permitted to sit in the bes midrash and study on his own. It was said of some young men that if one stuck a pin through a word on a page of the Talmud and through any number of further pages, the ilui could tell you which word was printed where the pin came through the other side.

Torah study was a way for a poor boy to acquire status and position in the community. Since the community admired learning above wealth, the wealthy attempted to associate themselves with the learned through marriage alliances. The wealthiest man would seek the best student as a husband for his daughter. The next wealthiest would acquire the next best student for his son-in-law, and so forth. The wealthy would support their sons-in-law so that they would be free to engage in study day and night. Some wealthy men established a bes midrash in their homes where ten indigent scholars would be maintained to study Torah all day.

It was said that Rabbi Elijah, the Gaon of Vilna, kept a notebook in which he recorded every minute that was idled away which could have been spent in study. Each year on Yom Kippur he would atone for that wasted time—and it never amounted to more than ten minutes in a year!

Talmud study and related studies in Jewish law assumed such importance in the shtetl that other topics fell by the wayside. In the nineteenth century there were attempts to broaden the curriculum. Elijah Gaon believed that mathematics and natural science should be taught in addition to Talmud. The Hasidic movement encouraged the study of Kabbalistic texts in place of the Talmud.

---

[3]Abraham Joshua Heschel, *The Earth Is the Lord's,* Farrar Straus Giroux, N.Y., 1978, pp. 46–47.

Rabbi Israel Lipkin Salanter (1810–1883) founded the **Musar** (Ethical) Movement. In the Musar schools the great ethical texts of medieval Judaism were studied along with the Talmud. What began as a modernizing movement became an extremist movement after the death of its founders. The Musar students practiced self-humiliation in public by wearing silly clothes and the like, in order to inure themselves to public opinion. To eliminate all self-interest from their ethical way of life, they learned to take no pleasure in performing good deeds. Rather than rely on their emotions, the Musar students learned right from wrong by studying in infinite detail those Jewish laws which govern behavior. A classic text from this movement is the *Hofetz Haim*, published in 1873 by Rabbi Yisroel Meir Kagan. The *Hofetz Haim* lists all of the laws and rules concerning forbidden speech, gossip and tale-bearing. It was said of the author of this book that even though he was a man of affairs, very involved in community politics, he was never heard to say a single bad word about anyone. In old age Rabbi Kagan became somewhat deaf. He declared this to be a benefit, since a person might try to whisper gossip to him but would never dare to shout it.

The Social Order of Polish Jewry

When the Polish kings in the sixteenth century were trying to attract Jews to Poland, they offered the Jews generous terms of self-government. The Jews paid their annual dues to the king, but they were ruled and judged by their own leaders. The supreme council of Polish Jewry was the **Council of the Four Lands,** the "Va'ad Arba Ha-aratzot." The four lands were the four provinces of the Polish kingdom: Lithuania, Galicia, Volhynia and Podolia. The council met twice a year, at the great fairs in Lublin and Cracow. At their meetings the council handled the administrative and legal matters of the Jewish community and distributed the burden of taxation among the different communities, each according to its capacity.

The Jewish community of each city or shtetl had its own government, the kahal. The leading Jewish householders of the community elected the town council, which selected a mayor. The council collected the taxes owed to the government and those for the support of the community itself. The chief source of revenue was the tax on kosher meat. This tax fell most heavily on the well-to-do, since the poor ate very little meat. The council oversaw the community institutions and appointed the religious professionals who served the community. These included the **rav** (the town rabbi), the **hazzan** (who led prayers in the synagogue), the **shammas** (the synagogue overseer), the **shoket** (the kosher slaughterer), the **dayyanim** (the rabbinic judges who ran the Jewish courts), the town crier who woke the people up every morning, and sometimes other officials as well. The social institutions of the community included the synagogue, the bes midrash, a school, a hospital, and a poorhouse.

The kahal enforced its decisions without a police force. They had the power to impose fines, to deny public honors to wrongdoers, and to ban those who did not obey their decisions. In a close-knit community ruled by tradition, this was sufficient to maintain public order. Besides the power of tradition and reputation in a close-knit community, the Jews were obliged by their precarious position in society to maintain an orderly and united community. The Jews were powerless and subject to persecution. A crime committed by any one of them could bring down the wrath of the Gentiles upon the entire community, endangering them all. Because of this, the most unforgivable crime was to inform to the government against a fellow Jew.

The kahal was abolished by the Russians in the 1830s as part of their ongoing program to restrict and oppress the Jews. Even after the Kahal was stripped of legal recognition, the Jews continued to handle their own affairs and resolve their disputes within their own community as much as possible.

Hasidism: The Legend of the Baal Shem Tov

In the early eighteenth century **Hasidism,** a movement of spiritual revival, swept through the Jewry of Southern Poland. The founder of Hasidism was Israel ben Eliezer, known as the **Baal Shem Tov,** or Master of the Good (Divine) Name. The title refers to the power to heal and perform miracles through the magical use of God's name. The Baal Shem Tov was an itinerant preacher who left no writings, but after his death his disciples wrote down stories about his life and parables from his teachings.

The Baal Shem Tov was born around 1700. As a youth he showed no interest in Talmud study, but he loved to go into the fields and commune with nature. It is said that, unknown to his townsmen, he became expert in the Kabbalah. He acquired the secret Book of Adam which gave him power over the natural and spiritual worlds. Israel was made a teacher's assistant, a lowly job. His main function was to bring the children back and forth to school each day. Sometimes he would take the children into the woods instead, where he would teach them to appreciate and enjoy the mystery of God's creation. This led to his being fired.

Israel married the sister of Gershom, a Talmud scholar. Gershom objected to the marriage of his sister to an ignoramus, but later he became one of the Baal Shem Tov's disciples.

The Baal Shem Tov became an innkeeper in an obscure place deep in the Carpathian mountains. There he waited until the time came to reveal himself. In his thirty-third year the Baal Shem Tov came out and revealed his spiritual powers. He went from town to town in Southern Poland, preaching his doctrines and gaining enthusiastic supporters everywhere.

The Growth of Hasidism

Despite the opposition of the learned rabbis, the Hasidic movement grew rapidly. By the time of the Baal Shem Tov's death in 1760 more than half the Jews of Poland were Hasidim. Those who resisted Hasidism were known as **Misnagdim,** "Opponents" or "Protestants." It is highly unusual in the history of religion for those who maintain the older traditions to be labeled as the protesters; this displays the extraordinary speed with which the Hasidic movement became the mainstream of Polish Judaism.

The Hasidic movement grew in fertile soil. Jewish life in Southern Poland had been devastated, first by the Chmielnicki rebellion and then by the disappointment of the Sabbatean movement. Living in poverty and despair, the Jews in this region were not able to maintain their yeshivas. Many Jews were unlearned, and they resented the attitude of superiority of the scholarly rabbis. In their dire straits, the people did not respond to a religious culture based on intellect. They wanted a religious gratification that was more immediate, that would bring healing to their wounded lives. Further, the people wanted a religious teaching that was grounded in the ideas of popular Kabbalism and that would respond to their messianic yearnings. Instead of going to the rabbis for spiritual guidance, the people were attracted to the **maggid,** the itinerant preacher who could stir them with his words, and to the **baal shem,** the wonder-worker who would heal them and intercede with God for the fulfillment of their wishes. The Baal Shem Tov gathered together the strands of religious thought that were out among the people; he wove these strands into a new fabric.

Among the early leaders of Hasidism some were learned in Torah and some were not. It did not matter; the Hasidic leader was valued for the quality of his soul and for his spiritual guidance, not for his knowledge. The Hasidim addressed their leaders not as rabbi but as **rebbe.** This new title signified a new and different kind of religious leadership.

The Doctrines of Hasidism

The Baal Shem Tov taught that the simple, ignorant man can relate to God as surely as the learned scholar. The joyful service of God is the most important thing. A person must make every single act of his existence a joyful service of God. If a person is a shoemaker, then let him make shoes in the service of God. If he is a woodcutter, then let him cut wood with the joyful awareness that he is doing this in the service of God. In one Hasidic tale, the Baal Shem Tov is told in a vision that he must go to learn from a certain person who is working as a shepherd. As the Baal Shem Tov approaches he sees that the man is jumping back and forth over a gully. With every leap the man shouts, "I am doing this for the love of God! I am doing this for the love of God!" The Baal Shem Tov now understands why he was sent to this man.

The Hasidim valued prayer above study. They would pray with great fervor, often gesticulating wildly. They made dancing an important part of their worship. A Hasidic tale which exists in many versions illustrates the Hasidic attitude to divine service through prayer:

> One day the Baal Shem Tov was leading his disciples in prayer. The room was crowded with worshipers. They prayed long and hard, but their prayers did not seem to be getting anywhere. In the room was a simple-minded boy. He did not even know the words of the daily prayers, so he kept silent, but his heart yearned to join in the worship. Finally he stood up and announced, "God, I do not know any of the prayers. The only thing I know how to do is to crow like a rooster. So, I will now do this for you." The boy crowed like a rooster at the top of his lungs. The horrified worshipers turned to remove the boy from the room, but the Baal Shem Tov stopped them. "This boy's prayer," said the Baal Shem Tov, "has taken all of our prayers and carried them up to heaven."

The Hasidim taught that whether a person has a high or low station in life, he has been placed there to redeem captured sparks of holiness that only he can redeem, and only within the exact circumstances in which he finds himself. The task of each person, then, is to accept his situation in life, and to raise that situation to holiness by sanctifying his daily activities. The Messiah will come only after every spark of holiness has been redeemed. The activity of the lowliest person within his station in life is, therefore, as necessary to the ultimate redemption as is the activity of the most honored person.

> Rabbi Zusya said: When I go to the bar of judgment in heaven they will not say to me, "Why weren't you Moses? Why weren't

you Isaiah?" They will say to me, "Why weren't you Zusya?" At the thought of that question I tremble.

A person can only fulfill the unique service for which he was placed into this world by being himself. But that is no easy thing.

The Way of Hasidism

The Hasid attempts to release the sparks of holiness that are to be found in every place, every time, and every situation. To accomplish this he performs acts of **yihud,** "unification." Yihud actualizes the holiness which exists everywhere in potential. Yihud is accomplished through a concentration of self, living in a state of wholeness and integrity. If one is wholly present to a situation, and one brings to that situation a determination to find God's presence, one accomplishes an act of yihud. The goal is to remove all the impediments to God's presence in the world, to extend the realm of the holy into the realm of the profane. In the end the realm of the holy will include all of creation, and God will be at one with his creation.

Hitlahavut is passion. The Hasidim taught that it is not sufficient merely to perform the mitzvot in a perfunctory way. The redemptive purpose of the mitzvot is not accomplished unless they are done with hitlahavut. Hitlahavut means taking a joyous and positive attitude to daily life. Hitlahavut also means the ecstasy felt by the mystic in his communion with God. Hitlahavut means that the heart must overflow with joy in the knowledge that with one's every act one serves the Creator.

Devekut is clinging to God. The Hasid attempts to remain eternally conscious of the presence of God. He attempts never to do anything which would remove him from the presence of God. Sin, half-heartedness, pride and hypocrisy drive God's presence, the Shekinah, out of the world. Integrity, good deeds and humility, with proper consciousness, keep one always close to God. The following story is told:

The Baal Shem Tov was traveling over a mountain to go to preach in a certain town. He brought one of his young disciples with him. As the wagon crested the mountain and began to go down the other side, the harness broke, the horse ran away, and the wagon began to careen crazily down the twisted path. At any moment the wagon might crash into a tree and smash into splinters, killing its occupants. The young disciple was screaming in terror, but when he looked to his side he saw that the Baal Shem

Tov was sitting in complete serenity. Miraculously, the wagon
came to rest safely at the bottom of the mountain. "How could
you remain calm at such a moment?" asked the disciple. Replied
the Baal Shem Tov, "Once you know the only thing in life worth
being afraid of, nothing else can make you afraid."

There is nothing to fear except for the absence of God. As long as one
is in God's presence, one need have no fear of what may occur. There is no
assurance that we will not suffer or even die, but God is present with us
whether matters turn out for good or for ill, as long as we cling to him.
    In rabbinic Judaism **kavannah**, "concentration," means the aware-
ness that one is performing a mitzvah in response to God's command. In
the Lurianic Kabbalah, kavannah came to mean the esoteric knowledge of
how the fulfillment of a particular mitzvah helps to bring about the messianic redemption. The Kabbalists had composed little prayers to be recited
before saying the blessing over the performance of a mitzvah. By the time
Hasidism came on the scene, the concept of kavannah had deteriorated to
mean a rote recitation of these Lurianic prayers. The Hasidim gave a new
meaning to the idea of kavannah. In Hasidic doctrine kavannah means that
whatever one is doing, however mundane it may seem, one raises that act
to holiness by directing his heart to the service of God. This new meaning
is illustrated in the following Hasidic tale:

The Baal Shem Tov planned to blow the shofar himself on a
certain Rosh Hashanah. He asked one of his followers, a simple
man, to call out the notes to him. The follower attempted to
memorize the kavannot (the Lurianic prayers) for each blast of
the shofar. For fear that he would forget, he made notes on a
small slip of paper. The disciple was very anxious that everything
should go well and that there should be no slips on his account.
When the time came for the blowing of the shofar the man
reached into his pocket, but he could not find his slip of paper.
In his panic the man forgot everything that he had learned.
Broken-hearted, he called out the notes without reciting the
kavannot. Afterward the Baal Shem Tov said, "There are many
doors in heaven, and to each door there is a key. A broken heart
is an axe that breaks down every door."

Another tale:

A Hasid went off to visit a certain holy man. When he returned,
another Hasid asked him, "What did you learn from the mouth

of the wise?" The first Hasid replied, "I did not go to hear what he had to say, but to observe how he washed the dishes."

With kavannah, the act of washing the dishes can be an act of service to God as much as is prayer, Torah study or the performance of mitzvot.

The Generations of Hasidism

When the Baal Shem Tov died he left behind him millions of followers and an inner circle of disciples, but no movement. Hasidism was organized into a movement by Dov Baer, the Maggid of Mezeritch. Dov Baer was a brilliant organizer. He sent emissaries to every town and city to organize the Hasidim there. In the time of Dov Baer Hasidic teachings were put into writing, in collections of stories and parables and in written sermons. The Hasidim wrote in Yiddish instead of Hebrew, so that the common people would be able to read their literature. The prayers, doctrines and practices of Hasidism were firmly established. The Hasidim prayed in their own prayer-house, called a **shtibl**. They used a different prayer book from that of most Ashkenazic Jews. The differences in liturgy would seem slight to us, but they were enormous and scandalous to the rabbis of the time. Misnagdim and Hasidim did not pray together. The Hasidim also had their own way of slaughtering meat, which meant that Hasidim and Misnagdim did not dine together. Hasidim made little headway in Lithuania, despite the efforts of the Maggid, but everywhere else in Eastern Europe Hasidism predominated. In Lithuania the yeshiva system remained strong, and Torah study was still prized above passion and prayer.

After the death of Dov Baer the Hasidic movement broke up into numerous sects. In each region a Hasidic leader established his own center and sought to attract his own followers. Each Hasidic group was known by the town where its leader lived. Thus, there were Lizenskers and Bratzlavers and Lubavitchers and Lubliners and so forth. Each rebbe had his own style of leadership. Each rebbe chose to emphasize certain aspects of Hasidic teaching and Jewish practice. The Lubavitcher movement was known as **Habad**, an acronym based on three Hebrew words for knowledge. The Habad Hasidim restored the traditional emphasis on Jewish learning, though they still maintained the value system and mystical concerns of Hasidism.

Rabbi Elimelekh of Lizensk was an important leader in the third generation of Hasidism. He established the kingly mode of leadership that became common in many Hasidic groups. He built a sumptuous palace where he held court for his followers. He traveled in a coach pulled by four white horses. Rabbi Elimelekh named his son to be rebbe after him. For the first time since antiquity, Jews had dynastic leaders. Son followed father, regardless of individual qualifications.

In the later generations of Hasidism there were always rebbes who were sincere and who served for the benefit of their followers. Unfortunately there were others who were charlatans, living sumptuous lives on the contributions of their impoverished followers. In the eyes of many, later Hasidism fell away from the grand vision of the early generations.

Tzaddik and Hasid

The later Hasidim called their leader the **Tzaddik,** meaning "righteous one" or "saintly one." The follower of the Tzaddik is a Hasid, a "pious one" or "holy one." Because of his spiritual insight, the Tzaddik understands how each person's soul is rooted in the divine form of the sefirot. The Tzaddik therefore understands what sacred task each of his followers is assigned to fulfill on this earth. The Hasidim go to their Tzaddik not only to hear his teachings, but also for advice in all earthly matters: Whom should my child marry? Should I go into a certain business venture? How much should I give to charity this year? These questions are directed to the Tzaddik, who understands and reveals the divinely appointed destiny of each human being.

Hasidim, Misnagdim and Modernists

In the early nineteenth century the Hasidim and Misnagdim were the two major sects of world Jewry. This situation changed almost as suddenly as it began when the ideas of modernism began to creep into Eastern Europe from the West. The ideals of the American and French revolutions had transformed society in Western Europe. Life was radically changed for those Jews, relatively few in number, who lived in lands where modernism took hold. In Eastern Europe most of the monarchs of Russia and of Austria-Hungary did their best to deflect the winds of change. Jewish religious leaders in Eastern Europe likewise attempted to discourage modernism. They feared that modernism would be destructive to the traditional Jewish way of life, as it had been in Western Europe. Whatever the differences between Hasidim and Misnagdim, they were tiny compared to the differences between themselves and the modernists. The two movements never merged into one, but they joined forces in the battle against modernism. Despite their efforts, modernism with its promise of equal rights and material prosperity proved irresistible to most Jews.

The Hasidic groups which survived the onslaught of new ideas stood right in the path of the onslaught of Hitler's troops. When the Nazis invaded Poland and, later, the Ukraine, they rounded up and killed the Jews who were living in the last bastion of traditional Judaism. A movement that had once claimed millions of adherents could number its survivors in the thousands after the Second World War.

Some Hasidic rebbes survived, along with a smattering of their followers. Since they could not return to Communist Poland, they re-established themselves in little enclaves in Jerusalem, Israel or in Brooklyn, New York. They are in, but not of, the countries of Israel and the United States. They continue to speak Yiddish rather than Hebrew or English, and they live as if they were still in old Poland. An exception is the Lubavitcher movement. They have established an active outreach program which has drawn many formerly modernist Jews into the fold of Hasidism. Hasidism, which began as a revolution against Jewish tradition, has become the last stronghold of the traditional pre-modern Jewish way of life.

PART FOUR:

Judaism in the Modern Age

19

The Road to Modernism

The Origins of Modernism

Between the fourteenth and the eighteenth centuries the countries of Western and Central Europe underwent a gradual transition from the medieval to the modern world-view. The significant stages in this transformation are known as the Renaissance, the Reformation and the Enlightenment.

The Renaissance of the fifteenth and sixteenth centuries began with the rediscovery of the literary, cultural and scientific achievements of the ancient world. This led to a flowering of the liberal arts, with great new achievements in science and the arts. The Renaissance initiated the new spirit of Humanism, which was concerned with human life in the here-and-now. Humanism contrasts with the medieval concern for the afterlife and concentration of the intellect on purely religious matters.

The Reformation of the seventeenth century began with Martin Luther's rebellion against the authority of the Roman Church. The central authority of the Church was broken by the rise of Protestant religions, particularly in Northern Europe. Even in those countries which remained predominantly Catholic, the Reformation led to a questioning of old authority, secular as well as religious. The parallel hierarchies of the Church and the nobility lost power to the rising merchant class of the cities. Capitalism began to overtake the feudal economy with its emphasis on land and agriculture. The Reformation was a political and economic revolution as much as it was a religious revolution.

The Enlightenment of the eighteenth century was the intellectual vanguard of the modernist revolution. The proponents of Enlightenment believed that human reason could answer all questions and solve all problems. They looked to human reason rather than to divine revelation as the source of authority. The groundwork of the Enlightenment was laid with the scientific discoveries of Isaac Newton and the rational philosophy of Spinoza and Descartes. The champions of Enlightenment encouraged a secular view of the world in which the overthrow of irrational beliefs and social institutions would lead to an era of progress for humankind. The political philosophers of the Enlightenment envisioned a new kind of government in which reason rather than tradition would guide human affairs. The individual in society would be granted liberty so that he could realize his economic and intellectual potential.

The ideals of the Enlightenment influenced and helped to generate the American Revolution in 1776 and the French Revolution in 1789. In the eighteenth century all the nations of Western and Central Europe were transformed by the Enlightenment. Napoleon spread the Enlightenment as he conquered many of the countries of Europe. In some places the kings and princes adopted the principles of Enlightenment and attempted to be "enlightened despots." Resistance to change was met with revolution against the old political order. With the First World War (1914–1918) and the Russian Revolution (1917) all of the medieval monarchies were either transformed into modern constitutional monarchies or overthrown by violence. The Enlightenment came later to Eastern Europe because economic conditions were not ripe for it, and because the monarchs of Eastern Europe fought to keep out the new ideas.[1]

The Exclusion of Jews from the Process of Modernization

We have seen that the transformation from medievalism to modernism took place over many centuries. The Jewish people were excluded from participating in this gradual process. There are two primary reasons for this—the oppression of the Jews, and the fact that there were few Jews living in the lands where the process of modernization was occurring.

Jews were banished from England and France in the fourteenth century. After this time Jewish life centered in Eastern Europe. Almost no Jews remained in Northern and Western Europe, the areas most affected by the Reformation and the Enlightenment. Some Sephardic Jews, exiles from Spain, made their way into England and Southern France, where they were allowed to quietly revert to Judaism. Holland, which had fought

---

[1]The "Iron Curtain" which Soviet Russia uses to keep out Western influences has its origin in the attempts of the czars to keep the ideas of the Enlightenment from influencing the people under their rule.

a bitter religious and dynastic war against Spain, welcomed Jewish exiles from that country. A prosperous Sephardic Jewish community arose in Amsterdam, a community immortalized in many of the paintings of Rembrandt. The Spanish and Portuguese Jews of Holland participated fully in the process of modernization. Spinoza, the first modern philosopher, was one of their number. As we have noted, the Jews of Spain were influential in sparking the Renaissance through their work as translators. But, important as these Sephardic Jews were in the process of modernization, they were relatively few in number. They had no influence on their Jewish brethren in the East.

There were a few thousand Jews in the Americas at the time of the American Revolution. Most of these were Sephardic Jews, with a few German Jews among them. These Jews were cut off from contact with other Jewish communities in the world, and many of their descendants assimilated and disappeared from the rolls of the Jewish people.

There were more Jews in central Europe, in the various principalities of Germany and in the city-states of Italy.[2] These Jews were locked behind ghetto walls. Their social and intellectual intercourse with the outside world was severely restricted by the ghetto. Within the ghetto walls, Jewish life did not change much from century to century. Most Jews received only a medieval-style religious education. They were unaware of the new intellectual currents in the outside world. Some of the great Humanists were interested in Jewish teachings, particularly Bible commentaries and Kabbalah, but their interest was only in how they could reinterpret these teachings for Christian society. They were not interested in improving the social condition of the Jews, nor in introducing new ideas into Jewish education.

The first exposure of a sizable Jewish community to the ideas of modernism came in the late eighteenth century, when the Enlightenment came to Germany. The Jews of Germany were struck all at once by the full force of centuries of social and intellectual change. They had no way to prepare themselves for their entry into a radically new world.

Moses Mendelssohn (1729–1786): The First Liberated Jew

The proponents of Enlightenment proclaimed the value of the individual human being. After all, reason belongs to the individual, not to society or its institutions. Any person is equally capable of reason, regardless of

---

[2]Germany and Italy were not unified into nation-states until the nineteenth century.

social class. The Enlightenment political philosophers taught that the state must treat its citizens as individuals. The caste system of the medieval state, with its nobility, peasantry, freemen, and other classes, must be replaced by a society of equal citizens, each one respected for his own accomplishments.

The Jews suffered as much as any class from the corporate system of government, which had a separate set of laws governing the rights and privileges of each caste. The Jews of Germany were allowed to live only within the confines of the ghettos. They were restricted from nearly every form of gainful employment. Jews were not allowed to emigrate from one German city to another. Many cities strictly limited the number of Jews permitted to live within their boundaries. Jews were granted a permit to live in the city only if they were economically useful.

The Jews presented the greatest challenge to the liberal ideals of modernism. If society was truly to treat every person as an individual, regardless of social class and other accidents of birth, would that treatment extend even to the Jews?[3] This challenge came to the fore when there arose in Germany a great philosopher of the Enlightenment who was also a Jew.

Moses Mendelssohn was born to a poor ghetto Jewish family in Dessau. He was frail and hunchbacked, but he had a brilliant mind. He was educated in the classics of Western literature as well as in the sacred texts of Judaism. As a young man he came to Berlin, where he furthered his secular education. Mendelssohn soon became renowned for his philosophical writings.[4] In 1763 Mendelssohn won first prize in an essay contest sponsored by the Berlin Academy. The great Immanuel Kant took second. Mendelssohn acquired fame with his *Phaedon*, a philosophical defense of the immortality of the human soul.

Mendelssohn came to Berlin in 1743. According to legend, he was already known to Germans as a philosopher. He came seeking entrance to the city not as a Jew, to be counted in the Jewish quota, but as a person. He stood outside the city gate for three days until King Frederick the Great, touched by the irony that a great philosopher should be mistreated only because he was a Jew, allowed him entry. The legend is not, strictly

---

[3]We might compare this to the question of civil rights for blacks in America in the 1960s. A person's attitude toward civil rights revealed not only, or even primarily, a person's attitude towards racism, but rather that person's commitment to all of the ideals of liberalism.

[4]In that time philosophy was the most revered of the intellectual disciplines. All educated people tried to keep in touch with the latest currents in philosophy, just as educated people in America today attempt to maintain a level of sophistication in psychology. Philosophers were the intellectual heroes of Germany, and the darlings of high society.

speaking, true.[5] The story is true, however, in a certain sense. The plight
of Mendelssohn and his later fame opened the way for the acceptance of
Jews into modern society as individuals and citizens.

The renowned German philosopher Gutthold Lessing took an interest
in the young Mendelssohn. He became the model for Lessing's *Nathan the
Wise*, a renowned play which pleaded for the extension of human rights to
the Jews.

Mendelssohn's Philosophy of Judaism

As Moses Mendelssohn acquired fame, he acquired the admiring acceptance of many of the leading intellectuals of Germany. They were ready to
befriend this extraordinary person despite his Jewishness, but it bothered
them that he clung to his Jewish ways and would not become a Christian like
them. In 1769 the philosopher Lavater published an open letter to Mendelssohn. Lavater said that now that Mendelssohn had been accepted in
Christian society, it would only be proper for him to return that acceptance
and be baptized. Lavater implied what many "enlightened" Christian intellectuals were to say, that in a modern society Jews should not stick to the
"medieval superstition" that was Judaism. In other words, the spread of
Enlightenment ideals was to be accompanied by the assimilation of the Jews
into general society. The Jews were expected to prefer a modern, enlightened Christianity over their own traditional religion.

Mendelssohn was hurt that his friend would extend this challenge to
him in public. Mendelssohn was now in a difficult spot. If he were to
appear ungrateful or critical of Christianity in his refusal to convert he
would endanger not only himself, but all the Jews of Germany. Rather
than reply directly, Mendelssohn wrote an argument for the eternal truth
and validity of Judaism.

Mendelssohn's defense of Judaism amounted to a new, modern philosophy of Judaism. He described Judaism not as a law, a nation, or a way
of life, but as a philosophy and a religion. As a philosophy, Judaism is the
highest expression of the liberal ideals of the modern age. As a religion,
Judaism is a confession of faith in the one God.

Mendelssohn distinguished the ethical laws in Judaism from the ritual
laws. The ethical laws, said Mendelssohn, were the property of all rational
human beings. By having these as divine law from an early time, the Jews
came to live an ethical way of life millennia before human reason, the

---

[5]Mendelssohn was not yet well known, and he was permitted entry to the city as a
student of the Chief Rabbi.

Enlightenment, would draw other societies to an equal level of ethical living.

The ritual laws, said Mendelssohn, were also part of the divine revelation to Israel. Unlike the ethical laws, these were intended for the Jews alone. Just as no rational human being should reject the ethical laws which are rooted in God, no Jew should reject the ritual laws which derive from the same root.

Ethical and Ritual Mitzvot

The ancient sages and the medieval rabbis recognized that the mitzvot in the Torah could be divided into ethical rules and ritual rules, but they did not allow this or any other distinction to be made between various types of commandments, lest some commandments be deemed unworthy of observance. The traditional attitude is expressed in these words from the Talmud: "Be as zealous in the fulfillment of a minor commandment as a major commandment, for you do not know the divine reward of each commandment."[6]

By making a distinction between the rational, ethical commandments and the ritual commandments, Mendelssohn made it possible for Jews to reject the rituals which distinguished them from their Gentile neighbors, preserving of Judaism only the pure faith and the ethical laws, which no Gentile could object to. Even though that is not what Mendelssohn intended, that is what the enlightened Jews of Germany made of his philosophy. Mendelssohn himself observed all of the strictures of Jewish religious ritual, but those Jews who redefined Judaism as "ethical monotheism" and rejected Jewish religious ritual saw Mendelssohn as the father of their movement.

Mendelssohn and the German Haskalah

Mendelssohn could not win acceptance for the Jews among the modernists of Germany, although he made the first steps in that direction. Mendelssohn's major achievement was among his own people. He spread the doctrines of the Enlightenment among the Jews of Germany. The Jewish proponents of Enlightenment believed that not only would Enlightenment be a benefit for the Jews in itself, but also once the Jews adopted

---

[6]Avot 2:1.

the perspectives of the Enlightenment they would win acceptance in general society.

The Jews called their own Enlightenment movement the **Haskalah.** This is a Hebrew word which means something like "the acquisition of wisdom." Mendelssohn's primary means for spreading Haskalah among the Jews was a translation of the Bible into modern German. The Jews of Germany spoke Yiddish, the Jewish dialect of medieval German. If Jews would learn modern German by studying Mendelssohn's Bible translation, they could begin to interact with the society around them. They could begin to read the Enlightenment literature which was available in the German tongue. Mendelssohn's Bible was widely distributed, and it quickly led to the intended effect. The Jews of Germany learned to speak the language of the land, and they immediately began to absorb its culture.

Mendelssohn's circle of followers initiated a Hebrew language journal to spread the ideas of the Haskalah. Hebrew had long been the language of intellect and scholarship among the Jews. The **Maskilim** (proponents of the Haskalah) hoped to reach the learned Jews who did not know German through this vehicle. This journal, entitled *Hameassef,* had a short life. It was not effective, and the rapid spread of the German language among the Jews of Germany made it unnecessary. The importance of *Hameassef* is that it represents the first attempt to use the Hebrew language for a modern, non-religious purpose.

The French Revolution, Napoleon and the Jews

In 1789 the French overthrew their king and established a republic. The French Revolution represented the political victory of the forces of the Enlightenment over the forces of medievalism, the Church and the landed gentry. France was reconstituted as a secular state. The state guaranteed the individual human rights of all of its citizens, regardless of social class. The slogan of the revolution was "liberty, equality and fraternity for all men."

The French were slow in extending this guarantee to the Jews who lived in France. A year after the revolution citizenship was granted to the Sephardic Jews of Southern France, who were valued for their potential contributions to the nation. The Ashkenazic Jews, concentrated in the Eastern part of France, had to wait another ten years for their enfranchisement.

The Jews had always lived as guests in France, not as Frenchmen. The Jews, as their name implied, were citizens of Judah, living in exile, awaiting the return to their homeland. Jews were a corporate group within

France, living under their own laws, and this arrangement had been satisfactory to Jews and Gentiles alike.

The conservatives in the French government believed that the Jews should continue in their former status. The liberals believed that Jews should be granted citizen's rights, but only if they were willing to give up their communal status. As one leading liberal said, "To the Jews as individuals—everything! To the Jews as a people—nothing!"

When Napoleon became ruler of France in 1799 he initially retracted the rights which had been granted to the Jews. Then, in 1807, Napoleon made himself the champion of the Jews. He called together an assembly of rabbis and leaders in the Jewish community, which he called the Great Sanhedrin. The name of this assembly was no accident. Napoleon wished this group to have the authority, in the eyes of the Jews, to overrule the laws of the Talmud. Only a new Sanhedrin could do this, and no Sanhedrin had existed since the fourth century.

Napoleon presented a series of questions to the Assembly, to be answered yes or no. The questions amounted to asking the Jews to give up their sovereignty and national identity to become one with their fellow Frenchmen. Would Jews bring their lawsuits to French courts and abide by the decision of these courts? Would they serve in the army of France and fight against the enemies of France? Would Jews submit to the authority of the state and live by its laws? Would they consider all Frenchmen their brothers?

The Great Sanhedrin gave Napoleon the answers he wanted, with one exception. They could not give their blessing to marriage between Jews and non-Jews. Still, their answers were sufficient for Napoleon, and he made the Jews citizens of France. From this time on, Judaism was not to be a way of life, but the private confession of faith of the French Jew. In every aspect of their public life, Jews were to be indistinguishable from their fellow Frenchmen. In time, this was to be the pattern followed by modernist Jews everywhere.

Napoleon enfranchised the Jews in all the lands which he conquered— in Germany, in Italy, in Eastern Europe. He tore down the ghetto walls and encouraged Jews to enter society. He became a hero to the Jews. Napoleon may have hoped that the Jews would supply his troops when he made his disastrous foray into Russia in 1812, but the Russian Jews followed the age-old Jewish pattern of doing nothing to assist the enemies of their host country, and the Jews assisted in denying food to the invading French army.

After the defeat of Napoleon in 1815, the forces of the old order regained strength, but they could not entirely undo the work of Napoleon. The Jews could not be placed back into the ghettos. Many new restrictions against the Jews were set in place, but from then on the Jews were a part of modern society in Western and Central Europe, and they had to be dealt with as a part of society. Throughout the nineteenth century the battle raged in every country between the forces of the Enlightenment and the forces of the old order. The liberals favored extending rights to Jews, the conservatives favored restricting the Jews. In no country on the continent of Europe did Jews achieve full and equal citizenship in every respect, but in virtually every country the Jews achieved some degree of acceptance in society. The "Jewish question" remained a central item on the political agenda of the emerging modern states.

The Haskalah

As the liberals and conservatives of Europe debated about what to do with the Jews, a parallel debate took place within Jewish society. Some Jews were devoted to the old way of life. Jews were poor and socially disabled, but they were able to live according to their sacred laws without outside interference or influence. Other Jews saw the Age of Reason as the dawn of a new age for the Jewish people, and they wanted the Jews to prepare for this new age and come out to meet it. The Jewish Enlightenment, the Haskalah, attempted to change Jewish society from within according to the patterns of modernism. The **Maskil** (pl. Maskilim) attempted to spread Haskalah among the Jews.

Jewish Philosophy

The Maskilim studied the writings of the philosophers of Enlightenment. They then attempted to explain and redefine Judaism as a philosophy. German Jewry in the nineteenth and early twentieth centuries generated philosophers of Judaism unequaled since the Golden Age in Spain. Hermann Cohen, Franz Rosensweig, Leo Baeck, Abraham Joshua Heschel and Martin Buber stand out as the great lights of modern Jewish philosophy in Germany. This great flowering of Jewish philosophy was brought to an end by the rise of Nazism in Germany. Heschel fled to America and Buber to Palestine, while Baeck miraculously survived World War II in a concentration camp.

The Jewish way of life was defined by the halakha, Jewish law. Judaism as defined by the philosophers of modern Judaism was "ethical monotheism," an ethical way of living based on faith in the one God who was the father and guarantor of morality. The ethical monotheist need not live by the halakha, which was now seen as an outmoded way of fulfilling the ethical

goals of Judaism. The standards of the Enlightenment were seen as a sufficient replacement for the guidance of Talmudic law. Following the classic
presentation of Judaism by Mendelssohn and Cohen, many Jews saw historic Judaism as a sort of proto-Enlightenment. Even as they assimilated to
Western culture, they believed that in the Enlightenment the whole Western world was becoming "more Jewish." The Jews were fulfilling the task
assigned to them by God by adopting the cause of Enlightenment.

The Historical Study of Judaism

The first stages of the Enlightenment were ushered in by advances in
pure philosophy and in the hard sciences. These were followed by the
development of the social sciences—political science, sociology, and history. The social scientists believed that they could do for human society
what the hard sciences had done for technology and the human economy—
generate great progress in a short period of time. The social sciences would
show enlightened governments how to engineer a society of perfect equality, peace and social harmony. Humankind, enriched by technological
progress, would learn to distribute these riches properly in order to avoid
the wars and social upheavals which had destroyed earlier societies.

The Jews were particularly influenced by Hegel's development of the
modern discipline of history. The modern historian establishes criteria for
the analysis of the past. His purpose is to discover the patterns behind
historical events, in order to reveal the lessons of history.

Hegel and other early historians ignored or denigrated the historical
significance of the Jews. In response to this, and in search of a justification
for modernizing Judaism, Jewish scholars established the **Wissenschaft
des Judentums,** the "Science of Judaism," for the historical study of
Judaism.

The first great historical scholar of Judaism was Leopold Zunz. Zunz
wrote his first great work, *The Sermon in Israel,* to defend the practice of
the modernist German Jews of having their rabbis give instructive sermons
in the German language during the Sabbath worship service. The traditionalists accused the modernists of shamelessly copying the practice of the
Gentiles.[7] Zunz proved in his historical study that many of the ancient
midrash texts originated as sermons delivered in the synagogue. Zunz
discovered—truthfully—that the Jews had invented the sermon. We cannot deny that the Jewish reformers were copying the pattern of the Ger-

---

[7]Sermons were not given in the traditional synagogue in Europe, but they were
common in the Protestant churches.

man church in their own worship, but Zunz's discovery gave them ammunition for a defense of their practices. Above all, the historians proved that Judaism had changed over the course of time. This justified the desire of the Maskilim to change Judaism in their own time according to the new patterns of modern society.

Politics

The Maskilim struggled to acquire full rights for Jews in society—civil rights, economic rights, political rights. In pre-modern times the Jews were not able to engage directly in the political process in order to preserve or extend their rights. When it needed a political voice, the Jewish community depended on "court Jews." Certain Jews had access to powerful Gentile leaders because they served them as aides or physicians. The Jewish community would bring its requests to its most powerful court Jews, who would work behind the scenes in an attempt to influence the government to alleviate the grievances of the Jews. If the rulers were not amenable to the Jews' petitions, they had no recourse but had to suffer the consequences of the government's decisions.

Now that they were entering society, Jews were emboldened to form organizations that would work directly to influence the political process in defense of Jewish rights. The first such organization of importance was the Alliance Israelites Universalle, centered in France. In 1848 a blood accusation was brought against the Jews of Damascus, then part of the Turkish empire. The Alliance successfully lobbied the enlightened governments of Western Europe to pressure the Turks into admitting the falsehood of the charges and punishing the persons responsible for the libel.

The Jews in Society

The Maskilim admired modern society, and they wanted the Jews to adapt their own way of life to modern culture. Certain aspects of the self were to remain uniquely Jewish, but in all respects of outward culture the desire was for Jews to assimilate, to become indistinct from their neighbors. The Maskilim believed that a Jew should dress like the Gentiles, eat as they eat, mingle in their society, and enjoy the same expressions of "high" culture—great literature, the symphony orchestra, opera and theater. The Jews of Germany and the West needed little urging—almost without exception they adopted the cultural standards of their host nations. The Jews became so attached to high culture that they became essential to it. In Europe before World War II, and to this day in America, the patronage of Jews is essential for the support of museums, theaters and concert halls. Many of the great composers, performers, authors, and artists of modern society are Jews. The Jews adopted modern culture so thoroughly that they virtually made it their own.[8]

The key to assimilation into Western culture was education. Jews abandoned the restricted Jewish curriculum in order to study the liberal arts. Some Jews attended the public schools, despite their Christian orientation, while other Jews attended Jewish schools established by Maskilim for the teaching of secular subjects. Many Maskilim encouraged practical education in the trades in order to expand the Jewish role in the economy beyond that of petty trading. This was especially so among Jewish socialists. The socialists believed that only manual labor was productive for society. They despised the middle class, the traders and shopkeepers, as an unproductive class who lived off the labor of others. Through practical education they hoped to move the Jews into the class of workers.

The traditional Jewish love of learning was transformed into a passion for higher education. Jews flocked to the "gymnasia," or academic high schools, and to the universities. Many a young Talmud scholar ran away from his yeshiva in Eastern Europe and into the great universities of Germany and Austria. With the diligence they acquired in their Talmud studies, it was not unusual for such students to master the subjects of university scholarship in a surprisingly short time. Jews encountered much anti-Semitism in the German universities, and were generally not permitted to become professors, but still Jews flocked to the halls of higher learning. With many professions, such as the law, closed to them, a disproportionate number of educated Jews became medical doctors and research scientists. To this day in Western countries a high proportion of doctoral degrees are earned by Jews, and Jews have won an extraordinary percentage of Nobel prizes.

The Maskilim believed that education would cure Western society of its hatred against the Jews. As Christians became enlightened they would see the irrationality and foolishness of their prejudices; they would embrace the Jews as brothers and sisters. As Jews became enlightened they would drop the distinctive rituals and medieval attitudes that made them unacceptable to the Gentiles. The Jews would make themselves productive and welcome members of society at large, enriching the society around them both economically and culturally. The Jews would become the bea-

---

[8]One might see a contemporary parallel in the enthusiasm with which the Japanese have adopted Western culture since the end of the Second World War. It is interesting to note that many of the great performers of classical music who are not Jewish are Oriental.

cons of enlightenment through the rationality of their faith in one God and their practice of ethical religion.

The Russian Haskalah:
The Modernization of Jewish Culture

The modernist Jews of Germany wanted to assimilate into Western culture. In Eastern Europe the Maskilim had a different goal, to modernize Jewish culture, to make Jewish culture equal in glory, achievement and enlightenment to the cultures of Germany, France and England.

There are a number of reasons why the Haskalah in Eastern Europe took this different direction. Haskalah began in the West and worked its way slowly eastward. The Haskalah did not begin in earnest in Eastern Europe until the 1860s, a full fifty years or more after the German Jews entered modern society. By that time the Jews had become aware of the negative effects of assimilation. Many German Jews, perhaps half the total, completed their assimilation by being baptized as Christians. In a society where religion was no longer taken seriously, it was easy for insincere Jews to become insincere Christians in order to escape from the restrictions which prevented a Jew from rising in society. Not one of Moses Mendelssohn's grandchildren remained Jewish, including the famous composer Felix. Such famous Jews as the author Heinrich Heine and the British Prime Minister Benjamin Disraeli accepted baptism as the price of their rise to fame, despite their continuing attachment to the Jewish people. The Jews of Eastern Europe recoiled in horror at the apostasy of the German Jews. They did not want to repeat this experience in Russia.

Assimilation was less attractive as a social option in Eastern Europe. Society was not as advanced nor as enlightened as in the West. A Jew may be enticed to be a German or a Frenchman, but there was little to entice him to become a Russian or a Pole.

There were many more Jews in Eastern Europe than in Germany, and they lived in greater proximity to one another. The Jews maintained a social cohesion in the East that became impossible in the West after the ghettos were eliminated.

In the early days of the Enlightenment the individual was glorified. The world was perceived as an aggregate of individuals. This cosmopolitan view went out of fashion in the later nineteenth century. Nationalism took the place of individualism. The individual was prized not so much for himself as for his participation in the life and spirit of his nation. The Maskilim of this time tended to be Jewish nationalists. For many of them, the restoration of the spirit and the national rights of the Jewish people took precedence over the pursuit of individual rights for Jews.

The people of Eastern Europe were more devout in their religion than the people of post-Enlightenment Western Europe. The Russians were devout Orthodox Christians; the Poles were devout Roman Catholics. The Jews, too, remained pious. Even those Jews who adopted the modern program of secularization remained much more traditional in their attitude to life than the secular Jews of the West. They may scoff at traditional faith and law, but Shabbat was still Shabbat. Instead of rejecting the traditional Jewish way of life, the Eastern Maskilim attempted to re-establish it on a secular, cultural basis.

The Western nations reorganized themselves as nation-states. The empires of the East, Russia and Austria-Hungary, were multi-national states. The Jews were only one of many minority peoples living under one government. In the East, the idea of citizenship did include the idea of a uniform national culture. The Eastern Jew believed that he could be a citizen and retain his national and cultural identity as a Jew.

The "Reawakening"

The proponents of a modernized Jewish national culture distanced themselves from the religious program of the German Haskalah. They declared themselves part of a new project, the **Tehiyyah,** or "reawakening" of the Jewish national spirit. This movement strove to give dignity and self-respect to the Jews of Europe. It strove to bring Jews out of the world of the Talmud and into the modern world, without abandoning Jewish identity. While the German Maskilim rejected Jewish nationality and projected modern Judaism as a religion, the Russian Maskilim rejected religion and projected modern Judaism as a national movement. The Reawakening led to the Zionist movement to restore sovereign Jewish statehood in the Land of Israel.

The Revival of Jewish Literature

The nationalists of the European nations gloried in their language and its great literature as the highest expression of national culture. The Jews believed that they could stand on an equal footing, for didn't they have a language and a literature that was recognized by all nations for its greatness? The language was Hebrew, and the literature was the Bible. The Russian Maskilim rejected Yiddish, the Judeo-German dialect, as an impure borrowing from another culture. The pure spirit of the Jewish nation could only be expressed in Hebrew. They attempted to revitalize Hebrew as a language for high cultural expression. As the English had Dickens, the Germans had Goethe and the Russians had Tolstoy, the Jews too must produce great writers and poets who would capture the spirit of the Jewish nation and give it a modern expression. By the turn of the twentieth century, the Jews had produced some superb Hebrew writers. Ahad Ha'am wrote essays in a clear, sparkling Hebrew style. Berditchevsky wrote classic short stories in Hebrew. Hayyim Nahman Bialik proved to be the greatest Hebrew poet since Judah Halevi. These were the fathers of modern Hebrew literature. The last Hebrew writer to write in the unique literary style of the Haskalah was S.Y. Agnon, an Israeli from Poland who won the Nobel Prize for literature.

Even though the Maskilim despised Yiddish, many an author turned to writing in Yiddish. They did this because of the frustrations of writing in a dead language that for centuries had been used only for religious writing, and also because there was a much larger audience for Yiddish literature. Mendele Mokher Seforim (Mendel the Bookseller) was the first short story writer in Hebrew and in Yiddish. He became the father of two different modern literary traditions. He used a pen name so that his friends would not know that he was writing in Yiddish. After Mendele came the world-renowned Yiddish humorist and story-teller, Sholom Aleikem. The audience for Yiddish literature was destroyed in the Holocaust. Isaac Bashevis Singer is the last of the great Yiddish writers. Although he writes in Yiddish, his stories are immediately translated into English and European languages, for there are hardly any Yiddish readers left. Singer, like Agnon, won a Nobel Prize for literature. Both literary traditions of modern Jewish culture, Hebrew and Yiddish, have received this ultimate recognition.

Religion and the Haskalah

In pre-modern times religion was one aspect of the Jewish way of life, inseparable from law, custom and culture. The modernist Jews of Western Europe redefined Judaism as a "religion"—that is, as a set of ultimate beliefs. These Jews rejected the national and cultural aspects of Judaism. Some even rejected the use of the term "Jew" because it had a national connotation, a person of the nation of Judah. They called themselves "Germans (Frenchmen, Americans) of the Mosaic persuasion." These Jews were indistinguishable from their countrymen except in matters of religious belief, matters which are found only in the human heart and not in any outward expression.

The modernist Jews of Eastern Europe took exactly the opposite view toward religion. They promoted an anti-religious Jewish nationalism. In the East the traditional rabbis were the authority figures in Jewish society, with the backing of the Russian government. The czars desired that all of their subjects, including the Jews, would live by their traditional religions. This would make them less likely to adopt revolutionary ideas. The Russian Maskilim fought against "clericalism" just as the leaders of the American and French revolutions fought against the established (government-sponsored) churches of their own nations.

There were some attempts to create "enlightened rabbis" of the German type in Eastern Europe, and seminaries were set up for that purpose. These rabbis never acquired any authority among the Jews of the East. The traditional Jews did not accept them because they were tainted by secular learning and not sufficiently immersed in the Talmud. The Jewish nationalists did not accept them because they taught that Judaism was a religion and not a nationality. The czarist government supported this movement because they hoped that it would lead to the assimilation and conversion of many Jews, as it had in Germany. The Jews understood this motive and remained suspicious of the attempts of the czars to "modernize" their Jewish subjects. The Jews would not assimilate unless they were offered citizens' rights, and the czars were not about to do this.

The Character of the Maskil—Summary

The Maskil believed in a modern intellectual education. The Jews should become learned in philosophy, social science, the natural sciences, and the useful arts. The Maskil admired the Bible and the study of Hebrew, but rejected Talmudic dialectics. He was usually learned in the Talmud from his childhood education, but he had rejected his own past to enter the wide world.

The Maskil remained a Jew, but he rejected Judaism as it was in his time. He had a vision of a new Judaism, purified of those "medieval" elements which he believed were holding the Jews back in modern society.

Although the Maskil encouraged assimilation, he was shocked and often deeply hurt by the attitude of the younger generation who grew up without Jewish education and showed no devotion to their people. Only a very few Maskilim welcomed the total assimilation and disappearance of the Jews as a solution to the Jewish problem. Many Maskilim turned to writing anthologies and encyclopedias in their later years, to preserve for the future the wisdom of the rabbinic writings which they had once rejected.

The Maskil believed that Judaism had an eternal core and a changing exterior. He used the evidence of historical study to prove that Judaism had changed in the past. To him, this justified his own determination to change Judaism. The German Maskilim believed that religion was the eternal aspect of Judaism. The Russian Maskilim believed that the national spirit of the Jewish people was the eternal core of Judaism.

The Maskil dedicated himself to the spread of Enlightenment among the Jews. He established schools and meeting groups. He wrote books and articles for journals. He engaged in politics both within the Jewish community and with the government. Among his own people, he encouraged them to adopt the ideals of the Enlightenment. He lobbied the government to extend rights to Jews and to place the modernist Jews in power over their communities.

The Maskil believed in progress. He believed that the coming age would be the best ever for humankind and for the Jews. He believed that the spread of Enlightenment among Gentiles and Jews would bring anti-Semitism to an end.

The Maskil believed in the individual. He wanted the Gentiles to recognize each Jew as a unique person, not as one of a class of people. Like the Gentile proponents of the Enlightenment, he believed that the highest thing in creation was the individual human being, with his reason and free will. The Maskil Y.L. Gordon coined the phrase which became the watchword of the Maskilim, "Be a Jew at home and a human being when abroad."

Responses to the Haskalah

The Maskilim were the elite few in the Jewish modernist movement. Many Jews welcomed the new opportunities which the modern world granted them, but they did not trouble themselves to work toward a new, modernized Judaism. They simply left behind them any aspect of Judaism which they found inconvenient in their rush to avail themselves of their new freedom. Many Jews simply disappeared from the fold, especially those intent on rising to the highest levels of society. From the dawn of the modern age until the present, assimilation has drained much of the strength and depleted the numbers of the Jewish people.

In response to the threat of assimilation and the destruction of their way of life, traditionalist Jews drew together and turned inward. They established psychological and religious barriers around themselves to replace the legal barriers and walls that once separated the Jew from the outside world. The traditional rabbis clung to the Shulhan Aruk, the sixteenth century code of Jewish law, as the definition of what it is to live as a Jew. One observes the law according to the codes without fail, or one has removed himself from being counted among the Jews! One traditional rabbi, Moses Sofer of Hungary, decreed that everything new is forbidden by the Torah, just because it is new. He taught that Jews should not ride in trains or use telephones.[9]

Not all traditional Jews were so opposed to anything modern. Many believed that it was acceptable to use modern inventions and even to study modern academic subjects, as long as this did not interfere with the observance of Jewish law. Nevertheless, since modern Jews did not live within a legally constituted Jewish society, the areas of Jewish law which a Jew could apply in life became restricted largely to matters of ritual and observance, faith and ethics. If a Jew made a business contract, for instance, that contract had to meet the legal requirements of the law of the land rather than the requirements of Jewish law. Except in an ever more restricted arena of life, the time when a Jew could bring his lawsuits to a Jewish court was coming to an end.

Many Jews who rebelled against their background and embraced modernism later in life came to regret the loss of the beautiful traditional Jewish way of life. The first generation out of the ghetto ended up living between two worlds and not quite belonging to either. The majority of Jews embraced modernism with passion as soon as they were granted the opportunity, but some Jews went in the other direction. They attempted to return to an enclosed Jewish society and to live according to ancient Jewish tradition as much as possible.

Considering how late the Jews came into modern Western civilization, the impact they have had on it is amazing. Sigmund Freud, Albert Einstein and Karl Marx were all Jews, though Marx rejected his Jewish background and Freud had no Jewish learning. Jews have been dominant in all the arts, as patrons and as creative artists. Any novel which captures the interest of Jews is sure to become a best-seller, for Jews constitute a major portion of the book-buying public. The movie industry was virtually a creation of American Jews. Jews have had a remarkable influence in shaping and directing the course of modern society, perhaps because they had to struggle so hard to become a part of it.

---

[9]This attitude to modern technology was not unique to traditional Jews. In America we still recall the attitude of many people to the invention of the airplane: "If God had meant man to fly he would have given him wings."

20

The Three Movements
of Modern Judaism

Three Movements

The Jews of America have divided themselves into three separate movements—Orthodox, Conservative and Reform. A fourth movement, the Reconstructionist movement, began as an offshoot of the Conservative movement, and is poised to be recognized as a fourth major movement of American Judaism. Those Jews who choose to recognize their Jewish identity through membership in a synagogue, about half the total of American Jews, define themselves by the affiliation of their synagogue with the ideology of one of these movements.

The division between the three movements of Judaism has no relationship to the various divisions and sects of the Jews in pre-modern times. All three movements trace their origins to traditional Judaism as it was practiced in pre-Enlightenment Europe. The three movements arose principally in Germany, in the nineteenth century, as part of the civil emancipation of the Jews in that country. They grew out of the varying responses of Jews to the process of modernization. The religious attitudes of these movements were transplanted to America by Jewish immigrants.

The three movements have certain things in common which derive from their origin in Western, post-Enlightenment culture. All three movements define Judaism in religious terms. Religion may include aspects of culture and law, but it is taken for granted that Jews will live as citizens of their country and participate in its public life. For this reason the three movements did not find a home in Eastern Europe. There, the Jewish modernists preferred anti-religious nationalism, while the traditionalists rejected participation in Gentile culture and customs. In the State of Israel the Reform and Conservative movements have found only a few adherents. The majority of Israelis came from Moslem countries or from Eastern Europe and were not influenced by the social forms of the West European Enlightenment. Israelis define themselves as "observant" (of traditional law) or as "secular," not as members of a Jewish religious movement. The three movements help a Jew define his or her Jewishness in a secular, democratic state with a predominantly non-Jewish culture. The United States, Canada, England, and Australia are the home of most such Jews. Small Reform and Conservative movements exist in Western European countries, although Orthodoxy is predominant among those European Jews who survived the Holocaust. The Nazis utterly destroyed the Jewish community of Germany, the birthplace of the three movements. Since the Second World War, the United States has been the center for all three movements.

The movements appeared, as organized movements, in reverse order of their attachment to historical Jewish tradition. The Reform movement arose first. The Conservative and Orthodox movements arose later, in negative response to the radical changes in Judaism proposed by the Reform movement. The early reformers did not set out to create a separate sect of Judaism. They intended their reforms for all Jews, at least for all the Jews of Germany. When it became apparent that there could be no compromise among the attitudes of those who wanted radical change in Judaism, those who wanted moderate change, and those who wanted no change, the German Jews divided into movements. Each movement established its own synagogues and its own rabbinical seminaries.

Division and Unity

The division of German Jewry into separate movements was limited by the fact that in most German states the Jews still had something like a kehila to run the religious institutions of the community. The German states had a religious head tax, paid by all citizens. The tax money was returned to the leaders of each religious community to maintain its institutions and to pay the salaries of the professional religious leaders. Jews did not want to remove themselves from their official community, and very few could afford to support a second set of religious institutions out of their own pockets. Therefore, the fight over the religious stance of the synagogue had to be fought internally, within the community.

Even where the differences in religious belief and practice are extreme, the movements of modern Judaism cannot be compared to the different sects of Protestantism. Jews of different religious movements all relate to the same past and claim it as their own. All Jews are part of the same ethnic community, with social customs that are recognizable to one another regardless of denomination. Jews join together for social, charitable and political causes, especially to fight for rights for endangered Jewish communities. Many Jews are not attached to any particular movement; they choose their synagogue on the basis of proximity and social relationships rather than on the basis of religious doctrines and practices. The break into three distinct movements has strained Jewish unity, but the Jews still consider themselves to be one people and one religion.

The Beginnings of Reform

The initial impetus for the reform of Judaism came from lay persons, and later spread to modern-minded rabbis. Although the principles of reform applied to all areas of religious life, the form and content of the worship service was the symbol of the movement for reform and the center of controversy between reformers and traditionalists.

Israel Jacobson was a leading Jew in the city of Seesen in the state of Westphalia. He ran a school for Jewish boys. In 1805 he began to hold worship services for his students at the school. The services were shorter than the traditional service. They included hymns sung in German, and an inspirational sermon. Many townspeople began to attend the services at the school, preferring them to the traditional services of the synagogue. The services attracted many Jews who had long since ceased to worship, since they found no inspiration in a lengthy service conducted in a language they no longer understood. This gave an indication that religious reform might be a good response to the problem of assimilation and the abandonment of Judaism.

In the city of Hamburg some Jews established a Temple which advanced new reforms in its worship service. The congregation published its new prayer book in 1819. The service was shortened and many prayers were in the vernacular (the common spoken language, German). The reformers eliminated prayers containing doctrines which they considered outmoded.

The new format of the worship was more radical than the change in the liturgy. The congregation adopted Western standards of decorum in worship. The pulpit was moved to the front, facing the congregation. The rabbi read the prayers or led the congregation in unison recitation. This pattern of strong leadership was different from the traditional synagogue, in which the cantor maintained a loose unity among worshipers, each of whom recited his prayers individually. The Hamburg congregation eliminated the **aliyot,** the calling up of congregants to the pulpit for various honors. Hymns were sung to the accompaniment of an organ, although Jewish tradition forbade instrumental music on the Sabbath. The rabbi gave a sermon. These innovations became common in many German synagogues as the movement for reform spread.

Rabbinical Synods

In the 1840s the liberal rabbis of Germany called a series of rabbinical synods. In these synods the rabbis debated the changes which should be made for a modernized form of Judaism. Thirty or forty German rabbis attended these synods. They considered themselves equal in authority to the great rabbis of antiquity, or even higher, since they had the wisdom of the Enlightenment which had been denied to the rabbis of old. They therefore felt qualified to overrule the teachings of the Oral Torah which had been the basis of Judaism for two millennia.

The rabbis voted to eliminate the laws of keeping kosher. This had the practical effect of allowing Jews to mingle freely with their Gentile neighbors. The rabbis voted to eliminate the necessity for religious divorce when a marriage had been dissolved in the civil courts. The more radical rabbis spoke in favor of eliminating the custom of circumcision, a custom that was looked upon with distaste by German Gentiles. In all of their deliberations the rabbis placed the Talmud in an advisory capacity. They gave it a vote, but not a veto, in their decisions.

Positive Historical Judaism

The traditional rabbis of Germany naturally did not attend the synods. There were other rabbis who believed in change and did attend, but were outraged by the ease with which the liberals were voting down ancient Jewish traditions. Rabbi Zekarias Frankel (1801–1875), a great Jewish historian, walked out on the Frankfort conference of 1845 in protest. He founded his own modernist movement, which he called **Positive Historical Judaism.** This movement is the forerunner of the American movement of Conservative Judaism.

The term "positive" meant "progressive." Frankel believed that Judaism had changed over time, and that this change represented progress to more advanced modes of religious belief and action. The term "historical"

meant that progress must occur in accordance with the process of history. Historical change does not take place by the vote of leaders, nor by the rational process of philosophy. Religious change, like all historical change, is evolutionary and often not self-conscious. The key to historical change is the constantly developing spirit of the nation. This spirit is revealed in the beliefs and practices of the folk, the people as a whole. Religious leaders must adjust to change as it occurs in the spirit of the people; such change cannot be legislated.

Frankel's movement was in accord with the ideals of the Romantic movement, which had gripped Germany. The German people were turning away from philosophy and the dictates of reason. The Romantic movement idealized the past, particularly the Middle Ages, before modernity had destroyed the faith and security of traditional life. Romanticism went hand in hand with a resurgence of nationalism, the feeling that each person played out his role in life as a member of his nation, not just as an individual. Allegiance to the traditions of the people was therefore more important than the lonely quest of the individual to assist progress through the use of scientific reason.

Samson Raphael Hirsch and Neo-Orthodoxy

Samson Raphael Hirsch (1808–1888) grew up in an Orthodox home in Hamburg. As a young man he had an excellent Talmudic education. After his rabbinic ordination he earned a doctoral degree at the University of Bonn. There he established a close friendship with Abraham Geiger, who was to become the scholarly and intellectual leader of the Reform movement. After he earned his degree, Hirsch went on to a career as a rabbi. He held a number of important rabbinic posts.

Hirsch's first posts were in the eastern part of Germany. This region was still under the sway of the traditionalism of the Jews of the East. Hirsch was considered as a reformer there because of his openness to new ways. Hirsch moved on to Frankfort, where he reinvigorated the Orthodox community and established a number of day schools for Jewish students. In his schools Hirsch strove to give his students an excellent education in both traditional Jewish studies and modern subjects.

While still a young rabbi Hirsch published a book, *The Nineteen Letters of Ben Uzziel*, which became the manifesto of modern Orthodox Judaism. The book was written in the form of a literary dialogue between a young rabbi and his friend, who was confused by the temptations of the modern world and had abandoned Jewish practice. The young rabbi explains to his friend how he can best fulfill the ideals of the Enlightenment by clinging to the laws and practices of traditional Judaism.

Hirsch's educational philosophy was "Torah im Derekh Eretz," meaning "Torah combined with worldliness." Hirsch taught that a Jew can dress and act as a member of modern society, learn the practical and intellectual subjects of the modern curriculum, and still live by the laws of Judaism. Hirsch taught that the ritual and ceremonial laws of Judaism, so opposed by the reformers, were not bound by time and circumstance but were unchangeable laws given by God. As such, we must have confidence that observance of these laws will mold a person into the best kind of citizen that the Enlightenment had envisioned. When the laws and rules of Judaism seem to us to be opposed to the spirit of the times, we must struggle to understand them in new ways rather than reject them. Hirsch taught that the civil emancipation of the Jews presented a new opportunity to advance the original purposes of Judaism in the world. This opportunity should not be rejected. Hirsch therefore criticized the traditionalists who would not accept even those changes in Jewish society which were not contrary to law, and who insisted that the Jews remain completely separate from Gentile society. Hirsch welcomed contact with the modern world, as long as the Jews were not tempted to forget the distinctions that God had placed upon them. Hirsch believed that the Jews would bring ultimate benefit to all humankind if they would remain true to the special revelation that God had granted them.

The Reform of Doctrines

The Reform movement in Germany represented a rejection of the essential idea of rabbinic Judaism—the twofold Torah. Reform Jews believed in a continuously unfolding revelation which was brought about by "divine inspiration" upon the human mind. This replaced the idea of the written Torah, spoken by God, and the Oral Torah, revealed through human reason but also deriving from God. One might say that to the reformers, all Torah was Oral Torah. All Torah derived from the interplay between God's will, as revealed in human reason, and the forces of history that shaped human society. Reform Jews revered the Bible, especially the ethical books of the Prophets, and tended to denigrate the Talmud. Positive Historical Jews viewed Torah and Talmud equally as aspects of the progressive revelation of the spirit of Judaism.

The reformers rejected or revised other essential doctrines of rabbinic Judaism in addition to the doctrine of the twofold Torah. These doctrinal changes are revealed in the new liturgies of the Reform congregations. The reformers eliminated or revised those ancient prayers which contained doctrines that they thought were unscientific or which had no place in modern religion. Among these doctrinal shifts are:

☐ the elimination of mysticism, replaced by an emphasis on human reason, eternal truths, the uplifting of the emotions, and spirituality.

☐ de-emphasis of the special status of the people Israel, with new emphasis on the unity of all humankind and the universal mission of the Jewish people to better the world.

☐ elimination of the doctrine of angels. All mention of angelic beings was expunged from the prayer book.

☐ elimination of the belief in the Messiah as an actual human being who would someday bring peace on earth. This was replaced by a new emphasis on the Messianic Era, which would be brought about by human effort to live ethically and to create a just society.

☐ elimination of the doctrine of bodily resurrection, replaced by an emphasis on the eternity of the human soul.

☐ elimination of the hope for a return to the Land of Israel. As citizens of their country, Reform Jews believed that the Jews could seek a solution to their troubles by working for equal rights where they were, rather than by hoping for a return to sovereign Jewish statehood. The Jews were no longer a nation, and they no longer had national hopes.

☐ elimination of the doctrine that the Exile was a punishment for sin. The scattering of the Jews across the world was perceived as part of God's plan to spread the teachings of Judaism to all humankind. Israel was properly a nation only in her early history, when national life was necessary to form the people and strengthen their faith in God. A return to Zion would be contrary to God's will.

As time went by, many of these doctrinal changes were accepted by Conservative and Neo-Orthodox Jews, even though they would not accept any changes in the liturgy. The last two doctrinal changes we mentioned are an exception. The Conservative movement from its beginning in America in the early twentieth century was favorable to Zionism, the attempt by modern Jews to restore Jewish sovereignty in the Land of Israel. One party of the Orthodox, the Mizraki, was founded in the early twentieth century to support the cause of Zionism. Another party, the Agudat Yisrael, rejected Zionism and clung to the belief that the Jews would be restored to the land when, and only when, God sent the Messiah. Eventually, most Reform Jews also came to favor the work of the Zionist movement, even if they had no desire for themselves to leave the lands where they now lived.

In 1937 the Reform movement in America made its first public proclamation in support of Zionism.

The Reform of Worship

The Reform Jews changed the outward form of their worship to make it more like the worship of the people around them, and to confirm their new doctrines. They made the service shorter by eliminating traditional repetitions of certain prayers and by eliminating the medieval poetry which had been added to the liturgy. They prayed in unison, with the rabbi as leader. They used the vernacular in addition to Hebrew in their worship. The rabbi gave a sermon on the Sabbath. They sang newly composed German-style hymns in their worship. In America and in the more radical German congregations, Reform Jews prayed with heads bared, following Western social custom in place of the old Jewish custom of covering the head indoors as a mark of respect. Reform Jews sat in the synagogue in family groups, women sitting together with the men. Mixed seating is also usual in Conservative synagogues.

The Reform Jews called their house of worship a "temple" rather than a synagogue. This term symbolized the break with the rabbinic Judaism of the past. It also symbolized the rejection of the doctrines of the Messiah and the return to Zion. Traditional Jews prayed for the rebuilding of the Jerusalem Temple, which would take place after the Messiah brought the Jews back to their land. The Reform Jews announced that the synagogue is their Temple, and they do not need or look forward to any other. The rabbi, in his new role of worship leader, was perceived as the priest of the Temple, performing his sacrifical service by leading the congregation in prayer. The Reform movement eliminated from their temple the few honors which had been reserved by the ancient rabbis for the descendants of the Temple priests. The "cohen," or priest, was no longer the first to be called up to the pulpit for the recitation of Scripture, and the priests were no longer called to the pulpit to recite the priestly blessing (Numbers 6:22–27) over the congregation on the Festivals. The rabbi, as the functioning priest, recited the priestly blessings himself, regardless of his ancestry. The reformers declared the priesthood to be no longer valid, and members of priestly families were no longer required to observe the special marriage and burial laws prescribed by the Torah.

The changes which Reform Jews made in the style of Jewish worship generated more protest than their revision of historical Jewish doctrines. Many Jews had little interest in doctrinal matters, but they still objected to seeing Jews pray with heads bared, or in a language other than Hebrew.

There are even many non-practicing Jews who object to any changes in the traditions which they do not observe.

The Reform of Law and Practice

Traditional Judaism was based on practices that were founded in Jewish law. Jewish faith and practice were defined in the halakha. Orthodox Jews uphold the eternal sanctity of the law, although as citizens of the secular state the realm in which the law applies to their lives is for the most part restricted to religious matters. Reform Jews reject law as a basis for Judaism. The Reform movement emphasizes the freedom of the individual in deciding how to practice his religion. Each Jew must study the teachings of Judaism and then decide how he or she will live based upon an educated personal decision. The Reform movement declared that only the ethical laws of Judaism, which are common to all humanity, are part of the eternal law of Judaism. Religious rituals are tied to time and circumstance, and in different times Jews are free to change or reject old rituals. In recent years many Reform Jews have shown a renewed appreciation for ritual and tradition, but there is no body in the Reform movement with the authority to require certain practices. The Conservative movement agreed that religious practices change over time, but they denied that the individual person is free to decide what to practice or not practice. The Conservative movement taught that religious practice is grounded in the life of the people as a whole. Historical tradition plays a big role in determining the way in which the people express their relationship to God. Jews must observe the law, but the law is not eternally the same. It evolves with the life of the nation.

The Reform of Social Customs

Nearly all German Jews adopted the social customs of the German people. In this lies the primary distinction between Neo-Orthodoxy (also called Modern Orthodoxy) and traditional Judaism. The Jews who reject modernism entirely, the ultra-Orthodox, believe that Jews must remain distinct from all other peoples even in those matters which are not required by the halakha. The ultra-Orthodox retained the old Polish costume even when the Polish people around them switched to the modern German way of dressing, in a short suit coat instead of a long caftan. The ultra-Orthodox attempt to limit their relationship with Gentile society to the greatest extent possible. They continue to speak Yiddish. They teach their children only traditional Jewish subjects in their schools. The modern Orthodox observe the same religious laws as the ultra-Orthodox, but they wear the same clothes and speak the same language as their Gentile neighbors. They attend the symphony and the opera. They read modern literature and study modern secular subjects in addition to Jewish subjects. To a traditional Jew in Eastern Europe all German Jews in their short coats, even the Orthodox, seemed overly assimilated to Gentile culture.

Reform Judaism in America

By the mid-nineteenth century most American Jews were of German origin. The Jews of America did not think of themselves as members of any sect or movement in Judaism. They were fairly unanimous in accepting a modernist point of view. There were few rabbis in America, and most American Jews had very little religious knowledge. Individual Jews might be more or less observant of tradition. Being German, and being those who were willing to venture the journey to America, the general tendency was not to be too strict in ritual matters. There were some few congregations which actively adopted the principles of Reform Judaism as they had developed in Germany. Most congregations practiced a liberal form of Orthodoxy.

Rabbi Isaac Mayer Wise (1819–1900) came to America in 1846. After serving in a few pulpits, Wise settled in Cincinnati. The Ohio River valley had attracted many German immigrants, Jewish and Gentile. Cincinnati at that time was a major center of Jewish settlement in America.

Wise established the institutions that became the heart of the Reform movement of Judaism in America. In 1875 he founded the Hebrew Union College, the first lasting rabbinical seminary in America. Two years earlier Wise had helped organize the Union of American Hebrew Congregations[1] (U.A.H.C.) to support the seminary. In 1889 Wise founded the Central Conference of American Rabbis (C.C.A.R.) to bring together the graduates of his seminary and other Reform rabbis. Wise ushered in a period in which Reform Judaism became dominant in American Jewish life.

Wise established a Jewish newspaper, the *American Israelite*, which represented the modernist point of view. He also published a prayer book,

---

[1]Many American Jewish organizations identified themselves as "Hebrew" rather than "Jewish." There were two reasons for this. The term "Jew" was still used in an uncomplimentary way by Gentiles. Also, the term "Jew" has a national connotation, and the reformers used another term to symbolize their belief that the Jews were no longer a nation, but a religion only.

Minhag America, "The Jewish Custom of America." Wise's prayer book excluded those prayers which contradicted Reform Jewish doctrine. In most other ways, *Minhag America* was a fairly traditional prayer book. It was much more traditional than many of the early prayerbooks published by individual Reform congregations, prayer books which often had virtually no relationship at all to the traditional Jewish liturgy.

Wise did not intend to establish a separate movement for Reform Jews. He envisioned a moderate reform, respectful of tradition, which would be acceptable to nearly all American Jews. Wise believed that he was developing the form of Judaism which was appropriate to life in free, democratic America. Just as there had been Ashkenazic and Sephardic Judaism, there would be an American Judaism, with its own religious forms and customs.

The Division of American Judaism

Wise's vision of a single form of American Judaism was not to be. One reason is that the radical reformers in the Union of American Hebrew Congregations would not be content with Wise's limited reforms. Many of those German rabbis who had come to America were among the most radical reformers from Germany. Often, they came to America precisely because their radicalism made them politically unacceptable in Europe. Religious radicals in that time were likely to be political radicals as well. Some radical Reform rabbis escaped to America after the revolutions of 1848 failed to overthrow the conservative governments of central Europe.

When the C.C.A.R. published a prayer book for its member congregations, the *Union Prayer Book*, the radicals controlled the committee which wrote the book. They went far beyond the moderate reforms of Wise's prayer book.

The American Jewish community became less homogeneous after 1881, when large numbers of Eastern European Jews began to come to America. These Jews were much more traditional than their German brethren, who did not all welcome their arrival. Many German Jews did not want these Eastern Jews in their congregations, for fear that they would demand a return to traditions which the Germans did not wish to accept. Thus, many German Jews saw a split in the organization of American Jewry as desirable.

The split came in 1883, at a dinner celebrating the ordination of the first graduates of the Hebrew Union College. Oysters, an unkosher food, were served as an appetizer. The more traditional rabbis were outraged. They walked out of the dinner and severed their connections with Wise's organizations. The organizers of the infamous "treife banquet" claimed that the caterers had made a mistake, but many thought that this "mistake" was arranged by the radical reformers to force out the traditionalists.

Conservative Judaism

The Conservative movement of Judaism in America claims Isaac Leeser (1806–1868) as its founding spirit. Leeser was a liberal-minded Orthodox Jewish leader. He was probably the most influential of all Jewish leaders in mid-nineteenth century America. He was the hazzan, or prayer-leader, of the Sephardic congregation Mikveh Israel in Philadelphia. Leeser thought of himself as a traditional Jew, but he introduced moderate reforms in the worship, reforms which he felt were in tune with the spirit of the times. He gave sermons in English. He translated the prayer book and the Bible into English so that they could be understood and studied by American Jews. Leeser founded the Jewish Publication Society, still in existence, to publish literary works on Judaism in the English language. Leeser established the first American Jewish newspaper, *The Occident*, which represented a traditionalist point of view.

Leeser's successor at Mikveh Israel Congregation, Sabato Morais (1823–1897), was the founding president of the Jewish Theological Seminary, which opened in New York in 1887 to train rabbis for what eventually became the Conservative movement of American Judaism. The seminary struggled for many years. In 1902 it received generous financial support from some wealthy Reform Jews. These Jews recognized that Reform Judaism could never satisfy the religion needs of East European Jews. They wanted to help establish an institution that would encourage the new immigrants to accept modernism, even while retaining many of the forms and practices of traditional Judaism. The Jewish Theological Seminary took a great step forward when, in 1902, the great English Jewish scholar Solomon Schechter accepted the presidency of the school. Under Schechter the school stopped vacillating between the Reform and Orthodox congregations and established the principles of Conservative Judaism in America, following the pattern of Frankel's Positive Historical Judaism. In 1913 Schechter founded the United Synagogue as a Conservative parallel to the U.A.H.C. and the Union of Orthodox Jewish Congregations. In 1919 the alumni of the Jewish Theological Seminary established the Rabbinical Assembly, accepting into membership other rabbis who accepted the principles of Conservative Judaism.

The Conservative movement did indeed prove attractive to East European Jewish immigrants. By 1920 the great majority of American Jews were East Europeans. Very few of these joined the Reform congregations. Not only were the Reform congregations too non-traditional for these Jews, but there was a great social distinction between the Germans and the East Europeans which lasted until the third or fourth generation in America. The German Jews considered themselves to be socially superior—more Westernized and more cultured. Having come to America earlier, they were certainly more materially successful. Many of the differences between Reform and Conservative Judaism in America were more ethnic than religious.

Conservative Judaism proved attractive to many of the children of Orthodox Jewish immigrants. After the Second World War, when many American Jews moved to the suburbs of the big cities, the greatest number of suburban Jews affiliated with Conservative congregations. The Conservative movement became the largest of the movements of American Judaism, though recently the Reform movement has overtaken it.

Orthodoxy in America

In 1860 there were about two hundred Jewish congregations in the United States, some Sephardic and some German Ashkenazic. As a matter of course, the members of these congregations used the traditional Jewish liturgy in their worship. To the extent that American Jews were observant, they observed traditional Judaism. Traditional Judaism was difficult to observe in America. There was little Jewish education; there were few learned rabbis. Saturday, the Jewish Sabbath, was a workday for most Americans. When the Reform and Conservative movements were organized, only a minority of congregations remained Orthodox.

The number of Orthodox Jews in America increased with the East European immigration. Although many of these immigrants were not religious and many found a home in Conservative Judaism, there were also many who clung to Orthodoxy in the new land. These immigrants founded many Jewish day schools for the traditional education of their children.

Ultra-Orthodox Jews did not immigrate to America, which was known as a land that tempted Jews to assimilate, the "treife medina" or "unkosher nation." When Hitler left them with no choice, some ultra-Orthodox Jews did come to America. More came from among the survivors of the Holocaust. Various areas of Brooklyn, New York became ultra-Orthodox enclaves. Various Hasidic rebbes re-established their courts in America. The most numerous ultra-Orthodox group are the Lubavitcher Hasidim. Their rebbe has become a well-known figure on the American Jewish scene. Other ultra-Orthodox groups are reclusive and less well-known.

Unlike the Reform and Conservative movements, Orthodoxy in America is not a unified movement. There are many shades and gradations of Orthodoxy. Each Orthodox movement has its own day schools and yeshivas, its own seminaries, its own rabbinical and congregational organizations.

One of the outstanding institutions of Modern Orthodox Judaism in America is the Yeshiva University in New York City. As the name implies, Yeshiva University is a school for both traditional Jewish studies and modern secular studies. The university follows the modern Orthodox philosophy of Samson Raphael Hirsch.

Yeshiva University began in 1896 as the Rabbi Isaac Elchanan Theological Seminary, a rabbinical yeshiva where Talmud was taught in the traditional manner. The school became Yeshiva College in 1928, with the addition of a course of secular studies leading to a bachelor's degree. The school became Yeshiva University in 1945 with the addition of graduate and professional schools.

The leading body of Orthodox congregations in America is the Union of Orthodox Congregations. Among other activities, the Union is the primary body in America for establishing standards of kashrut. The symbol of the Orthodox Union on packaged foods means that the foods have been inspected in preparation and found to meet the standards of Orthodox Judaism. There are many other kashrut-supervision organizations as well, but none of them has as much visibility in the kosher community as the Orthodox Union.

The two major Orthodox rabbinic organizations in America are the Rabbinical Council of America and the Agudat Harabbanim, or Union of Orthodox Rabbis. The latter organization has among its members a great many European-trained rabbis. The former organization, with American-trained rabbis, tends to be more open to modern changes which do not undermine halakha.

The Hasidic sects do not participate in any of these organizations. They each have their own complete set of institutions, so that their members can live a full religious life within the bounds of their own community. Many of these groups continue to speak Yiddish among themselves. The adults learn English to conduct their business with the outside world. They do not watch television or movies and have little contact with Gentiles. These groups continue to wear the long black coat, broad hat, and white shirt without tie that was customary in Europe. The women dress according to traditional standards of modesty, covering their necks, elbows and legs. Married women cover their hair with a wig or a kerchief; only their husbands are permitted to gaze upon their natural hair.

The Baalei Teshuvah Movement

In general, the movement of American Jews has been away from tradition and toward a modernist interpretation of Judaism. The children of each succeeding group of immigrants have moved away from Orthodoxy, either into Conservative and Reform congregations or else out of religious life altogether. There was an economic component to this movement. The Reform were the most well-to-do, the Conservative less so, and the Orthodox Jews were the poorest.

Since the 1970s there has been a small but accelerating reversal of this trend. Many Orthodox Jews who succeed economically are remaining Orthodox. A small but significant number of assimilated Jewish youth are seeking a more spiritual way of life by returning to Orthodox Judaism. Some Orthodox organizations, particularly the Lubavitch Hasidim, have established special institutions to encourage this phenomenon. The Lubavitch Hasidim have established outreach centers on college campuses and in cities and towns. They send speakers wherever they are invited to explain the Orthodox way of life to other Jews and encourage them to try it. In America and in Israel there are special yeshivas established to train newly Orthodox Jews in the traditional Jewish way of life.

The Orthodox call a former assimilated Jew who returns to Orthodoxy a **baal teshuvah,** a "penitent."

It is difficult to judge the true numerical strength of Orthodoxy in America today. About half of all American Jews belong to a religious congregation. Between a fourth and a fifth of these belong to Orthodox congregations. Many of these members are not practicing Orthodox Jews, however. Some join out of family tradition, and some because they believe that Orthodoxy is the correct form of Judaism even if they do not observe it. What the Orthodox lack in numbers they make up in energy and devotion. Every true Orthodox Jew has a good Jewish education. The Orthodox place Jewish living above all other goals in life, and are willing to give a great deal of their time, money and energy to support the cause of traditional Judaism.

Reconstructionism

The Reconstructionist movement is the youngest and most volatile movement of American Judaism. It is the only movement whose roots are in America rather than Europe. This movement came about as a result of the work and teachings of one man, Rabbi Mordecai Kaplan (1881–1984). Kaplan was a member of the faculty of the Jewish Theological Seminary.

In 1934 he summarized his ideas on Judaism in his book, *Judaism as a Civilization*. Kaplan's views led to a gradual separation between himself and the Conservative movement. By 1960 the Reconstructionists had their own synagogue and rabbinical organizations and their own rabbinical seminary, in Philadelphia. The Federation of Reconstructionist Congregations and Havurot (Fellowships) has sought recognition in national Jewish organizations as a fourth movement of American Judaism, equal to the other three.

Mordecai Kaplan taught that Judaism is the civilization, the culture, of the Jewish people. Not God, but the people themselves, are the generators of the Jewish way of life. Kaplan rejected the concept of the Chosen People; the Jews generated their own concept of themselves, he taught. Kaplan analyzed Judaism according to the teachings of the sociologist Durkheim, who described religion as a projection of the ideals of a people. Jewish peoplehood is therefore primary in Reconstructionist Judaism, while faith and traditional piety are secondary. In some ways Reconstructionism encourages traditionalism, since the traditions are sanctified as the culture of the Jewish people. In other ways Reconstructionism is the most radical movement in Judaism. A people is free to change its life and customs as it wishes, especially if the customs derive from them and not from a commanding God. To Kaplan, Judaism was not a religion but a religious civilization, a culture which was centered around its response to faith. In modern times the faith must be updated. Kaplan believed in a "Power which makes for salvation" toward which we strive rather than in a God who establishes rules and commands obedience.

In recent years the Reconstructionist movement has been closely associated with counter-culture Judaism and with the Havurah movement. The presidency of the Reconstructionist Rabbinical College was taken over by Arthur Green, one of the founders of this movement. A Havurah is a small, intense fellowship group. Its members meet for worship, study, celebration, and the religious education of their children. The Havurah is characterized by respect for experimentation with tradition, and by an openness to "new traditions" which may enhance Jewish spirituality. This movement has attracted many young, devoted Jewish spiritual seekers.

A Summary of Distinctions Between Orthodox, Conservative and Reform Judaism

Reform Judaism is based on philosophy, the religion of reason. Conservative Judaism is based on history, the historical development of a people which progressively reveals the divine spirit. Orthodox Judaism is based on law, the law of the eternal and unchanging Torah which God gave at Mount Sinai.

Reform and Conservative Jews apply the methods of historical study to the Bible and other sacred Jewish texts. Orthodox Jews believe that the entire Torah was given to Moses at Mount Sinai and cannot be subjected to historical analysis.

In Reform Judaism it is taught that each generation of Jews is free to revise the practices of Judaism in order to express the eternal values of Judaism in keeping with the spirit of the times. Each individual Jew may decide for himself what he will or will not practice. Conservative Judaism teaches that Judaism slowly evolves, and every Jew must stay in step with the practices of the Jewish people. Orthodoxy teaches that a Jew is obligated to live by the halakha. The halakha is interpreted in response to new situations, but in principle it never changes.

Conservative Judaism was always favorable to Zionism, the modern Jewish nationalist movement. Reform Jews originally rejected Zionism as not being consistent with the Jewish acceptance of citizenship in the Diaspora. Most Orthodox Jews originally rejected Zionism because they believed that the Jews must await the Messiah to restore them to nationhood. Today all three movements are favorable to Zionism except for a very small group of Reform Jews (the American Council for Judaism) and the most ultra-Orthodox sects.

The Orthodox believe that Jews must remain a distinct people, separated from the general community as much as possible. Conservative Jews believe that they must have a strong sense of community, but they are also free to mingle in the wider society. The Reform are universalists, encouraging Jews to mingle in general society and to put their Jewish ideals into practice in working for social justice for all people.

21

Anti-Semitism and the Holocaust

Anti-Semitism in Modern Society

Anti-Semitism is the national-racial hatred of Jews. In the pre-modern world Jews were subject to suspicion and hatred as a result of their unique and different religion. A Jew who adopted the religion of the majority in his nation was no longer subject to anti-Jewish persecution. In fact, such a Jew was often given a lofty position in society as encouragement to other Jews to follow his example.[1] The anti-Judaism of the Middle Ages must be distinguished from the modern phenomenon of anti-Semitism, which arose in the nineteenth century. The anti-Semite considers the Jew to be genetically distinct from other peoples; he believes that the Jew is either inferior or dangerously superior to other races. The anti-Semite therefore believes that the Jews must be suppressed, restricted from access to power, wealth and position, or even eliminated altogether.

The Enlightenment spread the idea of individual human rights, guaranteed by Nature, as the basis for government and society. No people benefited more from this ideal than the Jews. The Jews had been the

[1]There are exceptions to this rule. The New Christians of Spain were persecuted as Jews at the time of the Inquisition. Although this persecution was rooted in ethnic jealousies, it was justified by standard medieval religious arguments. The New Christians, having been denied the opportunity to assimilate into old Christian society, stuck together and were suspected of harboring in their hearts a continued attachment to Judaism. Despite the Spanish emphasis on "limpieza," or purity of blood, no argument was raised that Jews were hereditarily incapable of becoming Christians.

official underclass of Europe. After the Enlightenment some Jews achieved wealth and high status in general society, while the mass of Jews continued to press for continuing social change which would lead to full equal rights for themselves.

There were many groups in European society who did not benefit from the changes brought by the modern revolution. These groups fondly recalled their position in the hierarchical, pre-modern society. They opposed liberalism, modernity, and social change. Included in this conservative opposition to the ideals of the Enlightenment were the old nobility, the military, many of the clergy of state-supported religions, and peasants who lost their land and became part of the impoverished urban masses. Also included were members of the middle class who found themselves unable to compete successfully in the new capitalist economy which valued individual ability above nobility of birth. Anti-Semitism became the unifying doctrine for these disparate groups which opposed the principles of modernity.

This perspective means that we cannot blame anti-Semitism on the work of a few insane fanatics such as Adolf Hitler. To the question "What if there had been no Hitler?" we must reply that even without Hitler things would have been very bad for Europe's Jews in the twentieth century. Anti-Semitism grew out of the reaction to the Enlightenment to become one of the driving forces of modern European society. This perspective also means that anti-Semitism includes much more than just a personal hatred for Jews. Anti-Semitism is a whole world-view which includes a morbid, negative fascination with Jews.

Pseudo-Science and Racism

The term "Semite" was coined in the nineteenth century to describe the Jews as a race, possessing a distinct set of inherited characteristics. Many people believed at that time that humankind could be easily divided into distinctive racial types. It was believed that blood lines determined not only a person's physical traits, but also his or her personality, character, morality, and innate abilities. The pseudo-scientists of racism believed that a person's moral character could be defined by the physical characteristics of the skull and face. There were charts which showed what were believed to be the typical facial features of the "criminal type," so that one could identify a probable criminal by appearance alone. The Jew was described as having beady eyes, a long, hooked nose, a bent posture and a lascivious look, indicative of the "shrewd and immoral" character of his race.

The science of racism meant that a Jew could not erase the negative elements of his character through religious conversion. A Jew was still a Jew by virtue of his inherited blood, still to be despised and feared. The goal of the anti-Semite was not to convert the Jew nor to cause the Jew to assimilate into society. It was, rather, to totally isolate the Jew so that his race could not affect society and his blood would not mingle with that of the "pure" North European races.

Charles Darwin had published his *Origin of the Species* in 1859. Darwin taught that species evolved to higher forms through natural selection. The competition between members of a species led to the survival of the fittest. The weakest failed to reproduce and disappeared, to the benefit of the species as a whole.

Many people came to believe that Darwin's theory could be applied to the competition among individuals for success in society. This is the theory of "Social Darwinism," which is well known to readers of American literature through the writings of Theodore Dreiser and Jack London.

Those who believed in the pseudo-science of racism came to believe that the various races of humankind were engaged in a constant competition for world domination. They taught that the Germanic peoples must strive to overcome the "inferior" races of the Mediterranean peoples, the Slavs, the dark races, and the Jews. If the Aryan nations did not overcome these races, they themselves would be overcome in the competition for survival. On the one hand, these racists depicted Jews as the most inferior of nations, lacking the human qualities necessary for participation in proper society. On the other hand they depicted the Jews as a superior race, strong in cunning and intelligence, determined to dominate the world, and therefore the most dangerous opponent of the Aryan nations. We must note that the racists accused the Jews of doing exactly what they themselves most fervently wished to do—to dominate and control all the peoples of the world.

Romanticism and Nationalism

The Romantic movement of the nineteenth century placed an emphasis on the "folk," on the history and the customs and lore of the nation. Under the influence of Romanticism, national identity was considered by many people to be more important than individual identity. This was something of a reversal of the idea of the Age of Reason, in which the individual human being, the rational creature, was most prized. Instead of society serving the needs of the individual (government of the people, by the people and for the people), the individual was expected to subsume his own needs to those of society. The individual achieved importance only to the extent that his own life reflected the spirit of the nation and advanced its cause.

The rise of nationalism resulted in part from the reaction to Napoleon's conquests. Following the defeat of Napoleon the political conservatives came to power in the nations which had opposed his attempts at empire. The Congress of Vienna restored the old order to power in Europe. They encouraged nationalism in opposition to the cosmopolitan internationalism of liberals and Socialists.

As individuals, the Jews were qualified to be citizens of the European nations in every respect. If genuine citizenship were dependent upon identification with the history and folk spirit of the nation, then Jews could not be genuine citizens. The ancestors of the Jews did not come out of the forests of Northern Europe. The ancient gods of the Germans were never worshiped by the German Jew. Jews could not identify with the castles, the nobles and Christian knights of Romantic literature. The folk spirit of the Jews was not at all one with that of the Germans. The Jews came to be perceived as outsiders who could never be full participants in the culture and national life of the European nations.

The Political Uses of Anti-Semitism

Left to themselves, the common folk usually had no trouble accepting and dealing with Jews as members of society. Whenever anti-Semitism became a problem, it was usually fostered and encouraged by powerful people who saw anti-Semitism as a means to consolidate their own grip on the reigns of society. Anti-Semitism came down from above, not up from popular sentiment.

The czarist rulers of Russia used anti-Semitism as a weapon in their campaign to prevent the kind of revolution that had overthrown the other medieval monarchies of Europe. The czars held on to power until 1917, while other monarchs lost their heads or became figurehead rulers. As absolute monarchy became an anachronism, the czars depended more and more on their campaign of anti-Semitism to divert the attention of the peasants away from the true causes of their misery. In 1881, following the assassination of Czar Alexander II, there were bloody pogroms throughout Russia. The government did nothing to stop these pogroms, and in many ways encouraged them. The government was active in encouraging the infamous Kishinev pogrom of 1905 in which hundreds of Jews were killed.

In Western Europe, conservative political parties made anti-Semitism the central plank of their party platform. Karl Luger, the mayor of Vienna for many years at the turn of the century, was leader of the Anti-Semitic Party in Austria. In America, too, fear of Jews and other "foreigners" became a significant factor in politics. In the early twentieth century Congress passed the first restrictive immigration laws in the United States, with the intent of stemming the influx of Jews as well as Slavs, Italians and Irish. When the Nazi party used anti-Semitism to rally the German people around their banner they were following a practice which had become usual.

The "Protocols of the Elders of Zion"

In 1905 the czarist government commissioned a work which could be used to spread anti-Semitism among the masses. The result was "The Protocols of the Elders of Zion." This book was purported to be the minutes of a secret meeting of the leaders of world Jewry. The Jewish leaders are said to have a plan to dominate the world. They will do this by secretly manipulating the world economy and by corrupting world leaders through bribery and sexual immorality. The Jewish leaders are said to have invented liberalism and Socialism in order to spread chaos among the Gentile nations, thus weakening them for the Jewish takeover. Even though this work was an obvious fake and fantasy of a sick mind, it was accepted as truth by many. The "Protocols" was translated into many languages and continuously reprinted.

Henry Ford, the automobile magnate, was a leader of the anti-Semitic movement in America. He used his newspaper, the "Dearborn Independent," to spread anti-Semitic beliefs to the American people. Ford had the "Protocols" translated into English and published them in his newspaper.

Later in life Henry Ford regretted his role in spreading anti-Semitism. He publicly retracted and attempted to gather and destroy the anti-Semitic works he had published.[2] Unfortunately, it was too late to undo the damage. The "Protocols of the Elders of Zion" is still printed in English and distributed by various hate groups.

The "Protocols of the Elders of Zion" is widely distributed today in many Arab nations, such as Saudi Arabia, which are opposed to the State of Israel. Copies were distributed free at the entrance to the Saudi exhibit at the World's Fair in Knoxville, Tennessee in 1982, until they were removed due to American protests.

---

[2]For many years no Jew would buy a Ford automobile. This changed after Ford's retraction, and the Ford Motor Co. of today is not in any way held responsible for the anti-Semitism of its founder.

The Dreyfus Affair

In 1894 French Military Intelligence discovered that there was a spy somewhere in the officer corps of the French Army. The army chose to identify Captain Alfred Dreyfus as the culprit. There was not much evidence against him, but it was enough that he was a Jew. Certain generals who wished to discredit the French Republic and increase the independence of the Army used Dreyfus' court-martial as an opportunity to whip up an anti-Semitic campaign throughout France. Dreyfus was convicted and sent to Devil's Island. A few years later the real culprit was discovered, a certain Esterhazy. In 1899 Dreyfus was brought back to France for a new court-martial—and again convicted!

Under pressure from the liberals of France, Dreyfus was pardoned. Seven years later he was exonerated. He was eventually raised to the rank of major, and decorated with the Legion of Honor.

The Dreyfus Affair was a cause célèbre throughout Europe. Not only Jews, but liberals of all stripes, rallied behind Dreyfus. The French journalist Emile Zola published a newspaper article, "J'accuse," in which he exposed the entire plot of the French military to frame Dreyfus, and demanded that justice be done. On the other side, royalists and churchmen all over Europe joined the campaign against Dreyfus and the Jews. They accused the Jews of an "international conspiracy." They claimed that the Dreyfus Affair proved that Jews would not be loyal citizens and could not be accepted as citizens of any country.

If something like the Dreyfus Affair had occurred in Russia or even in Germany, no one would have been unduly surprised. That such a thing could happen in France, the Mother of the Revolution, the champion of liberalism and democracy in Europe, this came as a great shock to Jews. The Dreyfus Affair revealed that anti-Semitism was not withering away, but becoming stronger, as the pace of modernization increased. The Dreyfus Affair was a portent of what Europe held in store for Jews in the twentieth century.

The Rise of the Nazis

Adolf Hitler was the leader of the Nazi Party, originally a small fringe party in Germany. Germany had been made a republic by the Allies after the First World War. Hitler increased his power by making political capital of the sting of Germany's defeat in the Great War and the poverty and disruption caused in Germany by the Great Depression. Hitler accused the Jews of engineering both the Depression and the defeat of Germany. Many

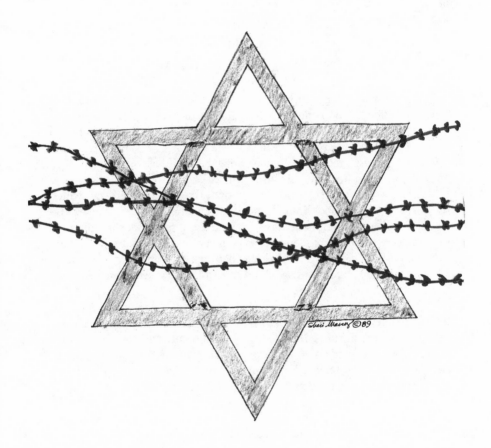

Germans desired a strong leader to pull them out of the social and economic chaos of the Weimar Republic. Certain wealthy German industrial-
ists backed Hitler, seeing in him a man they could manipulate to restructure Germany according to their own tastes. The Nazi party grew to be one
of the largest in Germany, well represented in the Reichstag, the German
Parliament. Hitler manipulated the German government so that by 1933
he was the ruler of Germany. He dissolved the Republic and had himself
declared "Fuhrer," the dictator of Germany.

The Nazi Campaign Against the Jews 1933–1939

The German people supported Hitler because he promised to renew
German military and economic strength, but they were also enthusiastic
about his anti-Semitism. The Nazis ran a massive propaganda campaign
against the Jews. Hitler railed against the Jews in his speeches. Attacks on
Jews were encouraged and often organized by Hitler's henchmen. The
Nazis organized a boycott of Jewish businesses.

Along with their propaganda campaign, the Nazis passed laws which
restricted the Jews and limited their participation in German society.
These so-called "Nuremberg Laws" restored the medieval disabilities of
the Jews. Jews were forbidden to engage in various professions. They were
driven out of the universities. Marriage between Jews and "Aryans" (pure-
blooded Germans) were outlawed. In 1935 the Jews were removed from
German citizenship altogether.

On November 9, 1938 the Nazis organized a nationwide pogrom
against the Jews. On this "Kristalnacht," the "Night of Broken Glass,"
synagogues were burnt to the ground, Jewish homes and stores were van-
dalized, and thousands of Jews were beaten, many to death. The Jews of
Germany were then fined a huge sum to pay for the damages. All Jewish
property was expropriated and handed over to Germans.

The Jewish Response

The wariest Jews left Germany as soon as Hitler took power. Many
Jews stayed in Germany and attempted to wait out the Hitler episode. The
Jews of Germany had learned to love their country. Many had fought for
Germany in the Great War. They took pride in German culture and intellectual achievement. They did not believe that "the most civilized nation
on earth" would go so far as to do harm to its Jews. Many Jews still
believed that the Enlightenment meant better times for Jews were ahead,

and Nazi anti-Semitism was just a passing, unfortunate phase on the way to a more glorious future for Germany and her Jews.

The Jews had so much faith that the Enlightened nations of the West were the Jews' best hope, that when Germany and Russia invaded Poland some Jews moved westward to enter the German occupied zone. Despite the rhetoric of the Nazis, they expected better treatment under the Germans than under the Russians.

The Jews had a long history of dealing with violently anti-Jewish rulers in Europe. Past experience had shown that quiet waiting and low-key political maneuvering led to the best possible result for the Jews. Jews did not have much political power or public sympathy, and could only hope that the event of Nazism would pass with minimal long-term damage and loss of life. In historical hindsight the blindness of Jews to the danger of Nazism seems naive. We must remember that before it happened, no one dreamed that Germany would set out on a policy of mass extermination on a level never before conceived.

By 1938 virtually all German Jews wanted to get out of Germany, but it was difficult for them to find a place to go. The Germans were not alone in their anti-Semitism, their vehement nationalism and hatred of foreigners. Virtually all the nations of the world had closed their borders to immigration, including the United States. One shipload of Jews reached America on the very eve of the Second World War, only to be refused permission to land. Finding no other port, they returned to Germany and their death. Many German Jews who did escape ended up in other European countries where they were later swept up in the Nazi net.

The Second World War: Phase One—The Ghetto

The Second World War began in the fall of 1939 with the German invasion of Poland. Poland fell to the German onslaught in less than a month. The world's largest Jewish community, some three million in number, were in the hands of the Nazis.

The Jews of Poland were herded into walled-in ghettos in the larger cities of Poland. The Jews were put to work as slave laborers for the Nazis, working in exchange for a near-starvation diet. Many Jews died of hunger and disease. The Nazi guards killed anyone who tried to escape or got out of line; sometimes they killed at random for enjoyment. Most Jews worked hard, believing that only by being valuable to the Germans could they spare their lives.

Despite the tremendous difficulties of ghetto life, the Jews in most ghettos managed to organize schools for children, cultural activities and study groups for people of all ages. This was the only kind of rebellion available to them—to be human in the face of inhumanity.

Those few Jews who were able ran off to the forests and joined partisan groups, fighting the Nazis from behind the lines. Most Jews did not have this option. They were caught up in the Nazi dragnet, with no way of escape. Partisans need the cooperation of the local populace to survive, and the Jews did not have this. Many Poles assisted the Nazis in rounding up the Jews, and Polish partisans often shot escaped Jews when they found them. Eventually, when it became clear that the Nazis intended to liquidate the ghettos, there were organized rebellions in most ghettos. The most famous and successful of these was the Warsaw ghetto uprising of April and May 1943. The Jewish fighters, with only a few rifles and pistols and Molotov cocktails at their disposal, tied up two German divisions for two months until the entire ghetto was turned into rubble and hardly a Jew was left alive.

The Invasion of Russia

In 1941 Hitler broke his treaty with Stalin and ordered a surprise attack on Russia, opening up a new front in the war. About two thirds of Russia's three million Jews managed to retreat behind Russian lines, but another million were caught by the Nazis. Especially in Lithuania and in the Ukraine, large numbers of Jews were caught by the Nazis. The Nazis systematically gunned down the Russian Jews, community by community.

Close behind the regular army came the SS, special units designated to carry out the slaughter. When the SS came into a town they ordered all the Jews to appear at a certain time in the town square. They marched the Jews to the forest outside the town and made them dig pits. They then lined up the Jews in front of the pits and mowed them down with machine guns. The Jews had no option but to join the death line so that they could die in family groups, comforting their children, rather than be gunned down trying to escape.

In the major city of Kiev in the Ukraine, some 30,000 Jews were marched to Babi Yar, a deep gully outside the town. The guns fired non-stop for three days until all the Jews were killed.

The Death Camps

At a conference of top Nazi leaders at Wansee in 1942, the Nazis decided upon "the final solution of the Jewish problem"—the execution of all the Jews. The machine gun method used in Russia was deemed too slow, messy, and bad for soldiers' morale. The Nazi leaders decided to build death camps, concentration camps where Jews would be sent to die. The most able would be worked to death; the rest would be immediately killed with poison gas. The earliest death camps used carbon monoxide from engine exhaust to kill Jews. The later camps built special gas chambers and used Xyclon B, a gas which was easy to handle and which killed rapidly. At the largest death camp in Auschwitz-Birkenau the gas chambers could handle 6,000 Jews a day. The bodies were burned in huge ovens, making way quickly for the next load of victims.

Death camps were built in various locations in Poland. Jews were transported in cattle cars from the ghettos to the camps. One ghetto after another was emptied out. The Germans organized the deportation of Jews from Greece, from France, from every nation which they invaded. The Nazis showed the greatest knack for efficiency in transporting and murdering millions of people. The Holocaust is unique among massacres not just for the large number of victims, but also for the mechanical efficiency with which the killing was carried out.

The Nazis depended on local cooperation for their success. They received this cooperation almost everywhere. In those few places where the conquered nation would not cooperate, many Jews were saved. The Danes worked together to remove the entire Jewish population of Denmark to safety in neutral Sweden. The Romanians refused to cooperate with the Nazis, despite their history of anti-Semitism, and many Romanian Jews were saved. The Bulgarians also resisted. Many Dutch people risked their lives to try to hide Jews, but Holland was occupied for a long time and very few Jews were saved. In virtually every other country, the government and the people assisted the Nazis in killing Jews. Most of the guards in the death camps were not Germans but Poles and Ukrainians.

Even the Allies cooperated in the Holocaust. They refrained from criticizing Hitler for his anti-Semitic campaign, both before and after the outbreak of war. They closed their borders to Jewish immigration. They refused to bomb the gas chambers in the death camps, despite the pleas of Jewish leaders in America and Palestine. Every day Allied planes flew over Auschwitz to drop bombs on military and industrial targets, while one bomb that would put the gas chambers out of commission for even a single day could have saved 6,000 lives.

Some historians believe that Hitler planned the mass extermination of the Jews from the very beginning. Others believe that Hitler moved step by step. When he saw no resistance at each step he was encouraged to go on to another step against the Jews. Hitler was convinced that the Allies and all the occupied nations secretly thanked him for what he was doing to the Jews.

The Final Stages

The tide of the war turned in 1943. From that time on, the defeat of Germany was inevitable. The Germans made the killing of Jews their top priority, ahead of the war effort. If a troop or supply train encountered a deportation train, the troop train was under orders to wait on a siding and allow the deportation train to pass without interruption.

In 1944, when the Germans were already retreating on many fronts, they invaded Hungary. They immediately began the deportation of Hungary's 400,000 Jews. Adolf Eichmann, the Nazi in charge of the mass murders, offered the Allies a trade—Hungarian Jews for trucks, ten Jews per truck. The offer was declined.

As the Allies advanced, the Germans attempted to cover up their activities. When the Allied forces advanced on a death camp the Germans killed any inmates who could not travel and forced the rest to march into the interior, while they burned the camps. Only the rapidity of the Allied advance prevented the destruction of all the death camps. The Germans continued to kill until the very last moment.

After the Liberation

Many inmates of the death camps who survived until the Allied conquest were too weak to live. Many died of disease and starvation in the following weeks, despite attempts to save them. The remaining survivors were put into displaced persons camps along with numerous other refugees. Some of these Jews attempted to return to their home villages, only to find that everyone they ever knew was gone. Gentiles now lived in their homes. Some Jews were killed when they tried to reclaim their property. Poland was no longer a home for Jews. The whole country was "one vast Jewish graveyard."

The majority of Jewish survivors ended up behind the Russian lines. Many of these attempted to cross over to the American sector, from which they could emigrate to America or Palestine. The U.S. Army quietly assisted many Jews to cross the lines, even though this was against the rules.

The British closed Palestine to Jewish immigration in respect of Arab wishes. Many Jews attempted to immigrate illegally. Those who were caught were placed in British concentration camps on the island of Cyprus. After the State of Israel won her freedom in 1948, Israel became a home for many survivors.

The Yiddish-speaking Jewish culture of Eastern Europe was gone forever. A Jewish culture which had thrived for four centuries was utterly wiped out in a few short years. Those Jews who remained in the East found themselves in Communist states which discouraged religion in general, and the separate identity of the Jewish people in particular. In all, some six million Jews were murdered—three million from Poland, a million from the Soviet Union, over 200,000 from Czechoslovakia and again from Hungary, 160,000 from Germany, 135,000 from Lithuania, 106,000 from Holland, 83,000 from France, 65,000 from Greece, and more from every other country which had been occupied by the Nazis.

Response to the Holocaust

In the first few years after the Holocaust there was very little public response to what had occurred. Perhaps the world was too shocked to admit what had happened; how can one deal with such atrocities on such a level? Holocaust awareness increased in the Western world with the publication in 1959 of the novel *The Last of the Just* by the French Jewish novelist, Andre Schwarz-Bart (published in English translation in 1960). Elie Wiesel published his first Holocaust novel, *Night*, in 1960. Since that time Wiesel, A Holocaust survivor himself, has written extensively on the Holocaust and its meaning for humankind. He has become something of a spokesman for all the Jewish people and has been recognized with a Nobel Peace Prize as a spokesman for the cause of humanity in a cruel and dangerous world. Wiesel has keyed his message on the moral obligation that comes with being a "survivor." He has encouraged all Jews and all people to perceive themselves as survivors, and to live in response to that perception.

As time has gone by, the Holocaust and its victims have been memorialized in monuments, study centers, documentation centers and museums. The most important of these is Yad Vashem, the Holocaust museum in Jerusalem. It is seen as vitally important to document the Holocaust as fully as possible, because already anti-Semites have arisen to claim that it never happened. It is seen as vitally important to study and understand the Holocaust, to make sure that such a thing never happens again, neither to the Jews nor to any other people. To further this goal, many school districts in the United States have made the Holocaust a part of the curriculum for high school students.

Understanding Anti-Semitism and the Holocaust

Was the Holocaust an aberration of history, the work of madmen in extraordinary circumstances? Or was the Holocaust merely another example of the evil of which humans are capable, made more destructive by the application of modern technology? There is much disagreement over this question. Some theologians and moral philosophers believe that the Holocaust requires us to forge an entirely new concept of God and of humankind. Some Jews believe that in response to the Holocaust Jews must change their idea of what it means to be a Jew and what it means to serve God. Others believe that life goes on as before, only with a new determination to thwart the enemies of the Jewish people.

Whatever the ultimate meaning of the Holocaust, it should not be trivialized into just another example of "man's inhumanity to man." Every instance of inhumanity is not another Holocaust, and to overuse the term is a dishonor to the six million victims. In memorializing the victims, we cannot overlook the specific causes of the Holocaust. The Holocaust was directed against the Jewish people, and one cannot deal with the Holocaust unless one deals with the causes of anti-Semitism in the modern Christian world.

Some have attempted to explain the extraordinary vehemence of modern anti-Semitism in psychological terms. The philosopher Jean-Paul Sartre described anti-Semitism as a problem that arises in the mind of the anti-Semite.[3] Anti-Semitism is the outlet for the mediocre person who cannot bear his lack of distinction. He takes out his frustration with himself upon the Jews. There is nothing about the Jew himself to cause anti-Semitism, except that he has been singled out by society to bear this burden. Anti-Semitism cannot be cured by changing or eliminating the Jew; society must be cured—not just for the Jews' sake, but for the sake of the health of society.

Anti-Semitism has been described in Freudian terms as an Oedipal neurosis of Christian society. A child competes against his father for his mother's love; he comes to fear that the father will learn of his competitive urges and kill him. This is the "Oedipus complex." Just so, it has been suggested, Christians who worship the "Son" compete against and fear the people who are identified with the worship of the "Father." This fear is expressed as anti-Semitism.

Anti-Semitism has also been described as a displaced hatred for Jesus. It is suggested that many Christians subconsciously hate Jesus for placing

---

[3]Sartre, *Anti-Semite and Jew*, Schocken, N.Y., 1948. First published in French in 1946.

upon them the burden of "turning the other cheek," so opposed to the notions of vengeance and personal honor which predominated in the pagan society of pre-Christian Europe. To hate Jesus is unbearable, and so the hatred is sublimated and displaced onto the people of Jesus. The Nazis and other anti-Semites openly claimed that Christianity was a fiction foisted upon the Aryan nations by the Jews, with the intent of weakening them through Christian ethics. It is possible that professing Christians with unacknowledged ambivalent feelings toward Jesus could express that ambivalence through hatred toward Jews.

Christian Responses to the Holocaust

The Catholic Church was the first to publicly recognize the role that traditional Christian teaching played in setting the stage for the Holocaust. Pope John XXIII acknowledged that while the Nazis were anti-Christian, they played on attitudes toward Jews that were encouraged by Christian doctrines. He taught that anti-Semitism was opposed to Christian doctrine, and he initiated steps to eliminate anti-Jewish statements from Catholic liturgy and Catholic education. He showed personal regard for the Jews and respect for their religion. John XXIII convened the Second Vatican Council in 1960 and instructed the Council to make a statement on the Jews. The Council declared that the Jews of today are not to be blamed for the death of Christ. This was a significant first step in the long road to Christian-Jewish reconciliation.

Since that time, many major Protestant churches have also taken steps to eliminate anti-Jewish teachings from their doctrines. Many churches have begun to teach that Judaism is not just an incomplete form of Christianity, but a complete religion which is valid for Jews. They have ceased to blame the Jews as a whole for the death of Christ. The Catholic Church and many Protestant churches have initiated interfaith dialogue with Jews in the attempt to eliminate ancient hatreds through education and increased understanding. Many Christian theologians have sought a new appreciation for the Jewish roots of Christianity, finding a common ground in the shared Judeo-Christian heritage.

As individuals and as organized churches many Christians show empathy for the Jews by giving strong support to the State of Israel. Unfortunately, since Israel's victory over her enemies in 1967 the support of many churches has weakened. The Jews have lost the sympathy that came to them as underdogs.

Ironically, the greatest support for Israel today comes from those churches which are least likely to recognize Judaism as a valid religion.

Many of the churches which support Israel teach that the Holocaust was a divine punishment brought upon the Jews for not believing in Jesus. They teach that the State of Israel is a prelude to the Second Coming which will see the final conversion of all Jews. The liberal churches, which have been the most progressive in trying to change historical church teachings against Judaism, have also on the whole been the least friendly toward Israel. This is a dilemma for contemporary Jews. Who are their true friends—those who give political support to Israel and her three million Jews, or those who are willing to recognize the validity of Judaism and to repudiate anti-Jewish teachings? Naturally, Jews would like Christians to accept the validity of their religion and to support the Jewish state.

Contemporary Anti-Semitism

Since the end of the Second World War, the Anti-Defamation League of B'nai Brith has taken an annual survey of anti-Semitism in America. Initially, the survey showed that two thirds of Americans held anti-Semitic attitudes ranging from mild to severe. That proportion has decreased every year since. Today, only about one third of Americans hold anti-Semitic attitudes, and very few of those are extremists. The evidence seems to indicate that anti-Semitism is still a problem in America, but a decreasing one. Some American Jews believe that they must constantly struggle against a potential resurgence of anti-Semitism, while others believe that anti-Semitism will continue to fade until it is entirely a thing of the past.

Informal surveys in Germany and in Poland have shown that anti-Semitism still exists in these countries even though all the Jews are gone. Apparently, anti-Semites do not need actual Jews around them in order to maintain their attitudes. The persistence of anti-Semitism in these countries is a matter worth pondering.

Until recent times, anti-Semitism was not an issue in Islamic countries. Jews were treated as second-class citizens in Islamic countries. Jews suffered indignities and periodic persecutions, but nothing like the mass persecutions and killings that were common in Christendom. This situation has changed since the end of the Second World War and the founding of the State of Israel. As an aspect of their war against Israel on all fronts, many Arab states have adopted the methods and attitudes of European anti-Semitism.[4] The governments and official presses of these states have

---

[4]Arabs, like Jews, are Semites, but we must remember that the term "anti-Semitism" was coined to describe not a hatred of all Semites, but a racial hatred of Jews. An Arab can potentially be an anti-Semite, within the meaning of the term.

carried on a consistent campaign of anti-Semitic propaganda.[5] Many Communist countries, notably the Soviet Union, have joined in this campaign. Perhaps the most significant factor which these nations have in common is that their governments want a monolithic culture, with no room for dissent or individualism. For these nations the Jews may be a symbol of distinction, a people that wishes to live in the midst of others while insisting on the right to be different.

Anti-Semitism and Anti-Zionism

The campaign against Israel has brought about a new type of hatred against Jews—anti-Zionism. As anti-Judaism is hatred of Jews as a religion and anti-Semitism is hatred of Jews as a race, anti-Zionism is hatred of Jews as a nation. Since the Second World War, racism is no longer acceptable in polite society. Racial hatred of Jews is forbidden. To hate a nation is considered acceptable, however. Anti-Zionism creates a publicly acceptable forum for the expression of hatred against Jews.[6] In fact, the Zionist Jews are themselves condemned as "racists," making hatred against Jews not only acceptable, but a moral imperative. Under the guise of anti-Zionism, the Soviet Union has renewed its persecution of Jews in ways remarkably similar to the pattern of czarist persecutions. Jews are once again restricted from advancement in Russian society.

In public statements, anti-Zionists claim to harbor no hatred against Jews as a religion or a people. Their propaganda gives the lie to this claim. Israel is portrayed in exactly the same way that Jews were portrayed in Nazi propaganda—as a nation of immoral devils, overly powerful, intent on world domination. Anti-Zionism is clearly the descendant and the inheritor of anti-Semitism.

Jewish Determination

Jews may differ in their interpretation of the Holocaust, but on one matter they are all united. Never again! Never again shall such a thing be allowed to happen to the Jews! To insure this, contemporary Jews have worked to have a greater hand in the determination of their own fate. They

---

[5]By no means have all Islamic states or all Arab states participated in this propaganda campaign.

[6]Every Jew is a Zionist. This is virtually true in reality, and definitely true in the mind of the anti-Zionist.

have done this by working to strengthen Israel as a homeland for Jews and as a refuge for Jews in distress. Jews have come to Israel from Iraq in 1949, from Argentina in the 1970s, from Ethiopia in 1987, from the Soviet Union from 1967 to the present. If Jews were persecuted where they live, they now have a sovereign state of their own which can take them in.

In free and democratic countries, Jews have become willing to engage in the democratic process as citizens to preserve their rights and to protect Jews in other lands. American Jews lobby actively with their government for human rights and for support for the State of Israel. It is hard for today's Jews to remember that before the Second World War, American Jews were afraid to stand out by petitioning their own government with their grievances.

Jews work not only to defend themselves but also to fight anti-Semitism through education and dialogue. Jews work to expose anti-Semitic fringe groups before they enter the mainstream of society. They attempt to teach about Judaism to non-Jews, in the firm belief that knowledge leads to friendship and understanding. This book which you are now reading was written for a college course funded by the Jewish Chautauqua Society with the goal of increasing interfaith understanding.

22

Zionism and the
State of Israel

Jews in the Land of Israel

There have been three sovereign Jewish states in the Land of Israel. The first Jewish state began with the conquest of Canaan under Joshua, about 1200 BCE. The tribes of Israel united into one kingdom under King Saul. After the death of King Solomon the kingdom divided into two kingdoms, Israel in the North and **Judah** in the South. Israel was conquered by the Assyrians and her leaders were exiled in about the year 622 BCE. The people of the northern kingdom became known as the "Ten Lost Tribes," disappearing from the scene of history. Judah was destroyed by the Babylonians in 586 BCE. In that year the Babylonians burned the Temple, destroyed the city walls of Jerusalem, and led the leaders and many of the people into captivity in Babylon.

The Babylonian captivity was short. After about seventy years the Persians conquered Babylon and restored the kingdom of Judah as one of the provinces of the Persian empire. The second kingdom of Judah lasted until the year 70. After the Romans put down the Jewish uprising in that year they removed Judah's status as a province of the Roman empire and attached Judah administratively to the province of Syria. The Romans renamed Judah (the Land of Israel), calling it **"Palestine"** after the ancient Philistines, in their determination to destroy the memory of Jewish independence in their own land. Except for a brief period during the Bar Kochba rebellion (132–135) the Jews never again had sovereignty in their land until the creation of the modern State of Israel in 1948.

During the nearly two thousand years of the Second Exile, Jews continued to pray for a return to sovereignty in their land. The central Jewish hope for the Messiah was that he would bring the Jews back to their homeland and rule over them in freedom and independence.

Through all these years, no other state arose in the territory of the Land of Israel. Palestine was ruled from outside, as a conquered possession, by a succession of empires—Roman, Byzantine, Persian, Arab, Crusader, Mameluke and others. From the fourteenth century until 1918 Palestine was a province of the Turkish empire, which had its capital in Istanbul (Constantinople). After the First World War Palestine became a British possession.

There is a myth that the Romans exiled all the Jews from the Land of Israel and that no Jews lived there again until the rise of the modern movement of Zionism in the nineteenth century. This is not the case. The Jewish population of the Land of Israel underwent a slow decline from the first century into the Middle Ages. Persecutions and the destruction of the economy by uncaring overlords accounted for the population decline. There were always some Jews who remained in the land. In all of those centuries Jerusalem was devoid of Jews only briefly, when the Crusaders conquered Jerusalem and slaughtered every Jew living in the city. Within a few decades of that slaughter new Jews had arrived to re-establish a Jewish community in the Holy City of the Jewish religion.

In every generation there were Jewish pilgrims who came to settle in the Land of Israel. Many were discouraged by the extreme poverty of the land and the danger of life there. Roving bandits and corrupt imperial politicians made life difficult and dangerous. A great many of the Jews in the Land of Israel were scholars who studied all the time and depended for their livelihood on charity from world Jewry. The rich and powerful Dona Gracia Nasi attempted to establish a Jewish agricultural colony in the Galilee in the sixteenth century, but her plan came to naught. The Jews of the Land of Israel remained poor, oppressed and few in number. The Jewish desire for a return to the land remained a passive hope, expressed through faith and prayer rather than action.

The Rise of Zionism

In the nineteenth century some Jews began to call for a Jewish return to the Land of Israel. They rejected the notion that Jews must await the Messiah before God will permit them to return to their land. They suggested that nothing but their own inertia was preventing the Jews from returning to full nationhood. This movement came to be known as **Zion-**

ism after the term "Zion," a poetic name for the city of Jerusalem. Zionism is the modern national liberation movement of the Jewish people.

Zionism represents a particular way of being Jewish in the modern world. The Zionists rejected the notion that modern Judaism should be a religion. Many Zionists believed that religion is not relevant in the modern world. The Zionists believed that the Jews are above all a nation. Rather than seek acceptance in modern nations as citizens of the Jewish faith, Jews ought to seek to restore their own status as a nation among the nations of the world. Religious Judaism became the dominant mode of modern Judaism in Germany, the United States and other Western countries. In Eastern Europe, Zionism had the largest appeal to Jewish modernists.

The Zionist movement advanced on a number of fronts from the mid-nineteenth century on. There was an ideological front, to reinterpret Judaism as a modern nationalist movement and to win over Jews to the Zionist cause. There was a political front, to gain the backing of Turkey and the European nations to favor and allow a Jewish return to Zion. There was a financial front, to raise funds for the purchase and development of land. Most important was the actual immigration of Jews to Palestine, with the intention of building up the land and restoring the Jewish national presence as a creative force in their own land.

The Earliest Settlements

Sir Moses Montefiore, a wealthy British Jew, toured the Land of Israel in the 1850s. Upset by the destitute condition of Jerusalem's Jews, Montefiore constructed a housing development and a windmill where the Jews could make a living milling grain. This was the first housing to be built outside the walls of the city.[1] When Jews would not live in his development for fear of bandits, Montefiore actually paid people to live in his houses.

The first Jewish agricultural settlement was Petah Tikvah ("Glimmer of Hope"), founded in 1878. The Rothschild family, wealthy Jewish bankers in Europe, helped to fund this project and other early agricultural settlements. The Rothschilds established a modern wine-making industry in the Land of Israel. Jewish agricultural settlements sprang up in all parts of the Land.

---

[1]These walls were built by the Turkish emperor Suleiman the Magnificent in the sixteenth century. They stand upon the foundations of ancient walls. The walled city is very small, and today contains only a small portion of the population of Jerusalem.

The city of Tel Aviv was founded in 1909. When Arabs would not allow Jewish settlers to live in the coastal city of Jaffa, the Jews moved a mile up the beach, pitched their tents in the sand, and began to build their own city. Today the city of Tel Aviv and its suburbs contain over a million people.

In that same year the first **kibbutz**, Kibbutz Degania, was founded on the shores of Lake Kinneret (the Sea of Galilee). A kibbutz is a collective farm. The members work each according to his ability and share equally in the proceeds. They have no private property. The members eat in a communal dining hall. Their children live in children's housing and are raised in a group by the whole kibbutz. The kibbutz is governed through town meetings, with elected officials carrying out the daily leadership functions. The kibbutz came to symbolize the idealism of the Zionist movement, just as the frontier pioneers came to symbolize the spirit of America.

By the time the State of Israel came into being in 1948, there were 600,000 Jews in the Land of Israel. Through extensive immigration in the early years of the state that number quickly rose to about three million, about a fourth of the world's Jews.

Early Zionists: Hess, Smolenskin and Pinsker

Moses Hess was one of the founding fathers of European Socialism. He was a teacher and friend of Karl Marx. Hess broke with Marx over the issue of nationalism. Marx and other socialists looked for all national boundaries and identities to fall away in the Socialist future. Hess noticed that the German Socialists had an idea of what a non-nationalistic person would be like, and that person closely resembled a German Socialist. Hess saw that the internationalism of the European Socialists was in fact a kind of cultural imperialism. The Socialists expected all other nations to drop their own identities and become like them in order to have unity between all peoples.

Hess preferred a different version of Socialism, in which every nation would advance toward Socialism in its own way, while retaining its unique identity and cultural institutions. Hess hoped that the Jewish nation would be restored to sovereignty and would lead the way for all the nations to a perfected, class-less Socialist society.

In the mid-nineteenth century many nations were returning to sovereignty after years of imperial rule. In the 1850s Italy was reunited after centuries of being broken up into city-states which were ruled by other European powers. The unification of Italy gave Hess hope that the Jews could accomplish something similar, to restore their ancient nation by modern political means. In 1862 Hess published his book, *Rome and Jerusalem*, in which he suggested that the Jews follow the example of the Italians. He outlined his vision of the new Jewish state as a Socialist utopia. Hess suggested that if Jews would lobby with France, the "Mother of Revolution," then France would support this plan and use her power to see it through to fruition.

Peretz Smolenskin was one of the leaders of the Hebrew Haskalah of Eastern Europe. He founded "Hashakhar" (1868–1885), one of the earliest journals in the Hebrew language. In his magazine and in books Smolenskin presented his thoughts on the Jewish future. Smolenskin believed that the Jewish Enlightenment should lead to a revival of the unique Jewish cultural identity, rather than to assimilation into Western European culture. He believed that to accomplish this the Jewish people must revive their language, Hebrew. They must reinvigorate their traditional religion with the spirit of modernism. They must return to their land, the Land of Israel. All of these factors must be brought together to bring about a modern revival for the Jewish people.

In the time of Smolenskin the philosophy of Pan-Slavism was popular in Russia. The Pan-Slavists taught that the Slavic peoples must be united in their language, under the Russian Orthodox Church and the czarist government. Smolenskin taught a kind of Pan-Judaism in which people, land, religion, culture and language are one, and each receives its perfection in relation to all of the other elements.

Leo Pinsker was a Russian Jewish doctor, a proponent of the Haskalah. Pinsker was profoundly affected by the anti-Jewish pogroms which swept through Russia in 1881. In response to these events Pinsker wrote his book *Auto-Emancipation*. Pinsker wrote that the Jews were sadly mistaken in believing that the Enlightenment would lead the European nations to emancipate their Jews. Following the pseudo-science of his day which taught that human character was "in the blood," Pinsker wrote that the European nations were genetically pre-disposed to anti-Semitism. Nothing could cure them of the disease of anti-Semitism except an absence of Jews. The only hope for the Jews was to emancipate themselves by leaving Europe and establishing their own state. There the Jews would be free to enjoy the fruits of the Enlightenment, free of the burden of anti-Semitism. Pinsker wrote that when the Jews were a nation on equal footing with other nations they would gain the respect that they could never gain as a people living on tolerance among the European nations.

Pinsker proposed that the Jews set up a practical program of action to bring about their new state. They must have leaders and raise funds. They must educate the Jewish people to the goal. Pinsker believed that it would take generations, perhaps centuries, to accomplish the restoration of Jew-

ish nationhood, but the project should begin immediately. Pinsker did not believe that the Jewish state must be in the Land of Israel. Any land would do for him, as long as Jews could go to it to escape from anti-Semitism. Pinsker was not the only early Zionist to propose establishing a Jewish state elsewhere than in the Land of Israel, but these other plans were soon abandoned. The majority of the Jews who were interested in Jewish statehood had retained their traditional piety, even in a modern secular form. They did not just want to escape from Europe and be free; they wanted a secular fulfillment of the messianic ideal of a Jewish return to the Promised Land.

Eliezer ben Yehuda and the
Revival of the Hebrew Language

One of the major goals of Zionism was the revival of Jewish national culture. The same term, "ruah," was used to mean both national "spirit" and national "culture." The Jewish culture was at a low level because of the "mentality of Exile" that Jews had adopted. Jewish culture was full of impurities that had accrued to it from being mingled with the cultures of other lands, or that had developed out of the lowly social position of the Jews. The best way to purify Jewish culture was through a return to the pure Jewish language, Hebrew. The Zionists rejected the Yiddish language as symbolic of impure culture and the Exile mentality. They worked to revive the Hebrew language as the vehicle of Jewish culture. This revival took place in a series of steps.

From late antiquity on, Hebrew was "lashon hakodesh," the "holy tongue." The people spoke the common language of their country in daily usage. They used Hebrew only for religious purposes.[2]

The first stage in the revival of Hebrew was the use of the language to spread the ideas of the Enlightenment. Hebrew was used as a temporary expedient until the Jewish people could become familiar with the modern European languages in which the philosophy and literature of Enlightenment were to be found.

The next step was the attempt to develop Hebrew for "belles-lettres," for poetry and fine literature. This was a secularization of the concept of the holy tongue. Hebrew would be the high cultural language of secular Jewish culture, while in everyday use people would continue to speak the common languages.

---

[2]The one exception to this general rule is that, during the Golden Age of Spain, some Jewish poets wrote secular poetry in Hebrew.

Eliezer ben Yehuda was a Zionist settler who believed that the Jews of the Land of Israel could only be united into a true nation if they shared a common language. He believed that Hebrew should be the language. Eliezer ben Yehuda labored to restore Hebrew as the common spoken "street language" of the Jewish people.

Ben Yehuda began working on a modern dictionary of the Hebrew language. He had to invent words for the newspaper, the airplane, the salt-shaker, the myriad objects which had no name in sacred Hebrew writings. At his death in 1923 he had published a few volumes of his dictionary and was working on the rest.

Eliezer ben Yehuda's oldest son, Itamar, was the first native Hebrew speaker since ancient times. He had a lonely childhood, since his parents allowed him to hear no language but Hebrew. There were no other children who could speak to him. By the time of Itamar's death there were three million Hebrew speakers in the world, half of them native speakers. Eliezer ben Yehuda's dream had become a reality in a single generation. Hebrew is used in modern Israel not only for everyday speech but also as a language of instruction in every subject matter, no matter how technical or scientifically advanced. Hebrew is the only "dead" language ever to be successfully revived.[3] Immigrants to Israel since the founding of the state are given six months of intensive instruction in the Hebrew language. Every Israeli, regardless of national origin, is able to communicate with every other Israeli in the uniquely Jewish language.

A.D. Gordon and the Religion of Labor

The Hebrew term for immigration to the Land of Israel is **aliyah**, "going up." Jewish immigrants came to the Land of Israel in waves. The first wave, or First Aliyah, took place around 1881. The Second Aliyah, around 1903, included most of the young people who were to become the first leaders of the State of Israel. Among all of the young Jewish idealists who made up the Second Aliyah there was one older man who became the spiritual father of the settlers. This man was A.D. Gordon. Gordon had been impressed by the agrarian utopianism of Leo Tolstoy. He believed that a return to working the land was the best means for the rejuvenation of the Jewish people. Gordon believed that the clustering of Jews in the cities and in middle class occupations was the result of oppression and was holding Jews in the Exile mentality. Gordon taught that hard labor in

---

[3]Irish people who are struggling to restore Gaelic as the language of Ireland look to Israel's success with Hebrew for their inspiration.

farming and restoring the land was a spiritual activity, the highest act of spirituality a Jew could perform. This doctrine of national rebirth through farming and land development is called the "religion of labor." This became the social ethic of the kibbutz and of the Zionist pioneering movement in general.

By the early twentieth century the Zionist movement had already come into conflict with the Arab population of Palestine. Many Arabs feared the result of a large Jewish influx into the land. They fought against the Jews and attempted to discourage them. The Arabs hoped to overthrow the Turks and restore the united Arab nation of the Middle East that had existed in the first century of Islam. They did not want a Jewish state in the middle of the Pan-Arab nation.

Battles over who has a right to the land, Jews or Arabs, broke out then and have continued ever since. Gordon rejected religious arguments based on divine promises, historical arguments based on past realities, and political arguments based on international agreements. Gordon taught that the land belongs to those who show their love for it by working it. The Land of Israel had suffered from deforestation, overgrazing, and neglect. As a result the land had lost its fertility, and much of the land was either desert or swamp. Gordon taught that Jews and Arabs must work together to develop the land and restore its beauty and fertility. As they did so they would develop a unity between them. They would own the land together and live in peace. Gordon's idealism inspired hope for peace and a better future among the Zionist pioneers. Unfortunately, few Arabs could ever be found who were willing to work alongside the Jews. The Jews had to carry out their land development projects on their own. In this they were successful. Swamps were drained and turned into farmland. Forests were planted. The land is able to support a much larger population now than a century ago, thanks to this work.

Gordon encouraged the Jewish settlers to be anti-materialistic, to value hard work for the good it does for the soul rather than for the material gains it brings. This idealism inspired the early generations of Israeli pioneers to work hard and make sacrifices for the good of the country. Now that Israel is more secure her people have acquired a better standard of living, but many Israelis still idealize the early days when people sacrificed all comforts in order to build their state.

Theodore Herzl—The Father of Modern Zionism

Theodore Herzl (1860–1904) was an assimilated Jewish newspaper journalist from Vienna. In 1891 Herzl was assigned by his paper to cover the Dreyfus Affair in France. Herzl was shocked by the strength of anti-Semitism in Europe, which was revealed in the events of the Dreyfus Affair. Herzl's great desire was to assimilate into European culture. It seemed to him now that the European nations would never allow him or any other Jew a full place in European society.

Herzl decided that the only solution was for Jews to have a state of their own. He was so unlearned in Jewish affairs that he did not know that many other Jews had proposed such a solution before him. Working only from his own thoughts, Herzl went home and wrote a book, *The Jewish State*, in which he outlined his proposal for a Jewish state.

Herzl showed in his writing a virtually prophetic understanding of the force of anti-Semitism in modern society. The Jews, said Herzl, believe that Enlightenment will bring an end to anti-Semitism. The Jews believed that as they became more like their neighbors they would become acceptable to them. Actually, said Herzl, Enlightenment is the cause of anti-Semitism. The anti-Semite might tolerate a ghetto Jew who keeps to himself, but he cannot stand the Jew who dresses like him and sits next to him at the opera. Anti-Semitism is so enmeshed in contradictions, said Herzl, that the Jews can never overcome it by their own actions. The Jews are at once criticized for being capitalist and for being Communists, for being too rich and for being too poor, for controlling the economy and for being a drain on the economy. The Jews can do nothing about anti-Semitism but escape from it by removing themselves to a country of their own. There they will be free to live as modern people.

Herzl was not a Jewish intellectual, but he was a great publicist. In his writing and in his travels Herzl managed to put the question of a revival of Jewish statehood into the minds of Jews and of European national leaders. Herzl attempted to gain an audience with all of the great heads of state of the European powers, hoping to gain their support for the Zionist cause.

Herzl was the prime mover behind the organization of the First World Zionist Congress, held in 1897 in Basle, Switzerland. The Congress brought together Jewish nationalist leaders from all over Europe. The delegates established the World Zionist Organization to carry on its work between meetings. At a later Congress the Jewish National Fund was established to purchase and develop land for Jewish settlement. These organizations created the structural foundation for the establishment of the Jewish state.

At the First Zionist Congress Herzl declared in a speech that the goal of Jewish statehood was attainable. He said, "If you will it, it is no dream." Even Herzl could not have imagined that in only fifty years the dream would become a reality.

Ahad Ha'am—The "Secular Rabbi"

Ahad Ha'am (1856–1927) was, in his youth, a Talmudic genius. As a young man he abandoned the religious life and became a Hebrew journalist. His essays were not only thoughtful and thought-provoking, they also did a great deal to advance the modern Hebrew language. Ahad Ha'am (literally, "one of the people") was his pen name; Asher Ginsberg was his given name.

Ahad Ha'am and Theodore Herzl became the leaders of the two opposing schools of Zionist thought. Ahad Ha'am was the leader of the Cultural Zionists, while Herzl was the leader of the Political Zionists.

The Political Zionists (also called the practical Zionists) wanted the "normalization" of the Jewish people; they wanted Jews to lose their unique status in the world and become just like everyone else. The Political Zionists conceived of Zionism as the Jewish response to anti-Semitism. They believed that the Jews must have an independent state as soon as possible, in order to have a place of refuge for endangered Jewish communities. The Political Zionists were not much concerned with Judaism; they wanted the Jewish state to reflect the culture of Western Europe and the political ideals of modern European liberalism.

The Cultural Zionists had as their goal the restoration of the spirit of the Jewish nation. They believed that the way to do this was to establish a Jewish presence in the Land of Israel. The Jewish settlement, the **yishuv,** would develop ways to express the eternal spirit of Judaism in a modern national context. They would overcome the mentality of Exile, removing the tarnish that was dulling the luster of Jewish national culture. The other Jewish communities of the world would imitate the forms of Jewish culture as they developed in the yishuv. Ahad Ha'am compared the future world Jewish community to a wagon wheel. The yishuv was the hub, with spokes of cultural influence radiating out to the Diaspora Jewish communities on the circumference.

The cultural Zionists believed that the goals of Zionism could be accomplished by a strong Jewish presence in the Land of Israel even without sovereign statehood. They believed that it was best for sovereignty to come many generations down the road, as the final stage of Jewish renewal. Ahad Ha'am urged the Political Zionists not to rush their political agenda, but to concentrate their energies on strengthening the yishuv.

The difference between the Political and Cultural Zionists is demonstrated in a statement by Golda Meir, later to become prime minister of the State of Israel. Meir once said, "When we have our own state we will have Jewish criminals, and Jewish police to catch them." This was an expression of the dream of normalization for the Jewish people. The Cultural Zionists, on the other hand, dreamed of a state where police would be unnecessary, because the Jewish genius for ethical living would permeate the social life of the Jewish citizens.

Schools of Zionist Thought

All Zionists agree that the Jews are first and foremost a nation. All other aspects of Judaism derive from or are dependent on Jewish national identity. All Zionists agree that the only way that Judaism can be properly expressed in the modern world is through a national mode of expression. Zionists disagree among themselves, though, on the meaning of Jewish nationhood. As we have seen, the Political Zionists wanted the Jewish nation to be like all other nations, while the Cultural Zionists wanted a modern secular expression of the eternal spirit of Judaism, a spirit which had formerly been expressed in the context of national religion. There were sub-groups within these schools of Zionism, and there were other groups as well. Religious Zionism deserves special mention.

Most religious Jews were opposed to Zionism at first. Orthodox Jews objected to the secularism of Zionism, and to the rejection of the doctrine of the Messiah. Reform Jews objected to the definition of the Jews as a nation at a time when they were seeking full acceptance as citizens of the Western nation-states. There was a significant group of liberal Orthodox Jews who adopted Zionism. The major parties of Orthodoxy in Europe were the Agudas Yisrael, which opposed Zionism, and the Mizraki (Oriental) party, which favored Zionism.

Rav Kook (1865–1935) was Ashkenazic Chief Rabbi of Palestine under the British. Rav Kook taught that the Zionists were fulfilling God's will, even if that was not their intent. By taking the first steps for a Jewish return to the Land of Israel, the Zionists were hastening the coming of the Messiah. God would intervene and fulfill his Messianic promise once the Zionists had laid the groundwork, and at that time the Zionist pioneers would return to Jewish religious life.

Religious Zionism has become a growing political force in Israel in the past few decades. Religious Zionists believe that a Jewish state ought to reflect the traditional Jewish way of life. Halakha should be the law of the land, with Orthodox rabbis as the final judges and arbiters of the law. Law should develop through rabbinic scholarship, as in the Jewish past, rather than through the votes of a secular, elected Parliament.

Another movement, Revisionist Zionism, represents the right wing of Zionism. Most of the early Zionists were Socialists, but the Revisionists believed in strong central government, state capitalism, and militant nationalism. Zeev Jabotinsky was the founder of the Revisionist movement. Jabotinsky was the leader of the Jewish regiment which fought in the First World War. He believed that raw power determined the outcome of world events, and so the Jews must strive to be as powerful as possible. The Jews must use that power unabashedly to win the conflict for Jewish statehood. Unlike the Socialists who favored compromise with Arab national aspirations, the Revisionists longed to see a Jewish state comprising all of the territory of the Land of Israel, from the Mediterranean Sea to the Jordan River.

The Revisionist movement became the Herut (Freedom) Party after the establishment of the State of Israel. A tiny minority party for many years, the Herut Party was voted into power in 1977. Menahem Begin, Jabotinsky's former young lieutenant, became prime minister of Israel. The Herut party was favored by many Israelis from Arab lands who did not relate to the secular, humanistic, European Socialism of the Labor Zionists. The Herut Party had moderated considerably over the years, but it still represents the political right wing of Zionism. Now that the Revisionist Zionists are in the mainstream of Israeli political life, it is doubtful that Socialism will ever again dominate as it did in the first thirty years in Israeli politics. Since the mid-1970s there has been a rough balance in Israel's **K'nesset**, or Parliament, between the Herut and Labor (Socialist) parties, with the religious parties holding a swing vote of about ten percent.

The old division between Political and Cultural Zionism became less meaningful with the establishment of the actual State of Israel. This fulfilled the agenda of the Political Zionists. Considering the urgent need for a Jewish place of refuge in the decade after the Second World War, it was probably a good thing that the Political Zionists had their way in quickly establishing a sovereign Jewish state. Even so, the argument between these two views of Zionism still persists. It now takes the form of a debate over the way the government and Israeli society function. The argument between Herzl and Ahad Ha'am was carried on after the establishment of the State of Israel between Prime Minister David ben Gurion and Martin Buber, the famous philosopher. Ben Gurion announced in a speech that with the establishment of the Jewish state, Zionism was at an end. Buber responded that Zion, the ideal Jewish state, was the goal of Zionism, and the establishment of the state was merely a step toward that goal.

Today Jews continue to debate whether Israel is to be a normal state or a special state which reflects the character of Judaism. Shall the government of Israel act to maximize the security of her citizens, or shall Israel take security risks in order to display compassion toward her enemies? This is not asked of any other state, but it is asked of Israel. Shall the citizens of Israel seek to maximize the comforts of their life, as people do in all places, or does the Jewish nature of the State of Israel call on all of her citizens to sacrifice personal advancement for the sake of the public good? These questions and others make the meaning of Zionism a still significant issue even after forty years of pragmatic national life.

From Zionism to the State of Israel

The World Zionist Organization worked on the political front, seeking support for Jewish statehood from world Jewry and from the European governments, which had the power to influence events in the Turkish Empire. Meanwhile, Jews continued to come to the Land of Israel to be **halutzim,** "pioneers" in resettling the Land. Central to the philosophy of Zionism is the idea that the Jews can determine their own destiny. The Zionist pioneers believed that a Jewish state would be inevitable if they would establish an active presence in the Land.

The First World War broke out in 1914. The Turks, who controlled Palestine, entered the war on the side of Germany. Jews fought on both sides in this war, some for Austria and Germany, some for England, Russia, France and the United States. Both sides were anxious to win over the public opinion of world Jewry.

In 1917 the British foreign secretary, Lord Balfour, asked the Anglo-Jewish scientist Haim Weizmann what could be done to honor him for his contribution to England's war effort. Weizmann replied that all he wished was for England to favor the establishment of a Jewish state in Palestine. This request fit in with current English policy. In November 1917 the **Balfour Declaration** announced that England favored "the establishment of a Jewish homeland in Palestine," short of advocating Jewish statehood but still a significant statement. In December 1917 the British army marched into Palestine, having defeated the Turks. After the war ended France and England divided the Middle East between them, with England gaining control of Palestine.

During the war the English had courted the Arabs of the Middle East as well as the Jews. They had made contradictory promises to both groups concerning their national aspirations. In the 1920s the English found themselves in the middle of an expanding conflict between the growing Jewish yishuv and the increasingly angry Arab population of Palestine. Anti-Jewish riots broke out in 1929. The English did little to control the rioters.

In the 1930s Hussein, the ruler of Arabia, was ousted by the Saudis. The English felt indebted to Hussein for his assistance in fighting the Turks during the First World War. The English took all of Palestine east of the Jordan River, comprising more than half of the territory of Palestine, and gave it to Hussein as the kingdom of Transjordan.

As the 1930s progressed, the English tilted more and more toward the Arabs. The Jews had no choice but to support the English against Hitler, while the Arabs had strong sympathies for the Germans now that England was the colonial power in the Middle East. The English allowed the Arab revolt against the Jewish presence to grow unchecked until, in 1938, it threatened to become a full-scale rebellion. At that point the British put down the rebels with military force. A Jewish unit, the "Night Raiders," trained by the English officer Orde Wingate, helped to put down the rebellion. Many of Israel's later military heroes, including Moshe Dayan, came out of this group of soldiers.

By the 1930s the yishuv was well organized. The **Jewish Agency** for Palestine acted as the self-government for the Jews. There was a secret Jewish defense force, the **Haganah,** which defended Jewish settlements against Arab attacks. The Haganah did not attack the English or peaceful Arabs. There was a more militant Jewish militia, the Irgun, which carried out military operations against the British army. A small group, the Stern Gang, used guerrilla warfare against the British. They blew up the King David Hotel in Jerusalem, which served as British military headquarters. The Jewish Agency and the Haganah opposed the Stern Gang, who had to hide out from the Jewish as well as the British authorities. In Israel's War of Independence the Irgun laid down their arms and accepted the authority of the Jewish Agency. Their members were incorporated into the Haganah. Thus, Israel was spared the internal strife which has been the bane of many post-colonial nations. The Jews in Israel knew their history; they knew that the Jews had defeated themselves through civil warfare in their rebellion against Rome. They were determined to remain united.

In 1939 the British acquiesced to Arab demands by severely restricting Jewish immigration to Palestine. As a result, Jews fleeing from the Nazis were not allowed to enter Palestine. The British White Paper restricting Jewish immigration remained in force until Israel's independence in 1948. Jewish Holocaust survivors who were caught sneaking into Palestine were arrested and deported to concentration camps in Cyprus. The English held them there until the new State of Israel opened its borders to them.

In 1947 the English, tired of adjudicating the dispute between Jews and Arabs, turned over the question of what to do with Palestine to the United Nations. The U.N. voted to partition Palestine. The Jews accepted the partition plan, but the Arabs of Palestine and the Arab nations did not. A war between Jews and Arabs broke out even before the British pulled out. The British, expecting the Jews to be utterly defeated, did nothing to stop the fighting. On May 14, 1948, the day before the British pullout, the Jewish Agency announced Israel's Declaration of Independence. All laws currently in force were declared still in force,[4] except for those restricting freedom of religion and Jewish immigration. The very next day the newly independent Jewish state was invaded by the armies of Egypt, Saudi Arabia, Jordan, Syria and Lebanon. Israel survived the attacks and even managed to improve to some extent the unworkable borders of the U.N. partition plan. Since the Arab states would not make peace with Israel, the war ended in an armistice. The armistice lines became the de facto border of Israel until 1967. The Old City of Jerusalem, containing all the holy sites, fell into Jordanian hands. The Jordanians annexed the West Bank of the Jordan River, which had been assigned by the U.N. as an Arab state. The Egyptians held onto the Gaza strip along the Mediterranean coast. This area was also supposed to be part of the Arab state in partitioned Palestine. Arabs who had fled their homes during the fighting, many under threat from the Arab armies, were not allowed to resettle in Arab countries. They were placed permanently into refugee camps to serve as a political embarrassment to Israel and to serve as a constant reminder that the Arabs would not accept a Jewish state in their midst.

The Six Day War of 1967

In the spring of 1967 the Egyptians mobilized their army on the borders of Israel. They blockaded the Strait of Tiran, Israel's exit to the Red Sea. Tensions mounted also on the Syrian border. With her army vastly outnumbered in manpower and in every category of weaponry, Israel's friends feared the worst for her.

On June 5, 1967, Israel's air force made an early morning preemptive strike which destroyed the air forces of Egypt, Syria and Jordan. The Israeli army began to advance in the Sinai peninsula against the Egyptians and in the Golan Heights against the Syrians. On the third day of the war the Jordanians entered the battle, despite repeated warnings by the Israelis to stay out.

In six days the war ended with a complete victory for the Israelis. The Israelis conquered the Sinai peninsula up to the Suez Canal from the Egyptians. They took from the Syrians the Golan Heights, from which the Syrians had for years rained artillery shells upon the Israeli civilian settle-

---

[4]Primarily Turkish common law, which remains the basis for law in the State of Israel.

ments in the upper Jordan River valley. The Israelis took from the Jordanians all the territory west of the Jordan River which they had conquered in 1948, including the city of Jerusalem.

Israel's victory electrified the world. The Jews had won a major military victory for perhaps the first time since the time of the Maccabees! When Jews in the Soviet Union heard the news they began to rise up and demand the right to live as Jews. This was the beginning of the movement for Jewish emigration from the Soviet Union, and the movement for Jewish study and practice within the Soviet Union. In the United States, many Jews who had never acknowledged their Jewishness before suddenly felt pride in being Jewish. Many who had never before made a Jewish commitment of any kind began to get politically involved on behalf of Israel and other Jewish causes and to make charitable contributions to Israel. Many American Jews were moved to explore their heritage, to join a synagogue, and to renew their practice of Judaism.

Israel found herself militarily secure for the first time since her founding. Although Israel now controlled much more territory, her borders were much shorter, and they were defensible. Israel had removed the threat which had hovered over her head since the beginning of the state in 1948. The Israelis quickly developed a new doctrine for relations with their neighbors; they would hang on to the conquered territories and their Arab populations and wait for their neighbors to sue for peace. The Arab states responded with a doctrine of "no negotiation, no recognition, no peace." The Arab states gave support to the recently founded Palestine Liberation Organization to war against Israel through terrorist actions.

For the Jewish spirit, even more important than Israel's newfound security was the establishment of Jewish sovereignty over the holy places— most importantly, the site of the Temple Mount in the Old City of Jerusalem. Jewish tourists began to flock to Israel to see the historic sites and to revel in Israel's glory. Many American Jewish youth came to Israel to study in one of her universities or to work for a time on a kibbutz. This pilgrimage became a source of new religious and ethnic inspiration for many Jews from America and elsewhere in the Diaspora.

The Israelis immediately annexed the Old City of Jerusalem to the new city, reuniting the city which had had a military armistice line running through it since 1948. They restored the Jewish holy places which had been desecrated by the Jordanians. The city of Jerusalem has undergone tremendous growth since that time, outpacing Tel Aviv to become the largest city in Israel. The mayor of Jerusalem, Teddy Kollek, and his administration have striven to make Jerusalem a cultural and religious center for people of all religions and nationalities.

The Yom Kippur War of 1973
and the Peace with Egypt

On the Jewish Day of Atonement in 1973 the Egyptian and Syrian armies made a surprise attack on Israel. The Israeli army was pushed far back. The State of Israel was in great danger during the first few days of the war, before Israel's civilian army could be fully mobilized. It took the Israelis twenty-three days, many lost lives, and a massive airlift of American arms to defeat the Arab armies, who were armed and advised by the Soviet Union. When the Israeli army finally regained the initiative and crossed the Suez Canal in a bold strike, the Russians imposed an immediate cease-fire, with U.S. agreement.

The war was a sobering event for Israel. It showed that the status quo, which was acceptable to Israel, could not be maintained. The war had an eventual good outcome for Israel, though. President Sadat of Egypt saw that the Russians could not deliver victory to the Arabs. The Egyptians threw out their Russian advisors and moved toward the United States. The U.S. government sponsored the disengagement talks which followed the cease-fire, helping to establish a basis for negotiation between Egypt and Israel.

In November 1977 Sadat flew to Jerusalem. In an address to the Knesset, Israel's Parliament, he offered Israel peace in exchange for the return of Egyptian territory in the Sinai and movement toward a solution to the Palestinian problem. President Carter of the U.S. sponsored the peace talks between President Sadat of Egypt and Prime Minister Menahem Begin of Israel. The result was the Camp David Agreement, signed in September 1978. This was the basis for the peace treaty between Egypt and Israel, signed in March 1979. The Israelis agreed to withdraw their army from the Sinai Peninsula. Egypt became the first Arab state to recognize the State of Israel. The treaty was in the best interests of all three countries involved, but it cannot be ignored that the religious devotion of the Christian President Carter, the Moslem President Sadat, and the Jewish Prime Minister Begin had a great deal to do with their urge to make peace.

Unfortunately, the other Arab states have not followed the example of Egypt in making peace with Israel, and the Palestinian problem still festers. Even so, Israel has been much more secure since making peace with her most populous neighbor.[5]

---

[5]Egypt has a population of over sixty million, more than the other Arab states of the Middle East combined.

Daily Life in the State of Israel

Although Israel continues to live under a threat from her neighbors, particularly Syria and the Palestinian terrorist organizations, daily life in Israel is not much different from life in any modern democratic country. The poverty of the early years, when great sacrifices were necessary to build the country and welcome a mass of impoverished immigrants, is now just a memory. The standard of living is well below that of the United States, but comparable to that in many European states. Virtually all Israelis have adequate housing and plenty of food to eat. The level of literacy is high, and many Israelis study in Israel's thriving university system. Israel has become a world leader in agricultural and medical technology, as well as military technology.[6] Israel is a net exporter of food, supplying the winter market for fresh fruit and vegetables in Europe. Cut gems are another source of export income, as Jews skilled in this craft came to Israel after the Second World War. Tourism continues to be an important industry.

The Jewish character of the State is evident even in its secular forms. Saturday, the Jewish Sabbath, is the day off from work (most workers work a five and a half day week, quitting at noon on Friday to prepare for the Sabbath). The fall and spring Festival weeks of Sukkot and Passover are the national holiday times. The schools are closed for Jewish holidays, which are the national-cultural holidays of all Israelis.

The State of Israel has become a comfortable home for her three million Jews. Israel continues to extend a welcome to Jews from all over the world, whether they come as refugees from persecution or out of devotion to living in a Jewish state. It is the fervent wish of the Israelis that someday all the Jews in the world will come to live in Israel.

---

[6]This became a necessity on account of Israel's overwhelming need for military security.

23

The Jews of America

Waves of Immigration

The Jewish population of the United States since the mid-twentieth century has stood at between five and six million—two or three percent of the total population of the country. Jews came to America in three waves of successively greater size. The first wave consisted of Sephardic Jews who came in the colonial period. The second wave consisted of German Jews who came in the mid-nineteenth century. The third and greatest wave was of Eastern European Jews who came to America between 1881 and 1920.

Jews in Colonial America

The first Jewish community in America was in the Dutch settlement of New Amsterdam (later New York). In 1654 a boatload of Spanish and Portuguese Jews came to New Amsterdam. They had settled in Brazil when the Dutch briefly conquered it from the Portuguese, then moved on to the Caribbean, and from there to North America. The Dutch governor, Peter Stuyvesant, did not want to let the Jews in, but he was overruled by the directors of the Dutch West India Company, which had many Jewish shareholders. The Jews established their own cemetery and, after the British took over the city, their own synagogue. This congregation, Shearit Israel, is still flourishing. Their current synagogue building is on the Upper West Side of Manhattan. The religious ritual of the congregation is Sephardic Orthodox.

By the time of the American Revolution there were about 2,500 Jews in the thirteen colonies. They had established congregations in some major cities: Touro Synagogue in Newport, Rhode Island,[1] Mikveh Israel in Philadelphia, Pennsylvania, Beth Elohim in Charleston, South Carolina, and Mickve Israel in Savannah, Georgia. The location of these congregations was not accidental. Jews came to those colonies which practiced religious toleration. Either by principle or to attract colonists, these colonies tolerated dissenting and minority Protestant sects and, by extension, Jews. Religious toleration had not yet become religious liberty or equality. Even after the American Revolution it was some decades before all states allowed Jews to vote and to hold public office.

Nearly all of these Jews were Sephardim who had come to North America from Holland, England, or elsewhere in the Americas. There were a smattering of Ashkenazic Jews, but these joined the existing congregations and adopted the Sephardic religious ritual. No Jewish community was large enough to support two separate congregations. After the American Revolution, when more Ashkenazic Jews came from Germany, they began to assert themselves and demand the observance of their own ancestral customs. On one occasion a riot broke out in the Touro Synagogue between the Ashkenazic and Sephardic groups, and the police had to be called in to restore order.

Haym Solomon, a Philadelphia Jew, assisted the Revolutionary War effort by selling war bonds. The new government of the colonies did not have much credit and the revolution had no assurance of success. It was no easy task to get investors to buy the bonds. Solomon's efforts helped to finance George Washington's army. He also used his own small fortune in the war effort. Solomon was only one of many who helped broker war bonds, but his efforts came to represent to American Jews their dedication to their new country. There were also Jewish soldiers in the ranks of the revolutionary army.

When George Washington was elected the first President of the United States, he received a letter of congratulations from the Jewish congregation in Newport. Quoting this letter in his letter of reply, Washington wrote that the government of the new Republic "gives to bigotry no sanction, to persecution no assistance, requires only that they who live under its protection shall demean themselves as good citizens in giving it on all occasions their effectual support."

---

[1]This congregation is still in their original building, the oldest synagogue building in North America. The site is open to tourists.

Religious Liberty in America

In 1789 the states and Congress passed the Bill of Rights, the first ten amendments to the Constitution. The First Amendment guaranteed the separation of church and state, meaning that there could be no official government-sponsored religion in the United States, nor could the government interfere in the affairs of any religion. The separation of church and state was proposed by Thomas Jefferson, who had passed a similar bill into the Virginia constitution.[2]

Many of the founding fathers of the Constitution were Deists. They believed in a Supreme Being but they did not believe that any specific religion had a hold on truth. They also believed that religion was only meaningful when it was practiced as a free expression of the individual human conscience, unfettered by government compulsion. Because of these beliefs the founding fathers resisted those who wanted to make America an officially Christian country. In America, unlike any European nation, a Jew could be a citizen as fully in every way as a Christian American. In the atmosphere of religious liberty that prevailed in America, many Protestant sects flourished. In this atmosphere the Jews were perceived by their neighbors not so much as people of a different and alien religion, but as practitioners of yet another variation of that general "religion" which made people good citizens.

This attitude was exemplified by Benjamin Franklin, the leading citizen of Philadelphia in the time of the American Revolution. Franklin was a member of every church in the city; he was one of the subscribing members of Mikveh Israel Congregation. Franklin believed that the practice of religion was good for the social order, and he therefore cheerfully encouraged it in any of its forms.

All of this made Jews feel especially at home in America. On the other hand, it also made it easy for Jews to assimilate to the general society and to lose their specific identity as Jews. It was difficult for a Jew to remain Jewish. There were not many other Jews to provide spouses. There was no Jewish religious education in America and there were no rabbis. Rebecca Gratz of Philadelphia founded the first Jewish Sunday school in 1831, in imitation of the Protestant mode of religious education. The Sunday school taught Bible stories and basic Jewish doctrines—a far cry from the intense education of European Jews. With small numbers and little Jewish education, many of the Jews of the colonial period left no Jewish descendants.

---

[2]Up until that time the Anglican Church was the official church of the Commonwealth of Virginia.

The German Immigration

The small Jewish population of the United States was reinvigorated by a wave of generally pious immigrants from Germany. From the 1820s to 1880, the period of German immigration, the Jewish population of the United States grew from about 50,000 to about 250,000. Many new congregations were formed. The German Jews settled in the new frontier as well as in the established cities of the East Coast. Many German Jews settled in Cincinnati and elsewhere in the Ohio Valley and the upper Midwest, following the mass of other German immigrants. Many settled in the South. Jews fanned out into all the small towns of the interior. When the Civil War came Jews fought on both sides, though most Jews and most Jewish sympathies were with the North.

In central Europe Jews had lived on the margins of society, making a living by filling niches that were new or that no one else cared to fill. Jews found similar niches on the frontier in America. The typical Jewish immigrant from Germany started out as a backpack peddler. An outfitter, generally an earlier immigrant, would set him up with a backpack and a supply of manufactured goods. He would walk from farm to farm, selling his goods. When he saved up enough money the peddler would buy a wagon and increase his stock. As soon as he had saved enough money and scouted out a good location, he would settle in a town and open up a shop of his own. Many of the great department stores in America, including Gimbel's and Macy's, were started by German Jews who had begun with a peddler's backpack.

The German immigrants were shunned by the Sephardic Jews. The Sephardim considered themselves superior in ancestry and in culture. Also, having been in America longer, they were much more Americanized than the Ashkenazic newcomers. The German Jews developed their own aristocracy, though, as they quickly climbed the economic ladder in America. The rapid industrialization of the United States presented new economic opportunities, and the German Jewish immigrants were well situated to contribute and benefit from America's increasing wealth. Jews were excluded from most major industries and from commercial banking, but there were other opportunities on the economic frontier. Besides the retailing giants, there were Jewish investment bankers such as David Seligman, Marcus Goldman, Joseph Sachs, Solomon Loeb, and Jacob Schiff. Meyer Guggenheim and his sons made a fortune in mining. These new aristocrats built themselves great homes on New York's Fifth Avenue. They built the great, cathedral-like Temple Emmanuel as their house of worship. Joseph Seligman was a personal friend of American presidents. He was offered—and turned down—a cabinet post during the term of President Grant. The German Jews clearly had made it in America.[3]

As the frontier moved westward, Jews went with it. There were many Jews in the new towns and mining camps of the far West. Following the usual pattern, most of these Jews came not to mine or raise cattle but to open retail shops. Jews were involved in the founding of the city of San Francisco from the very beginning, and were very active in its civic affairs. There were two congregations there already by 1849. One Jewish peddler, Levi Straus, came to California to sell denim tent material to the Gold Rush miners. When he got there he decided to make pants instead of tents with his material. Blue jeans were born.

The German Jewish immigration was spurred by the failed Revolution of 1848 in central Europe. The failure of liberalism sent many Jews to America, looking for freedom and an escape from poverty. Among the immigrants after 1848 were the first ordained rabbis to come to America. These were mostly Reform rabbis, many of them radical reformers. In the latter part of the nineteenth century the majority of American Jewish congregations adopted the Reform ritual, which had developed in the Germany of their ancestry. Until the appearance of the next wave of immigrants from Eastern Europe, it appeared that Reform would become the Jewish ritual of America.

Social Restrictions Against Jews

Even though America was a land of freedom and legal equality for Jews, certain avenues of economic life were always closed to them. No Jews were appointed to the boards of major corporations or given upper management positions in such companies. Jews were excluded from corporate law firms, from college professorships, from commercial banking, and other high status occupations. Because they could not rise in these occupations, ambitious Jews preferred entrepreneurship. By working for themselves or in small, Jewish-owned companies they avoided the effects of corporate anti-Semitism. In the mid-nineteenth century a new form of anti-Semitism arose in America—the social exclusion of Jews.

In 1877 Joseph Seligman, the leading Jew in America, was turned away from the Grand Union Hotel at Saratoga. The Seligman family had frequently vacationed there in the past. Judge Henry Hilton, executor of the estate of the hotel's former owner, announced that henceforth the

---

[3]The story of the German Jewish aristocracy is well told by Stephen Birmingham in his book *Our Crowd*, Harper and Row, N.Y., 1967.

Grand Union Hotel would not accept Jews. The practice of restricting Jews became commonplace. Jews were not allowed into the resorts, social clubs and philanthropic organizations of the Gentile elite. Jews were restricted from living in many towns and neighborhoods. All of this was accomplished quietly for the most part, in "restrictive covenants" or "gentlemen's agreements" by which no Jew would be proposed for membership, brought as a guest, shown a home, etc. In the 1920s many of America's elite colleges established quotas limiting the number of Jews who would be admitted as students.

This was a change from the openness and general good will which had existed in American society in the early nineteenth century. Why the change? As the number of Jews in America increased and as some of them became wealthy and successful, the old elite began to see Jews as a threat to their own hegemony over American society. America was subject to the scourge of anti-Semitism which was growing strong in Europe at this time. Americans were also becoming fearful of the great wave of immigrants who were coming to America from Ireland, Italy, and Eastern Europe. Previous immigrants to the United States had been mostly Northern Europeans. They were similar in appearance, culture and religion to the English.[4] The new immigrants were ethnically distinct and were largely Catholic or Jewish. A strong nativist movement arose, warning that America would be inundated and destroyed by the foreigners who were flocking to her shores. In this atmosphere, anti-Semitism increased.

Despite the growth of social and economic barriers, discrimination against Jews never became law or official government policy. The values of religious liberty and respect for diversity were sufficiently ingrained in American society that personal and social prejudices were not allowed to publicly contradict them. America remained a land of opportunity for Jews, if not in every area of society then at least in enough areas to provide an outlet for economic and social aspirations. Jews responded to social restrictions by founding their own social clubs, country clubs, college fraternities, charities and resorts.[5] Jewish resort areas grew up in the Catskill Mountains, in certain towns on the New Jersey shore, and elsewhere.

Social restrictions against Jews subsided after the Second World War. The unity of army life was a great leveler for American society. Colleges

---

[4]The term "WASP," White Anglo-Saxon Protestant, was coined in the twentieth century to describe the members of the old elite, the descendants of the early immigrants from England and other Germanic peoples.

[5]Restrictions have been falling away since the 1960s. Many of the originally Jewish clubs now are attractive to many Gentiles who seek to join them, even as Jews join clubs once closed to them. Today, elite clubs and resorts may be predominantly Gentile or predominantly Jewish, but fewer and fewer are exclusively one or the other.

dropped their Jewish quotas to accept returning Jewish veterans. Jews bought houses in ethnically integrated suburbs which were built to meet the demand for housing of the veterans. Restrictions fell further as a result of the Civil Rights movement of the 1960s and the subsequent view which arose that America is not a "melting pot" but a multi-ethnic society in which each ethnic group has its rightful place. Today it is no longer rare for a Jew to sit in upper management circles in a large corporation or to sit on the board of a symphony orchestra or museum. There are now many Jewish college professors in every field. More and more country clubs, fraternities, and other elite social organizations are open to Jews who may wish to join.

The East European Immigration

As we have seen, the Jews of Eastern Europe ceased to hope for Enlightenment to solve their problems after the pogroms of 1881. That year began the flood of East European Jewish immigration to America. From 1880 to 1900 nearly a million Jews came to America. From 1900 to 1920 over a million more came. Altogether, perhaps half the Jews of Eastern Europe transferred to the United States in those years. The tide was finally stemmed in the 1920s by a series of restrictive immigration laws that Congress passed to limit immigration from Southern and Eastern Europe.

The East Europeans changed the face of American Judaism. They arrived in far different circumstances than their German predecessors. Most of these Jews were poor and had no education or skills which were useful in the American economy. The kind of economic opportunities that had existed in the mid-nineteenth century for German Jews were no longer available. The immigrants crowded into terrible slums in the major East Coast cities, especially New York. They became workers in the factories that were sprouting up to take advantage of cheap immigrant labor. Jewish labor was especially dominant in the garment industry. Some Jews set up small shops or pushcarts, while others became painters, carpenters and the like.

New York City was the destination for most Jewish immigrants. They sneaked across the Russian border and received transit visas in Germany. They made their way to Hamburg, where they booked their passage on steamships to America. The crossing, in steerage, was brutally difficult. The ships were crowded and the skimpy provisions were not kosher, so that many Jews ate nothing but what little they had with them. The earlier immigrants landed at Castle Garden in lower Manhattan. Later, because of the great numbers of immigrants, the American immigration authorities set up a large complex on Ellis Island in New York Harbor. The authorities generally showed great kindness to the terrified and confused immigrants. If the immigrants showed no signs of communicable diseases and were able to work, they were admitted. Often the immigration authorities would give a new, more American-sounding name to the immigrants, as the first step in their process of assimilation to American society.

The Lower East Side

Most of the new immigrants found their first home on the Lower East Side of Manhattan. This area was a horribly overcrowded, greatly impoverished slum. Often there was only one sink or toilet for an entire apartment building, and no hot water. To pay the rent, immigrants took in large numbers of boarders. A family with many children and as many as a dozen boarders would crowd into a few small rooms.

The streets of the Lower East Side bustled with activity. The social climate of Eastern Europe was reproduced in the Jewish butcher shops, groceries, and cafeterias. Poor peddlers with pushcarts sold their wares on the street corners. Many shops sold Jewish books and religious articles. There were many store-front synagogues. Some of these were **landsmanschaften,** "old-country associations" of Jews who had come from the same village or region in Eastern Europe. These synagogues maintained the social customs and religious melodies of the former home. Yiddish was the common language in the streets, though Jews strove to learn English as quickly as possible. The immigrants read Yiddish-American newspapers; the most popular was the "Jewish Daily Forward." Yiddish theater and Yiddish literature flourished for a time, until the second generation of English-speaking Jews became dominant.

Despite the poverty, very few Jews returned to Europe. Only about ten percent of the immigrants went back, a much lower percentage than for any other immigrant group. Italy or Ireland, Germany or England might still be home to an immigrant from these countries; Russia had never been home for Jews. From the day they arrived on these shores, the Jewish immigrants were determined to do whatever it took to become Americans.

Americanization

The German Jews were not happy to see all of these Eastern Jews coming to America. They had tried to stay out of the public eye, believing that obscurity was a necessary element in the acceptance they had found here. The immigrants were numerous and seemed uncouth in all of their ways. The Germans feared that they would generate anti-Semitism. Despite their feelings, and to some extent because of them, the German Jews did whatever they could to help the Eastern Jews become Americans as quickly as possible. They established organizations such as the Hebrew Immigrant Aid Society and Settlement Houses to provide basic education and social services to the immigrants. While they learned English, the newcomers were taught the manners and polite social customs of American society—how to use a handkerchief, how to use a knife and fork, how to be demure rather than brash. Besides helping the immigrants, the German Jews formed the Joint Distribution Committee after the First World War, to help the Jews still in Eastern Europe in their struggle against persecution and poverty.

This mass of poor immigrants worked their way up the economic scale and into American society more rapidly than any other immigrant group in American history. The immigrant generation sacrificed themselves and their own lives so that their children could have a better life. Their primary weapon in the struggle was education. The Eastern Jews took the Jewish cultural admiration for learning and made it a secular trait of American Jews; a boy who had a college education could get ahead. Some of the children, and most of the grandchildren, of the immigrants became professionals with a college degree. The grandchildren of low-paid factory workers became doctors, lawyers, dentists, engineers and accountants. Many became school teachers and social workers. Especially after colleges dropped their restrictions, many became scientists and professors. The first and second generation Jews worked their way out of the factories to become successful small businessmen, but their children usually declined to enter the business. More often, they went off to college and became professionals.

When the immigrants had their first taste of success, they moved out of the Lower East Side and into Brooklyn or the Bronx. By the 1920s large middle class Jewish communities existed in pleasant neighborhoods in the boroughs of New York, with comparable areas in Philadelphia, Baltimore, Boston, Chicago, and other cities. After the Second World War these neighborhoods broke up as Jews moved out to the suburbs. Most New York Jews no longer live in the city, but in Long Island, southern Connecticut and northern New Jersey. The situation is similar in other large cities. The Jewish population of the United States today is almost entirely to be found in the suburbs of the largest cities, with half the total living in the New York metropolitan area.

Judaism and Jewish Identity in America

Jewish immigrants to America were by and large the least religious Jews from the European communities. America was known as the "treife medina," the "unkosher country," where Jews did not observe the laws and traditions. As soon as they arrived on these shores, most Jews dropped the distinctively Jewish style of haircut and dress and dressed as ordinary Americans. The passion to be "American" was intense. Most of the immigrants made certain that their children would not know how to speak Yiddish. They wanted their children to speak only English, like real Americans. The immigrants did not and could not distinguish between the ways of the old country that they wanted to leave behind, and the Jewish beliefs and religious practices that they may have wished to preserve. On the other hand, the immigrants could not imagine an "un-Jewish Jew." They were so immersed in Jewish culture from their childhood and within their Jewish neighborhoods in America that **Yiddishkeit**, "Jewishness," was an inescapable fact of life. An immigrant Jew could not eat unkosher food or ignore Jewish holidays or avoid a sense of community responsibility to fellow Jews without great self-consciousness. They could abandon Jewishness if they tried, but they could not be indifferent to it.

The generation born in America was able to escape from the Jewishness that was their parents' lot in life. Many chose to do so, rejecting their parents' way of life to fulfill their parents' goal of having truly "American" children. Assimilation still seemed like the highest goal to many Jews. Synagogue membership and Jewish knowledge and observance fell to an all-time low among second-generation Americans. Even so, the children of immigrants, still living in Jewish neighborhoods, continued to feel the fact of their Jewishness. Some experienced this as a burden, some enjoyed it, and many just took it for granted.

The move to the suburbs meant that third-generation Jews were raised in a more heterogeneous society. Yiddishkeit was no longer part of the environment of the streets. In this environment Jews could just disappear into the undifferentiated mass of individual Americans, and some did. Many Jews, though, found that they wanted a new mode of Jewish identity to replace the lost feeling of the ethnic neighborhood. Jews established synagogues in their new suburban communities—generally large, impressive noticeable structures which seemed to announce to the world that Jews were no longer self-conscious about their identity, but were proud to take their place in the social landscape of American religion and cultural identity. In the decade after the Second World War, when the new suburbs were built, synagogue affiliation went up from a fourth to a half of all Jews. Many of America's synagogues were founded in this period.

Ethnic and Religious Identity

Synagogue membership became the primary mode of establishing Jewish identity in America. About half of all American Jews are synagogue members at any one time, and many Jews join a synagogue at least for the years that their children are young. When one considers that synagogue membership is entirely voluntary, this is a remarkable figure. On the other hand, the fact that a Jew belongs to a synagogue does not mean that he or she participates actively in Jewish religious life. Most members use the synagogue only for the religious education of their children leading to Bar Mitzvah, and for worship on the High Holy Days. It is not participation but membership itself that establishes Jewish identity. There is, of course, a core of active members in every congregation, but these usually make up only a small percentage of the total membership.

The American synagogue is a Jewish version of the American church. The European synagogue was primarily a house of study. It was a community institution, supported by involuntary community dues. The American synagogue is primarily a house of worship. It is a voluntary association, as it must be by American law. Membership identifies one as a believer in the Jewish religion, though as we have mentioned the unique Jewish sense of ethnic-cultural community is also expressed in synagogue membership.[6]

As a religion, the Jews of America have achieved a status beyond what their numbers would suggest, the status of one of the three major religious groupings in American culture—Protestant, Catholic, Jew. There is much in American life to encourage Jews to perceive their Jewish identity as a religious identity—the prominence of the synagogue as an institution, the openness of American society to varieties of religious expression, the fact that religious identity may be more resistant to the forces of assimilation than ethnic identity. Also, the society as a whole seems comfortable with categorizing Jews as a religion rather than an ethnic or national group.

Historically, Judaism as a religion was always dependent upon membership in the Jewish people. As we have seen in the previous chapter, for Zionists the national identity of Jews remained primary. Few American

---

[6]Many Gentiles are surprised to discover that a synagogue's members are not all or nearly all present at worship services. A Gentile probably would not join a church unless he or she were a Christian believer, while Jews join synagogues for the other reasons we have mentioned, aside from belief and commitment to religious practice.

Jews perceive themselves as members of a Jewish nation, but many Jews perceive their identity more in ethnic terms than in religious terms. As there are Afro-Americans and Italian-Americans and Chinese-Americans, they are Jewish-Americans. The ethnic identity of Jews is expressed in a variety of ways that do not all depend on membership in a religious institution. An ethnic Jew may express Jewish identity by eating the foods that his ancestors brought over from Europe, such as lox and bagels or pickled herring or luxen kugel (noodle pudding). A primary mode of ethnic identity for American Jews is taking pride in the State of Israel and displaying concern for Israel through philanthropy and political activism. For many Jews making an annual gift to the United Jewish Appeal for social services in Israel is their primary mode of Jewish identification. Ethnic identity is also expressed in joining Jewish Community Centers, where secular activities such as sports, children's day camps and counseling services take place in a Jewish social environment. While religious identity is primary in outlying areas, many New York Jews feel that just living in the New York area is sufficient for a Jewish ethnic identity. Ethnic Jews may express their identity by reveling in seemingly minor but highly significant (to them) Jewish cultural traits such as loquacity, excitability, serving much food and little liquor at parties, decorating their homes and dressing in the styles preferred by Jews, and the like.

Assimilation and Identity

Many American Jews who display no outward signs of Jewish identity are nevertheless very anxious for their children to remain Jewish, though they may not be sure what that means. Jews tend to feel an obligation to pass on Jewish identity and a devotion to the Jewish people to their children. Even those Jews who have lost all positive identification with Judaism are usually anxious to keep their children from the last step in the abandonment of Jewish identity, that of formally adopting another religion.

The urge to assimilate which was so visible in the immigrant generation is largely a thing of the past. The third and fourth generation Americans who make up the bulk of the American Jewish community today are comfortable with their identity as Americans. Their problem is not becoming American, but remaining Jewish. Jews have achieved a sufficient level of acceptance in American society that Jewishness is seldom perceived as a burden, and is often perceived as a benefit (the particular pleasures of being ethnic, the honor of belonging to an ethnic/religious group that is prominent in American society, etc.). In former times, Jews who married out of the faith nearly always adopted the faith of their spouse. There is much more inter-marriage today, but most inter-married Jews keep their religion and identity, and nearly half raise their children as Jews.

There is a Yiddish saying that "what the children try to forget, the grandchildren try to remember." We may be seeing something of this phenomenon among young American Jews today. There are signs of a revival of observance of traditions, of study of traditional Jewish texts, of Jewish affiliation in general. Studies have shown that the ethnic identity of immigrants to America is generally lost by the third generation. Most young Jews growing up in America today are fourth and fifth generation Americans. There are signs that many of these Jews will defy the pattern and remain Jewish, either because of the strong pull of Jewish ethnicity, or because a newly discovered religious identity keeps them Jewish. Studies done by the Reform movement show that fourth generation Reform Jews are more apt than their parents and grandparents to observe rituals, to study Judaism and to identify themselves in a variety of ways as a Jew.

The Protestantization of American Judaism

It can be argued that all Americans believe in the same religion. American Catholicism, American Judaism and the different sects of American Protestantism are merely different forms of that same religion. All of these forms hold in common the originally Protestant belief that religion consists of the values and beliefs that are held privately within the mind and soul of each individual. Religion is not, then, immediately relevant to public life. It is expected that every religion, regardless of its peculiarities, will lead its adherents to similar public values of good citizenship. It is important in America to be religious, but the particular religion is of no public concern.

This view of religion has made the total integration of Jews into American society possible, but it has also created an internal conflict about the meaning of Judaism. Judaism was historically a complete way of life. Every aspect of daily life, public and private, was directed by Jewish laws, customs and teachings. Jews valued their uniqueness not only in matters of doctrines and values, but in every aspect of human life. Many American Jews feel that their Judaism has been diminished by being reduced to a mere religion as defined in American society. Unless they are among the few who choose to live entirely separate from the mainstream of American society, they must struggle to find ways that, as Americans, they can continue to find a role for Judaism in every aspect of their daily life.

Jewish Scholarship in America

Judaism is a religion based on knowledge. A high level of learning, among leaders and among all Jews, is presumably necessary to keep Judaism alive and meaningful. During the nineteenth and early twentieth centuries the Jews of America had difficulty in meeting this challenge. The Sunday schools and afternoon Hebrew schools transmitted very little knowledge, and generally failed to instill the joy of Torah study in their students. The number of genuine Jewish scholars in America was small, and consisted almost entirely of immigrant Europeans.

Since the Second World War this situation has changed. The rabbinical seminaries no longer depend on European imports for their faculty; they develop their scholars here in America. America has become a world center of Jewish scholarly research and Jewish book publishing, in many ways even surpassing Israel.

Brandeis University in Waltham, Massachusetts, founded in 1948, is the only Jewish-sponsored secular university in America. Brandeis attracts many Jewish students, and has a strong Judaic Studies department. Since the 1960s, many other American colleges and universities have developed courses in Judaism and even full departments of Judaic studies, including the most prestigious colleges in the country. Harvard and Yale both have strong Judaic Studies departments. Books of Jewish scholarship are printed by many university presses, even in states without large Jewish populations. Over three hundred colleges and universities in America now offer at least one course on Judaism.

This amounts to a recognition on the part of American society that Jewish knowledge and culture are an integral aspect of American civilization and of Western civilization in general. Jewish studies courses also provide an opening for young Jews who did not learn much in their childhood religious education to learn more about Judaism. The strength of Jewish scholarship in America demonstrates that the American Jewish community has become self-sustaining, no longer dependent on an influx of more pious and learned immigrants to keep itself going.

On the elementary and secondary school level, a small but increasing number of young Jews are receiving a more intensive Jewish education. The Orthodox Jews who came to America before and after the Second World War established an extensive system of Jewish day schools, where traditional Jewish subjects are studied for a part of each day. The Conservative movement has established its own national network of day schools, and in recent years some Reform congregations have established their own Jewish day schools. Jewish young people may receive an occasional input of intensive Jewish learning through summer camps, weekend retreats, or periods of study in Israel during high school or college. Alternative institutions have sprouted up to provide Jewish learning opportunities for Jews of all different ages. These include "free universities" which offer evening classes, retreat centers, and conventions. There are retreat centers in Israel and in America where Jews in mid-life or after retirement can take six months or a year and dedicate that time to intensive Jewish study.

Is America Different?

No Diaspora community in all of world history has been as free, as successful by every standard, as integrated into the general culture as the Jewish community of the United States. American Jews do not for the most part believe that they are living in the Exile. America is their home.

Some would warn that American Jews should not feel too much at home in America. They remind us that Jews once felt at home in Babylon, and in Spain, yet eventually they were cast out from these places. There do seem to be some fundamental differences, though, between the United States and other places where Jews felt welcome for a time.

No matter how much at home Jews were in Babylon, Spain or Poland, they were never thought of as Babylonians, Spaniards or Poles. They were always distinguished from the "native" population. The natives had their own religion, customs, and ancestral memories which distinguished them from the "foreigners" who lived among them on tolerance.

America has no natives other than the American Indians, who are hardly in a central position in American society. Jews are as native to America as the other elements of the population. In the multi-ethnic, multi-racial society of America, the Jews are just another of many subgroups, and not one that stands out very much at that.

In the age of nationalism, when the European nations gloried in their past and their ancient customs, Americans keenly felt their own lack of an ancient history. To make up for this, they adopted the Bible as their own history. Americans saw themselves as another Israel coming out of Egypt to found a new nation. The Bible played the role in American literature and culture that the medieval past played in the culture of the European nations. A Jew could not identify with the pagan history of the ancient Germanic, Celtic or Slavic tribes of the European nations, but the Jews are the central characters in the Bible, America's adopted past. This helps to make Jews comfortable in the American culture. Besides, American Jews feel no contradiction between the democratic, liberal, rational values of Americanism and the historic values of Judaism. The two have become one in their eyes, so that to be a good Jew is a way to be a good American.

It is of course possible that someday America will change to become inhospitable to Jews, but such an America would be so utterly different from the America that exists that it is difficult to imagine. It would take a complete reversal of all that America has stood for since the very beginning of its history.

Not only do Jews feel at home in American culture, they have had a large role in creating it. The movie industry was created almost entirely by Jews. The early movies were peopled with upper-class WASPs and with rugged cowboys. The Jewish movie moguls self-consciously kept Jewish characters and Jewishness out of their films. Nevertheless, it was their feel for the American people and culture that created the classic characters of American film. Jews have played a large role in the development of other media of American culture, including television, journalism, the twentieth century novel, symphonic music, and the musical theater. Jews also play a role beyond their numbers in developing such everyday aspects of American culture as styles in cuisine and clothing. Jews have contributed greatly to the medical, technological and scientific advances of America; nearly a third of the Nobel Prizes won by Americans have been won by Jews. It is difficult to imagine American culture without the contributions of American Jews.

24

The Present and Future

Judaism in the Late Twentieth Century

Three events have changed Judaism enormously since the beginning of the twentieth century. These three are the Holocaust, the founding of the State of Israel, and the rise of the Jewish community in the United States as the most free, prosperous and socially integrated community in the history of the Diaspora. At the beginning of the twentieth century Eastern Europe was the center of the Jewish world. The Jews there were just beginning to come to terms with the challenges of modernity. Jews who were still intimately acquainted with ancient traditions constantly flowed out of Eastern Europe, generating a constant relationship to tradition among the more modernized and assimilated Jews of Western Europe and America.

In the latter part of the twentieth century the Jewish people find themselves facing a whole different set of issues from an entirely different perspective than anyone could have imagined a hundred or even fifty years ago. Jews in Israel must figure out what it means to be a Jew in a sovereign state. Jews in the Diaspora must figure out what their relationship to that state might be, and how that relationship affects the meaning of their own Jewishness. Jews in the United States and other democratic countries must figure out what it means to be a Jew in a society in which every individual Jew is completely free to identify as a Jew or not. The Jews must respond to these issues without the benefit of a natural flow from the past into the present. The Holocaust completely cut off the Jews of the late twentieth century from their immediate past. It took from the land of the living nearly all of those Jews who were still living in a natural relationship to that past.

351

The Jews are one of the most ancient peoples on the earth, and Judaism is one of the oldest of the world religions. Even so, on account of the great changes we have mentioned, contemporary Jews are in the position of having to define almost from the beginning what it means to be a Jew and live as a Jew in the life situation in which they find themselves.

Where the Jews Are

There are about eleven million Jews in the world today. Three million Jews live in the Land of Israel. Between five and six million Jews live in the United States, nearly half of these in metropolitan New York. Most of the rest of the world's Jews, about two million, live in the Soviet Union. There are nearly half a million Jews in France and in Great Britain. Canada and Argentina each have a few hundred thousand Jews. There are significant Jewish populations also in South Africa, Uruguay, Brazil and Chile, and most of the democratic nations of Europe.

Before the Second World War there were significant Jewish populations in many more countries. Most of the European communities were destroyed in the Holocaust. Most of the Jewish communities of North Africa, the Middle East and Asia disappeared when their members went to Israel, seeking relief from persecution, isolation and poverty. Jews in the Soviet Union are cut off from contact with other Jewish communities and are prevented by their government from studying or practicing Judaism. Thus, the world Jewish community of the late twentieth century essentially has only two poles, one in Israel and one in the United States.

Soviet Jewry

The Soviet Union is officially an atheistic country. All religion is suppressed, and those who insist on practicing their religion are denied advancement in Soviet society. The Jewish religion is suppressed along with all others. In addition, the Soviet Union since the 1950s has denied Jews access to institutions of Jewish culture that are constitutionally guaranteed to them as one of the recognized nationalities of the Soviet Union. As time has passed, the government of the Soviet Union has come more and more to resemble the czarist government in its attitude to Jews.

Although Jews are persecuted for being Jewish in the Soviet Union, most Jews have very little understanding of what it means to be a Jew. Those Jews whose ancestors have been Soviet citizens since the Bolshevik Revolution in 1917 have virtually no Jewish knowledge at all. Those Jews who live in areas such as Lithuania which were added to the Soviet Union after the Second World War can still learn from their older family members something of what it means to be a Jew, but this resource will not be available for long. Jewish books are not printed in the Soviet Union. Jewish ritual objects are unavailable. Very few synagogues are still open. It is a punishable crime in the Soviet Union to teach Hebrew to children! Some Soviet Jewish activists have gone to great lengths to learn and teach Judaism, but for most Soviet Jews the result of their situation must be that Judaism becomes increasingly irrelevant while being Jewish remains a social impediment.

A Jewish emigration movement began in the Soviet Union in 1967. Jews in the free world have held mass demonstrations and done whatever they could politically to encourage the Soviet Union to allow Jews to emigrate. The United States government has helped by raising the issue of Jewish emigration in its relations with the Soviets, as one aspect of America's concern for human rights. For a brief period in the 1970s Jewish emigration reached the tens of thousands per year, but then the gates were closed and many Jews became **refuseniks,** Jews who are stuck in Russia after applying for an exit visa. The refuseniks lose their jobs and are treated as outcasts, while they may languish for many years before getting out. Some Jewish activists have become **prisoners of conscience,** sent to Siberia for organizing Jewish study groups and political organizations.

The long term hope of the Jewish people is that all those Soviet Jews who so wish will be allowed to leave. It is hoped that most of these will choose to live in Israel. Whether they choose Israel, the United States or another country, it is hoped that Jewish organizations will be able to provide them with the positive Jewish identity they lack while helping them adjust to their new freedom. It is further hoped that those Jews who choose to remain in the Soviet Union will someday be allowed the freedom to study Judaism and to establish institutions for Jewish cultural expression.

Endangered Jewish Communities

From time to time one of the remaining Jewish communities in the world is placed into danger due to anti-Semitism or general political instability. When they are free to do so, the response of Jews in these communities is usually to move to Israel. When these endangered Jews are not able to leave their homes, Jews in Israel, the United States and other free countries use whatever political influence they can muster to try to alleviate the sufferings of their fellow Jews.

Between 1949 and 1952 Jews left Syria, Iraq, Morocco, Yemen, Egypt and other Arab countries when the birth of the State of Israel led to anti-Jewish riots and government-sponsored persecutions. The few Jews who remained in these countries were treated well in most places, but the few hundred remaining Jews of Syria are held as virtual hostages. There are not enough young Jewish men available to marry the available young women. These women have not been allowed to leave the country to marry, and some have been forcibly married off to Moslem men.

Most of the few remaining Jews of Poland and other East European nations left during the 1960s and early 1970s during a period of rising anti-Semitism in these countries. Some of these states, such as Romania and Bulgaria, were helpful and sympathetic with the desire of their remaining Jews to rejoin the mass of their people in Israel.

Many young Jews in Argentina were caught up in the battle between rightists and leftists in the 1970s. Many young Jews were among the "desaparecidos," those who were arrested by the military government and murdered in secret prisons.

When the Ayatollah Khomeini took over in Iran, that country became inhospitable to its 80,000 or so Jews.

The most sadly persecuted Jewish community in the world since the Second World War is that of the Ethiopian Jews. Once numbering over a hundred thousand, by the 1980s there were only twenty thousand left alive. Famine, civil war, wandering bandits, and the constant persecutions of their Christian and Moslem neighbors all took a toll on this ancient Jewish community. The Jews of Ethiopia had lost touch with the outside world in antiquity. They developed many of their own unique customs. Since their rediscovery they have shown themselves most anxious to learn Hebrew, to learn about the rest of the modern Jewish world, and to learn the pious practices of Talmud-based Orthodox Judaism. They all desire to go to Israel, but Ethiopia does not allow emigration. About half of the Ethiopian Jews have been spirited out of the country and into Israel. It is hoped that the remainder can be brought out before they all perish.

The Jewish Demographic Problem

At the close of the Second World War there were about twelve million Jews left in the world. Since that time the world population has more than doubled, while the world Jewish population has decreased. Some of this decrease can be attributed to the loss of Jewish identity by assimilated Jews. The major factor, however, is the low Jewish birthrate in Israel, the United States, and most other Jewish communities. Exact statistics are not available, but it seems that the world Jewish birthrate is slightly below the replacement rate.

There is no reason to believe that Jews have fewer children because they are Jews, although the tendency of Jews to political liberalism and to concern for such issues as world over-population may have some effect. Most Jews live in urban areas and have a high level of education. This is the type of person most likely to prefer a small family to a large family.

Some demographers have predicted, based on recent trends, that the Jewish population of America will all but disappear by the mid twenty-first century. Most would now say that such dire predictions are exaggerated, and that the Jewish population of America will shrink to between three and five million before stabilizing.

The Jewish people have always been few in number, so it may seem surprising that Jewish leaders would be extremely concerned about Jewish numbers. They fear that there is a critical number below which the Jewish community will not be able to sustain its institutions or retain the group loyalty of its remaining members.

Some Jewish leaders have urged Jews to have three or more children "for the sake of the Jewish people." The most committed Jews may answer this call, but it is unlikely that more than a few will make such a personal decision on the basis of the requirements of their people as a whole. Some Jewish leaders have proposed making larger families more attractive to Jews by raising funds to provide free day care, day school, camp and college tuition to Jewish children. Some Jewish leaders, mostly Reform, have responded to the population challenge by urging Jews to be more active in recruiting new Jews from among the intermarried and from among the large group of Americans who are religious seekers. This is a reversal from the Jewish position of the past thousand years, which discouraged proselytizing. The Reform movement has recommended not an active mission, but an effort to make information on becoming Jewish more readily available to those who express an interest.

Assimilation and Intermarriage

In a society which grants freedom of choice in virtually all matters, will Jews continue to identify themselves as Jews in any meaningful way? This is one of the great questions confronting Jewish leaders today. How can they make Judaism meaningful to a group which displays little Jewish piety or knowledge? We have seen that in the first stages of entry to modern society many Jews chose to abandon Judaism. Anti-Semitism was an impediment to assimilation, but it no longer is. A Jew can easily disap-

pear into the undifferentiated crowd. Jews will only continue to be Jewish if they want to be—that is, if they find Jewish identity to be meaningful to them on their own terms.

Most Israelis expect that all American Jews will assimilate and disappear in a generation or two. They believe that without a national identity Jews cannot persist as Jews in the modern world. Some American Jewish leaders share this pessimistic view. Many believe, though, that the tide of assimilation has turned. They can point to a revival of Jewish study and practice. With the waning of anti-Semitism, being Jewish is no longer an impediment to social advancement. There is no pragmatic reason for Jews to abandon their identity, although many Jews may still feel self-conscious about their minority status. Among Jews who admit their Jewish identity, even the least religious seek rabbis to officiate at important moments in life such as birth, death and marriage. This shows some sense of continuing attachment to Judaism. There is reason to believe that most American Jews will retain their Jewish identity, and many will cherish it.

As long as Jews marry other Jews their children will probably identify themselves as Jews, even if the family does not actively practice Judaism. With the move of Jews out of ethnic neighborhoods and the complete integration of Jews into general American society, the intermarriage rate has greatly increased. It is estimated that since the 1960s nearly a third of all Jews getting married have married a non-Jew. Even if the Jewish partner continues to identify as a Jew, the children may be lost to Judaism. Thus, intermarriage is perceived as a threat to the continuity of Judaism.

Orthodox and Conservative leaders have faced this issue by attempting to educate Jews on the importance of marrying within the faith. Reform leaders, while acknowledging the importance of marrying a fellow Jew, have taken a different approach. They have accepted intermarriage as an inevitable fact of life in an open society. This is a reversal of Jewish tradition; a person who married out was considered by virtue of that marriage to have abandoned Judaism and the Jewish people. The Reform movement has initiated an outreach program to encourage conversion of non-Jewish spouses and to encourage interfaith couples to raise their children within Judaism. With controversy and with great outcries from traditional Jews, the Reform movement has voted to accept the children of a Jewish father and a non-Jewish mother as Jews, if the children are raised in the Jewish faith. According to the Talmud, the identity of the mother alone determines whether or not a child is Jewish.

The problem of Jewish identity is qualitative as well as quantitative. In a society where Jews are much like everyone else, what makes a Jew Jewish? Is being Jewish just another way of being human, or is there something special about being Jewish? Most American Jews do not accept the traditional concept of the "chosen people." It is difficult for Jews to decide today in what way they are like everyone else and in what way they are unique as Jews. On the extremes we find Jews who reject all association with general society and believe that Jews are a completely different sort of human being, and we find Jews who believe that there is nothing special about being Jewish and that whether or not the Jewish people exist is a matter of indifference. Most American Jews take a position between these extremes. They struggle with the ambiguity of their Jewish identity.

Who Is a Jew?

The difficulty of defining Jewish identity in an open society, and the increase of intermarriage, has led to what may be the most intractable of all problems facing the Jewish people today—the problem of determining who is a Jew. In former times Jews could tolerate great diversity in doctrines and practices largely because all Jews were fundamentally united as members of the Jewish people. A "bad" Jew could always change his ways and return to the fold, as long as he was recognizable as a Jew to himself, to other Jews, and to the surrounding community.

The legal definition of a Jew is one born of a Jewish mother or one who has converted to Judaism according to halakha. Many people today who consider themselves Jewish do not fall into this category. There are children of Jewish fathers who consider themselves Jewish. There are Jews who converted to Judaism under the aegis of the Reform movement, which does not observe the halakha for religious conversion. There are people who simply choose to identify themselves as Jews. In an open society in which Jews are not distinguished by language, clothing or custom, who is to say whether a person who arrives in town and joins a synagogue is a Jew or not? One cannot judge on the basis of Jewish knowledge and practice, since many born Jews lack these attributes.

Most Jews agree that it would be a great disaster for Judaism if the Jewish people were to become two peoples—one people that is Jewish according to halakha, another that is Jewish by some contemporary standard. The two different groups would not be able to marry each other or practice Judaism together. Eventually they might not be able to work together for Jewish charitable, social and political ends. While all Jews wish to avoid such a schism, neither traditional nor modernist Jews have shown a willingness to break with their own dearest principles for the sake of Jewish unity.

Interesting cases arise from the modern separation of Jewish identity into religious, national, cultural and legal components. A Catholic monk,

Brother Daniel, once applied to the State of Israel for citizenship. He was born Jewish, and he pointed to the Jewish law which states that "once a Jew, always a Jew." He claimed that despite his change of religion he had as much right as any Jew to claim his national identity. The Israeli Supreme Court, after much deliberation, declared that although Brother Daniel was a Jew, he could not claim the benefits of being Jewish as long as he was an active practitioner of another religion.

Some Jews take the most open possible attitude toward the question of who is a Jew. They say that anyone willing to claim in public that he or she is a Jew is one. While this is not the official stance of any Jewish body, it is in a sense true.

Anti-Zionism

Anti-Semitism is not currently a great problem for American Jews, and Israelis obviously do not experience anti-Semitism in their daily lives. It has not happened, though, that Jews have become totally accepted in the world, a people like any other. On the contrary, the Jews as a nation have been singled out for negative attention by the nations of the world. Anti-Zionism has become a problem of world proportions for Jews, and it could become a danger to them. In public forums throughout the world, especially in Moslem and in Communist countries, Zionism is decried as one of the great evils of the world. The political far left in America and Europe has taken up cudgels against Israel. Israel is subjected to intense media scrutiny. She is criticized for actions that are accepted when performed by other nations. Although Palestinian refugees are a tiny proportion of the world's refugees since 1948, well under one percent, people who show no concern for other refugees express great concern for homeless Palestinians as "victims of Zionism." Anti-Zionism has led to terrrorist attacks against European Jews as well as against Israelis. It would be a great tragedy for Israel and for the Jewish people if the intensive propaganda campaign against Israel led to an erosion of support for Israel in the free world, or to an increase of persecution against Jews.

The Continuing Challenge of Modernity

The Jewish experience with modernity is now nearly two hundred years old. This is not a great deal of time for an ancient tradition to adjust to the great changes brought about by modern conditions. It took longer than two hundred years for the transition from biblical to Rabbinic Judaism to take full shape. It should not surprise us, then, that there are still so many different and contradictory ideas of what it means to be a Jew in the world today.

In the twentieth century Jews have had to deal with both the greatest persecutions in their history and the greatest freedom they have ever known. While millions of Jews were made into helpless victims, millions of others have been able to take their fate into their own hands as never before, deciding for themselves what being a Jew means to them.

In America, Judaism has entered the marketplace of ideas. Judaism will continue to have a hold on Jews if they find that it answers their questions about life and responds to their need for a religious and personal identity. To be a Jew in the world today is an act of conscious choice.

The French Jewish playwright Edmund Fleg (1874–1963) was one modern Jew who came to find great meaning in Judaism. He grew up in a moderately observant home, but became completely estranged from Judaism as a young man. In his essay "Why I Am a Jew" (1928) Fleg describes his return to Judaism. At the conclusion of the essay Fleg gives his Jewish credo. It stands as a fine summary of what Judaism can mean to a Jew living in a modern society:[1]

I am a Jew because the faith of Israel demands of me no abdication of the mind.

I am a Jew because the faith of Israel requires of me all the devotion of my heart.

I am a Jew because in every place where suffering weeps, the Jew weeps.

I am a Jew because at every time when despair cries out, the Jew hopes.

I am a Jew because the word of Israel is the oldest and the newest.

I am a Jew because the promise of Israel is the universal promise.

I am a Jew because, for Israel, the world is not completed; we are completing it.

I am a Jew because, for Israel, humanity is not created; we are creating it.

---

[1]Quoted here in English translation from *Gates of Prayer*, CCAR, N.Y., 1975, p. 705. Used by permission. Translated by Laise Waterman Wise and first published in English by Block Publishing, 1929

I am a Jew because Israel places humanity and its unity above the nations and above Israel itself.

I am a Jew because, above humanity, image of the divine Unity, Israel places the unity which is divine.

Glossary

Akeda: The binding of Isaac; Genesis Chapter 22.

Aliyah: Going up to the bimah to perform an honor in the Torah service. Going up to live in the Land of Israel.

Amidah: The second major portion of the Jewish worship service, containing prayers of praise, petition and thanks. Also called the "Shemoneh Esre" and the "Tefilah"; to be recited morning, afternoon and evening every day.

Aninut: The mourning period from the moment of the death of a near relative until the moment of burial; no condolences may be granted in this period, and the mourners are excused from all religious obligations except for burial arrangements.

Anti-Semitism: Racial hatred of Jews.

Apocalypse: The supernatural cataclysm which will bring a sudden end to the world as we know it and usher in the Time of the Messiah; a belief of some Jews in various times and places.

Aron Hakodesh: Holy ark; repository of the sefer Torah in the front wall of the synagogue.

Ashkenaz: Jewish name for the region of Germany and Northern France in the Middle Ages.

Avelut: "Grief," "mourning." The condition and obligations of mourners during the periods of mourning—the week, the month, and the year following the burial of a near relative.

Avodah: A Hebrew term for worship, especially through sacrifice. The name for the liturgy of Yom Kippur which recalls the sacrifices performed by the High Priest in the ancient Temple.

Baal Teshuvah: A former sinner who has reformed his deeds.

Bar Mitzvah: "Liable for the commandments"; the religious status of a Jew beyond the age of thirteen years. The attainment of this status is recognized by calling the child to the bimah for the public reading of Scripture in the synagogue.

Beraka: A blessing, beginning with the formula "Blessed be Thou, Lord our God, Ruler of the universe . . ."

Bet Din: A court of at least three rabbis, authorized to make legal judgments and to recognize changes in personal status (conversion, divorce, etc.).

Bet K'nesset: "Assembly hall"; a synagogue.

Bet Midrash: "Study hall"; a library for informal Jewish study by individuals or groups.

Bimah: The pulpit in the synagogue; the platform or table from which the Scriptures are read.

Blood Accusation: The libel, periodically leveled against the Jews by anti-Jewish agitators, accusing Jews of using Christian blood in the manufacture of Passover matzoh.

B'rit: The covenant; the contractual relationship between God and Israel.

B'rit Milah: The "covenant of circumcision"; the circumcision of Jewish boys on the eighth day after birth as a sign of entry into the "Covenant of Abraham."

Conservative: Movement to modernize Judaism gradually while remaining within the confines of Jewish law.

Dayyan: A rabbinic judge; a rabbi who serves on a Jewish court.

Diaspora: The dispersion; all the places where Jews live outside the Land of Israel. Called in Hebrew "galut," "exile."

Dreidle: A four-sided top used for games of chance on Hanukah.

El Male Rahamim: Prayer recited in memory of the departed at funerals and at Yizkor services.

Essenes: First century sect of Jews; desert-dwellers who dedicated their lives to personal purification.

Etrog: A citron, a precious kind of citrus fruit; one of the "four species" which are waved on Sukkot.

Gan Eden: The Garden of Eden, Paradise; the place where the souls of the good go for eternal reward.

Gaon: Title of the head of a rabbinic academy in Babylonia, third century to eleventh century.

Gehinnom: The Valley of Hinnom, Purgatory; the place where the souls of the wicked go for punishment, or where the souls of those who are middling go for purgation before eternal reward.

Gemarra: Along with the Mishnah, the contents of the Talmud.

Get: A Jewish divorce decree, written in the presence of a bet din and presented by the husband to the wife, by mutual consent.

Ghetto: In central Europe from the sixteenth century, a walled-in area of a city in which all Jews were required to reside.

Giur: The ceremony of conversion to Judaism, traditionally consisting of milah, tevilah and kabbalat ol hamitzvot (circumcision, immersion and acceptance of the commandments). Some modern-day Jews do not require the first two of these requirements for conversion.

Haftarah: The reading from the biblical books of the prophets which follows the Torah reading in the synagogue on Sabbaths and holy days.

Haganah: Jewish defense militia in the pre-state Land of Israel.

Haggadah: The book which contains the liturgy for the Pesah seder.

Halakha: The body of rabbinic law; any individual Jewish law.

Hallah: A braided loaf of white egg bread, eaten in celebration of the Sabbath and holy days.

Halutzim: Zionist pioneers in the Land of Israel.

Hametz: Leavened bread, the opposite of matzoh; may not be eaten on Pesah.

Hanukah: The eight day festival of lights celebrating the victory of the Maccabees; observed around the time of the winter solstice.

Hanukiah: A Hanukah candelabrum, with space for nine candles or oil lamps.

Haskalah: The Jewish Enlightenment in the nineteenth century.

Hattan: The groom at a Jewish wedding.

Havdalah: The ritual which marks the conclusion of Shabbat.

Havurah: In modern Judaism, a democratically run, informal group that gathers periodically for study, worship or celebration.

Hazzan: The cantor who chants the liturgy in the synagogue, leading the congregation in worship.

Heder: Jewish elementary school. In traditional society Jewish boys went to heder from age five to ten, approximately. There they learned the Hebrew Bible.

Hesped: The eulogy at a funeral.

Hevra: In Jewish communal life, a voluntary society to perform good deeds.

Hevra Kaddisha: A burial society which prepares the dead for proper burial. In traditional Jewish society, membership in the hevra kaddisha was granted only to the leading citizens of the community.

High Holy Days: See **Yamim Nora'im.**

Holocaust: Murder of six million Jews during World War II.

Huppah: The canopy under which the bride and groom stand at a Jewish wedding.

Intercalation: In the calculation of the Jewish calendar, the addition of an extra day in certain months, or an extra month in certain years, in order to harmonize the lunar calendar with the solar year.

Israel: The Jewish people. The Land of Israel, at the intersection of Africa and Asia. The State of Israel.

Judah: Southern kingdom after split of kingdom of twelve tribes. Name of Jewish province in time of the "Second Commonwealth," from the return from Babylonian Exile to the Roman Destruction.

Kabbalah: Late medieval form of Jewish mysticism.

Kabbalat 'Ol Hamitzvot: "Acceptance of the yoke of the commandments"; one of the requirements for conversion to Judaism, consisting of a degree of knowledge of the commandments of the Torah and their rewards and punishments, and a display of willingness to obey the commandments.

Kadisha: A prayer for the speedy coming of God's rulership over the earth, recited in numerous places in the Jewish liturgy and, especially, by mourners in memory of the departed.

Kallah: The bride at a Jewish wedding.

Kashrut: The laws concerning permitted and forbidden foods.

Kavannah: Intention; purposeful fulfillment of God's commandments.

Kehila: The officially constituted Jewish community. The organized institutions which govern the Jewish community.

Keriat Shema: The first major portion of the worship service, containing three paragraphs from the Torah surrounded by prayers praising God as Creator, Revealer and Redeemer; to be recited morning and evening every day.

Ketubah: A Jewish marriage contract; the ketubah spells out the financial obligations of bride and groom and establishes the rights of the bride in the event of divorce or widowhood.

Kiddush HaShem: "Sanctification of the name of God." Any ethical act of a Jew which raises the reputation of God in the eyes of Gentiles. The giving of one's life in martyrdom rather than to repudiate Judaism.

Kiddushin v'Nisuin: Engagement and marriage; the term for the Jewish marriage ceremony which includes both engagement—the ring and legal obligations—and marriage—the right to live together as husband and wife.

Kipah: A small hat worn to cover the head in worship in accordance with Jewish custom; worn all the time by very traditional Jews, and not at all by very modernist Jews; also called a yarmulke.

K'nesset: The democratically elected Parliament of the State of Israel.

Kol Nidre: "All vows"; the prayer which opens the Yom Kippur eve worship, known especially for the melody by which it is sung.

Kosher: "Ritually acceptable"; especially, food which may be eaten in accordance with Jewish ritual law.

Lag B'Omer: The thirty-third day of the counting of the omer; a minor holiday in the springtime.

Landsmanschaft: In America, a synagogue or club made up of immigrants from the same European city or region.

Latkes: Fried potato pancakes, eaten especially on Hanukah.

Lulav: A palm branch; one of the "four species" waved on Sukkot.

Mahzor: The prayer book for the High Holy Days, containing all the special prayers for these days.

Maror: Bitter herbs, horseradish; eaten at the Pesah seder.

Mashiah: The Messiah, the rightful king; the descendant of King David who will rule over the Jewish people with justice in a future time.

Maskil: A proponent of the Haskalah, nineteenth century.

Matzoh: Unleavened bread, eaten on Pesah in commemoration of the Exodus from Egypt.

Mazal Tov: "Good luck!"; traditional Jewish salutation, especially at weddings.

Menorah: A candelabrum; a seven-branched menorah stood in the Temple in Jerusalem; a nine-branched menorah, called a hanukiah, is used in the celebration of Hanukah.

Mezuzah: A scroll in a decorative container which is nailed to the doorpost of a house as a reminder of God's presence and God's commandments.

Midrash: Rabbinic homilies on scriptural verses; the non-legal interpretation of Scripture.

Mikraot Gedolot: "Expanded Scriptures"; a Bible printed with the biblical text in the center of the page, surrounded by a variety of commentaries.

Mikveh: A proper ritual bath, of dimensions allowing complete immersion, and containing at least a percentage of rainwater or fresh spring water (as opposed to well water or piped water).

Minhag: Community custom, which has the force of law.

Minyan: A quorum for worship; traditionally, a group of ten or more adult male Jews.

Mishnah: Rabbi Judah's encyclopedia of rabbinic law, composed ca. 200 CE; the basic text of the Oral Torah.

Mishneh Torah: Maimonides' code of Jewish law, thirteenth century.

Misnagdim: In eighteenth and nineteenth century Eastern Europe, Jews who opposed the new Hasidic movement; centered in Lithuania.

Mitzvah: A commandment of God, given in the Torah.

Mohel: A Jewish professional skilled in the ritual and the medical aspects of b'rit milah.

Musaf: The additional recitation of the Amidah said in the traditional synagogue on Sabbaths and holy days in commemoration of the ancient sacrifices.

Nasi: "Prince"; head of the Sanhedrin in Roman times.

Neilah: The concluding service on the late afternoon of Yom Kippur.

Nusah: The proper scale in which the liturgy is traditionally chanted; the nusah varies with the different kinds of holy days.

Omer: The sheaf of grain which was brought to the Temple each of the fifty days from Pesah to Shavuot. This fifty day period is called the days of the counting of the omer.

Oneg Shabbat: Joy of the Sabbath. A social gathering and repast in joyous observance of Shabbat, following worship services.

Orthodox: Movement to maintain Jewish law and tradition in the modern world; movement opposed to extra-legal changes in Jewish practice and belief.

Pale of Settlement: Region in Western Russia where Jews were permitted to settle, away from the center of the country.

Palestine: Name given by the Romans to the Land of Israel, and used by later colonial powers into modern times.

Paroket: The curtain that covers the aron hakodesh in the synagogue.

Parve: Food which is neither "fleishig" (meat) nor "milchig" (dairy) and may therefore be eaten at either meat or dairy meals.

Pesah: The spring festival commemorating the Exodus from Egypt; observed with the seder ritual meal and eating matzoh.

Pharisees: First-century sect of Jews; forerunners of the rabbis.

Pilpul: Drawing out the meaning of the Talmudic text through logical debate; scholastic study of the Talmud.

Piyyut: A prayer-poem composed in late antiquity or in the Middle Ages as an addition to or commentary on the liturgy.

Pogrom: Slavic term for a riot; an organized riot against Jews, especially in early modern and modern Eastern Europe.

Purim: Festival in late winter celebrating the events told in the biblical Book of Esther.

Rashi: Great eleventh century commentator on the Bible and the Talmud. The words of these commentaries, as in "the Rashi to Genesis," etc.

Rav: "Rabbi"; the appointed rabbinic leader of a community.

Rebbe: A Hasidic leader, whose position is based on charisma or heredity rather than on rabbinic knowledge.

Reform: Movement to recreate Judaism according to modern principles.

Refusenik: Soviet Jew denied permission to emigrate.

Responsa: Legal essays written by rabbis in response to questions of practice. The total body of this literature.

Rosh Hashanah: The Jewish new year; the Day of Judgment.

Sadducees: First century sect of Jews, rivals of the Pharisees; upheld the ancient priestly concept of Judaism.

Sanhedrin: High court of seventy-one elders or rabbis which ruled over the Jews of the Land of Israel from about the second century BCE to the fourth century CE.

Seder: The liturgical meal observed at the family table on the first (and often second) nights of Pesah.

Sefer Torah: A scroll of the five books of the Torah, handwritten on parchment in the ancient manner.

Sefirot: In Kabbalah, the emanations of God.

Selihot: Penitential prayers recited in preparation for the High Holy Days.

Sepharad: Jewish name for Spain in the Middle Ages.

Shabbat: The Sabbath; the seventh day, dedicated to rest.

Shadkan: A marriage broker.

Shalosh Regalim: The three pilgrimage festivals; Pesah, Shavuot and Sukkot; when the Temple stood those Jews who could do so went to Jerusalem for these festivals.

Shammas: The caretaker of a synagogue. The candle which is used to light the others in a hanukiah.

Shavuot: The spring harvest festival of first fruits; commemorates the giving of the Torah at Mount Sinai.

Shekinah: The "Indwelling"; God in the feminine aspect of closeness to the world. The lowest of the Kabbalistic sefirot.

Sheloshim: The "thirty" day period of mourning during which mourners must refrain from public celebration and observe other rules of the intermediate level of grief.

Shema and Its Blessings: See "Keriat Shema."

Shemini Atzeret: The Festival of Conclusion on the eighth day after the beginning of Sukkot; the end to the fall holiday season.

Sheol: In biblical times, the place where it was believed the dead slept with their ancestors for eternity.

Sheva Berakot: The "seven blessings" which constitute the Nisuin, the Jewish marriage ceremony.

Shiva: The "seven" days of mourning during which mourners remain at home and receive condolence calls from visitors.

Shofar: The horn of an animal, usually a ram, which is blown in the synagogue on Rosh Hashanah.

Shoket: A Jewish professional expert in the kosher slaughtering of meat.

Shtetl: A Jewish village in Eastern Europe.

Shtibl: A Hasidic synagogue. A small study house.

Shulhan Aruk: Sixteenth century code of Jewish law written by Joseph Caro.

Siddur: A Jewish prayer book, containing the liturgical prayers for weekdays, festivals and the Sabbath.

Simhat Torah: The celebration, on Shemini Atzeret, of the conclusion and new beginning of the annual cycle of Torah readings in the synagogue; observed with joyous processions around the synagogue.

Sukkah: A temporary harvest booth, roofed with greens, in which Jews reside and dine during the week of the festival of Sukkot; a reminder of the booths in which the Jews lived during their forty years of wandering in the desert.

Sukkot: The week-long fall harvest festival, coming two weeks after Rosh Hashanah. Plural of "sukkah."

Tahara: "Purification"; the washing of a body before dressing in shrouds for traditional Jewish burial.

Tallit: The prayer shawl in which a traditional Jewish male wraps himself in morning worship; also called a tallis.

Talmud: Basic text of the Oral Torah, composed ca. 500 CE; book of ongoing rabbinic interpretation of the Mishnah.

Tefilin: Leather boxes containing words of Scripture which are tied onto the arm and forehead with leather tongs during the recitation of the morning liturgy.

Tehinas: Prayers of supplication recited by women in traditional Judaism; usually composed in the Yiddish language.

Teshuvah: "Return"; repentence.

Tevilah: Immersion in a mikveh, a properly constituted ritual bath. The ceremony of tevilah is traditionally used for conversion and for ritual purification. In antiquity it was required for those who would attend the sacrifices.

Talmud Torah: Literally "Torah study"; a community-supported school for the education of the young.

Tenaim: A contract establishing the intent for engagement and marriage.

Tikun Leil Shavuot: The mystical custom of studying all night on the night of Shavuot in the hope of hastening the Messianic redemption.

Tisha B'Av: A fast day in summer, commemorating the destruction of the first and second Temples and other sad events in Jewish history.

Tosafot: Medieval commentary to the Talmud composed by the Tosafists, disciples of the school of Rashi.

Tractate: One of the sixty topical sections of the Mishnah or Talmud.

Treife: Not kosher; specifically, meat from a kosher animal which has not been slaughtered, inspected and prepared in accordance with the laws of kashrut.

Tu B'Shevat: The new year of the trees; a minor holiday in late winter.

Twofold Torah: The concept that the Torah contains two parts, one written and one oral. Rabbinic tradition is the Oral Torah.

Tzaddik: "Righteous one"; in Hasidism, the charismatic leader; the rebbe.

Tzidduk Hadin: "Justification of the divine judgment"; the prayers which are recited at graveside at a funeral service.

Wissenschaft des Judentums: The "Science of Judaism"; the modern study of Judaism according to the principles of university scholarship, as developed in Germany in the nineteenth century.

Yahrzeit: The annual observance of the death of a parent, spouse or child through the lighting of a candle and the recitation of the Kaddish prayer.

Yamim Nora'im: The "Days of Awe"; the period of the Jewish Holy Days in the fall, centering on Rosh Hashanah and Yom Kippur.

Yeshiva: An advanced traditional Jewish school, equivalent to high school or college, where students learn the Talmud.

Yetzer: An impulse in the human psyche. There are two yetzers, the yetzer tov, or good yetzer, and the yetzer ra`, or evil yetzer. The integration of these two yetzers determines human moral character.

Yiddish: Language of Ashkenazic Jews from the Middle Ages until modern times; a Jewish dialect of medieval German.

Yiddishkeit: "Jewishness"; the Jewish culture of Eastern Europe.

Yishuv: The Jewish settlement in the pre-state Land of Israel.

Yizkor: A liturgy in remembrance of the dead and especially the martyrs of Israel, recited on Yom Kippur and, in some places, on the last day of festivals.

Yom HaAtzma'ut: Israel independence day; observed as a holiday by modern Israelis.

Yom HaShoah: Holocaust memorial day; a modern Jewish observance.

Yom Kippur: The Day of Atonement, ten days after Rosh Hashanah.

Zemirot: Songs for the Sabbath, sung at the family table in observance of the day.

Zionism: Modern national liberation movement of the Jewish people.

Zohar: Thirteenth-century book of Kabbalah.

Student Bibliography

The following books are recommended for additional reading, study and research.

General and History

Abrahams, Israel, *Jewish Life in the Middle Ages*, Atheneum, N.Y.

Baron, Salo, *A Social and Religious History of the Jews*, 18 vols., Columbia/ J.P.S., N.Y., Phila., 1937–1983.

Ben-Sasson and Ettinger, *Jewish Society Through the Ages*, Schocken, N.Y., 1969.

Eban, Abba, *My People: The Story of the Jews*, Behrman House / Random House, N.Y., 1968.

Encyclopedia Judaica, Keter, Jerusalem, 1972.

Glatzer, Nahum, ed., *The Judaic Tradition*, Behrman House, N.Y., 1969.

Graetz, Heinrich, *History of the Jews*, 6 vols., J.P.S., Phila., 1956.

Hallo, Ruderman, Stanislawski, *Heritage: Civilization and the Jews*, Study Guide, Reader, Praeger, N.Y., 1984.

Katz, Jacob, *Exclusiveness and Tolerance*, Schocken, N.Y., 1961.

Marcus, Jacob R., *The Jew in the Medieval World*, Harper, N.Y., 1938.

Margolis, Max & Marx, Alexander, *A History of the Jewish People*, Atheneum, N.Y., 1969.

Neusner, Jacob, *Between Time and Eternity: The Essentials of Judaism*, Dickenson, Encino, 1975.

Potok, Chaim, *Wanderings: History of the Jews*, Alfred A. Knopf, N.Y., 1978.

Prager & Telushkin, *The Nine Questions People Ask About Judaism*, Simon and Schuster, N.Y., 1975.

Roth, Cecil, *A History of the Marranos*, Schocken, N.Y., 1974.

———, *Dona Gracia of the House of Nasi*, J.P.S., Phila., 1977.

———, *History of the Jews*, Schocken, N.Y., 1961.

Schwartz, Leo, ed., *Great Ages and Ideas of the Jewish People*, Random House, N.Y. 1956.

————, ed., *Memoirs of My People*, J.P.S., Phila., 1943.
Steinberg, Milton, *Basic Judaism*, HBJ, San Diego, 1947, 1975.
Steinsaltz, Adin, *The Thirteen Petalled Rose*, Basic Books, N.Y., 1980.
Wouk, Herman, *This Is My God*, Doubleday, Garden City, N.Y., 1959.

Customs and Holidays

Agnon, S.Y., *Days of Awe*, Schocken, N.Y., 1948, 1965.
Cohn, Jacob, *The Royal Table*, Feldheim, N.Y., 1973.
Gaster, Theodore H., *Passover: Its History and Traditions*, Henry Schuman, N.Y., 1949.
————, *Purim and Hanukkah in Custom and Tradition*, Henry Schuman, N.Y., 1950.
Gittelson, Roland B., *My Beloved Is Mine: Judaism and Marriage*, UAHC, N.Y., 1969.
Heinemann, Joseph, *Literature of the Synagogue*, Behrman House, N.Y., 1975.
Heschel, Abraham Joshua, *The Sabbath*, Farrar, Straus and Giroux, N.Y., 1951.
Lamm, Maurice, *The Jewish Way in Love & Marriage*, Harper and Row, S.F., 1980.
Millgram, Abraham, *Jewish Worship*, J.P.S., Phila., 1971.
————, *Sabbath: The Day of Delight*, J.P.S., Phila., 1944.
Munk, Rabbi Dr. Elie, *The World of Prayer*, 2 vols., Feldheim, N.Y., 1963.
Reimer, Jack, ed., *Jewish Reflections on Death*, Schocken, N.Y., 1974.
Schauss, Hayyim, *The Jewish Festivals*, Schocken, N.Y., 1938.
————, *The Lifetime of a Jew*, UAHC, N.Y., 1950.
Strassfeld, Michael, *The Jewish Holidays*, Harper and Row, N.Y., 1985.
Trepp, Leo, *The Complete Book of Jewish Observance*, Behrman House / Summit Books, N.Y., 1980.
Waskow, Arthur, *Seasons of Our Joy: A Handbook of Jewish Festivals*, Bantam, N.Y., 1982.

Judaism and Christianity

Asch, Sholem, *The Nazarene*, G.P. Putnam's Sons, N.Y. 1939.
Baeck, Leo, *Judaism and Christianity*, Meridian, Cleveland and J.P.S., Phila., 1958.

Klausner, Joseph, *Jesus of Nazareth*, Macmillan, N.Y., 1926.

Parkes, James, *The Conflict of the Church and the Synagogue*, Atheneum, N.Y.

Rankin, Oliver Shaw, *Jewish Religious Polemic*, Ktav, N.Y., 1970.

Sandmel, Samuel, *We Jews and Jesus*, Oxford U. Press, N.Y., 1973.

Vermes, Geza, *Jesus the Jew*, Fortress Press, Phila., 1973.

Weiss-Marin, Trudy, *Jewish Expressions on Jesus: An Anthology*, Ktav, N.Y., 1977.

Zeitlin, Solomon, *Who Crucified Jesus?* Bloch, N.Y., 1964.

Rabbinic Judaism:
History and Texts

The Babylonian Talmud, in English translation, Soncino, London.

Danby, Herbert, trans., *The Mishnah*, Oxford U. Press, 1933.

Finkelstein, Louis, *Akiba*, Atheneum, N.Y., 1970.

Freehof, Solomon B., *The Responsa Literature*, J.P.S., Phila., 1955.

Ginzberg, Louis, *The Legends of the Jews*, 7 vols., J.P.S., Phila., 1968.

Glatzer, Nahum, *Hillel the Elder*, B'nai Brith Hillel Foundations, N.Y., 1957.

Golden, Judah, *The Living Talmud*, Mentor, N.Y., 1957.

Herford, R. Travers, *The Ethics of the Talmud: Sayings of the Fathers*, Schocken, N.Y., 1962.

Holtz, Barry W., ed., *Back to the Sources*, Summit, N.Y., 1984.

Midrash Rabbah, in English translation, 10 vols., Soncino, London, 1983.

Mielziner, Moses, *Introduction to the Talmud*, Bloch, N.Y., 1968.

Montefiore, C.G., and Loewe, H., ed. and trans., *A Rabbinic Anthology*, Schocken, N.Y., 1974.

Neusner, Jacob, *From Politics to Piety: The Emergence of Pharisaic Judaism*, Ktav, N.Y., 1979.

————, *Our Sages, God and Israel*, Rossel Books, Chappaqua, N.Y., 1984.

————, *There We Sat Down: Talmudic Judaism in the Making*, Abingdon Press, N.Y., 1972.

Spiegel, Shalom, *The Last Trial*, Behrman House, N.Y., 1967.

Steinsaltz, Adin, *The Essential Talmud*, Bantam, N.Y., 1976.

Yadin, Yigael, *Bar Kochba*, Random House, N.Y., 1971.

————, *Masada*, Weidenfeld and Nicolson, London, 1966.

Zeitlin, Solomon, *The Rise and Fall of the Judaean State*, 3 vols., J.P.S., Phila., 1967–1978.

Philosophy, Mysticism and Spirituality

Bleich, J. David, *With Perfect Faith: The Foundations of Jewish Belief*, Ktav, N.Y., 1983.

Buber, Martin, *Hasidism and Modern Man*, Horizon, N.Y., 1958.

————, *Tales of the Hasidim*, vol. 1, *Early Masters*, vol. 2, *Later Masters*, Schocken, N.Y., 1947, 1948.

————, *The Legend of the Baal Shem*, Schocken, N.Y., 1955.

————, *The Origin and Meaning of Hasidism*, Horizon, N.Y., 1960.

Dan, Joseph, ed., *The Early Kabbalah*, Paulist Press, N.Y., 1986.

Green, Arthur, ed., *Jewish Spirituality: From the Bible Through the Middle Ages*, Crossroad, N.Y., 1986.

————, ed., *Jewish Spirituality: From the Sixteenth-Century Revival to the Present*, Crossroad, N.Y., 1987.

Guttman, Julius, *Philosophies of Judaism*, Schocken, N.Y., 1964.

Hartman, David, *Maimonides: Torah and Philosophic Quest*, J.P.S., Phila., 1976.

Husik, Isaac, *A History of Mediaeval Jewish Philosophy*, Atheneum, N.Y., 1976.

Levin, Meyer, *Classic Hassidic Tales*, Penguin, N.Y., 1975.

Scholem, Gershom, *Kabbalah*, Keter, Jerusalem, 1974.

————, *Major Trends in Jewish Mysticism*, Schocken, N.Y., 1954.

————, *The Messianic Idea in Judaism and Other Essays on Jewish Spirituality*, Schocken, N.Y., 1971.

————, *On the Kabbalah and Its Symbolism*, Schocken, N.Y., 1960.

————, *Sabbetai Sevi*, Princeton U. Press, 1973.

————, ed., *Zohar*, Schocken, N.Y., 1949.

Three Jewish Philosophers: Philo, Saadia Gaon, Jehuda Halevi, Atheneum, N.Y., 1973.

Trachtenberg, Joshua, *Jewish Magic and Superstition*, Atheneum, N.Y., 1979.

Twersky, Isadore, *A Maimonides Reader*, Behrman House, N.Y., 1972.

The Zohar, 5 vols., Soncino Press, London, 1984.

Eastern Europe

Chagall, Bella and Marc, *Burning Lights*, Schocken, N.Y., 1946.

Dubnow, M., *History of the Jews in Russia and Poland*, 3 vols., J.P.S., Phila., 1918.

Grade, Chaim, *My Mother's Sabbath Days*, Schocken, N.Y., 1986.

Heschel, Abraham Joshua, *The Earth Is the Lord's: The Inner World of the Jew in East Europe*, Farrar, Straus and Giroux, N.Y., 1949.
Roskies, Diane and David, *The Shtetl Book*, Ktav, N.Y., 1975.
Shazar, Zalman, *Morning Stars*, J.P.S., Phila., 1967.
Singer, I.B., *In My Father's Court*, Farrar, Straus and Giroux, N.Y., 1962.
Zborowsky, Mark & Herzog, Eliz., *Life Is With People*, Schocken, N.Y., 1952.

Anti-Semitism and the Holocaust

Dawidowicz, Lucy S., *The War Against the Jews, 1933–1945*, Holt, Rinehart and Winston, N.Y., 1975.
Gilbert, Martin, *The Macmillan Atlas of the Holocaust*, N.Y., 1982.
Glatstein, Knox & Margoshes, eds., *Anthology of Holocaust Literature*, Atheneum, N.Y., 1980.
Hilberg, Raul, *The Destruction of the European Jews*, Quadrangle Books, Chicago, 1961.
Sartre, Jean-Paul, *Anti-Semite and Jew*, Grove Press, N.Y., 1948.
Schwarz-Bart, Andre, *The Last of the Just*, Atheneum, N.Y., 1961.
Steiner, Jean-Francois, *Treblinka*, Simon and Schuster, N.Y., 1967.
Wiesel, Elie, *Night*, Farrar, Straus and Giroux, N.Y., 1960.
Wyman, David S., *The Abandonment of the Jews: America and the Holocaust 1941–1945*, Pantheon, N.Y., 1984.

Literature

Anderson, Elliot, ed., *Contemporary Israeli Literature*, J.P.S., Phila., 1977.
Agnon, S.Y., *The Bridal Canopy*, Doubleday, Garden City, N.Y., 1937.
———, *Twenty-One Stories*, Schocken, N.Y., 1970.
Selected Poems of Jehuda Halevi, J.P.S., Phila., 1952.
Grade, Chaim, *The Yeshiva*, Menorah, N.Y., 1976.
Mintz, Ruth Finer, ed., *Modern Hebrew Poetry*, U. of Calif. Press, Berkeley and L.A., 1968.
Potok, Chaim, *The Chosen*, Simon & Schuster, N.Y., 1967.
Sholom Aleichem, *Favorite Tales of Sholom Aleichem*, Avenel Books, N.Y., 1983.
Singer, I.B., *The Family Moskat*, Farrar, Straus & Giroux, N.Y., 1950.
———, *The Manor*, Farrar, Straus & Giroux, N.Y., 1967.
Selected Religious Poems of Solomon Ibn Gabirol, J.P.S., Phila., 1952.

Zinberg, Israel, *A History of Jewish Literature*, 12 vols., Martin, Bernard, trans. & ed., HUC Press, Ktav, N.Y., 1978.

Modern Jewish History and Thought

Altmann, Alexander, *Moses Mendelssohn*, J.P.S., Phila., 1973.
Baeck, Leo, *The Essence of Judaism*, Schocken, N.Y., 1961.
————, *This People Israel: The Meaning of Jewish Existence*, U.A.H.C., N.Y., 1964.
Borowitz, Eugene, *Choices in Modern Jewish Thought*, Behrman House, N.Y., 1983.
Buber, Martin, *I and Thou*, Charles Scribner's Sons, N.Y., 1970.
————, *Israel and the World*, Schocken, N.Y., 1976.
Glatzer, Nahum, *Modern Jewish Thought*, Schocken, N.Y., 1977.
Hertzberg, Arthur, *The French Enlightenment and the Jews*, Columbia U. Press /J.P.S., N.Y., 1968.
Heschel, Abraham J., *Between God and Man*, Free Press, N.Y., 1959.
Hirsch, S.R., *The Nineteen Letters of Ben Uzziel*, trans. Drachman, Bloch, N.Y., 1942.
Jospe, Eva, trans. & ed., *Reason and Hope: Selections from the Jewish Writings of Hermann Cohen*, Norton, N.Y., 1971.
Koltun, Elizabeth, *The Jewish Woman: New Perspectives*, Schocken, N.Y., 1976.
Philipson, David, *The Reform Movement in Judaism*, Ktav, N.Y., 1967.
Raisin, Jacob S., *The Haskalah Movement in Russia*, J.P.S., Phila., 1913.
Rudavsky, David, *Modern Jewish Religious Movements*, Behrman House, N.Y., 1979.
Sachar, Howard Morley, *The Course of Modern Jewish History*, Delta, N.Y., 1977.

Israel and Zionism

Avineri, Shlomo, *The Making of Modern Zionism*, Basic Books, N.Y., 1981.
Bettelheim, Bruno, *The Children of the Dream*, Macmillan, N.Y., 1969.
Halkin, Hillel, *Letters to an American Jewish Friend*, J.P.S., Phila., 1977.
Hazleton, Lesley, *Israeli Women*, Simon & Schuster, N.Y., 1977.
Hertzberg, Arthur, ed., *The Zionist Idea*, Atheneum, N.Y., 1977.
Laperriere and Collins, *O Jerusalem*, Weidenfeld & Nicolson, London, Jerusalem, 1972.

Laqueur, Walter, *A History of Zionism*, Schocken, N.Y., 1976.
Simon, Leon, trans., *Selected Essays of Ahad Ha'am*, Atheneum, N.Y., 1970.
Spiro, Melford E., *Kibbutz: Venture in Utopia*, Harvard U. Press, Cambridge, MA, 1975.
Wiesel, Elie, *A Beggar in Jerusalem*, Random House, N.Y., 1970.

American Judaism

Birmingham, Stephen, *Our Crowd: The Great Jewish Families of New York*, Harper & Row, N.Y., 1967.
———, *The Grandees*, Harper & Row, N.Y., 1971.
———, *"The Rest of Us": The Rise of America's Eastern European Jews*, Little, Brown & Co., Boston, 1984.
Blau, Joseph L., *Judaism in America*, U. of Chicago Press, Chicago, 1976.
Dawidowicz, Lucy, *On Equal Terms: Jews in America 1881–1981*, Holt, Rinehart & Winston, N.Y., 1982.
Dimont, Max, *The Jews in America*, Simon & Schuster, N.Y., 1978.
Evans, Eli N., *The Provincials*, Atheneum, N.Y., 1973.
Howe, Irving, *World of Our Fathers: The Journey of the East European Jews to America and the Life They Found and Made*, Touchstone, N.Y., 1976.
Meltzer, Isaac, ed., *A Bintel Brief*, Doubleday, Garden City, 1971.
Plesur, Milton, *Jewish Life in Twentieth Century America: Challenge and Accommodation*, Nelson-Hall, Chicago, 1982.
Silberman, Charles E., *A Certain People*, Summit, N.Y., 1985.
Sklare, Marshall, *The Jews: Social Patterns of an American Group*, Free Press, N.Y., 1958.
Stember, Charles, et al., *Jews in the Mind of America*, Basic Books, N.Y., 1966.
Yaffe, James, *The American Jews*, Random House, N.Y., 1968.

Index

BM 155.2 .W95 1989

Wylen, Stephen M., 1952-

Settings of silver

BM 155.2 .W95 1989

Wylen, Stephen M., 1952-

Settings of silver

DEMCO